Media, Propaganda and Politics in 20th-Century Japan

SOAS Studies in Modern and Contemporary Japan

Series Editor: Christopher Gerteis, SOAS, University of London (UK)

Series Editorial Board:
Steve Dodd, SOAS, University of London (UK)
Andrew Gerstle, SOAS, University of London (UK)
Janet Hunter, London School of Economics and Political Science (UK)
Helen Macnaughtan, SOAS, University of London (UK)
Timon Screech, SOAS, University of London (UK)
Naoko Shimazu, Birkbeck, University of London (UK)

Published in association with the Japan Research Centre at the School of Oriental and African Studies, University of London, UK.

SOAS Studies in Modern and Contemporary Japan features scholarly books on modern and contemporary Japan, showcasing new research monographs as well as translations of scholarship not previously available in English. Its goal is to ensure that current, high quality research on Japan, its history, politics and culture, is made available to an English speaking audience. The series is made possible in part by generous grants from the Nippon Foundation and the Great Britain Sasakawa Foundation.

Published:
Women and Democracy in Cold War Japan, Jan Bardsley (2014)
Christianity and Imperialism in Modern Japan, Emily Anderson (2014)
The China Problem in Postwar Japan, Robert Hoppens (2015)
Media, Propaganda and Politics in 20th-Century Japan, The Asahi Shimbun Company (translated by Barak Kushner) (2015)

Forthcoming:
The Self-Defense Forces and Civil Society in Postwar Japan, Tomoyuki Sasaki (2015)
Contemporary Sino-Japanese Relations on Screen, Griseldis Kirsch (2015)
Japanese Taiwan, edited by Andrew Morris (2015)
Politics and Power in 20th-Century Japan, Mikuriya Takashi and Nakamura Takafusa (translated by Timothy S. George) (2015)
Debating Otaku in Contemporary Japan, edited by Patrick W. Galbraith, Thiam Huat Kam and Björn-Ole Kamm (2015)
Japan as a Maritime Power, Masataka Kousaka (translated by Paul Midford) (2015)

Media, Propaganda and Politics in 20th-Century Japan

The Asahi Shimbun Company

Translated and abridged by Barak Kushner

Foreword by Funabashi Yoichi

Bloomsbury Academic
An imprint of Bloomsbury Publishing Plc

B L O O M S B U R Y

LONDON · NEW DELHI · NEW YORK · SYDNEY

Bloomsbury Academic

An imprint of Bloomsbury Publishing Plc

50 Bedford Square
London
WC1B 3DP
UK

1385 Broadway
New York
NY 10018
USA

www.bloomsbury.com

BLOOMSBURY and the Diana logo are trademarks of Bloomsbury Publishing Plc

Originally published as 朝日新聞「検証．昭和報道」取材班著『新聞と「昭和」』
by the Asahi Shimbun Company, 2010.
© The Asahi Shimbun Company, 2010

This translation is published by Bloomsbury Publishing Plc by arrangement with Asahi
Shimbun Publications Inc. c/o Tuttle Mori Agency, Inc.

English translation © Barak Kushner, 2015

British Library Cataloguing-in-Publication Data
A catalogue record for this book is available from the British Library.

ISBN: HB: 978–1–4725–0956–7
        ePDF: 978–1–4725–1417–2
        ePub: 978–1–4725–1226–0

Library of Congress Cataloging-in-Publication Data
A catalog record for this book is available from the Library of Congress.

Series: SOAS Studies in Modern and Contemporary Japan

Typeset by RefineCatch Limited, Bungay, Suffolk
Printed and bound in Great Britain

Contents

List of Illustrations

Foreword

The trials and tribulations of journalism—withstanding the judgment of history.

Until now, I have never believed the axiom "History repeats itself." Does history really re-occur in exactly the same manner? That seems unrealistic. And yet, I have at times been taken aback by the feeling of previously having heard things like a sort of rhythm, or background music to one's experiences. Lately, this no longer just stops at the feeling of *déjà vu*. This refrain I keep hearing has grown to the point of unease and it has the same cadence, tone, and quality of something that I have experienced before.

In Japan and the world at large, newspapers, television, the internet, and blogs are surging with populism and nationalism.

Whether this is the Russian annexation of the Crimea Peninsula from Ukraine; the East and South China Sea conflicts between China and its neighbors regarding territorial rights; or Britain, France, Russia, and Turkey's responses to the civil war in Syria—what is stirring up this sentiment and behavior is, along with strategic interests, the hidden hand of history and memory in the background.

Media arouse a nation's memory and play an exceedingly important role in forming historical views and historical consciousness. If how the media report and editorialize is stained with populism and nationalism, the result is terrifying. We know that at one extreme going down this path leads to ethnic cleansing and war. Nonetheless, journalism's grasp on this is still rather limited. That I find is even more terrifying.

Reporters who write the first dispatch weave together their stories from all sorts of sources and eyewitness accounts at the scene, but these may not form a seamless whole. Those people at the heart of the affair—with their psychology, their loves, their hopes, their fears, their jealousy, and their pride all wrapped up in the story—settle into the sediment as memory. News is an element of history and gives life to memory. But how is that news crafted into an article and released into the public? What is the process it passes through to become memory and history? Moreover, to what extent can that news withstand the scrutiny of history?

In the case of Japan, early modern and modern history is even now casting its long shadow over Japanese domestic politics, education, foreign policy, and national security. This was especially true during the Showa era (1926–1989) when upheaval followed upheaval in the Sino-Japanese War, the Pacific War, defeat, the occupation, and the Cold War. Given these events, the telling of history and memory risked easily becoming confused, ideologized, and politicized. As we move into the twenty-first century, this has clearly started to become a problem in foreign policy. Comfort women, official visits to the Yasukuni Shrine, and other historical problems have started to grate against Japan's relations with neighboring countries. To directly face history, retrieve its lessons, and build on that for a brighter future, is even more than before the important responsibility and role of journalists and journalism.

In view of this, the *Asahi Newspaper* has investigated its own reporting over the Showa era and examined whether or not its reporting can stand up to history. Where and when during the Showa era did journalism, whose core mission is to keep an eye on power, lose its viability? Moreover, at what turning point did it lose its freedom to report? For the *Asahi Newspaper* was it the Manchurian Incident in September 1931 that was the moment when it lost both? The October 1, 1931 Osaka *Asahi* ran an editorial commenting on the birth of an independent Manchuria: "There is no reason we should oppose celebrating this event," thus easily accepting as a fait accompli the Manchurian Incident. A year later, the Lytton Report was released to the public and *Asahi* resolutely entered the "empty rhetorical realm ignoring history." With this decision, in one fell swoop, Japan deepened its international isolation.

Even so, on May 15, 1932, *Asahi* criticized the violence of the May 15 Incident, when a group of military officers attacked high-level Japanese officials. However, on February 26, 1936, during the attempted military coup, even though the Tokyo head office had itself been attacked by rebellious soldiers, immediately afterward the paper did not publish an editorial that directly excoriated the military. At this time, it was already apparent that articles that displeased the military would face censorship and not be published. In July 1937, when the Marco Polo Bridge Incident (also known as the China Incident) erupted, essentially the start of the Sino-Japanese War, the freedom to report, nay, the responsibility to report, had already died.

At the time of the May 15 Incident, public opinion sympathized more with the underdog terrorists than with the victims. A flood of petitions poured in asking for diminished sentences for the young officer assassins. *Asahi* walked in step with that public opinion. What threatens freedom of the press is not necessarily only official authority. Journalists have their own attitudes and stances, and their self-censoring and populism also hollows out from within the integrity of journalism.

I am very pleased that Bloomsbury Publishing is to produce the English translation of *Media, Propaganda and Politics in 20th-Century Japan*. For a long time, English journalism was the model for Japanese journalism and *Asahi* is no exception. My previous colleagues at *Asahi* drew many insights from Walter Bagehot, Wickham Steed and others, striving to create quality journalism. What motivated my predecessors at the newspaper was the British journalistic belief that without the freedom to report, democracy would not thrive. This book, which investigates the way in which *Asahi* reported the Showa era, is also an analysis of the failures of journalists who yearned to follow their beliefs and the trajectories of those who had to start all over again. This process is not only something necessary for *Asahi* to reflect on and admonish itself over. I firmly believe this is an important reference and set of lessons that should be in common to the world of media.

The English translation of the book was made possible by the generous endeavors of Dr Barak Kushner from the University of Cambridge. Barak came to Tokyo on the occasion of the Japanese publication of the original book to join an international symposium on the topic as a panelist, where he gave a speech. It is due to his scholarly insight into the modern history of Japan and northeast Asia and his careful attention to contemporary Japanese society that made production of this translation possible. Once more, I thank him for his efforts.

Funabashi Yoichi (former editor-in-chief of the *Asahi Newspaper*, and
Chairman of the Rebuild Japan Initiative Foundation, RJIF)
Tokyo, August 2014

Translator's Preface

The translation of this very detailed analysis from the *Asahi Newspaper* Company, concerning its own role and the impact of Japanese media on the course of Japanese history during the Showa era (1926–1989), grew out of a summer translation seminar hosted at the School of Oriental and Asian Studies (SOAS) in London. Under the sponsorship of Dr Christopher Gerteis and funded by the Nippon Foundation, we gathered a team for a week in September 2012 and got to work. Initially, the base translation was coordinated under my tutelage and completed by six very talented graduate student translators from various fields: Polly Barton (freelance translator), Angelika Koch (University of Cambridge), Sam Malissa (Yale University), Sherzod Muminov (University of Cambridge), Sara Osenton (University of Toronto), and Craig Smith (University of British Columbia). We also had the assistance of Asa Yoneda as a freelance translator during our week in London and Mujeeb Khan later joined to help check the names and fluidity of the text. The whole "Team Asahi" ably worked on their sections and in consultation with my efforts we brought the much longer Japanese version into an abridged length for English publication.

After countless months of hard work, the team passed the sections back to me for editing and checking. I was also assisted in this endeavor by Jōmaru Yōichi and his team at the *Asahi Newspaper*, who devoted hours of their own personal time drawing up a long list of readings for all the Japanese names that appeared in the original text. There were so many names of journalists and inside eyewitnesses unknown to the outside world that without Jōmaru-san's constant attention to assiduously following through on all my requests, we would not have been able to proceed. It is also, of course, due to the unwavering support of Funabashi Yōichi, now managing his own think tank in Tokyo, that this project got off the ground and that we secured the rights to the book. The *Asahi Newspaper* Company has fully supported this endeavor and we appreciate their patronage. We also have to thank, equally importantly, *Asahi* for permission to use many of the fine images that garnish the translation. We would have preferred to use them all, but in keeping the book a bit slimmer for English publication, I am particularly pleased that at least some of these historically key photographs are now available in an English language version. From the start, Bloomsbury Publishing has been very supportive of our effort to bring forth key Japanese texts into English and this is hopefully the first of many. A special note of thanks to editor Claire Lipscomb and her team at Bloomsbury for their long-term support.

As with many Japanese books of this length and nature, footnotes were often kept to a minimum in the original. In some areas where we felt it useful to English language readers, the graduate students tracked down the original source but frequently we left the notes slim to cut down on length but also to give interested readers a chance for further reading in Japanese. Because the original was also very detailed in parts for

Japanese readers, we reduced those sections or occasionally cut out sections that might have been a bit more superfluous for international readers in the English language. In short, while the translation is mostly faithful to the original, it should be considered abridged due to these careful omissions. Lastly, I must thank my partner Mami Mizutori who assisted me in the yeoman's task of checking the smaller details and finding inconsistencies in various spots. Without her eagle eyes, the final product would not be as polished.

Barak Kushner
Cambridge, August 2014

Note on Transliteration

Japanese, Chinese, and Korean names appear in the East Asian order, with family name first. Japanese words are normally printed in italics, except when the word, such as anime and samurai, has entered the English language. Long vowels in Japanese are indicated by a macron, as in *shōyu*, although this rule has not been applied to common place names, as in Tokyo, Osaka, and Kyoto.

1

The Last Days of an Era

The neon lights of Ginza go dark

It was 5:00 a.m. and lights from television cameras illuminated the front doors. *Asahi* journalist Sakurai Izumi, then 29 years old, jumped out of a shuttle bus shared by various news agencies awaiting news of the Emperor's condition. Chief court physician Takagi Akira had just emerged from his home with a grim expression on his face and got into a car headed for the Tokyo palace, led by a police escort. The condition of Emperor Showa (known more commonly in the West as Emperor Hirohito) had suddenly deteriorated. Sakurai rang the Tokyo main office with a mobile phone, rare in those days, and the reporter on night duty woke up other reporters one after another. This was how coverage of the last day of Japan's Showa Era (1926–1989) began on January 7, 1989.

At 7:55 a.m., Chief Cabinet Secretary Obuchi Keizō and Grand Steward of the Imperial Household Agency Fujimori Shōichi each assembled emergency press conferences. They announced that "His Majesty the Emperor passed away at 6:33 this morning in the Palace." On that day 18 million special editions were published according to the Japan Newspaper Publishers and Editors Association. As the time passed, newspaper headlines changed from "The Emperor is Critically Ill" to "The Emperor has Passed Away" and "The Start of a New Reign." On the same day in the evening edition of the *Asahi*, articles about the Emperor filled the best part of sixteen pages. An editorial under the title "Ushering out the Showa Era" graced the front page. Other pages were lined with commemorative articles about the Emperor, including one entitled "Highs and Lows of the Showa Era: a Record of the Emperor's Life." Stories on subjects unrelated to the Emperor's death were brief, limited to only eight items on the local news page. Advertisements were kept to a bare minimum.

Following the request of the government that "all ministries and agencies refrain from entertainment activities for six days, citizens should also observe mourning for two days," the neon lights of the busy shopping streets were switched off. This "refrain from entertainment" recommendation emulated practices after the Taisho Emperor passed away on December 25, 1926. At midnight, the electronic billboards over the dark of the Ginza streets lit up brightly with the Japanese phrase "The Heisei Era Begins." For the next couple of days, television stations continued to air commemorative programs under titles such as "Remembering His Majesty the Emperor," "The Emperor's Demise,"

Figure 1   Emperor Hirohito attending what was to be his last spring garden party, May 19, 1988, at the Akasaka Estate in Tokyo.

and "His Majesty and Me." TV commercials were not aired for two days. Although some saw this time as "a great opportunity to learn about modern history," video-rental shops were packed with customers who had tired of the monotonous programming.

During the 111 days starting in September 1988 when the Emperor coughed up large amounts of blood, the Japanese media, including the *Asahi Newspaper*, had meticulously covered the monarch's condition, noting his pulse rate and blood in his bowels. On the day he finally passed away, the media released a flood of pre-prepared articles and programs. The political scientist Shinohara Hajime used the term "conformity syndrome" in criticizing the newspapers caught up in writing exclusively about the Emperor on January 7 and 8. Touching on the issue of the Emperor's war responsibility, *The Times* editorial wrote, "Hirohito's personal role still remains discreetly veiled. [...] To Western sensibilities, the shared experience of the Japanese extended almost to a collective cover-up during the Emperor's lifetime."[1]

A question of terminology

"His Majesty's Demise" was the headline on the front page of the January 7, 1989 evening edition of the *Asahi*. The *Yomiuri* and *Mainichi* newspapers printed the same headlines. The Japanese word, *hōgyo* ("passing away"), was a special term used to denote the death of an emperor. But was it appropriate to use a term that belonged to the prewar era of imperial sovereignty in the period of postwar democracy? Was it not better to use the more general word, *seikyo* (passing), with only an honorific prefix added? This was the central dilemma newspapers faced at the time of the Emperor's death. Although *Asahi* used the term *hōgyo* in its headlines and the leads to articles and news stories, content employed more basic and simple terminology. Regardless, it was the front-page headline that usually set the overall tone. Among the regional press, there were newspapers that used less ceremonial terms, albeit comparatively few. The question, then, was why did *Asahi* use the more elaborate and prewar terminology?

Kishida Hideo, the long-serving senior staff writer responsible for covering the Imperial Household, compiled a confidential internal manual on his appointment in 1978. "The Showa Problem" was written as an editorial style guide in the event of the Emperor's death. Kishida wrote the following about word choice in case of an imperial death:

> Because the Imperial Household Law uses the Chinese characters [kanji] for *hōgyo* in passages such as "In case of the Emperor's passing away . . . ," it is permissible to use the word in newspaper headlines. However, within articles we should use simple terms, such as *seikyo* (passing), *shikyo* (death), *eimin* (eternal rest).

This was not, however, an official decision by the *Asahi Newspaper* company.

One of the background factors that eventually led to *Asahi*'s choice was how the February 1987 death of Nobuhito, Prince Takamatsu, the younger brother of Emperor Hirohito, was reported. Iwai Katsumi, then the *Asahi* correspondent responsible for coverage of the Imperial Household Agency, used a simple term when he submitted the line, "His Imperial Highness Prince Takamatsu [. . .] has passed away." This was the first death of a member of the imperial family since Prince Chichibu in 1953, another younger brother of the Emperor. *Asahi* had used the same term in the headline, "His Imperial Highness Prince Chichibu has Passed Away." Iwai Katsumi was apparently following that usage and Yoshikawa Toshio of the local news desk deemed this acceptable. Headlines in the *Asahi* Tokyo evening issue reported Prince Takamatsu's death by using the simpler term, while all other national newspapers employed the slightly more flowery vocabulary in their headlines.

A unanimous decision was never reached and heated discussions continued within the *Asahi Newspaper* company.

Drawing a line between the old Showa and the new

On March 2, 1987, not long after Prince Takamatsu's death, a division editors' meeting at the *Asahi* Tokyo office became the venue for a fierce dispute concerning the terms to be used in the event of the Emperor's death. Some argued: "There is an ideology behind every word. The term *hōgyo* is not appropriate for the symbolic Emperor of today. The situation today is different from the period when it was believed that honorific language was absolutely necessary to prevent disrespect toward the Emperor." Others voices still contended: "Is it acceptable to use the word *seikyo* in the headlines while all other media are using *hōgyo*?" Yet other voices contended, "*seikyo* is easily understood by the young generation, whereas elderly readers easily accept the term *hōgyo*." The debate was speaking to a conflict between those for whom the tenets of postwar democracy were sacrosanct, and those who prioritized the reaction of the Japanese public.

In September 1987, the Emperor was hospitalized with a bowel-related disease and underwent an operation, following which his condition started to improve. In March of the following year, Takagi Toshiyuki of the local news desk at *Asahi* received an internal memo from the reporter covering the Imperial Household Agency. The memo was a bulletin from an information exchange among the major newspaper companies and contained a list of terms to be used in the event of the Emperor's death. All companies planned to use the word *hōgyo* in their headlines.

Itō Kunio, the Tokyo office managing editor, handed down the final decision to use the term *hōgyo*. He remembers it as follows:

> At the time, personally, I felt it was acceptable to use the word *seikyo* [with an honorific prefix]. However, there was a danger of inviting public indignation if only *Asahi* went against the flow, and I wanted to avoid this reaction if at all possible. I decided it was not worth voicing a defiant opinion given the situation.

According to Gotō Fumiyasu, a committee member at the Japan Newspaper Publishers and Editors Association, an overwhelming majority of newspapers used the more traditional term *hōgyo* in headlines. Only seven papers utilized different terminology and the *Nagasaki Shimbun* managing editor, Iwanaga Hisashi, now says why:

> We belong to the generation that was impelled to join the war effort, the outcome of which was the atomic bomb. I opposed the word *hōgyo*, which acts as a reminder that we are still attached to the prewar imperial system. And the reaction toward the word *seikyo* was not as bad as we had expected.

During this time the debate carried on in the *Asahi* copyediting department, which was responsible for headlines. Hiroiwa Kunihiko, the department chief whose job was to explain the course taken by the company, remembers that "the rule to use the word *hōgyo* only once in the headline became the line separating us from the old Showa era." Based on the long debates that continued until the death of Emperor Hirohito, in March 1990 *Asahi* revised its list of standard words used for the Imperial Household. The revised version made it clear that "as a rule, the term *hōgyo* is not to be used," as it is "a word with which our current readers will be unfamiliar."

The illness kept secret

In Japan, there is a social debate about whether or not to inform patients that they have cancer. The case was not simple when it came to the Emperor. How much about his condition should be disclosed? On the night of September 16, 1987, the *Asahi*'s newly appointed reporter for the Imperial Household Agency, Shimizu Tateo, noticed that lights were still on in one of the agency's rooms. When he knocked on the door, he observed a group of court physicians having a discussion over an X-ray print. One of the more senior doctors then turned toward Shimizu and told him to "clear out immediately." Shimizu informed the senior staff writer Kishida Hideo, who "made a round of telephone calls to people in the know." On the morning of September 17, Kishida took a car equipped with a telephone and made hasty visits to the houses of the people concerned, according to internal *Asahi* records. Imperial Chamberlain Urabe Ryōgo wrote in his diary that he "deliberated with general affairs section chiefs concerning how to deal with the media. We need to be aware of Kishida's disquieting behavior. We should assemble materials detailing the condition of His Majesty's health."

So there were two parties involved, one that concealed the truth and the other that tried to reveal it.

On September 19, 1987, *Asahi* published a front-page scoop under the headline "His Majesty has an Intestinal Illness." On the 22nd, the Emperor underwent an operation, the purpose of which was to remove "an intestinal blockage." As then chief physician to the Emperor, Takagi Akira, wrote later in his book *111 Last Days of the Showa Emperor*, "Having opened the abdomen, I saw with my own eyes that the pancreas was swollen and understood that it was clearly cancer. I thought the certainty was as high as 90 percent." Yet in his statement to the public Takagi said, "As a result of the operation it seems that the Emperor has chronic inflammation of the pancreas." The imperial medical team chose not to reveal to the Emperor that he had cancer. However, the media suspected the truth. Bearing in mind that the doctors had not disclosed the nature of the illness, all the media companies kept their silence about the Emperor's cancer for around a year.

The debate on whether or not to report "the cancer"

Following his operation in September 1987, the Emperor's cancer became a fact known not only to the medical community and the Imperial Household Agency but many media outlets as well. Yet none of these media were willing to break the story first. The Emperor, who seemed to be on his way to recovery, coughed up large amounts of blood on September 19, 1988, almost one year after his operation. Afterward, his condition worsened. The September 24 evening edition of the *Asahi* ran a story, "His Majesty the Emperor is Seriously Ill." Next to the story was an article with the headline " 'Cancer' has Been Found in His Majesty's Pancreas." (Within the Japanese media, *Asahi* became the first to announce the true nature of the Emperor's illness.) In the May 1989 issue of *Newspaper Research* (*Shimbun Kenkyū*), at a roundtable discussion, senior staff writer Kishida Hideo explained the decision: "Fundamentally, the issue of why the Emperor was in a grave condition had to be made clear. This was based on the fact that the Emperor was the most 'public' of public officials and the facts had to be disclosed at that stage," he said.

Once *Asahi* broke the story, *Kyōdō News* released an announcement about the Emperor's cancer in its September 25 morning bulletin. However, many newspapers such as the *Yomiuri* adhered to a policy of not announcing these facts during the Emperor's lifetime. No nationwide consensus on whether to announce the truth existed because even though the Emperor was a public figure, he was thought to be different from the position of a politician. Factors leading to this disagreement differed from one newspaper company to another. Shortly after the news about the Emperor's cancer appeared, the Grand Steward of the Imperial Household Agency, Fujimori Shōichi, lodged a complaint against the *Asahi Newspaper* company. He said, "We have not mentioned to the Emperor out of concern that he was under treatment and such reports were inappropriate. The court physicians stated their decision to reveal the truth to the public only when the Emperor passes away, and I agree with them." Itō Kunio, managing editor of the *Asahi* Tokyo office, remembers it as follows:

> I heard that some members of the Imperial family were angry with us. Two or three days after receiving that phone call I paid a visit to the Imperial Household Agency and apologized to Fujimori for "causing trouble." I considered the Grand Steward's position and wanted to simply pay my respects. The aim of my visit was not to imply that we were ready to withdraw the article or issue a formal apology.

Nippon Television never broke its silence over the Emperor's cancer, nor did it immediately report the displeasure expressed by the Imperial Household Agency. Head of the Nippon TV news investigation team, Ishii Shūhei, reminisces:

> In breaking the story about the Emperor's cancer, *Asahi* showed a certain amount of good insight. This in itself deserves respect. I thought that publicizing the Imperial Household Agency's reaction would have ended up diminishing the space for future media rhetorical judgments.

Then the Emperor's health miraculously started to improve again. Suddenly, sections of the public judged that the *Asahi* news story had been rash, and public opinion ranged from the belief that revealing the name of the illness was what journalists do to that it was an inconsiderate piece of reporting. To this day, Japanese public opinion is still divided on whether or not it was a blunder.

Behind "excessive reporting"

On September 20, 1988, the *Asahi* published an article under a large-print headline, "Has His Majesty's Condition Suddenly Deteriorated?" For a week the newspaper published almost daily updates on the Emperor's condition on the front page. There were front-page reports about "new hemorrhages," but also stories reporting "No Changes in His Majesty's Condition." In the meantime, news of other events was secondary: medals being won in the Seoul Olympics, or the battle between the ruling and opposition parties on the introduction of the consumption tax. This excessive attention to the Emperor's condition attracted criticism about "over-reporting." Some also pilloried the abundance of news reports in the media for encouraging the cancellation of festivals and demanding restraint from the public. One of the reasons behind the deluge of news reports on the Emperor was that his serious condition was unpredictable. Tashiro Kikuo, president of TV Asahi, offered his take on the issue in an October 1988 press conference. His tone was contrite: "Having misjudged rapid changes in the Emperor's condition, media outlets have egged each other on, causing a sort of excessive reporting."

On January 7, 1989, the day Emperor Hirohito died, the newspapers were replete with related stories on the topic and television channels followed a special, commercial-free schedule for the next two days. At the end of the same month, *Asahi* conducted a survey of people's opinions on developments after the Emperor's health took a turn for the worse. The majority of those polled (57 percent) believed that "the media was overly excited." Compared with the detailed accounts of the Emperor's health, there were very few stories touching upon his war responsibility, a major topic for the overseas press. On December 7, 1988, mayor of Nagasaki, Motoshima Hitoshi, mentioned to the city assembly that he believed "the Emperor was responsible for the war." Right-wing propaganda trucks started to drive around the streets of Nagasaki proclaiming, "Divine punishment for Motoshima!" An *Asahi* editorial on December 19 disparaged this action, declaring that, "The use of threatening behavior in response to freely expressed opinions menaces the foundations of democracy." Yet the newspaper's own stance on war responsibility remained ambiguous and ultimately unresolved, as seen in the paper's statement that "whether or not the Emperor bears responsibility for the war is a problem that should be considered in a different venue."

The day after the Emperor's death, on January 8, 1989, the *Asahi* morning edition published a discussion about the Emperor by three scholars. The following day the paper printed a page-long special section devoted to the issue of war responsibility. On January 12, in a front-page series, senior staff writer Ishikawa Masumi wrote on the topic of war responsibility. But there were no editorials that addressed the issue directly. While media outlets were reluctant to take a stance, Nagasaki Mayor Motoshima, who made a stand with his statement, was seriously wounded when an ultra right-wing member shot him in January 1990. It was only on August 15, 2001 that an *Asahi* editorial stated:

When we consider that the Emperor was the supreme commander of the Army and Navy and that orders were handed down to the "Imperial Army" in his name, it is impossible to escape the conclusion that he is responsible for the war.

2

The Beginning of the Showa Era—Economic Depression

"Welcoming" the Wall Street crash

On October 24, 1929, the share prices of the New York Stock Exchange crashed. Known as "Black Thursday," this event touched off the global panic that developed into the Great Depression. The headlines of the Tokyo *Asahi* evening edition on the 26th read: "Great Confusion at the New York Stock Exchange as Shares Collapse All at Once. Unprecedented Number of Transactions." Although the words themselves were dramatic, the relevant article was in fact just a small section on the economics page. The article, which was not written by *Asahi* journalists, was a news feed from a different media agency. The news reported: "Immediately after the opening bell, as if jettisoned from an avalanche, shares plummeted in an instant," and "The market shuddered following this unprecedented tsunami and the closing prices continued to fluctuate in aftershocks." Next to this report was a short and optimistic article analyzing the impact these changes had on Japan under the headline, "Kabutochō [Japan's Wall Street] Welcomes Lower Interest Rates." The piece argued: "New York's high interest rates, which have long troubled global financial circles, seem to have returned to normalcy. It is a very propitious time to lift the ban on the gold standard in our country."

From the point of view of Japanese investors, the *Asahi Newspaper* went as far as writing that the fall of interest rates in the US, resulting from the stock market crash, was a development that "should be greatly welcomed." This was a one-sided look at things that ignored effects other than that on interest rates. Nonetheless, this is how the papers reported it. At the time, interdependence among countries was deepening through finance and trade. However, newspapers provided no analysis on background causes of the US stock market crash or the ways in which the crash might influence the world economy. On October 24, the day of the crash, share prices showed some recovery following large purchases in the afternoon. The average fall in share prices was not more than a third of that of the previous day because the banks were supporting the system by buying shares. The October 27 evening edition of *Asahi* reflected on these developments as if it were an action movie:

Amid this turmoil, a "Morgan broker," Richard Whitney, quietly appeared and suddenly yelled for a purchase of twenty-five thousand shares of US steel at 205 dollars. [...] This announcement ran through the market like an electric shock and immediately changed the state of the market. [...] It was a truly breathtaking and dramatic scene to behold.

The New York Times also shifted its focus from the crash to the intervention by the banks: the front page on October 25 read, "Worst Stock Crash Stemmed by Banks; 12,894,650-Share Day Swamps Market; Leaders Confer, Find Conditions Sound."[1] The fall in share prices continued, causing panic on a global scale but *Asahi*'s pages offered no recognition of the "crisis of the century." On October 31, the newspaper printed the following in the morning edition: "Although it is hard to deny that the decline in share prices will contribute to the depreciation of assets and to a fall in purchasing power [...] it is hardly a problem when viewed from the perspective of total American purchasing power." However, in Japan the banking bubble had already begun to deflate over the previous two years.

Geishas run on the banks

On the morning of April 18, 1927, almost four months after the end of the Taisho era, geisha ladies were lying in the spring sun in Kyoto's Maruyama Park and recovering from the fatigue of the previous night. A man came by and yelled, "If the Taiwan Bank goes bust so will the Mitsui Bank!" The geishas all returned home in a great hurry, picked up their bankbooks and rushed out into the streets again. "This is how the run on the Mitsui Bank branches began," reported the May 4, 1927 morning edition of the Tokyo *Asahi*. On April 18, the Bank of Taiwan, Japan's central colonial bank for Taiwan, had actually suspended operations. In the spring of 1927, two and a half years before the New York stock market crash, anxiety about the management of Japanese banks spread across the country. The rush of depositors withdrawing their money from banks soon swept successively through Japan. This came to be known as "the Showa era financial panic."

What triggered this crisis was an inappropriate remark by Finance Minister Kataoka Naoharu in March 1927. During a Diet session, he inadvertently said that the Watanabe Bank of Tokyo had "failed," although the bank was still functioning.[2] On April 21, following the closure of the Taiwan Bank, the Jūgo Bank, which enjoyed deep connections with and the trust of the nobility, also suspended operations. According to a collection of lectures, *Developments in Our Financial Circles During the Last Decade* by Yūki Toyotarō, who had worked both as a banker and finance minister, "almost all banks throughout Japan had completely lost the trust of their customers and faced mass withdrawals." Yūki delivered his harsh words to the newspapers: "If the media had taken a slightly more prudent attitude, maybe we could have got away without these serious disturbances reaching all sectors of the whole financial system." Indeed, as the run on banks spread, articles about the crisis filled the newspapers. Yet in the *Asahi*, reports about individual banks' potential managerial crises before they went bust were nowhere to be found and the general impression was that the newspaper was being cautious. Two major causes for the banks' instability were putting off dealing with losses and the collapse of the financial bubble. The paper graphically detailed the situation on March 24, 1927:

> During the great recession of 1920 and the losses suffered by the banks as a result of the 1923 Great Kanto Earthquake, temporary bandages were applied in vain when in reality drastic surgery was required. Losses gave birth to further losses, and within several years the financial tumor grew larger, swelling and putrefying into extensive losses. Finance Minister Kataoka's first measures lanced the wound but the pus that was silently building up inside suddenly erupted and leaked out all over the financial world.[3]

During the cheery economic climate of the First World War, businesses had quickly expanded the scope of their investments. Managers of companies concurrently held posts as executives of banks and financed themselves with bank loans instead of using company proper funds, and bad loans piled up. As *Asahi* noted on April 24, businesses were obsessed with new schemes, "which was akin to building 7-story reinforced concrete buildings on sites with no foundation. The industry has taken to heights of fancy based on exceedingly fragile foundations."

No banknotes left

Three days after the Taiwan Bank shut temporarily, the run on banks spread throughout Japan, causing pandemonium at tellers' windows. When Ikeda Shigeaki, managing director of the Mitsui Bank and Chairman of the Board of the Tokyo Clearing House, paid a visit to the Bank of Japan on April 21, 1927, he was taken to a separate room by Vice-President Hijikata Hisaakira. "Listen," said Hijikata, "we have run out of banknotes. There are not enough notes to lend." With each bank borrowing large amounts of cash from the Bank of Japan to cope with their withdrawals, even the central bank, which issued the banknotes, suddenly found itself running out of bills. Ikeda was shocked and angry: "Mitsui Bank itself has to borrow from 30 to 50 million yen (15 to 25 million US dollars in nominal terms at the time).[4] We cannot do without several hundred millions worth of notes. What on earth have you been doing?" According to the *Critical Biography of Takahashi Korekiyo* by Imamura Takeo, while the usual amount of bills produced was around one billion yen, on that day the demand for notes exceeded 2.3 billion yen. They could not cover the demand even by using old banknotes that were scheduled for incineration. The Bank of Japan hastily printed a large number of 200-yen notes but the backs of these notes were left blank. "Piled up at the teller windows, the main purpose of printing these notes was to put the depositors' minds to rest." It was also on April 21st that the Cabinet issued a decision declaring a moratorium on all payments. With this decision, banks could put holds on withdrawals for three weeks. The April 25 morning issue of *Asahi* printed Vice-President Hijikata's opinion on the new 200-yen note. Without mentioning the fact that the back of the note was blank, he said that "although it looks somewhat flimsy, it has the Bank of Japan watermark so there is no fear that it is counterfeit." The front page of the evening edition on the same

Figure 2 People queuing to withdraw their deposits from the Nakano Bank in Tokyo in March 1927.

day contained a photograph of heaps of new notes piled up at tellers' windows. As a result, the run on banks calmed down for a while.

The *Asahi* was consistent in its negative stance toward the government's support of the banks: "There are unreliable banks that have met the fate they deserved and are reaping what they have sown."[5] On May 9, the Bank of Japan announced special financial measures and passed a law to compensate those who had incurred losses. The next day's editorial criticized this decision:

> If the scope of the financial rescue initiative were limited to redressing the equilibrium in the financial sector, it could be carried out with minimal burden on the public. Yet the bill introduced by the government far and away exceeds this scope, aiming to rescue the numerous unreliable banks that are still operating. Consequently, it seems inevitable that the government will appropriate enormous public funds. [...] The people will shoulder the burden of repaying the bad loans, not the individuals really responsible for the failings of those banks.

In the same way, *Asahi* initially opposed the tax injection during the Housing Loan Corporation's failure in the mid-1990s. Following heated debates in the Diet, the decision to inject 685 billion yen was eventually passed. Should public money be used to rescue financial institutions that played around with money during the bubble era? Now, as in the past, this question remains a dilemma.

The gold standard

On a summer day in 1929, Finance Minister Inoue Junnosuke was delivering a lecture in Kyoto, passionately explaining campaign pledges to lift the gold embargo and the financial austerity measures by the Cabinet of Prime Minister Hamaguchi Osachi. The lifting of the gold embargo, a return to the gold standard system whereby the value of the currency was supported by gold, would put Japan on equal footing with the great powers. This was Japan's fervent wish at the time. During the First World War, the leading nations of the world suspended the gold exchange and banned the export of gold, thereby putting an end to the gold standard system to exchange paper money for gold. While other nations had returned to the gold standard after the war, Japan, whose economy had remained mired in chaos thanks to the recession, the Great Kanto earthquake and the "financial panic," had not yet done so. In this way, Japan lagged behind the rest of the world.

But how was the government to re-establish exchange rates once the gold embargo was lifted? Compared with the pre-embargo parity, the new exchange rate at the time would depreciate the yen. A devalued yen was considered a national disgrace for a country aspiring to become a great power. The government, therefore, aimed to lift the embargo at the rate from before the war, from when the yen was valued higher. All the major newspapers, including *Asahi*, also endorsed the pre-embargo parity. The lifting of the gold embargo based on the old parity would supposedly lead to a strong yen and it was expected this would have force a tight budget and cut public works. This was the Showa era's "structural reform." The government, the press and the people headed down the road of lifting the gold embargo because it was seen as the last resort to overcome the chronic recession of the post-First World War era. The Tokyo *Asahi* stated on November 16, 1929:

> The economy will rebalance itself only if this tumor is cut open in a major operation called the lifting of the gold embargo. [...] As it is a large-scale operation, some bouts of post-operative fever are inevitable [...] but it is not something to worry about.

However, some voices begged to differ with this interpretation. Ishibashi Tanzan, chief editor of *The Oriental Economist* (*Tōyō Keizai Shimpō*), who also became the Prime Minister in the 1950s, advocated lifting the gold embargo based on a new exchange rate with a weaker yen. He wrote:

> Because we do not know whether the financial system will be able to withstand this change, it is extremely dangerous. This sort of a gamble is not something a country worthy of the name should risk. [...] The people of this country worship concepts such as "consolidation" or "austerity" as if they were idols.

The US stock market crashed in the autumn of 1929, yet an *Asahi* editorial from November 22 of the same year wrote: "Even if the gold embargo were lifted, it is difficult to think this would cause further economic problems." On January 11, 1930, the day the gold embargo was lifted, headlines in the morning edition joyously proclaimed that, "The dark clouds of many years have finally cleared!" and "The time has come for the development of national strength." In reality, however, lifting the gold embargo dealt a major blow to the Japanese economy.

Tramps in camps

"Last Night Fifteen Hundred Vagrants Marched Out, with Brooms on Their Shoulders, to Clean the City Streets," read the front page of the *Asahi* evening edition on December 27, 1930, adorned with a photo of the event. The streets of Tokyo were being cleaned thanks to the "volunteering of fifteen hundred tramps" who lived in "the tent camp in Hamazonochō, Fukagawa Ward" and in "other places of residence for the Tokyo homeless." They "received a small remuneration of 50 sen and a meal coupon for 10 sen to be used in public eateries for their services." In Tokyo at the time, one could get a haircut for 50 sen and a serving of curry rice cost 10 sen. One year after the stock market crash in the US, when economic depression was spreading throughout the world, Japan was suffering rising unemployment and the subject of vagrancy frequently appeared in newspaper pages. *Asahi*, which had supported the lifting of the gold embargo and the government's austerity policies, took up the subject of unemployment in earnest in its March 17, 1930 morning edition. An unusually long special feature queried the policies under the headline, "What to Make of the Unemployment Hell that has Swept Across the Country Like a Tsunami?" This article marked a turning point in the newspaper's fundamental stance on plans to boost the economy.

The article claimed, "The economic depression has further worsened as a result of the lifting of the gold embargo, the curtailed budget and consumer savings." With this *Asahi* acknowledged that the policies it had previously supported had actually accelerated the depression. Moreover, it criticized the government when it said, "the policy to curb unemployment that is currently being implemented is nothing but a stopgap measure." Comments from intellectuals also revealed a critical stance toward the government, such as those from the anti-government side like Abe Isoo of the Social-Democratic Party and Kawakami Hajime of the Workers and Peasants Party. Their slogan was "Establish public work projects—rescue the workers!" "Tales of No Food and No Job—Told Through Tears by Workers in the Heartless World of Greater Tokyo" was the headline of the morning edition on May 20, 1930, which introduced readers to the tough lives of the unemployed. News correspondents interviewed some of the 3,500 applicants for unemployment relief funds. Headlines told of a former elementary school teacher who said, "my wife is in tears on her sickbed and I was forced to send my beloved children to an orphanage; we are surviving on a diet of rice given to us as alms." "Caring for my elderly mother, should I choose to die or commit a crime? Born into a millionaire family, the tears of a man who has gone from riches to rags," another one detailed. Long lines of the unemployed formed at job center offices in every region. A caption under a photo of one such queue, published in the December 20, 1930 evening edition read: "From seven in the morning this great serpent of a queue winds through one city quarter after another."

The first time that nationwide unemployment statistics were properly obtained was in the national census of October 1930. The results, including figures for all prefectures and major municipalities, were published on *Asahi*'s front page in the December 11, 1930 evening edition. Writing about the nation's 322,527 unemployed, the editorial on the following day dismissed this figure out of hand as "insignificant," claiming that "it would by no means be considered excessive even if the estimate were over a million people." In reality, however, if the number of unemployed really were a million, it would have equaled 1.6 percent of Japan's population and thus have surpassed the unemployment rate (1.2 percent) in the US, which was the epicenter of the global recession.

Only the bad news

An old man from Tochigi Prefecture was wandering around Ueno Station at night carrying his dead daughter on his back. Struggling against poverty, he had dispatched his 19-year-old daughter to work as a live-in worker in a liquor shop in Tokyo's Kameido district. The advance salary was 50 yen. In those days, the starting salary of a primary school teacher was around 45–55 yen. The girl had fallen seriously ill with a chest infection and her father had come to take her back home, giving her a piggyback to the station. But the girl died on the way to the station, drawing her last breath on her father's back. An article about this incident, under a tiny headline, "Tragic Stories of the Great Depression," was published in the May 10, 1930 morning edition of the Tokyo *Asahi*. In October 1930, *Asahi* organized a meeting of executives from its headquarters and regional bureaus. An internal newsletter about this meeting disclosed the aims:

> Vice-President Shimomura Hiroshi said: "There are lots of articles about family suicides and food poverty. When one looks at these articles, it is always talk of economic recession that is noted in the headlines as the main culprit." Head of the *Asahi* editorial department, Midoro Masuichi, expressed his view that, "It is impossible not to interpret the horrible social conditions as one of the manifestations of the current state of affairs in society." Yet Midoro also drew attention to the fact that, "as a result of these horrible social conditions a portion of society may easily turn nihilistic."

This sort of back and forth grew prevalent and the start of the 1930s saw the number of tragic news items in newspaper pages grow to the point that newspaper management teams began to discuss the phenomenon. Finding a job at the time was extremely difficult. The noticeboard for the law and economics faculties at Tokyo Imperial University displayed a lone announcement for a "Life Insurance Company seeking a number of applicants to fill several posts in the foreign relations team," as reported in the *Asahi* morning edition on October 16, 1930. Students, who had started to view stability as their foremost priority, began to find their way into the army. According to the morning edition on March 1, 1930, the number of applicants to military officer schools "stands at 30 to 50 times the capacity of these institutions." Students of law and economics, who had never before given any thought to the prospect of working in the military, "made early provisions to be student reservists and received monthly allowances for student fees of 50 yen." "Money! Money! Money! The Moneymaking Era—A Publication on Making Money Becomes a Big Hit" ran the headline from the morning edition on January 7, 1931. Dubious books with titles such as *How to Get Rich Quickly* "flew off the shelves." Street corners in Tokyo were inundated with "recession noticeboards" announcing "Going Out of Business so Selling it All." However, these noticeboards soon disappeared from the streets, replaced by ones in which the word recession was "omitted" because the Tokyo Metropolitan Police Department had banned the term. The evening edition on October 7, 1930 wrote: "Businesses plagued with pay cuts and layoffs. Strikes are becoming more frequent and labor disputes are commonplace in factories."

And then a man climbed a smokestack, carrying with him a red flag and some food.

Enter "the chimney man"

The man climbed to the top of a forty-meter tall smokestack early in the morning of November 16, 1930, at the Kawasaki factory of the Fuji Gas and Textile Company, where a workers' strike had dragged on for more than forty days. His climb up the chimney was to show his solidarity with the strike. Newspapers christened this 28-year-old union member "the chimney man," and they reported on a daily basis about "the spectacle of thousands of people gathering," "dozens of food stalls lined up in rows," and the way in which the strike leaders prepared provisions: "five rice balls, a pot of Japanese green tea and a bottle of wine." The man remained on the top of the chimney for more than 130 hours, eating and sleeping. In the end "the world below bowed its head" and the labor dispute "reluctantly dissolved." Another labor dispute came to an end at the same time. Female workers at the Kameido factory of the Tōyō Muslin Company, who had lost their jobs due to layoffs, organized themselves. One month earlier, the strike had drawn crowds of supporters and onlookers who engaged in "street fighting" with the police. Nakamura Kiyo, who had come from Niigata in search of a job, also took part in the strike. "Workers of all countries listen to the roar of May Day . . .!" Before the strike, the director of the company happened to be standing behind Nakamura one time while she was cleaning and had overheard her singing the May Day song to herself. Nakamura was later notified of her dismissal.

In 1930, large-scale labor disputes broke out one after another in almost every locality. With the lifting of the gold embargo, resulting in a stronger yen and subsequent budget cuts, general economic conditions floundered due to the spreading global economic depression. This was also because enterprises were conducting major corporate restructuring. "Out of the Blue, Big Salary Cuts—Incomes to Decrease by 23 Percent," stated the morning edition on April 6, 1930 reporting the outbreak of the Kanebō strike in a banner headline. The article pointed out that it was "absolutely sensational for Kanebō, a leading, top-flight company," and not some ailing enterprise faced with management challenges, "to decide to make the cuts." At Kanebō "female workers were referred to as 'ladies' and were not treated as laborers," in a company known previously for its "warm regard of its employees." In addition, before the strike the enormous sum of money given to the former president of the company, Mutō Sanji, as a retirement bonus for special services, had already become a topic of heated debate.

The April 9 Tokyo *Asahi* editorial called for a decrease in the distribution of dividends to stockholders: "The prosperity of a company is not solely dependent on capital or the skills of the managers. It requires the cooperation of all employees."

Furthermore, an article in the April 11 edition argued that "the three million yen given to ex-president Mutō as a retirement package could have provided a year and a half of stability for thirty thousand employees of the company." The article also criticized "Mutō and his cronies who have forgotten that the workers have 'woken up from their slumber.' [...] The disappearance of Kanebō's 'warm regard of its employees' might mark the death of the company." *Asahi* ardently advocated the importance of preserving jobs. However, having extolled austerity measures and the lifting of the gold embargo, it was difficult to revive economic conditions that could create such new jobs. The newspaper's pages did not offer any clear prescription on how to achieve this.

Villages without youth

"If You Come to Tokyo, You Will Starve to Death." This was a headline in the November 8, 1930 evening issue of the Tokyo *Asahi* about the Tokyo municipal authority's distribution of posters across the country. The posters aimed to stop migrants coming to Tokyo in search of work because their numbers were so large. The campaign was a strategy that sought to stem the influx by exposing the gravity of unemployment in the capital and with this policy "even the option of leaving in search of work from these impoverished villages was cut off." At the same time, just like today's "temporary workers," migrant farmers were used as adjustment valves to calibrate an appropriate labor force. The government also "encouraged the unemployed to return to their villages," explained the *Asahi* on June 7, 1930, when it wrote that the "issue in the city is not an insufficiency of labor. Rather, it is the increase of returnees to villages that are already gravely suffering. The already poor peasants are dragged into greater economic ignominy through the return of migrants which doubles the deleterious influence on villages." Yet poverty in farming villages only grew worse. Prices for agricultural products were in global decline due to the increased production possible thanks to mechanization. Farmers who increased their output in a bid to secure income were thus caught in a vicious circle, as this caused a further depreciation in prices. Moreover, the price of silk cocoons, which provided many agricultural families with cash, collapsed due to the Great Depression. The cost of rice also plunged after the abundant harvest of 1930, whereas in the following year the harvest was poor. Farming families were continually crushed by debt.

In November 1931, an *Asahi* reporter visited a mountain village in the Mogami region of Yamagata prefecture to prepare a report under the title, "Villages Without Youth." "Out of 467 girls between the ages of 15 and 24, as many as 250 have left the village due to poverty, to become geisha or prostitutes," the newspaper noted. An official from the Ministry of Agriculture and Forestry who visited Iwate Prefecture as part of an investigation was quizzed by schoolchildren there, who asked: "Is everyone suffering like this? Are there places where people do not have to worry about food?" The official reported: "When we were distributing emergency food to hungry children, they fought and scratched each other, scrambling to get a riceball." "They boil the remains of soybeans, normally used for fertilizer, with grass and give the liquid to the horses, while they eat the remains," he also wrote.[6] Newspapers and magazines sensationalized the

Figure 3   Children contributing to their families' income by working part-time twining ropes at school in 1934 Iwate Prefecture.

misery of farming villages. Images of children gnawing on raw *daikon* radishes were captioned with "hunger," although such behavior was not at all unusual.

Writer Ōya Sōichi, who visited the northeastern areas of Japan during the bad harvest, wrote in the *Current Events News* (*Jiji Shimpō*) on February 8, 1932 that, "it is not only this year that villagers are leading lives not befitting human beings." Newspapers had not paid attention to the region before, so it all appeared new. Yamashita Fumio, a researcher of local history who was born and raised in Iwate, wrote in his book, *Bad Harvests in the Northeast During the Showa Era*, about his own childhood experiences of extreme poverty. He criticized the reporting about farming villages:

> There are many girls who become live-in maids or domestics, but it is a callous exaggeration to say that the majority of them go into prostitution. Descriptions of misery are also considered normal for the northeast. Although the reporters believe they are being sympathetic toward the people, their reports are actually superficial and offensive toward the local people.

Censorship of the publishing world, including newspapers, increased in 1934 and a clause was added due to "fear that reports might have a provocative influence on the sentiments of people by exaggerating poverty in farming villages."

Deadly blow to heresy

In January 1930, the government had lifted the gold embargo at the old exchange rate, which rendered the yen stronger than the actual rate. This move added to the weight of the Great Depression and the amount of exports from Japan dropped sharply, resulting in dire economic consequences. Arguments in favor of re-imposing the embargo with the aim to lift it once again at a lower yen exchange rate began to appear. The advocates of these proposals for a new, lower exchange rate were the "heretics" of the time. Half a year after the US stock market collapsed, an editorial in the May 7, 1930 Tokyo *Asahi* accurately analyzed the state of the world economy, stating: "The global recession is truly a serious state of affairs with deep-rooted problems." The article explained:

> The interest rates of all the major countries heading toward their lowest levels provides an accurate depiction: the condition of industrial production in these countries is far from good. [...] One of the major causes of the global recession is the sudden fall in the market prices of agricultural production in Europe and the United States. [...] The decline in industrial trade has also given rise to an unprecedented unemployment problem in this country.

Regarding the lifting of the gold embargo, however, the newspaper did not only provide an excuse that "its impact has been exaggerated," but went as far to say that "the lifting of the embargo has created a sound footing to break through the current recession." The newspaper neglected to mention any of its negative impact.

On one side, confronting the government and major newspapers by advocating the lifting of the embargo based on a new exchange rate, were "the gang of four": Ishibashi Tanzan of *The Oriental Economist* (*Tōyō Keizai Shimpō*), Obama Toshie of the *Chūgai Shōgyō Shimpō* (the *Nikkei Shimbun* of today), Yamazaki Yasuzumi of the *Yomiuri Shimbun*, and economist Takahashi Kamekichi. They all argued that neither maintaining a strong yen nor budget cuts was necessary. In his book, *The Impact of the Lifting of the Gold Embargo and Measures to Counter It*, Ishibashi criticized the old exchange rate as a philosophy of "reliance on others." Quoting from speeches of Bank of Japan executives who advocated lifting the gold embargo using the old exchange rate, their thinking belied: "If we do something different the situation might improve," and "The relevant authorities will have to deal with the situation if something happens." The strains of the old exchange rate deepened the problems. In the same way as during the financial panic of 1927, Takahashi Korekiyo once again took over the Ministry of Finance during a crisis.

On December 13, 1931, immediately after Takahashi's inauguration and during a press conference at his official residence, he "unflinchingly answered" yes to the question, "Will you re-impose the embargo?" Reporters jumped to their telephones all at once, shouting "Extra!" to their headquarters.[7] The lifting of the embargo based on the old exchange rate ended in a fiasco. On December 14, the Tokyo *Asahi* editorial blamed the situation on the previous leadership, writing: "Suspension of the gold standard following the change in government is extremely regrettable." The newspaper never reviewed the policies it had supported earlier.

The turbulent relationship between two finance ministers

The day Finance Minister Takahashi Korekiyo and his predecessor, Inoue Junnosuke, started an all-out confrontation regarding financial policy, the House of Peers was so full that "there was no room even for standing observers."[8] When Takahashi criticized

Inoue's policies for causing "an increase in unemployment," Inoue "sharply turned toward the minister" and retorted: "Your opinion is mistaken and not based on facts!" At the time Takahashi was 77 and Inoue was 62. Both came from the central bank and in the past Takahashi had helped get Inoue promoted to high positions. They parted ways after Inoue became finance minister in Hamaguchi Osachi's government because Inoue resolutely lifted the gold embargo and introduced austerity measures. Takahashi was a proponent of an expansionary fiscal policy to spur the economy. *Asahi* supported the austerity policies of the Hamaguchi Cabinet.

At the time, the idea of "austerity" was taking root in people's lives as part of a nationwide movement advocating greater savings. "Having fully understood the policies of the Hamaguchi administration, I want to offer my services to the best of my abilities as a woman." These were the words of the wife of a university professor, published in the December 1929 issue of the magazine *The Housewife's Companion* (*Shufu no tomo*). There were critical voices too. Asking people with low income to save money, claimed one such voice, is "tantamount to demanding the 'curtailment of one's life'."[9] Eventually, Inoue's austerity measures suffered a setback. In December 1931, the Ministry of Finance moved from Inoue to Takahashi's leadership, following the transfer of power from the Minseitō Party (People's Politics Party) to the Seiyūkai Party (Friends of Constitutional Government Party). To cover the military costs that had increased due to the Manchurian Incident (July 1931) and to rescue impoverished farming villages, Takahashi went ahead with the unprecedented step of deficit spending by issuing government bonds. Japan's economy started to improve, leaving other countries behind.[10] The *Asahi*, however, remained critical of Takahashi's policies until the end, writing in its March 16, 1936 editorial: "Presently, when the profit of enterprises is rising, but the living standards of the general population have yet to improve, the essence of Takahashi's policies can be seen as characteristic inflationary measures and excessive favoring of capitalists."[11]

There was a rumor that *Asahi* "favored the Minseitō Party and disliked the Seiyūkai Party."[12] Indeed, the newspaper was often critical of the Seiyūkai. During the transfer of government power in 1931, an editorial described the fundamentals of the Seiyūkai as "buying votes, deceiving the public, and constantly mudslinging in the Diet." The paper ridiculed assembly members from the Seiyūkai, who bought new clothes before the opening of the Diet session, for wearing "sparkling new outfits that reveal their party colors." The government budget, filled by Takahashi's inflationary policies through deficit-covering government bonds, was spent on an expansion in armaments. The economist Arisawa Hiromi pointed out at the time: "What the outbreak of inflation is connected to in practice is already clear ... it is XX."[13] The censored word was most probably "war." The two finance ministers held very contrasting views on fiscal policy, yet both of them were felled by fanatical right-wing terrorism: Inoue in February 1932, in the midst of a campaign speech; Takahashi on February 26, 1936, during the so-called "February 26 Incident."

The G20 and G67

From April 1–2, 2009, leaders of the G20 met in London for an international financial summit and drafted a joint declaration: Overcoming the global financial crisis requires fiscal action and monetary policies based on international cooperation. Seventy-six years earlier, on June 12, 1933, leaders of 67 countries also gathered in London to discuss the ways to break through "the global financial crisis headed for a catastrophe."[14] It is perhaps appropriate now to name them "the G67." King George V of Great Britain delivered the opening speech. "Ladies and Gentlemen! Face-to-face with this global recession, we should cooperate for the well-being of the whole world," he proclaimed. An article in the June 11, 1933 morning edition of *Asahi* proclaimed in a banner headline: "The World Economic Summit Will Finally Start Tomorrow." There were also related articles titled, "A Splendid Venue" and "Our Head of Delegation Granted an Audience with the King."

Following the Manchurian Incident in 1931, Japan announced its decision to withdraw from the League of Nations and the country grew more and more isolated. The London summit filled the Japanese people with an uplifting sense that Japan had not been fully dismissed by the international community. However, the summit dragged on for a long time and expectations soon turned into disappointment. Headlines of the time read: "Is this the Birth of International Cooperation or its Death Knell?", and "Nationalists Behind Masks."[15] The major powers of the time prioritized their domestic situation over international cooperation in the areas of currency and customs tariffs. An editorial on July 13 seemed to abandon all hope early on for international cooperation: "We doubt the effectiveness of an international gathering on such a grand scale." The reason for this, according to the newspaper, was that a summit in which "numerous small countries" participated, moved away from the heart of the issues and would instead worsen the international situation. Touching upon the Manchurian Incident, the newspaper took a critical stance toward internationalism: "International meetings, such as the meeting at the League of Nations regarding the Sino-Japanese conflicts, reveal the damage and lacuna of international conferences." A wave of protectionism surged around the world. "Amidst Unpopularity on a Global Scale: the United States to Impose a New Customs Duty—Other Countries Considering Retaliatory Measures," *Asahi* wrote.[16] This was a new path that threatened to shrink global trade by imposing high tariffs.

Addressing the "tariff wars," an *Asahi* editorial claimed that, "to change the global economy for the better, some liberalization of commerce in each country is necessary."[17] Regarding Japan's own decision to increase trade tariffs, the newspaper took an opposing stance: "Industry has taken up double protective barriers of high trade tariffs and low exchange rates and become completely used to them. Will these measures instead not lead to an unhealthy industry itself?"[18] At the time, the importance of free trade was fully acknowledged but to achieve it international cooperation was necessary. Unfortunately, both Japan and the world at large were being carried away into an era of intolerance.

3

Supreme Command Violated!

The London disarmament conference begins

On November 30, 1929, Tokyo railway station teemed with people. Just after noon "a storm of cheers reverberated through the station."[1] With a party of more than thirty people on its way to the London Naval Disarmament Conference, former Prime Minister Wakatsuki Reijirō, head of the delegation, boarded a special train bound for Yokohama. Prime Minister Hamaguchi Osachi held out a hand to Wakatsuki and wished him "Good luck!," to which Wakatsuki nodded in response. Seeing off the delegation, Hamaguchi "stood rigid at attention, not moving a muscle," reported the *Asahi* on December 1, 1929. Hamaguchi was planning to cut military expenses, which were already taking up about 30 percent of the national budget, and aimed to cooperate with the United States and Great Britain in promoting disarmament. The Osaka *Asahi* took up the subject in a supportive editorial on November 30: "The extent to which the expansion of military expenses continues to cause hardship to the economy of each country is clear from the way the United Kingdom and the United States have taken the lead in organizing the London conference. This is even more the case in Japan, whose national wealth is one-fifteenth the size of America's." At the 1921–22 Washington Naval Disarmament Conference, Japan had tried to establish the gross tonnage of its main fleet at 70 percent of those of the US and the Great Britain. This effort failed and Japan had to make a compromise at 60 percent. Following this, a race to build auxiliary fleets had intensified. In 1927, a subsequent disarmament conference was held in Geneva but it soon broke down due to disagreement between the Americans and British. Wakatsuki, who had set sail from Yokohama, arrived in London on December 27, 1929.

At the same time in Tokyo, the Navy top brass—Navy Undersecretary Yamanashi Katsunoshin and Undersecretary of the Naval General Staff Suetsugu Nobumasa—invited representatives of several newspapers to Kinsui, an elite restaurant in Tokyo's Tsukiji district. The managing editor of the Tokyo *Asahi*, Ogata Taketora, threw a question to the Navy hands who "wanted to gain support for the bid to achieve the seventy percent level of gross tonnage of the supporting fleet." Ogata asked, "What if you fail in your bid to achieve the seventy percent compromise?" The Navy officials replied obliquely, "In that case, we shall review the matter thoroughly." The newspapers wanted to avoid having to change their editorial stance suddenly to one of supporting

Figure 4 A page from the evening *Osaka Mainichi* on April 3, 1930, with the headline "Violation of the Supreme Command."

a compromise in the case that "the seventy percent" bid failed.[2] Neither the politicians, nor the military officials, nor the journalists could have imagined that the stance taken by the Hamaguchi administration at the disarmament negotiations would later be criticized by the military as an attempt to "violate the supreme command."

On January 21, 1930, the London Disarmament Conference opened, attended by the US, Great Britain, France, Italy, and Japan. An editorial in the January 15 Osaka *Mainichi* was entitled "A Refutation of the British and American Opposition to Japan's Aspirations for 'the Seventy Percent.'" An editorial in the Tokyo *Asahi* on January 21 wrote about the "fierce arms race" that would break out if the negotiations broke down, and called all nations to demonstrate a "spirit of mutual concession."

Behind the scoop on why the disarmament conference stalled

More than two weeks into the London Disarmament Conference, a member of the Japanese delegation, Captain Satō Ichirō, was taking an evening bath when he heard a knock at his hotel room door. (Satō was the eldest brother of postwar prime ministers Kishi Nobusuke and Satō Eisaku.) When Satō opened the door he saw Ono from the *Jiji Shimpō*. Captain Satō thought that this was the ideal chance and let the reporter into his room. He told Ono about the "strictly confidential" proposal brought forward by the American side the previous day. Satō said that he wanted to let the Japanese people know about the "unreasonable and extremely egoistic nature" of the American proposal. This news leak occurred on the spur of the moment and was triggered by Satō's personal views about the American proposal.[3] On February 8, 1930, the *Jiji Shimpō* published a report on the front page of its evening edition under the title, "On the Issue of the Gross Tonnage for the Supporting Fleet: Japan to be Allotted Only Sixty

Percent—A Surprising Proposal from the United States." The report, the article said, was "based on information we unearthed from the American side." The *Asahi* followed with a story the next morning and the Foreign Ministry started a secret investigation into the source of the leak. "The special correspondent Ono is not a fluent speaker of English; from this one can guess the source of this leak," the Ministry concluded.

After reading the news, Admiral Katō Hiroharu, Chief of the Naval General Staff, wrote in his journal: "London: Stimson, the US representative, came out with a new proposal that rejected out of hand Japan's bid for the seventy percent. Japanese public outraged."[4] Katō, who was a staunch defender of Japan's bid for "the seventy percent," had a bad record when it came to disarmament conferences. As the head of the naval section of the delegation at the Washington Disarmament Conference in 1921, he had arbitrarily announced to the foreign press his decision to "withdraw from the conference."[5] Katō Tomosaburō, who was Japan's chief representative at the Washington Conference, believed that the disparity in naval power between the US and Japan would continue to widen without a disarmament treaty. He had therefore accepted the "sixty percent" agreement, and "more than ninety percent of Japanese special correspondents" supported his view.[6] Forced to accept "the sixty percent" threshold for the main fleet at the Washington Conference, the Japanese Navy was adamant not to yield in London when it came to achieving the seventy percent for the auxiliary. On one hand, the logic of the head of the delegation, Wakatsuki Reijirō, was that "it would be acceptable to come back with an agreement on sixty-five or sixty-seven percent."[7] Nakashima Yadanji, a secretary to Prime Minister Hamaguchi, remembered:

> It would have been appropriate if the ratio between Great Britain, the United States and Japan had been 5–5–1, or even 5–5–0.5. But the Naval General Staff at the time was blind to both the current of the times and the great discrepancy in national power between our country and the great powers.[8]

The leaked compromise proposal

The American and Japanese delegations at the London Disarmament Conference finally reached a compromise in March 1930. The gross tonnage of supporting fleets Japan could maintain stood within 69.75 percent of US gross tonnage, and that of large cruisers at 60.2 percent (although by the next conference in 1935 this number could rise to 72.26 percent). The gross tonnage of submarines was equal for both countries and stood at 52,700 tons. Although this compromise did not meet Japan's demand of 70 percent for the first two categories and 78,000 tons for the last, the Japanese negotiators recognized the consideration shown by the American side in coming up with this compromise. The Americans understood that accepting Japan's demand of 70 percent would be criticized as "surrendering to Japan" by critical US public opinion. The US was trying to accommodate Japan's wishes and avoid domestic criticism at the same time. The Japanese delegation recognized that pressing for more concessions would be difficult, and on March 14 they dispatched a top-secret telegram to Tokyo requesting a government decision on the proposal.

On March 17, Suetsugu Nobumasa, acting on Chief of the Naval General Staff Katō's orders, distributed a pamphlet at the Navy Headquarters press club explaining the compromise proposal. The handout asserted: "The Navy cannot possibly accept such a proposal."[9] Although Japan and the US developed the proposal through mutual concessions, Suetsugu still labeled it "America's final proposal." He misled the public by insinuating that the US was pushing Japan to accept. The evening edition of *Asahi* on March 18 flashed the following banner headline on its front page: "To America's Compromise Proposal, Our Navy is Resolutely Opposed." Newspapers in Japan were easily taken in by Suetsugu and others who were trying to use the media to direct public opinion against arms reduction. During the top-secret negotiations, specific numbers, which were still being negotiated, became widely known both inside and outside the country. On March 19, the English newspaper, *The Times*, published a somewhat cynical article on the topic from Tokyo. It said:

> Readers abroad may find it difficult to believe that officers can indulge in such "politics" and retain their posts if the views they publish are not in fact those of the Government or, at least, of the Navy Ministry, but public opinion in Japan is accustomed to see the Army and Navy go to great lengths in advocating their own views, even in opposition to the Government.[10]

On March 25, Prime Minister Hamaguchi Osachi expressed his conviction to implement disarmament to Navy Undersecretary Yamanashi Katsunoshin. "I am strongly determined not to concede to the military on this issue, even if it means losing the cabinet, the Minseitō and even my own life," Hamaguchi said. On March 27, Hamaguchi paid a visit to the Imperial Palace and 28-year-old Emperor Hirohito said, "For the sake of world peace make efforts to settle this quickly." This statement encouraged Hamaguchi even more to support the settlement on disarmament.[11] In a Cabinet meeting on April 1, the government passed a Cabinet decision to accept the compromise proposal and the next day, the headline "Supreme Command Violated!" appeared on the front page of the evening editions of the *Osaka Mainichi Newspaper* and *Tokyo Nichinichi Newspaper*.

"Supreme Command Violated!"

On April 1, 1930, as the Cabinet approved the instructions to the Japanese delegation to accept the compromise proposal between the US and Japan, the secretary general of the opposition party, the Seiyūkai, Mori Tsutomu, publicized his dissent:

> This decision does not represent only an utter disregard for the wishes of the military leadership. [...] It must also be acknowledged that the way in which this decision about the important issue of national defense [...] was made solely in a Cabinet meeting is also a blunder that is unacceptable along constitutional lines.

According to the prewar constitution of imperial Japan, "The Emperor has the supreme command of the Army and Navy" (Article 11), and "The Emperor determines the organization and peace standing of the Army and Navy" (Article 12). The Supreme Command—the authority to command the military—was under the direct control of the Emperor; legally, the Imperial Naval General Staff and the Imperial Army General Staff Office "counseled" the Emperor independently of the government. Moreover, the size of the military was closely related to the exercise of the supreme command. According to the constitution, therefore, the fact that the government decided the quantity of arms (in this case, the tonnage of supporting ships) without having taken into account the wishes of the military authorities constituted a major problem. This was Mori's point, although he did not use the phrase "violating the supreme command." Although Mori's talk was published on April 2 in several major morning edition newspapers such as the *Tokyo Nichinichi*, for some reason his comments did not appear in the Tokyo and Osaka *Asahi* or in the *Osaka Mainichi*. The following day, an article with no byline under the headline, "Will the Violation of the Supreme Command Pose an Obstacle to Ratification?", appeared on the front page of the evening edition of the *Osaka Mainichi*. The article read:

> In trying to approve an international agreement that in essence limits the national defense forces contrary to the wishes of the military command, the government violated the supreme command. This is a major problem and may be taken up at the Privy Council.

But had the government "violated the supreme command" simply because it ignored the wishes of the military leadership? The *Osaka Mainichi* article was the first time the phrase "violation of the supreme command" was published in a newspaper.[12] Although the *Tokyo Nichinichi*, funded by the same company as the *Osaka Mainichi*, published a nearly identical article in its evening edition, the paper did not include the phrase "violation of the supreme command" in its headline. One could imagine that at his press conference on April 2 Mori had actually uttered such a phrase but there is no evidence to prove this. On April 4, a group from the National Association of Citizens for Naval Disarmament, a right-wing group represented by Tōyama Mitsuru, who were strongly in favor of achieving "the seventy percent" threshold, paid a visit to the prime minister's office. They were protesting against the decision to accept the compromise, which they saw as "a clear violation of the supreme command." Harada Kumao, private secretary to the elderly statesman Saionji Kinmochi, on April 7 or 8, heard the head of the Naval General Staff Katō Hiroharu say, "Although many members of political parties have come asking to meet with me, I have already firmly decided and will not meet with anybody." However, in reality the Naval General Staff officers would "deeply conspire" with the Seiyūkai Party to topple the Hamaguchi government.

The Seiyūkai operates behind the scenes

"Neither in the Ministry of Navy nor in the Naval General Staff is there any interest in nor any research into constitutional law," wrote the Navy Undersecretary Yamanashi Katsunoshin in a memoir composed at the time of the London Disarmament

Conference. "Some wily old men see the 'supreme command' issue as a launching pad to overthrow the government. The opposition Seiyūkai Party has no shortage of such old foxes," he penned.[13] At the same time, a man named Kōno Tsunekichi was working as a guest writer for *Asahi*. As a retired Army major general, he could talk with military officers on a first name basis: whether it was "an undersecretary or an office chief, Kōno was extremely useful in gathering information about the Army." In a volume published posthumously, *Blackest Moments of the Nation's History,* Kōno provided an account of the relationship between the Seiyūkai and the Naval General Staff:

> The Navy Ministry learned the following from various intelligence sources. First, it was said that the rhetoric behind the "violation of the Supreme Command" first appeared within the Army General Staff Office and that party chief Mori Tsutomu passed it on to the Seiyūkai. Second, it is a fact that the Seiyūkai Party president, Inukai Tsuyoshi, along with members Suzuki Kisaburō, Hatoyama Ichirō, Mori Tsutomu and the Undersecretary of the Naval General Staff Suetsugu Nobumasa, had a meeting at the Tsurumaki hot-springs resort.

Although there is no record to prove that such a meeting occurred, Mori's biography suggests that he "worked on persuading the Naval General Staff."[14] Mori believed that naval power equaling 70 percent of that of the United States was "absolutely necessary" to drive US influence out of China. Mori was a "very wise, bold and forceful person who would go to any lengths to achieve his goal," according to the book *Sixty Years of Diplomacy* by former Foreign Minister Yoshizawa Kenkichi.

During the latter part of April 1930, the "violation of the supreme command" topic became a heated political issue. On April 20, the day before the Diet convened, the Osaka *Asahi* addressed the issue in an editorial for the first time. According to the article, the Seiyūkai emphasized the government's violation of the supreme command clause, which meant that the political party acknowledged the military's authority to decide its own strength. Such an admission was tantamount to a party cabinet curbing its own authority and thus was, for the Seiyūkai, "an act of suicide as a political party," according to the editorial.

The following day Tokyo Imperial University's *Imperial University Newspaper* published a piece on the arms reduction treaty by Minobe Tatsukichi, an authority on constitutional law. Minobe wrote:

> The issue of setting up an army is, as a matter of course, an act of a state and not of the army itself. [...] There is nothing unconstitutional in a government seeking Imperial sanction against the wishes of the military to agree to a compromise proposal on arms reduction.

Thus, Minobe directly refuted the argument claiming there was a violation of the supreme command. On April 22, the Naval Arms Limitation Treaty was signed in London and three days later, in a plenary session of the Lower House, Seiyūkai president Inukai Tsuyoshi took to the platform to speak.

Asahi criticizes the Seiyūkai

One can say the Prime Minister reached the judgment that his decision posed no threat to national security based on political, economic, and various other factors. However, the Naval General Staff, which is responsible for military strategy, disagrees with this decision. Which of them is correct?

With these words, on April 25 opposition leader and Seiyūkai president Inukai pressed Prime Minister Hamaguchi Osachi for answers. Hatoyama Ichirō of the Seiyūkai also attacked the government on the issue of violating the supreme command: "It is an outrage that an institution that is not a consulting body for the Emperor on military matters [. . .] should infringe on the opinion of the Chief of the Naval General Staff." By emphasizing the military authorities' right to decide their own strength, and by denying the superiority of politics over the military, the Seiyūkai paved the way for establishing the military's independence from the civilian government. Both the Tokyo and Osaka *Asahi* took a firm editorial stance criticizing the Seiyūkai. On April 26, the Tokyo *Asahi* wrote in an editorial:

It is the duty of the Cabinet in a constitutional government to decide matters of national defense, having understood the nature of international relations and considered the burden on the people. Sacrificing finance and diplomacy for the sake of preparing for an imaginary international war advocated by military specialists can only happen in a militarist state.[15]

And on April 30 the Osaka *Asahi* editorial stated:

In a time when the party cabinet system is finally taking root, the Seiyukai's support of an anachronistic doctrine [. . .] acknowledges the military cliques' superiority, and exposes to the outer world the reality of a dual government. At the same time, one cannot help but say that with this decision the Seiyūkai has doomed itself as a political party.[16]

In May, the *Asahi* published three pieces by Minobe Tatsukichi, an expert on constitutional law, concerning "the Conclusion of the Navy [Disarmament] Treaty and the Limits of the Supreme Command." In his article on May 5, 1930, Minobe asserted that: "The military authorities' position should only serve as a reference. It is absolutely necessary for the sake of the nation to what extent it wishes to accept this position or not is made solely by the government."

Prime Minister Hamaguchi's position was in line with that of Minobe. However, believing that "saying it openly, like Professor Minobe" would hurt the opposition party's feelings, the prime minister avoided specific rhetoric concerning constitutionalism in the Diet. An *Asahi* editorial questioned this stance: "Why does the prime minister not answer questions related to constitutionalism? [. . .] We urge him to present clear and open answers without holding back."[17] An editorial in the May 4 *Jiji Shimpō* masterfully criticized the rhetoric about the violation of the Supreme

Command: "Putting too much confidence in military officials' unilateral decisions for the sake of the country's militarization is nothing but ignorant. It is tantamount to building unnecessary walls based solely on the say-so of a bricklayer."

Devilish voices

The debate about the violation of the supreme command unfolded in the Diet with the opposition Seiyūkai stirring up the military's anger along with the right wing and nationalists. The correspondents from the Navy Ministry press club, the Kokuchōkai, also expressed their "sympathy toward the Chief of the Naval General Staff."

Immediately after Inukai Tsuyoshi and others verbally attacked the government on April 30, 1930, Undersecretary of the Naval General Staff Suetsugu Nobumasa, who opposed the treaty, gathered Kokuchōkai press club reporters at a first-class restaurant and other places in Akasaka, Tokyo. According to the records held at the Ministry of Defense Archives, a total of 686 yen and 45 sen was spent. This was a colossal sum given that the prime minister's monthly salary at the time was 800 yen. On May 20, Lieutenant Commander Kusakari Eiji, a staff officer of the Naval General Staff, committed suicide. The note he left behind did not clearly state his motives, and although he may have had a nervous breakdown, groups opposing the disarmament treaty became indignant as they took his suicide as a protest against the government. The Chief of the Naval General Staff, Katō Hiroharu, told the Navy Minister Takarabe Takeshi: "Kusakari was an exceptional man. What a shame it has come to this—now the arms reduction treaty has produced its first victim." From this moment on the phrase "violation of the supreme command" became a major weapon in the hands of groups opposing the disarmament treaty. People angrily yelling out the word "Violation!" managed to label their opponents "evil" without actual proof, basing their arguments on the Emperor's authority. On the other hand, those opposing this stance drew their rationale from the constitution and resorted to explaining things theoretically. The historian Imai Seiichi remembers hearing Hori Teikichi, Head of the Ministry of Navy's Naval Affairs Department who was in favor of arms reduction negotiations, say: "At the time it was easy to attack the government with the words 'violation of the supreme command,' while for those on the defending side it was more difficult to counter these attacks." The phrase "violation of the supreme command" was like the devil's voice, taking on a frenzied life of its own.

On April 1, the Emperor had actually sanctioned the decision to accept the US-Japan compromise and conclude the treaty. According to a postwar Ministry of Defense historical assessment:

> The Emperor, who possesses the supreme power to conclude treaties, the supreme command, and the supreme authority to form the military, had made his will obvious. There was no "violation of the supreme command" whatsoever.[18]

On June 18, the delegation headed by Wakatsuki Reijirō returned to Tokyo and the Tokyo *Asahi* reported the group's arrival: "The public is at the height of its emotions—

Figure 5   The Japanese delegation from the London Naval Disarmament Conference, headed by Wakatsuki Reijirō, was welcomed by enthusiastic crowds upon returning to Tokyo Station on June 18, 1930.

cries of excitement reverberate through the crowd, countless flags are flying and hats are thrown up in the air." The large majority of people greeted disarmament enthusiastically as they had been hoping for a reduction in their financial burden. An *Asahi* editorial on June 19 boldly described this sentiment: "Politics should control the military, not vice versa. Scenes of the public welcoming the returning delegation is a clear demonstration of that dictum."

Avoiding war is the best national defense

Dissatisfaction with the treaty emanated from a group of Navy officials, including Katō Hiroharu, and had started as early as the 1921–22 Washington Disarmament Conference. This was the conference where Japan was given the right to a gross tonnage of its main fleet at 60 percent of that of the US. Katō Tomosaburō, head of that delegation, saw it as follows:

> War requires vast expenditures. However, it is difficult to find a state other than the Unites States that would purchase large amounts of Japanese foreign bonds. [. . .] As a result, a war between Japan and the United States is unfathomable. [. . .] It is necessary that Japan avoid war with the United States.

He added, "Along with managing military power in a way appropriate to the nation's capacities, national defense is also about cultivating national resources by way of avoiding war through diplomatic means. I believe this is the true meaning of national defense at this time."[19] In 1930, the year the London Naval Disarmament Conference was held, the discrepancy between the national power of Japan and the United States was self-evident: "According to the Cabinet Bureau of Statistics, in 1930 the per capita national income in Japan was 165 yen, in the US it was 1,116 yen; in 1929 steel production in Japan stood at 2.1 million tons, in the US it was 55.03 million tons."[20]

The 70 percent figure was the proposal of the Japanese Navy. It represented the ratio at which the Japanese Navy would equal the US Navy's Pacific Fleet, if the fleet entered Japan's coastal waters to attack. However, the idea that with 70 percent of the US tonnage Japan would not be defeated by the US was irrational in itself because such a supposition did not address the nation's capacity to win the war. Inasmuch as there was a large difference in access to national resources and industrial potential, there was no other way but for Japan to avoid war. The *Asahi* did not join supporters of "the seventy percent" rhetoric. The newspaper's stance was that in case the treaty failed and an arms race ensued, the enormous burden on the people would only increase. As the September 2, 1930 edition of the paper revealed, national defense was not only about providing for the military. Easing the burden on people is in itself part of the national defense.[21] In October 1930, after the ratification ceremony in London, leaders of Japan, the US, and Great Britain addressed the world on radio. Japan's Prime Minister Hamaguchi proclaimed: "The London Disarmament Treaty marks the beginning of a new era for mankind. [...] We have now reached an 'age of stability' in which all countries can coexist in trust and mutual prosperity."

A supportive editorial in the Tokyo *Asahi* on the day the treaty came into effect, October 29, "ardently" celebrated the moment along with the nation. Hamaguchi successfully deflected military intervention and concluded the disarmament treaty and thus promoted international cooperation. This was one of the high points of party politics under the Meiji Constitution. The *Asahi* criticized the rhetoric about the violation of the supreme command idea and supported the realization of the disarmament agreement from the sidelines. However, this achievement also planted the seeds of crisis that eventually sprouted. In the autumn during the conclusion of the disarmament treaty, the ultra-nationalist Cherry Blossom Group (*Sakurakai*) formed.

Terror and coup d'état

"The government rendering decisions on the strength of the military is not tantamount to a violation of supreme command"—this was a line of thought advocated by newspapers in 1930 when the London Disarmament Conference reached its conclusion. However, the cries of "violation of the supreme command!" further inflamed the anger of the military, rightists and nationalists, and led extremists to plan several coup d'état and terrorist acts. "That the poisoned dagger in the hands of degenerate party politicians is pointed toward the military can be clearly seen in this 'London Treaty Issue,'" proclaimed the Cherry Blossom Group in its manifesto in the autumn of 1930. The Cherry Blossom Group was a collection of officers who attempted two coup d'états the following year. Prime Minister Inukai Tsuyoshi was suddenly attacked on May 15, 1932. The fact that Inukai was gunned down by Naval officers was somewhat ironic because he had attacked the Hamaguchi government in the past, accusing it of violating the supreme command and thus opening a path for the further independence of the military. This assassination virtually brought an end to party-ruled Cabinets. Ōkawa Shūmei, an ultra-nationalist involved in the incident, said the following in a public report:

> From as early as 1928–29, there was an extreme antagonism among young officers toward parliamentary and party politics and a belief that action was necessary to renovate the nation. These feelings became all the more vehement following the "Violation of the Supreme Command Issue."[22]

Within the Navy, ever since the debacle of the "violation of the supreme command" issue, the sort of rational thinking that had previously been dominant was slowly overtaken by "severe anti-Americanism" and a sort of "overzealous cultishness," which permeated the organization.[23] Between 1933 and 1934, Navy Undersecretary Yamanashi Katsunoshin, who had made every effort to support the conclusion of the disarmament treaty, and Hori Teikichi, Head of the Naval Affairs Department, who had also exhausted all efforts, were forced to resign. Admiral Yamamoto Isoroku, a close friend of Hori's, wondered which was more important—"losing one-tenth of the large scale cruiser fleet or losing Hori"—and called their dismissal "an utterly foolish act of personnel mismanagement by the Navy." On the other hand, Suetsugu Nobumasa, who was among those opposed to the disarmament treaty, was appointed Commander-in-Chief of the Combined Fleet. On February 26, 1936, a group of Army officers rebelled in an act that became known as the "February 26 Incident." Every one of their targets—Prime Minister Okada Keisuke, Lord Keeper of the Privy Seal Saitō Makoto, and the Grand Chamberlain Suzuki Kantarō—was a proponent of the London Treaty. Isobe Asaichi, who was sentenced to death for his involvement in this incident, wrote in his prison cell: "Why is avenging the traitors, who violated the imperial prerogative, not made part of protecting the national polity? [...] Is it not natural that the truly loyal Japanese show their fury and kill these violators of the supreme command?"[24]

Military circles used the inviolability of the emperor's supposed supreme command as a pretext to take control of Japanese politics and newspapers were seemingly powerless to stop the flow of events. Perhaps the history of the Showa period could have taken a slightly different course had the phrase "violation of the supreme command" not been introduced into public discourse.

But let us turn back the clock to November 14, 1930, when a young right-winger was standing on a Tokyo rail station platform, his eyes focused on Prime Minister Hamaguchi.

No slackening of Army criticism

Prime Minister Hamaguchi Osachi was walking on a platform of Tokyo Station on his way to Okayama Prefecture to inspect Army military exercises. At 8:57 a.m. on November 14, 1930, just before boarding his train, Hamaguchi heard the sound of a pistol shot. An instant later, he felt a sharp pain like he had been hit hard in his lower abdomen with a blunt object. Hamaguchi thought to himself, "I've been shot" and "I am too young to die." Also on that platform was the managing editor of the Tokyo *Asahi*, Ogata Taketora. He was seeing off Hirota Kōki, his schoolmate from the Fukuoka Prefectural Shūyūkan School. Hirota, a diplomat, was setting off for his new post as Japan's ambassador to the Soviet Union. After the incident, Ogata swiftly took a car to his office and the Tokyo *Asahi* hastily published the fastest special edition by 9:30 a.m. The man who shot Hamaguchi was 21-year-old Sagoya Tomeo, a member of the ultra-right-wing group "Patriotic Society" (*Aikokusha*). Before committing the crime he had heard the Undersecretary of the Naval General Staff Suetsugu Nobumasa, who was strongly opposed to disarmament, speaking about the government violating the supreme command.[25] Yet there are doubts that Sagoya clearly understood what "supreme command" actually meant. In a written report submitted to the head of the appellate court, Sagoya wrote: "I could not possibly explain what constitutionalism is."[26]

Figure 6 Photograph taken just after the assassination attempt on Prime Minister Hamaguchi Osachi (with white mustache in the center), November 14, 1930, Tokyo Station.

Prime Minister Hamaguchi narrowly escaped death. Throughout March, he continued to attend Diet sessions despite his weakened physical condition, but in April he resigned and Wakatsuki Reijirō became Prime Minister for the second time. Following his stepping down from office, the *Asahi* continued to advocate disarmament and to criticize the military. On May 5, 1931, the newspaper editorial read: "Arms reduction is not done at the request of military authorities, but is something the state demands of the armed forces. It has never been the responsibility of military officials in the first place—it is a task for politicians."[27] And in another editorial on August 8, 1931:

> The way in which the military sticks its nose into politics and diplamacy and tries to influence the situation makes one think that they are trying to exercise the power of the *shogun* in the present day. This is an extremely dangerous situation. [. . .] In today's world, military power is definitely not the ultimate solution in international relations.[28]

On August 26, 1931, Hamaguchi died at the age of 61. The *Asahi* wrote on the following day, "with Hamaguchi's death, our country has lost one of its greatest politicians."[29] At the time, the footfall of war in Manchuria, in northeastern China, was growing louder. Merely three weeks after Hamaguchi's death, on September 18 near Liutiao Lake on the outskirts of Mukden (modern day Shenyang), railway tracks of the South Manchuria Railway, operated by the Japanese, were blown up. It was the beginning of what came to be known as the Manchurian Incident.

4

The Manchurian Incident

The fallen king

Just west of the Forbidden City Palace Museum in Beijing, surrounded by walls red ocher in color, there is a large area that is off limits to both locals and tourists. This is "Zhongnanhai," the political center of modern-day China where Chinese Communist Party officials lead the country. More than 80 years ago, Grand Marshal Zhang Zuolin advanced into Beijing from Manchuria and chose this site as the seat of his government. However, after about a year as "the King of Zhongnanhai," he had no choice but to retreat from the capital.

From the evening of June 2, 1928 to the early dawn of the next day, cars exited Zhongnanhai one after another. Zhang himself was in one of the cars. He had given up resisting Chinese Nationalist General Chiang Kai-shek's Northern Expedition to unify China and was now withdrawing his troops to Mukden (modern-day Shenyang) in Manchuria. Trains packed with soldiers, ammunition, and personal goods streamed out of Beijing Station. "Dreams of a United China Shattered—The Fallen King's Departure—Zhang Zuolin Escapes Beijing" was the headline under which the June 4 Tokyo *Asahi* morning edition reported details of Zhang's retreat from Beijing. Carrying Zhang in a cobalt blue car reserved for dignitaries and reported to be have been used by the Empress Dowager Cixi in the past, the special train "quietly left the station at about 1:15 a.m., leaving behind only a faint sound and the white smoke of its steam boilers." A Japanese Army officer observed this pandemonium from the platform. The Japanese military deployed personnel at strategic stations, monitoring movements and the general state of affairs, such as the departure and arrival times of trains at stations all the way from Beijing to Mukden.

"Blow up Zhang Zuolin's train and make it look as if it was planned by the KMT" (Chinese Nationalist Party)—this was the plot drawn up and executed by Colonel Kōmoto Daisaku, a high-ranking officer in the Japanese Kwantung Army, stationed in Manchuria. The aim was to cause a large-scale armed conflict, thereby tightening Japan's grip on Manchuria. At 5:25 a.m. on June 4, as the special train with Zhang on board passed under a bridge of the South Manchuria Railway approaching the terminal station on the Beijing–Mukden Line, there was a thunderous explosion.

Figure 7 Zhang Zuolin's elite rail carriage was destroyed when his train was blown up just outside of Mukden (modern-day Shenyang) (*Asahi*, June 4, 1928).

A front-page headline in that day's Osaka *Asahi* evening edition placed blame on the KMT: "Plainclothed Soldiers of the Southern Army (KMT Army) Blow Up Zhang Zuolin's Train." The evening edition of the Tokyo *Asahi* avoided such hasty conclusions but also made it appear as an act committed by the KMT:

> At 11.00 p.m. on June 3, the night before the special train was destroyed, two suspicious-looking Chinese men were seen in the vicinity of a railway crossing on the Beijing–Mukden Line. [...] When they were pursued and their pockets searched, two letters containing information about the KMT Army were found in their possession, with a timetable of Zhang Zuolin's train to Mukden.

The *Asahi* added, "It seems that the plainclothed soldiers of the Southern [KMT] Army watched the train and blew it up at exactly the time it passed with Zhang Zuolin on board." After the incident, the Japanese Kwantung Army promoted the opinion that it was a crime committed by the Chinese Nationalist Army. Japanese newspaper articles corroborated this view.

The plot that was covered up

By pure chance, early in the morning of June 4, the poet couple Yosano Tekkan and his wife Akiko were in Mukden on a lecture tour, staying in the Yamato Hotel, when they heard the sound of the blast resounding throughout the city. In a travelogue, *Travels in Manchurian and Mongolia*, a collection of impressions and poems about the tour, Akiko recalled: "I arose early and wrote letters to our children in Tokyo. As I was writing I heard a faint but strange noise. My husband was washing his face and he heard it, too."[1] Later, they learned from acquaintances that a train had been blown up and that Zhang Zuolin and his entourage had met with disaster. Yosano Akiko further reflected:

> We then understood what the earlier strange explosion we had heard had been and we found ourselves frowning as a certain dreadful realization swept across our minds. [...] We heard all sorts of wild rumors. These were all stories that I, as a Japanese, could not bear to hear.[2]

The following day the couple paid a visit to Ōi Jirō, *Asahi*'s special correspondent in Mukden. Ōi's elder brother, Sōgo, had contributed poems to a journal titled *Bright Stars* (*Myōjō*), edited by Tekkan, and Ōi Jirō had been on good terms with the couple since his childhood. Yosano Akiko wrote:

> Ōi and his staff were all occupied hunting down the story and gathering information in the wake of the incident, not having had so much as even a short nap the night before, they claimed. [...] What Ōi told us about the incident was not largely different from what our intuition was telling us from the previous day.[3]

There is no doubt that the "unpleasant suspicion" the Yosano couple and Ōi had at the time was that the Japanese had carried out the explosion. However, no-one could be certain. At first, Ōi wrote articles based on the Japanese Kwantung Army official position, which strongly implicated the Chinese side but at the same time suspicions in that area were growing about whether the incident was a Japanese conspiracy. The evening edition of the Tokyo *Asahi* on June 5 contained an article from a Mukden special correspondent under a large heading that read: "Suspicions of Japanese Conspiracy Behind Incident—Dire Turn for Sino-Japanese Relations in Mukden":

> The agitation on the Chinese side regarding the bombing incident has reached a climax, as certainty grows amongst the Chinese that it was a Japanese maneuver. [...] The situation has deteriorated to the point that Chinese are even aiming their guns at Japanese newspaper reporters and threatening to shoot.

The paper's evening edition on June 6 underlined the differences between the Japanese and Chinese positions: "the Japanese and Chinese opinions diverge following on-the-spot inspections." The morning edition of the Osaka *Asahi* on the same day stated in a follow-up report entitled "Rising Antipathy Toward Japan": "There is a rumor on the Chinese side [...] that this is all the doing of the Japanese. [...] Ordinary citizens, the Army, and even the authorities are all jumping on the bandwagon." However, articles such as these, which touched upon the possibility of a Japanese conspiracy, started to disappear from newspaper pages several days after the incident. The newspapers were being influenced from the outside.

Censorship or self-censorship?

Zhang Zuolin, who was seriously injured during the train explosion, was transported to his residence inside the Mukden city walls but his condition was kept a matter of strict secrecy. The *Asahi*'s special correspondent in Mukden, Ōi Jirō, was on friendly terms with Zhang's son, Zhang Xueliang. Nine days after the incident, on June 13, Ōi succeeded in meeting the son. Zhang Xueliang was wearing a black necktie and Ōi offered his condolences; Zhang admitted that his father had died on the night of the incident and Ōi managed to publish this news in his scoop: "Zhang Zuolin Died on the Day of the Accident." It is difficult to imagine that Ōi, who was such an able reporter, had not sensed any involvement on the part of the Japanese Kwantung Army. Why, then, did he not pursue the truth?

One reason for this negligence was controls on the freedom of the press. The July 10, 1934 "Table of Newspaper Articles Liable for Prohibition" provided details of specific regulations concerning reporting on Zhang Zuolin, which originated from the Home Ministry and the Kantōchō, Japan's civilian government agency of Manchuria established in 1919:

> Articles speculating about the connection between the death of Zhang Zuolin and citizens of the empire have been appearing now and then on the pages of newspapers. [...] Because there is a danger that these may present serious obstacles to diplomatic relations between Japan and China [...] it is important to not allow publication of such groundless rumors.

In this way, the prohibition came into force through a stricter directive issued by the Kantōchō two days after the incident on June 6, and through a "warning" on June 7 issued by the Office of the Governor General of Korea.

Starting on July 3, Ōi wrote four serial articles under the title, "What next for the political situation in the three Chinese northeastern provinces?" In these reports he dissected the political situation and potential developments in Manchuria after the train explosion. It is unnatural and surprising, however, that Ōi scarcely mentioned the incident itself. It is probable that one of the reasons for this was the controls on the freedom of the press, but was this the only factor? In the "Foreign Ministry Documents on the Incident of Zhang Zuolin's Death," kept at the Ministry of Defense Archives, there is a letter sent on June 8, 1928, from Hayashi Kyūjirō, Consul General of Mukden, to Tanaka Giichi, who was the foreign minister (and, concurrently, prime minister) at the time. It reported on the positions taken by newspaper journalists on the Zhang Zuolin Incident:

> It is not merely one or two Japanese journalists who say, "Oh, I guess they did it," as soon as they heard the explosion. Within the Japanese community there are those who go as far as to suspect that the whole incident was planned by the Japanese, the South Manchurian Railway Company, or a part of the Army. However, because this is a diplomatic matter of utmost importance, there is a general feeling that it should not be freely discussed in public.

The report strongly indicated that although journalists sensed that the incident was a plot executed by the Japanese military, they exercised restraint in making the truth public supposedly for the sake of relations with China and Japan's international standing.

The truth leaks out

Nonetheless, the truth about Zhang Zuolin's assassination started to leak out immediately after the incident. As chance would have it, a group of Diet members from the opposition Minseitō Party, who had come to China on an observation mission, alighted from their train at Mukden station one hour after the explosion. The group, which soon found out about the incident, headed for the Japanese consulate. Hayashi Kyūjirō, the consul general, said: "It's terrible. It is that army lot who are responsible for this. This is not going to be a trifling matter to solve." Matsumura Kenzō, a member of the observation mission, retold the events in his postwar memoir *Recollections of Three Generations* (*Sandai kaikoroku*). The group stayed in China for a week gathering information. They discovered that: (1) the yellow-colored gunpowder used in the explosion was a kind not used outside Japan; (2) the corpses "found" at the scene of the incident, claimed by the Japanese to belong to the "KMT patriots," were actually those of opium addicts with injection marks all over their arms; (3) between the site of the incident and a Japanese observation point an electric wire, which somebody had forgotten to hide, was still in place. President of the Minseitō Party, Hamaguchi Osachi, received a detailed report from Matsumura after the latter's return to Japan and immediately stated the following: "It is indeed a serious issue because its importance goes beyond traditional party affiliation. I would therefore like to handle this material by myself."

The government and the ruling party were both informed about the incident within a few minutes of each other. Minister of Railways Ogawa Heikichi was informed by an acquaintance who was a *Manshū rōnin*.[4] According to Ogawa's source, the mastermind of the incident was Colonel Kōmoto Daisaku. Dead bodies of Chinese men were placed at the scene to make the explosion look like an act of the KMT. Ogawa communicated this information to Prime Minister Tanaka Giichi and Army Minister Shirakawa Yoshinori. In September, the commander of the military police (*kempeitai*), Mine Yukimatsu, was dispatched to Mukden. Mine confirmed that the explosion had been plotted by the Japanese and informed Prime Minister Tanaka about this in October.

Newspapers were now in a position to know the truth. A story by the *Asahi* special correspondent in Shanghai, published in the morning edition of August 16, reprinted sources from a British reporter's story that ran in Shanghai foreign and Chinese language newspapers: "Although the joint Sino-Japanese investigative commission has yet to make its findings public, according to foreign reports the act was clearly carried out by a Japanese group to which the Army offered every assistance." *Asahi* cleverly maneuvered in such a way to convey suspicion of the Japanese Army under the pretense of introducing content from foreign newspapers, but it also distanced itself from this position by describing the British reporter as having "an established

Figure 8   The scene of Zhang Zuolin's assassination, from the photographic archives of the Osaka *Asahi*.

reputation of being anti-Japanese." After this article, *Asahi* stories on the Zhang Zuolin incident gradually died down. The second time the newspaper took up this issue was in December 1928 when the Minseitō started to rattle the Seiyūkai-led cabinet by calling the explosion "A Certain Grave Incident in Manchuria."

A "ghost-book" is discovered in Japan

In May 1929, eleven months after Zhang Zuolin was assassinated in the explosion, a book was published in Shanghai under the title, *The Japanese Plot to Murder Zhang Zuolin*. The tome unreservedly announced that the crime had been committed by the Japanese. According to Hu Yuhai, a professor at Liaoning University, when the book hit the shelves the Japanese government thrice protested against it, demanding that its sale be banned. The protest statement sent by the Japanese Consul General in Mukden, Hayashi Kyūjirō, to Liaoning provincial authorities, claimed "the book contained utter nonsense" and demanded an immediate ban. Although the book seems to have disappeared in China, copies can still be found in Japan. The 224-page volume was exactly the one described by Professor Hu. The tome was authored by Cong Debo, who had studied in prewar Japan and worked as a journalist writing about the political situation in Japan. In 1950, he left China for Taiwan with the KMT and died in 1980, at the age of 88. It is unclear why the book can no longer be found in China, but Professor Hu believes that "maybe because the Liaoning provincial authorities did not comply with the Japanese demand to stop the sale of the book, the Japanese side bought up most of the copies, taking samples back to Japan." If this is true, not only did the Japanese side control reporting on the Zhang Zuolin incident within Japan but it went as far as trying to influence publishing activities in China. Were the contents of the book so dangerous? Pan Liang, an associate professor at Tsukuba University, analyzes the issue:

> The book does not reveal any definitive evidence pointing toward a conspiracy by the Japanese Kwantung Army, but the author's personal conjecture and basing his opinions on reports from news agencies such as Reuters, meant that its contents were actually quite close to the truth. One can therefore understand the Japanese side's nervousness about the book.

Professor Hu, too, believes that "without doubt, it was a book that was quickest in exposing to the Chinese public the truth behind the incident." Of the five major newspapers publishing at the time in Mukden, three (both in the Japanese and Chinese languages) were under Japanese influence, while the remaining two, although published by the Chinese side, reprinted the Japanese version of the events when reporting on the Zhang Zuolin incident. In such a situation there were people who feared that the Zhang Zuolin incident would be erased from history. Wang Jiazhen, who like Cong also had studied in Japan, worked as a private secretary to Zhang Xueliang. According to Professor Hu, Wang recalled in his memoirs before his death in 1984: "I not only passed on to Cong Debo all the information that I had from being there, but I also offered him funds to support the task of writing the book."

A roundabout approach to the truth

Half a year after the explosion in Manchuria killed Zhang Zuolin in June 1928, the incident began to be referred to in a rather unusual manner: "the grave incident in Manchuria." The first time this term made headlines in the Tokyo *Asahi* was in the newspaper's evening edition on December 25. The article related that in a meeting with the Parliamentary Vice Minister of Foreign Affairs, Mori Tsutomu, and others, Prime Minister Tanaka Giichi "exchanged views particularly concerning the grave incident in Manchuria, the main target for the Minseitō's pointed criticism of the government." The opposition party, Minseitō, had learned that the attack surrounding Zhang Zuolin was a Japanese-orchestrated plot and leading up to the 56th session of the Diet, convened on December 24, there were signs that party members were planning to expose this fact, waiting for the opportune moment to topple the government.

Prime Minister Tanaka took pains to look for ways to handle this situation. On January 22, 1929, he made an appeal to the leader of the Minseitō, Hamaguchi Osachi, and other members of the Diet, voicing his "sincere hopes that out of consideration for Japan's international relations, and for the sake of the nation, the so-called 'grave incident in Manchuria' would not be made a subject of parliamentary discussion." He also emphasized that "should there be any enquiries on the matter [...] the only reply the government would be able to give was that the incident was still under investigation."[5]

Minseitō president Hamaguchi, on the other hand, could have hardly failed to take into account the negative impact that such a revelation would have on Japan within the international community. He ultimately decided not to disclose the facts but rather to use them as a tool to topple the Cabinet. With both the government and the opposition party taking such a rather weak-kneed approach toward airing the true nature of the incident, contrary to what one would expect, a fully negotiated debate never managed to develop in Japan. It was in this context that the euphemistic expression "grave incident in Manchuria" made its appearance—although the terms employed in Japanese newspapers were by no means uniform, and even after this the *Asahi* used alternative phrases such as "Manchuria Incident" or "the incident of Zhang Zuolin's violent death."[6]

The newspapers carried biting criticism of the curious exchanges between the government and opposition parties. The *Tokyo Nichinichi Shimbun* (now the *Mainichi Shimbun*), for instance, wrote the following in an editorial on April 3, 1929:

> Despite the fact that the incident in question quite clearly refers to the assassination of Zhang Zuolin, it is labeled "a certain grave incident," and the like. This in itself seems to suggest that there are already grave suspicions against our nation and it is to no small extent giving rise to disadvantageous implications for Japan's foreign affairs. [...] Of course if there is any truth to these suspicions against the local military and civilian authorities, the responsible parties should receive their lawful and just punishment.

The Tokyo *Asahi* also wrote in an editorial on May 15: "This matter should be promptly clarified so as to dispel suspicions in Japan and abroad. If Japan holds no responsibility in the affair – fine. If it does, it is not too late to bring the responsible parties to account." This, however, was as far as the newspapers would go in their coverage. For not only were they subject to censorship by the government, as media organs the papers were likely also concerned about the potential repercussions such reports would have on Japan's foreign relations. In any case, the newspapers did not take it into their own hands to investigate and report the facts of the matter.

Condoning the actions of the military yet again

Emperor Hirohito knew the true circumstances surrounding Zhang Zuolin's assassination. In his postwar memoirs, he provided his rendering of events: "The leading mastermind behind the incident was Colonel Kōmoto Daisaku. When Prime Minister Tanaka Giichi first spoke to me about it, he depicted the affair as highly deplorable [...] saying that he intended to punish Kōmoto and express his regret to China." At the outset, Prime Minister Tanaka offered Emperor Hirohito a relatively frank report of the events, even going as far as mentioning punishment for the perpetrators. Strong opposition to his plan of action from powerful members of the Cabinet and the Army, however, forced the prime minister to reverse his position: "Tanaka came to see me again, now saying that he wanted to bury the matter and keep it unresolved. [...] I remarked that his opinion had changed since our last meeting, and recommended in a rather forceful tone that he consider resigning," the Emperor recalled.[7] Having lost the Emperor's trust, Tanaka's entire Cabinet stepped down on July 2, 1929 and in the end the Zhang Zuolin Incident was left covered up. The Tokyo

Asahi evening edition reported the following piece of news on that day: "The government, as well as the military authorities, are working hard to resolve the grave incident in Manchuria. [...] No details surrounding the incident itself were released, only the punishment for those on guard at the time of the assassination was announced after imperial approval on July 1." Kōmoto escaped court martial and was merely discharged from the Army on the grounds of "dereliction of duty." The fact that an officer was able to put such a daring plot into action with impunity was one factor that contributed to further strengthening the military in its independent decision-making and unilateral moves.

Three years after the Zhang Zuolin Incident, on September 18, 1931, an explosion damaged the Japanese-operated South Manchurian Railway at Liutiao Lake, only a few kilometers from the site where Zhang had been assassinated. The Japanese Kwantung Army made this out to be "the result of Chinese machinations" and used it as a pretext to occupy all of Manchuria. The leaders of this plot were two staff officers in the Kwantung Army, Kōmoto's successor Itagaki Seishirō and Ishiwara Kanji—although the complete details of the conspiracy did not come to light until after the war.

The Wakatsuki Cabinet declared a "policy of non-expansion" in reaction to the incident and the Osaka *Asahi Newspaper*, in an editorial on September 20, similarly drove home the point that "great care should be taken not to give more freedom of action to the Japanese military authorities in Manchuria than is necessary." The Kwantung Army, nevertheless, advanced its troops and on September 21 Japanese forces stationed in Korea (*Chōsen*) also deployed to Manchuria on their own initiative. Although this move represented a historical watershed, Prime Minister Wakatsuki only commented that: "They have already mobilized, there is nothing we can do about it now," and the Cabinet likewise condoned the campaign.

The *Asahi* now followed suit and changed its editorial tone concerning the situation in Manchuria. According to a report from a commander of the military police to a deputy staff officer, executives of the Osaka *Asahi* held a meeting on October 12, at which they "decided that as Japanese citizens at such a crucial time for the nation [...] we should support to the extent possible a policy of absolutely not criticizing or condemning the military and military campaigns." In this way, the Army acted independently and government authorization lagged behind, merely rubber-stamping military actions after they had occurred. The newspapers, although continuing to harbor doubts about a possible conspiracy, joined in this consensus of approval. This easy acceptance was a pattern that repeated itself in both the 1928 Zhang Zuolin Incident as well as the 1931 Manchurian Incident.

The memories of an old Chinese man

Around two hours after the explosion on the Manchurian Railway at Liutiao Lake on the outskirts of Mukden (present-day Shenyang), the head of the local news office of the *Asahi*, Takeuchi Ayayoshi, drove around the city providing urgent reports on the tense situation. The Tokyo *Asahi* evening edition of September 20, 1931, captured his impressions:

I thought to myself, "The hell with it!" and mustering all my courage I entered the city. There I repeatedly encountered armed guards on patrol, who ordered me to stop. They shoved bayonets in my face, sending shivers down my spine. [...] With the roar of Chinese and Japanese gunfire from the site of conflict and the materialization of the Japanese military's plan to occupy the city, danger neared and feelings of unrest between the Chinese and Japanese in the city reached a crescendo.

At the time, Mukden was divided into the zone around the South Manchurian Railway line, where approximately 20,000 Japanese lived, the Mukden city area, mainly inhabited by Chinese people, and the mixed living quarters located in between. The *Asahi* quite actively reported on the movements of the Chinese, the spread of the fighting and the trend toward an anti-Japanese movement, with headlines in the September 19 special edition reading: "All Japanese Civilians from within the City Retreat to the South Manchurian Railway Public Areas" and "Defense Against Chinese Incursion of Areas Near South Manchurian Railway." None of the articles, however, allowed readers to catch a glimpse into the situation surrounding the Chinese citizens of Mukden, whose lives and property were threatened by the military conflict.

One such citizen was Fang Zheng, who recalls the Manchurian Incident and its aftermath:

At the time the incident occurred, I was asleep and did not notice anything. I only realized that something terrible must have happened the next morning, from the tense looks of the grown-ups. Because I had two older sisters of marriageable age, we locked our front door and spent days inside, barely daring to move or breathe.

Fang Zheng was seven at the time. His father ran a business that traded silk fabrics in the city where he had built a shop in which the family also lived. When the Manchurian Incident erupted, the family was no longer able to go around and collect outstanding payments from customers and business ground to a halt. His father divided the cash he had at hand among his employees and closed shop, eventually moving the whole family to Xinjing (present-day Changchun), the "new capital" of the "Manchurian Kingdom," also known as Manchukuo.

"The Japanese education I received in Manchukuo decided the course of my life," Fang Zheng recounts. He put the Japanese language he had acquired during his time in Xinjing to use in his professional life, being involved for over twenty years in Japanese language education at a foreign language school in Shaoxing, Zhejiang Province, where he ultimately became principal and retired in 2007. It was, however, not until after the reforms and the Chinese economic opening had set in that Fang could settle in Shaoxing, from where his parents had originally hailed.

Up to that point, his life was a series of trials and tribulations; he was jailed as a political prisoner, sent to a *laogai*, a reform through labor camp, and his family was separated. As a young man, burning with national pride, he had joined the anti-Japanese resistance and had been active as an underground spy for the Kuomintang, the Chinese Nationalist Party (KMT). This personal track record became a burdensome legacy in the new China of the People's Republic after 1949, and would resurface every time a political movement arose. As Fang Zheng points out, "all of this happened because of the September 18 Incident [the Manchurian Incident]. Had it not been for that moment, I might have taken over my father's business and never gotten involved with the Kuomintang." After his retirement, he wrote his memoirs in Japanese under the title, *An Old Chinese Man Remembers: A Life Wandering through Turbulent Times.*[8] His life, he says, provides "merely one example of many in China." The most important thing of all, in his view, was "that the September 18 Manchurian Incident decisively changed the course of Chinese history."

The path toward isolation

As the Manchurian Incident erupted in September 1931, it prompted the *Asahi* to adopt an approving tone toward the Japanese imperial military campaign on the continent. Symbolic of this shift in the newspaper's stance was the editorial in the Osaka *Asahi* from October 1, which proclaimed that "the formation of a new independent state in Manchuria should be welcomed and there was no reason to oppose this development." Such a statement essentially meant that the paper completely abandoned the views it had hitherto upheld—that is, "the basic notion that the unification of China should be supported and Chinese nationalism encouraged," and its "recognition of Manchuria as a part of China."[9]

In March 1932, Japan established Manchukuo as an independent kingdom, while effectively taking hold of the reins of political power and setting up a "puppet state." Subsequently, a League of Nations Commission under the leadership of Victor Bulwer-Lytton from the United Kingdom investigated the circumstances that had led to the September 18 Incident (the Manchurian Incident), and released a report in October. This "Lytton Report" included the following conclusions:

1. The state of "Manchukuo" cannot be considered to have come into existence through a genuine and natural independence movement.
2. The rights and interests Japan holds in Manchuria cannot be disregarded.
3. An autonomous government should be established in Manchuria under Chinese sovereignty.

This report was not unsympathetic toward Japan—and yet the Japanese side, which had recognized Manchukuo as independent, was enraged. Japanese newspapers were especially furious and criticism abounded in various editorials on October 3. The headline of the *Tokyo Nichinichi Newspaper* read: "A Fantasy Report, League of Nations Suffering from Severe Delusion." The Tokyo *Asahi* similarly spoke of "delusion, specious rhetoric, a lack of awareness on the part of the League of Nations"—branding the report as "empty rhetoric that disregards history." As the public critic Kiyosawa Kiyoshi pointed out, "every newspaper was in an uproar."[10]

In December of the same year, 132 newspaper companies and news agencies, including the Tokyo and Osaka *Asahi*, the *Osaka Mainichi* and the *Yomiuri*, issued a joint announcement in which they rebuked the League of Nations: "It is hereby declared in the name of the Japanese organs of public opinion that the proposed solutions, [...] in as far as they jeopardize the stability and continued existence of the state of Manchukuo, are completely unacceptable." The uncritical exultation that had taken hold of the newspapers in the wake of the Manchurian Incident showed no signs of abating.

On the other hand, the anxiety of international isolation heightened when the League of Nations' proposals became public—which, based on the findings of the Lytton Report, recommended, for instance, the withdrawal of the Japanese Army from Manchuria. In an editorial of February 18, 1933, entitled "The recommendation is not a verdict," the Tokyo *Asahi* displayed a cautious stance toward a possible Japanese withdrawal from the League of Nations. However, the paper also made clear that "the report's recommendation showed no understanding of Japan's position and was unable to indicate effective measures for the establishment of peace in the Far East, which is highly regrettable for us."

In the end, this standpoint—clinging to Manchukuo, while at the same time seeking to avoid international isolation—proved to be untenable. The League of Nations adopted the recommendation with a forty-two to one vote, Japan being the only country to oppose. The Japanese delegation, led by Matsuoka Yōsuke, subsequently left the assembly and so Japan withdrew from the League of Nations.

5

The Age of Terrorism

A grisly tragedy in Wakayama City

It was April 16, 1928 and a slight chill had descended onto the night-time streets of Wakayama City. At a lawyer's office in the third district of the city not far from the courthouse, a group of people were deep in discussion. After eight o'clock in the evening several men entered the office and, after some negotiation, swords were drawn and the intruders cut down their victims one after another. Wada Uzen, a lawyer and member of the prefectural assembly, and Yonezaki Kyūichirō, a member of the election campaign office of the oppositional party Minseitō, were both stabbed and died instantly. Lawyer Sakaguchi Keiichi, despite putting up resistance, sustained wounds all over his body as he attempted to rush toward the phone. He perished soon after. Several other people who happened to be present suffered injuries of varying degrees.

The following day the evening edition of the Osaka *Asahi* dedicated the better part of page two to reporting this violent crime under the headline, "Three People, Including Lawyers, Stabbed to Death." The Tokyo *Asahi* also covered the case. According to these articles, the *History of Wakayama Prefecture* and other sources, six members of the right-wing group National Essence Society (*Kokusuikai*), including the leader of the Wakayama branch of the organization, turned themselves in to the police.

The year this incident occurred in remote Wakayama Prefecture has gone down as a moment of special significance. February 1928 saw the first universal elections in which men over 25 were given the right to vote for the representatives of the Lower House—an outcome of earlier moves toward democracy during the Taisho era (1912–1926). Moreover, 1928 also marked the year that trials by jury were instituted.

Asahi had continuously campaigned for the implementation of universal suffrage in its editorials, writing for instance in the Osaka *Asahi* on November 6, 1919: "The time is already ripe. The overwhelming majority of the Japanese people have come to realize that limiting the right to vote in a constitutional nation is unreasonable." Shortly before election day in 1928, the paper printed slogans in big, bold red characters that warned against the buying of votes, or government interference in the elections, cautioning for instance, "No to the buying of votes!" In this way, near the beginning of the Showa era, it seemed that Japan was treading the path toward freedom and democracy—if not always in the most straightforward manner. Together with the Universal Suffrage Law, however, the Peace Preservation Law was also promulgated. This law strengthened government control over political activities. At the same time, antagonism between political parties vying for votes grew more heated following the expansion of voting rights. In the first general election for the Lower House, the opposition Minseitō Party put up a valiant fight, closing in on the incumbent Seiyūkai Party. During the elections, police forces interfered repeatedly, targeting the opposition Minseitō Party and the proletarian parties, supported by workers and peasants.

Furthermore, the rampant domestic terrorism that had spread anxiety in Japanese society from the 1880s through the 1920s and onwards, was a harbinger of the escalation to totalitarianism. The lawyer incident in Wakayama City, which came two months after the elections, appeared as a terrible tragedy in newspaper reports. When tracing the background of this event, however, its deep connections to the oppression and antagonism surrounding the first general election are revealed.

A police-orchestrated plot?

"After the blood-soaked tragedy, everything went according to plan."

On April 18, 1928, the Osaka *Asahi* ran a report conveying the shock of the victims' families in the aftermath of the Wakayama Incident. At the home of the murdered lawyer Sakaguchi Keiichi (37 at the time), his wife seemed at a complete loss. Next to her stood their young daughter "who did not yet know her father was dead and, with a beaming smile, got up to some childish mischief—a sight that could not fail to bring tears to the eyes of the observer," the paper related. Only two years old at the time, Kawanishi Masako (now in her eighties) has no recollection of the incident. She only learned about the circumstances of her father's death at age 14 after she came across some old newspapers on a bookshelf. "Until that time, neither my mother nor my relatives had told me about the incident," she recounts. Why had her father's life been taken?

In 1928, the Seiyūkai ruling party faced a tough battle in the Lower House elections, the first ever general elections in Japan. In Wakayama Prefecture, Nakamura Keijirō of the oppositional Minseitō Party emerged the winner. Following the victory, police raised suspicions of election infringement against a large number of people connected to the Minseitō. According to an article in the Osaka *Asahi*, one victim of the terrorist attacks in Wakayama, Yonezaki Kyūichirō, was the accountant for Nakamura's election campaign office. Yonezaki claimed that he had been tortured over allegations of election fraud while in custody at the Wakayama police station and had subsequently pressed charges against the police officers responsible. The lawyers representing him in the case were Sakaguchi and the other murder victim, who died with Yonezaki. It seems that their attackers from the National Essence Society had in fact demanded that Yonezaki drop the lawsuit. Yonezaki's refusal had led to the ensuing violence.

Rumors circulated as to whether the Wakayama police chief had requested this "intervention" to cover up the police torture and force Yonezaki to withdraw his charges. The division chief of the prefectural police and others rejected such allegations in the *Asahi* but the newspaper cast doubt on the incident based on its own investigation. The following month in the imperial Diet the Minseitō Party attempted to pursue these allegations of a police conspiracy through a written query to the government, which stated: "The prefectural police authorities in Wakayama trampled on human rights and then turned to a criminal organization to force the victims to drop their legal action. This ultimately caused a tragic incident in which a number of people were brutally murdered." The government responded: "while it was unlikely that the police were unaware of the National Essence Society's efforts to make Yonezaki withdraw his charges, there is no foundation to the fact that the group moved on orders from the authorities."

In October 1928, the six defendants in the Wakayama City Incident were sentenced, receiving terms ranging from fifteen years to life imprisonment. At the time, the *Asahi* portrayed the incident primarily as a horrific tragedy but any suspicions and allegations against the police soon disappeared from its pages. Miura Hitoshi, grandson of the victim Sakaguchi Keiichi, heard the particulars of the incident from his father, who was born half a year after the event. In his opinion, "the newspapers probably could not fully grasp the magnitude of the problem, in part also because it was an incident in an outlying prefecture."

At that time, however, the grip of terror also seized the capital Tokyo.

Unprecedented crackdowns

On April 11, 1928, five days before the Wakayama Incident, the former committee chairman of the Laborers' and Farmers' Party (Rōdō Nōmintō), Ōyama Ikuo, fell victim to an assault at Tokyo railway station. As party well-wishers welcomed Ōyama on the platform, a group of people suddenly charged at him, screaming as they began to beat him. The government had previously given orders to disband the Laborers' and Farmers' Party, a proletarian party. The police were on watch at the scene of the commotion but rather than arresting any of the assailants, they instead detained two

Figure 9 Ōyama Ikuo (center) after the attack on him at Tokyo Station (*Asahi*, April 12, 1928, Tokyo morning edition).

people from Ōyama's party, claiming that these men had illegally handed out flyers. The chief of Hibiya police station, in charge of the police forces at Tokyo railway station, later declared: "I believe that the people of the former Laborers' and Farmers' Party should thank us because we were on our guard and protected them. [...] We did not take any of the people on the platform into custody because in our eyes there was no physical assault on Mr. Ōyama and others."[1]

What fueled this increasingly intense crackdown on the proletarian parties was partly the Lower House elections in February, the first general elections in Japan. Ōyama ran as a candidate for Kagawa Prefecture, the local constituency of Minister of Finance Mitsuchi Chūzō, but his bid for office was unsuccessful. Purportedly, this was not least due to the police's staunch suppression of his campaign. Ōyama's biography reveals the extent of these intrusions, which involved measures such as immediate suspension of his public speeches. Plainclothes policemen would hover around the inns where he was staying, repeatedly questioning the guests. The police also summoned the owners of the establishments and interrogated them in detail about Ōyama's activities.[2] On February 3, before the elections, the lecture hall at the Tokyo *Asahi* main office hosted the first event where representatives from each party made public speeches. Ōyama received a storm of applause when he rose from his seat to deliver his speech but within five minutes the police ordered him to stop. In Kagawa Prefecture, approximately a hundred of the leading members of the Laborers' and Farmers' Party were detained in police custody for election irregularities, according to the February 18 edition of *Asahi*.

Even though the elections in February 1928 were "general elections," women still did not have the right to vote and freedom of expression was fairly restricted. The buying of votes and election violence was supposedly also rampant. Irregularities uncovered up to election day included 63 involving the ruling Seiyūkai Party, 469 involving the oppositional Minseitō Party and 73 the Laborers' and Farmers' Party.[3]

Eighteen days after the incident at Tokyo railway station, the proletarian parties held a "People's Rally to Overthrow the Cabinet" in Tokyo. This time the police did not merely stop at suspending public speeches, as the *Asahi* reported: "The frantic authorities were extremely determined to suppress any coverage of the meeting in newspapers or other media and cracked down with unprecedented force on journalists and photographers from all papers."[4] The police destroyed the camera of a photographer from the *Tokyo Nichinichi Newspaper*, while a journalist of the *Yomiuri Newspaper* sustained injuries so severe that he was left with a walking impairment. Ōyama himself could not even get close to the venue due to the throngs of irate policemen.

1928 was also the year of the so-called "March 15 Incident," which saw mass arrests of members of the Communist Party. This was the year when the Peace Preservation Law was amended to include capital punishment and the time when the Special Higher Police, responsible for the suppression of dissident thought, was established within the police forces of all prefectures. The growing antagonism between the political parties that took part in the general elections and the suppression of unwelcome political thought paved the way toward more violent times. A year later in 1929 Japan would witness even more shocking acts of terror.

The assassination of "Yamasen"

On the night of March 5, 1929, Yamamoto Senji, a member of the Lower House for the former Laborers' and Farmers' Party, was stabbed at the Kōeikan Inn in Kanda ward in Tokyo. "He tumbled down the steps from the second floor. I was startled and wondered what was going on, and then I noticed that Mr. Yamamoto as well as this other man were both stained with blood," said the female manager of the inn in an eyewitness report in *Asahi* the next day. At the time of his assassination, Yamamoto was 39. Formerly a university lecturer in biology, he stood at the front line of the Laborer's and Farmer's Movement and the year before he had been victorious in the first general elections for the second district in Kyoto. He was known informally by his nickname "Yamasen." His attacker, Kuroda Hokuji, was a former police officer and member of the right-wing organization Seven Lives Righteousness Association (*Shichiseigi-dan*).

On March 5, the Lower House had passed a revision of the Peace Preservation Law, which made the formation of organizations whose aim was revolution of the national polity a crime punishable by death as its maximum sentence. Yamamoto, like all the proletarian parties in general, had strongly opposed this provision. According to the March 6 *Asahi*, Kuroda appeared at the inn at around 9:20 p.m. wearing an indigo-blue kimono with a white splash pattern and a short *haori* overcoat. He approached the reception and asked to see Yamamoto. Yamamoto turned him down but Kuroda persisted and was ultimately invited in to his room. Upon entering, Kuroda took out a prepared statement detailing his intentions from his breast pocket and demanded Yamamoto's resignation as a member of the Lower House. He thrust this piece of writing at Yamamoto and an argument ensued. After quarreling Kuroda stabbed Yamamoto in the neck with a dagger. Criticism in Kuroda's statement included, among other things, that he believed Yamamoto was paving the way for the "Bolshevik Movement" by opposing the revision of the Peace Preservation Law.

The head of the Special Investigations Section of the Metropolitan Police Office, who was in charge of the Kuroda case, explained the crime as the end result of a struggle between the two men: "They got into a tussle in Yamamoto's room and the moment Yamamoto pushed Kuroda against the wall the latter brought out a dagger he had secretly been carrying and stabbed Yamamoto in the right side of the neck."[5] News media subsequently reported that the Head of the Special Investigation Division had suggested the possibility that Kuroda acted in legitimate self-defense. The *Tokyo Nichinichi* of March 7 quoted the head police officer: "If I were to send Kuroda to prison it would not be for murder but for manslaughter." Such statements became quite problematic in view of the fact that the year before trials by jury had been instituted. The legal scholar Suehiro Izutarō criticized this public display of opinion on part of the investigators due to the influence it would have on potential jury members, pointing out: "it provided the public with foregone conclusions concerning the incident and fundamentally hindered the fair application of the Jury Law."[6]

Kuroda was eventually indicted for murder. However, the judge at the preliminary hearing, who was to decide whether or not a public trial would be held, made a surprising move. Amid much controversy the judge granted Kuroda bail. In view of this, the *Tokyo Asahi* from May 4 cautioned in an editorial: "such moves might arouse doubts as to whether even the court shows leniency in the case of crimes motivated by rightist ideology and is only very strict on people holding leftist beliefs." The next year Kuroda was sentenced to twelve years in prison for stabbing Yamamoto but his sentence was later reduced and he was released on parole after seven years. In the June 11, 1938 evening edition of *Asahi*, an inconspicuous article announced the special reduction of Kuroda's punishment.

The motive for the assassination

The assassination of Yamamoto Senji, a Diet member in office, threw the Imperial Diet into an uproar. The police, meanwhile, did not loosen their control in their continued clampdown on proletarian parties' activities and even interrupted the memorial address at Yamamoto's funeral halfway through the event. As a result, the proletarian parties' rage mounted. In the Diet, Asahara Kenzō of the Japan Mass Party (*Nihon Taishūtō*) pursued allegations against the police. He pointed out that the section head of the Metropolitan Police, who had portrayed Kuroda in such a favorable light to journalists, generally "entertained rather close personal connections with the perpetrator in the past" and was a drinking buddy.

In the plenary session of March 18, 1929, Asahara questioned Akita Kiyoshi, the Parliamentary Undersecretary of the Home Ministry, which had jurisdiction over the police forces:

Asahara:　"'The Seven Lives Righteousness Group' (*Shichiseigi-dan*) openly announced to its adherents the stabbing of a Diet member belonging to a proletarian party and yet the government has not banned the sale of this publication. Why are you not intervening in this matter?"

Akita:　"We could of course ban the bulletin. However, because this article is not so important, it should not be criticized for not being banned."

Asahara:　"The newspapers are running articles implying that Kuroda possibly acted in self-defense. Due to such descriptions, readers sympathize with the culprit and lose such empathy for Yamamoto. Moreover, it is the Metropolitan Police who are communicating these sorts of announcements. They have disclosed the contents of the criminal's statement behind his actions, in which he demanded Yamamoto's resignation from the Diet, and they even publicized the testimony the criminal gave in court."

Akita:　"There is no basis concerning the Metropolitan Police's description of self-defense to reporters; nor is it the case that they announced the contents of Kuroda's letter to the newspapers."

Asahara:　"When it is convenient for the police you subtly use the newspapers and when it is not so convenient you claim to hold no responsibility for their articles."[7]

It seems that the contents of Kuroda's testimony and the other news items that the media published did not actually stem from police announcements. Rather, journalists had extracted this information through interviews with the relevant authorities. Papers need to probe and report on suspects and their motives. In the case of Yamamoto Senji's assassination at least, there were no actual articles that were sympathetic to the terrorist attackers.

However, due to an incident three years later, Japanese public opinion drifted toward an unexpected direction, as the newspapers covered the "motives of the terrorists" in explicit detail. This incident occurred on May 15, 1932, when a group of Army and Navy officer school students stormed several locations including the Prime Minister's residence, the Metropolitan police station, and the headquarters of the Seiyūkai, shooting dead Prime Minister Inukai Tsuyoshi in the process. Shortly before these events, from February to March 1932, during the so-called Blood Pledge Corps Incident, former Finance Minister Inoue Junnosuke and the Director-General of Mitsui Holding Company, Dan Takuma, were murdered. The police determined that this earlier incident was connected to the May 15 Incident.

On the night of May 15, the Home Ministry invoked the Press Law and banned any coverage of "the culprits' names, their backgrounds, and other details." The public therefore had to wait a while to find out the full details of why the perpetrators had resorted to terrorist acts.

A mountain of petitions

In the summer of 1933, Japan was swept by a bizarre fervor. The public trials of the "Blood Pledge Corps" and the May 15 Incident, which had both occurred the previous year, opened in quick succession. In the case of the May 15 Incident, articles on the trials appeared virtually every day in the papers after they began in late July. This was due partly to a lifting of press regulations but also because the proceedings were divided into three separate trials: a court-martial of the Navy, of the Army, as well as a civilian trial. In their trial testimony, the defendants detailed their innermost thoughts and the newspapers reported on this at length: "We saw the impoverishment of farmers and the destitution of fishing villages, the people in the commercial and industrial sector, the workers...." "We heard about the famines in northeastern Japan, and felt the need to overcome the present situation as soon as possible—not least for the preservation of the Japanese Army's own position," the perpetrators testified.[8]

Overall, the coverage in the papers seemed supportive of the defendants' claims and actions. The Japanese mainly held an "innocent" image of the accused cadets and looked to them in the hope that they could help to improve Japan's situation at the time. The discontent with the *status quo* had only increased among the people after former Railway Minister Ogawa Heikichi had been found innocent in a bribery scandal in May. Sympathy for the defendants spread and it did so in the form of petitions to decrease their sentences. At the outset, this all was merely an initiative involving some nationalist organizations but in the blink of an eye this support turned into a sort of mass movement.

In *The May 15 Incident and the Japanese Mass Media*, Tamai Kiyoshi's research group at Keiō University summarized the news coverage from that time. According to their findings and other sources, the scale of this movement increased significantly: "A Flood of Petitions Calling for a Reduction in Sentence, 60,000 Mark Exceeded," "350,000 Petitions for Mitigation of Punishment," and finally "Petitions for Mitigation of Punishment Pass 1 million Mark."[9] By contrast, the granddaughter of Prime Minister Inukai Tsuyoshi, a victim of the May 15 Incident, recalled in an interview with the *Asahi Weekly* (*Shūkan Asahi*) how marginalized she felt back when she was a schoolgirl. Others told her that, "she was the granddaughter of an unpatriotic man because her grandfather had been 'done in' by the military."

Some support for the defendants took more extreme and bizarre forms. In one instance, Army Minister Araki Sadao received a package addressed to him from Niigata. On opening the wooden box, he found nine little fingers together with a petition for decreasing the punishment of the May 15 Incident criminals.[10] In another instance, a 19-year-old girl committed suicide by throwing herself on the tracks at a railroad crossing of the Tōbu Railway Line in Saitama Prefecture. Her farewell note read: "I don't want to let the May 15 members die."[11]

However, voices were also raised that this movement for mitigation could potentially come into conflict with the law. "Iron Broom" (*Tessō*), the section of readers' letters in the Tokyo *Asahi*, cautioned on August 17: "Hopefully in their deep sympathy people will not choose the wrong means of protest and lapse into rash or illegal action." A Tokyo *Asahi* editorial on November 10 also pointed out several issues related to current events: "In view of preserving law and order in our nation, nothing could be more worrisome than if a trend developed where people believed that they could immediately resort to rash and reckless action as an expression of their discontent, as soon as something ran counter to their own subjective interpretations."

Articles like this, however, which demanded level-headedness of readers, were drowned out by the wave of sympathy for the defendants, and ultimately went unnoticed. That summer the media clearly swam with the flow of terrorist fervor.

A judge in tears

There is a little booklet whose edges have now turned brown with age, entitled *The People of the May 15 Incident and Their Notes from Prison*. It was a supplement to the monthly magazine *Sunrise* (*Hinode*) of November 1933. *Hinode* was a mass entertainment magazine launched by the publishing house Shinchōsha to compete with Kōdansha publishing company's *King* (*Kingu*) magazine. The November issue of *Hinode* went on sale at the beginning of October just as the sentences in the May 15 Incident were being handed down. The 160-page supplement summarized the defendants' prison notes, alongside reports of family visits and observers' accounts of the military court proceedings. The highlight of the booklet, however, was its photos: portrait pictures of the defendants in uniform next to family photographs from their childhood, which introduced the young officers one by one in dual-page spreads. Rather than defendants on trial for the assassination of a Prime Minister, they were treated in the magazine as selfless saviors, like war heroes who had met their fate after distinguishing themselves in battle. Around the time the magazine went on sale,

Figure 10 Newspaper advertisement announcing the monthly magazine *Sunrise*'s special supplement on the May 15 Incident (Tokyo *Asahi*, October 9, 1933).

advertisements for the issue appeared repeatedly in newspapers. In white extra-large lettering that danced across half a page or a full page, these ads promoted the new issue in a bid to stoke the emotions of the population: "The big supplement dedicated to the patriotism that is moving the hearts of the Japanese!!"

Those directly involved in the trials were also not completely immune to the growing media frenzy. Whereas in the prior case of the shooting of Prime Minister Hamaguchi (in 1930), the perpetrators had been sentenced to death, in the Blood Pledge Corps and the May 15 Incident cases the defendants escaped capital punishment. In response, Hayashi Itsurō, a lawyer in the Blood Pledge Corps case, wrote: "This followed the dynamics at work in society at the time and in itself speaks eloquently more than anything else to what extent Japanese law and the courts have evolved and taken a leap forward."[12] Lawyer Kiyose Ichirō, an opponent of the Peace Preservation Law who also defended many put on trial for violations of that law, also showed an understanding of the situation in the November 1933 issue of the magazine *Reconstruction* (*Kaizō*): "Special privileges have to be laid to rest. [...] The farming villages must be saved. 'This incident was inevitable'—how should we understand the perpetrators' beliefs?"

In the Blood Pledge Corps and the May 15 Incident cases, the sentences were in general far more lenient than the punishments demanded by the prosecution. Fujii Goichirō, the judge of the Tokyo district court who presided over the trial of the Blood Pledge Corps Incident, even addressed the defendants immediately after he had pronounced the verdict: "If the punishment is settled and you accept your sentences, please all take good care of yourselves. . . ." However, "before he could finish his sentence his eyes moistened and he bit his lip while lowering his face."[13] Even the judge, whose aim was to be calm and impartial, failed to suppress his emotions.

Four years after the May 15 Incident, the February 26 Incident erupted. The uncompromising journalist Kiryū Yūyū wrote in reaction to these events in the magazine *Tazan no ishi* (*Lessons Learned from the Experience of Others*): "Have I not told you so? If parts of the population in their utmost blindness are full of praise for the culprits of the May 15 Incident, these copycat actions are the inevitable result." The British newspaper, *The Times*, pointed out the day after, on February 27:

> The most disquieting feature of the current situation is the attitude of public opinion towards the terrorism practised by the patriotic societies, especially by those of the younger officers. The epidemic of political assassination four years ago [...] roused only a passing indignation. Sympathy was freely expressed for the young officers who had resorted to murder.... The sincerity of their patriotic fanaticism was held to explain, almost indeed to justify, the crimes of which they were guilty. [...] This toleration for methods of violence is a curious trait in a nation possessing so strong a feeling for discipline in most departments of life.[14]

"*Asahi*, traitor to the nation!": the newspaper under attack

On February 26, 1936, it snowed from morning until evening in Tokyo, which was still covered in white from a heavy snowfall three days earlier. At daybreak rebellious troops stormed several sites including the residence of the Prime Minister, killing Minister of Finance Takahashi Korekiyo, Lord Keeper of the Privy Seal Saitō Makoto, Inspector General of Military Education Watanabe Jōtarō, and severely wounding Grand Chamberlain Suzuki Kantarō. This was the so-called "February 26 Incident." Around 8:50 in the morning, approximately fifty Imperial Army officers arrived in cars in front of the *Asahi* office in Tokyo's Yūrakuchō ward. When Editor-in-Chief Ogata Taketora received them, the officers showered him with angry shouts of "We will tear down the *Asahi*, this traitor to the nation!" and ransacked the typesetting cases. On that day the Tokyo *Asahi* did not publish an evening edition.[15]

It was not the first time the *Asahi* had come under attack. In March 1928, a month after the first general elections, a dozen or so people in cars flying the banner of the Seiyūkai Party Supporters Group had barged into the Osaka *Asahi* main office. They beat the guards with sticks and destroyed equipment inside the editorial bureau. The attack was in reaction to a mistaken news report on the death of a member of the imperial family, which gave the impression that the Empress had passed away. Some editions containing this misleading error had been distributed and were the cause of this violence. A few days later, several individuals armed with pistols forced their way into the Tokyo main office where they injured the guards and poured sand over the presses. The attackers handed two employees in the printing department over to the Hibiya police station, though the police released them immediately.[16] In another instance in April 1934, a thug gained entry to the Tokyo *Asahi* office and slashed with a sword at the general affairs director of the news department, Suzuki Bunshirō, severely injuring him. Amid this growing tendency to resort to violence as an expression of political dissatisfaction, the media became yet another target for terrorist acts as newspapers gained ever more power to influence people in the general elections.

Shortly after the February 26 Incident, a problem occurred in the *Asahi*'s branch office in Moji, Fukuoka Prefecture. One of the employees at the office received a visit from the Imperial Military Reservist Association, which was collecting donations for the construction of a firing range. The employee turned the request down, saying: "I absolutely don't support the military. Reservists do not need to fire arms anyway. I am under no obligation to give a donation." The head of the military police informed *Asahi*'s managing editor, Harada Jōji, that the Reservist Association was outraged at this affront and reported the matter to managing director Tatsui Umekichi. According to internal *Asahi* records, it seems that this problem rose to the forefront while the military police conducted an investigation of anti-military thought. In the end, the two sides smoothed over their differences through mediation by an *Asahi* executive who was on friendly terms with the military police. The branch office employee responsible for the uproar wrote in a letter to Tatsui that "he was intending to make a payment to the Reservist Association in a day or two." As these events suggest, after the February 26 Incident a growing sense of urgency spread throughout the company that incurring the displeasure of the military was best avoided.

Two public speeches

The military's failed attempt at a *coup d'état* in the February 26 Incident left the country reeling and dealt a serious blow to the press. At the time of the May 15 Incident four years earlier, *Asahi* had immediately criticized the violence in its editorials. As the February 26 Incident unfolded, however, none of the paper's editorials that appeared directly after the events openly put the military authorities on the spot—despite the fact that the company itself had come under fire this time.

Two months after the incident, the Imperial Diet opened under martial law. In the plenary meeting of the Lower House on May 7, 1936, Saitō Takao of the Minseitō Party voiced criticism of certain trends within the military in his so-called "Army Purge Speech": "Unrest in our country clears the path for an absolutist rule of military men and therefore it is necessary to strictly prohibit political movements in the military."[17] In theory, Japanese law proscribed military officers' political involvement but after the 1931 Manchurian Incident the tendency to debate politics had spread, particularly among younger soldiers in the armed forces. What had prompted the recent incidents was this attitude among some elements of the military, Saitō claimed in his speech. In his opinion, the mindset of the defendants in the May 15 Incident was naïve, their viewpoint narrow-minded, and their punishment light.

Four years later, Saitō incurred the wrath of the military authorities with his "Anti-Military Speech" in which he severely criticized the war against China. This oration resulted in his expulsion from the Lower House. In his earlier "Army Purge Speech," Saitō asserted the political "non-involvement" of the Army without even meeting opposition from Army Minister Terauchi Hisaichi, who did not offer a rebuttal and furthermore made it clear that the military "should not interfere in politics." The *Asahi* was full of praise for both Saitō's speech and Terauchi's reply in an editorial on May 8 but nevertheless a certain mistrust of politics seeped into the newspaper's argument:

"Politicians should reflect on their own behavior as well when it comes to establishing why such radical thought and actions emerged among some of the military sectors. . . ."

Seven days after Saitō delivered his "Army Purge Speech," a problem arose at the plenary session of the House of Peers. The catalyst was a statement by Diet member Tsumura Jūsha. Criticizing the military in connection with an incident the year before in which officers had killed the head of the Bureau of Military Affairs in the Army Ministry (known as the Aizawa Incident), Tsumura asked if "common soldiers did not have more of a Japanese spirit than officers?" Moreover, he made an example of officers' salaries, suggesting: "it might be better to abolish monthly wages and instead pay for actual expenses."[18] Tsumura, founder of a pharmaceutical company, dedicated the latter part of his speech to his pet views on the development of airplanes and automobiles; but it was the first part with his comments on the "Japanese spirit" that piqued the anger of Navy Minister Nagano Osami. The *Asahi* announced this incident at the very top of its front page: "Military Authorities Extremely Outraged at Inappropriate Affront to their Dignity." In its editorial the paper leveled criticism at Tsumura—once again directing the brunt of its verbal assaults at a politician. The paper commented: "In getting carried away and pushing for a purge of the Army, Tsumura has shown an extreme lack of self-reflection on his part." The following day Tsumura decided to resign from the House of Peers.

Saitō and Tsumura's two speeches differed in their rhetoric as well as in the points they made but the most marked contrast lay probably in the reactions they elicited from the military. The line of argumentation that *Asahi* adopted *vis-à-vis* both of these speeches can be seen as a result of the paper merely following the military's lead. As military pride and popular enthusiasm gave rise to a climate of tolerance toward violence, newspapers increasingly lost their power to speak against such trends.

On the Road to Developing a
National Mythology

Two declarations to clarify the nature of the
Japanese imperial state

On August 3, 1935, Okada Keisuke's Cabinet released a declaration "to clarify the nature of the Japanese national polity." The declaration stated: "It is evident that the supreme governing power of the Great Japanese Empire lies strictly with the Emperor." Furthermore, "those who consider the Emperor merely an organ for exercising the right to govern are misconstruing the fundamental principle of our national polity (*kokutai*), which is unique among all nations." Prime Minister Okada himself explained the "national polity" of Japan in the Diet as "the eternally unbroken line of Emperors ruling over the country and the citizens reverently offering their loyalty as children would to a parent. This is our national polity."

When famed Tokyo Imperial University legal scholar Minobe Tatsukichi's treatise on the *Theory of the Emperor as an Organ of Government* became a matter of discussion several years previously, Okada had initially argued that, "surely the concept of the national polity as proposed by Professor Minobe does not differ greatly from our views."[1] However, as the voices denouncing the theory gained strength within the military and in the Diet, Okada, who believed it "to be his duty to protect constitutional politics," was forced to react.[2] The result was an August 3 pronouncement clarifying this rather vague national concept. An editorial in the August 4 edition of the Tokyo *Asahi* aligned the newspaper's position with the government, stating that if "the declaration encourages aspirations of loyalty and love for our nation," this was "highly desirable." For the opponents of the "Emperor as Organ Theory," the newspaper delivered some words of caution: "It can only be hoped that in rushing to attack others they will not hurt the pride of our nation's citizens who all stand united in spirit." In this regard, *Asahi* did not openly come to the defense of constitutionalism.

On the other hand, critics of the "Emperor as Organ Theory" were dissatisfied with what they considered to be a lack of clarity in the wording of Okada's declaration. In September 1935, Army Minister Hayashi Senjūrō informed Prime Minister Okada that "approximately one thousand young officers had banded together, seemingly planning to take action," and asked if the prime minister "could not do more concerning the matter of the Emperor as Organ Theory" and if "the government could not take further measures?"

On September 18, the prosecutor's office decided to suspend charges that had been brought against Professor Minobe for having violated the Publication Law. Concerning the other charge of *lèse-majesté*, the prosecutor's office came to the conclusion that there was no intentional irreverence against the Emperor discernible in his remarks. Thus, the case against him was dropped and on the same day Minobe resigned from the House of Peers. Prime Minister Okada assured the media that his policy was to eradicate scholarly theories that ran counter to the notion of the "national polity," but the anger of Minobe's opponents showed no signs of abatement. Military authorities again pressed the government to issue another declaration and on October 15 the prime minister announced a second declaration that would "clarify the nature of Japan's national polity."

This second statement stressed, "It is the fundamental principle of our nation, as well as the absolute and unshakable belief of the imperial subjects, that the Emperor wields the right to govern." The announcement stipulated: "the theory of the Emperor as an organ of government [...] needs to be completely eliminated." In this way, the "absolute and unshakable belief" that the Emperor should be revered as divine had overpowered any rational interpretation of the constitution.

The cowardly *Asahi*

In 1935, as the movement against Minobe's "Emperor as Organ Theory" gained strength, Iwanami Shigeo, the head of the Iwanami Publishing Company, sent the *Asahi*'s readers' column *Iron Broom* (*Tessō*) a lengthy "letter to the editor" where he openly rebuked Minobe's opponents:

> The scholar's way to devote himself loyally to his ruler and his country lies in living according to his own convictions, as a faithful servant to the truth. It is most dangerous to brand others as unpatriotic out of a narrow-minded sense of loyalty and a biased view of the nation.

Having learned of Iwanami's submission to *Asahi*, his son-in-law Kobayashi Isamu (chairman of the Iwanami Publishing Company after the war) made his way to the *Asahi* Tokyo main office where he met with prominent journalists Kaji Ryūichi and Ōnishi Itsuki. Even the people responsible at *Asahi* were "at a loss as to how to handle the situation because publishing the piece could get the company, as well as Iwanami, into trouble." Kobayashi asked them not to print the letter but Iwanami Shigeo, who was unaware of these exchanges, later complained to his son-in-law, "the men at *Asahi* are cowards."[3]

Asahi certainly took a very cautious stance on the matter. During the London Naval Disarmament Conference in 1930, the paper had openly criticized the opposition who believed that signing the naval treaty would infringe on the Emperor's supreme command but this time the paper did not take such a public stand. Although the *Asahi Newspaper* was sympathetic to Minobe, it did not directly voice support for his constitutionalist interpretation, which held that even the Emperor as the highest organ of the state was subject to the limitations imposed by the constitution. Only Miyazawa Toshiyoshi, a scholar of constitutional law, spoke out loudly in an *Asahi* column on March 5, 1935. Miyazawa declared, "If after having heard Professor Minobe's explanations there are still people who claim that he is against our national polity, this can only mean that they are either an irredeemable bunch of idiots or else a lot with nothing on their mind but character assassination under the pretext of defending our 'national polity.'" Behind *Asahi*'s hands-off approach and that of all the other newspapers was the concern that if they came to Minobe's defense, "they could themselves be subject to accusations of being against the nation or of lacking respect for the imperial family."[4]

However, this timidity does not mean that critical voices against Minobe's opponents were completely non-existent. The February 25, 1935 *Law News* (*Hōritsu Shimbun*), for instance, claimed that "it is impossible academically to explain sovereignty through the monarchy" without contradicting oneself because our current national polity is a system of constitutional monarchy. Even the Emperor himself said that "[Minobe's theory] is not contrary to our national polity," as his Chief Aide-de-camp, Honjō Shigeru, recorded in his diary.[5]

On February 21, 1936, Minobe was shot in his own home by a right-wing nationalist and suffered a leg injury. Violence smothered rational debates about the Emperor and only five days later the February 26 Incident exploded. In the meantime, the Japanese invasion of China continued and plans to bring the northern regions of the Chinese mainland under Japanese control advanced. In July 1937, the Sino-Japanese War began.[6]

The ousting of Yanaihara Tadao

In July 1937, Japanese and Chinese troops clashed at the Marco Polo Bridge on the outskirts of Beijing, marking the beginning of the Sino-Japanese War. At the outset of the conflict, *Asahi* expressed in its editorials "strong hope that a last effort will be made to head more toward a peaceful solution as quickly as possible."[7] In August, as the fires of war rose over Shanghai, the paper shifted to a more unyielding line of argumentation, proclaiming: "now all that is left is to strike a major blow."[8] In a Cabinet meeting on August 24, Prime Minister Konoe Fumimaro decided on a "Basic Outline for the Implementation of National Spiritual Mobilization," aiming for "the realization of national unity by boosting the Japanese spirit."

Immediately after the incident at Marco Polo Bridge, Yanaihara Tadao, Professor at the Faculty of Economics of Tokyo Imperial University, contributed an essay entitled "National Ideals" to the September issue of the magazine Central Review (*Chūō Kōron*). Yanaihara asserted that "true patriotism is not found in blind 'national unity' that is uncritical of actual political measures." Moreover, he claimed, "the visionary who resists blind consent and criticizes the political reality based on the ideal of the nation is the true patriot who shall guide the political actions of the country for a thousand years."[9] The Home Ministry banned the sale of that issue of Central Review (*Chūō Kōron*).

On the heels of this article, Hijikata Seibi, head of the Faculty of Economics, attempted to oust Yanaihara from the university claiming the latter to be a critic of "national unity." On November 25, Tokyo *Asahi* reported on these developments as the top story in its local news section: "Clash with China stirs up sudden winds of change at Tokyo Imperial University. Faculty of Economics overcomes indifference toward our nation within its own ranks and is determined to contribute to the country's current situation." Yanaihara's name was not mentioned but the article related that a movement was afoot in the faculty to revise indifferent attitudes concerning the nation's current state of affairs. Judging from the content, the information for the article had clearly been gathered from the faction surrounding the faculty head. It was also clear that Yanaihara had prepared a response in which he wrote: "Please lay this country to rest for the time being so as to bring to life the ideal Japan!" On December 1, Yanaihara handed in his letter of resignation to the university. Meanwhile, Minoda Muneki and supporters in the right-wing True Japan Society (*Genri Nihon-sha*) mounted fierce verbal attacks against Yanaihara, publishing an essay with the rather cumbersome title, "On Yanaihara Tadao's Twisted Theories Against the Nation, Against the Military, Against the War, on the Abandonment of the Colonies, and on the Unscholarly Nature of his Thought."

On December 13, 1937, Japanese troops occupied Nanjing and on December 17 the evening edition of the *Asahi* included the following news item:

> To celebrate the Imperial Army on its triumphant entry into the city of Nanjing all the staff at Tokyo Imperial University, including president Nagayo Mataro and approximately 9,000 students from six faculties (Law, Medicine, Humanities, Agriculture, Sciences, Economics), participated in a celebratory march that took place on December 16th at 9:30 a.m. This was the first event of its kind involving the whole school since the founding of the university.

In January 1938, the Konoe Cabinet issued its declaration that it "would no longer deal with the Chinese Nationalist government," thus effectively blocking the path toward peace by its own hand. A month later, the Japanese government introduced the bill for the National Mobilization Law to the Lower House.

Giving in to the National Mobilization Law

"The first thrill in this parliamentary session!" Thus announced the opening line of an article entitled "Yesterday's Diet Meeting" in the February 25, 1938 Tokyo *Asahi*. Although this was the first regular session of the Diet since the beginning of the Sino-Japanese War, up until then dull verbal sparring had dragged on in the Lower House. Suddenly, a new sense of urgency arose because the bill for the National Mobilization Law had been laid before the house. The bill contained provisions that would allow the government, "when necessary in terms of mobilization," not only to control resources but also to draft or mobilize citizens for labor. Because the decision of what was "necessary" lay with the government, this potentially linked to the issue of whether the Diet was unnecessary. The point of contention in the Diet centered on whether this broad mandate for the government was in fact constitutional.

At the forefront of those opposing the bill in the Lower House stood Saitō Takao of the Minseitō Party, who argued that, "anything that corrupted the great spirit of Japan's Constitution needed to be rejected by any means." On the other hand, Prime Minister Konoe Fumimaro, who should have been there to confront the opposition, was absent at the plenary session due to illness. It seems there was not much will to push the bill through. In fact, when he heard that the elder statesman Prince Saionji had remarked that, "in the end the bill ignores the constitution so it would be better if they didn't pass it," Konoe remarked, "I could have just dropped the initiative."

The *Asahi* at first took a critical stance toward the bill. Before its introduction to the Lower House, the paper pointed out in an editorial on January 25 that "the strengthening of state control envisioned in the bill would give considerable powers to the authorities. . . . The fact that officials will have virtually free rein is cause for concern." In a three-part series the newspaper debated the main points of contention, that is "extensive powers and authority for the government," "the drafting of ordinary Japanese subjects for labor," and "wide-reaching controls on the freedom of speech." What particularly irked the newspaper was a newly introduced ban on the printing of newspapers and other publications, together with an extension on the parameters increasing the already existing ban on the sale of publications. These were to be changed from "when disturbing public peace and order" to "when necessary in terms of mobilization." In light of these proposed alterations, the so-called Society of the 21st (*Nijūichinichikai*), which comprised editorial executives from major newspapers including *Asahi*, decided to oppose the bill. Bowing to such pressure, the government dropped the section covering the issue of the sales ban.

This was as far as *Asahi*'s efforts went. Nomura Hideo, the vice director of the editing bureau at the Tokyo *Asahi*, reflected: "Were they satisfied because the ban on publication had been removed? Had their zeal to defend the freedom of newspapers cooled off? [. . .] Where had the initial vigor gone? It all but disappeared."[10] After this the paper gave vivid accounts of the heated controversies surrounding the National Mobilization Law but its comments were rather supportive of the bill. In March 1938, Prime Minister Konoe said in a public speech in the House of Peers: "Our esteemed national polity is most vividly captured in the articles of our Imperial Constitution." The editorial in the *Asahi* the next day concluded that "this announcement inspired trust that, in a state of emergency, the government would not overstep the limits set by the articles of the constitution." Moreover, as the Diet session came to an end on the 26th, *Asahi* summed up its views: "Finally, several pieces of legislation are aligned to the nation's transition from a semi-wartime system to a wartime one."

The editor-in-chief's participation in the mobilization movement

Asahi could not fully oppose the National Mobilization Law, which was passed in 1938, partly because the top tier of the newspaper itself was deeply involved in the National Spiritual Mobilization Movement begun the year before. The Konoe administration had called for such a movement based on the start of the Sino-Japanese War in July 1937.

With an aim to achieve "national unity" concerning what was going on, the movement created an order that sought to coordinate propaganda campaigns in line with the reality of people's everyday lives, leading to a "boost in the Japanese spirit." As the institution responsible for implementing this goal, the Central League of the National Spiritual Mobilization Movement was launched in October. On the board of directors were the editor-in-chief of *Asahi*, Ogata Taketora, Takaishi Shingorō of *Mainichi* and Furuno Inosuke of the *Dōmei* News Agency. Moreover, the Cabinet Information Committee had now been upgraded from its previous status as a research group within the Cabinet, to the Cabinet Information Office (later to become the Cabinet Information Bureau). Ogata was an advisor to the Cabinet Information Office along with *Yomiuri Newspaper*'s Shōriki Matsutarō. Allegedly, Ogata participated in the movement because he judged that if a government of national unity could prevent a military dictatorship, this was the "best way to secure the continued existence of the newspaper." He supposedly expected this move to "eventually bring an end to the Sino-Japanese War."[11]

The government designated the period from September 9 to October 12 as "stage one in the implementation of National Spiritual Mobilization" and designated the following week, October 13 to 19, as "focus week." The basic guidelines for realizing the plan included strategies such as "seeking out the cooperation of every organ of public opinion" or "making use of the radio." In the meantime, the Tokyo *Asahi* published one article after the other on the "mobilization"—no less than 59 in total. On September 10, an editorial explained that citizens "need to cultivate calmness, composure, persistence and unshakeable integrity." On the first day of "focus week," *Asahi* significantly highlighted that "citizens whole-heartedly follow the will of the Emperor and desire the establishment and achievement of peace in East Asia, [...] making an effort to be second to none." Subsequently, such enlightening articles filled the pages of the paper for each of the seasonal festivals, Emperor Meiji's Birthday (November 3), National Foundation Day (February 11), Army Memorial Day (March 10) and Navy Memorial Day (May 27). In March 1939, the National Spiritual Mobilization Committee was formed under the direct authority of the Cabinet. One of its members was the managing editor of the Tokyo *Asahi*, Midoro Masuichi.

Ariyama Teruo, Professor of Media History at Tokyo Keizai University, has previously compared this anomalous situation to "a spider getting caught up in its own web of 'showing loyalty and repaying one's debt to the nation'—a web it had spun itself." What were the editorial writers thinking at the time? According to Kaji Ryūichi's biography, *Ogata Taketora*, about the former *Asahi* editor, there were two camps. One faction believed that "*Asahi* should cooperate more with the fanatical National Unity Movement under Konoe's New Order." The opposing faction held that "joining Konoe and taking part in a movement that facilitated the slide toward fascism needed to be avoided at all costs." Ogata, "unable to take either side, was completely befuddled."[12]

Supporting projects for the 2,600th anniversary of the imperial reign

In the realm of Japanese mythology, the year 1940 marked the 2,600th anniversary of the enthronement of the first Japanese Emperor Jimmu at the foot of Mount Unebi in the city of Nara. On National Foundation Day (February 11), two years earlier, at the yearly national holiday commemorating this historical event, the Osaka *Asahi* made a large company announcement on its title page: "Projects for the 2,600th Anniversary of the Imperial Reign. Boosting the Spirit of Our Nation's Founding. Proposing a Movement for Our Great Nation's People." Details of the plans became public in March. The Celebration Committee of Nara Prefecture would build a martial arts training hall in the outer garden of Kashihara Shrine, where the minds of Japanese youth could be fortified.[13] The Osaka *Asahi* would make an appeal for voluntary labor and also manage fundraising for the project.

The Cabinet had already set up the Committee for the Preparation of the 2,600th Anniversary Celebrations in 1935. The main projects were to fête and commemorate the event, so the committee designated maintenance works on the approach to the Kashihara Shrine, as well as promoting the investigation, preservation and publicization of historical sacred sites connected to Emperor Jimmu. A National History Museum was also constructed in line with this push. Any other large-scale undertakings for the anniversary required the authorization of the Celebrations Office, which also prohibited fundraising and such by newspaper companies, since it was held that such activities could be abused as a means of boosting newspaper sales.

The Osaka *Asahi* was granted unusual permission to cooperate in the celebratory works for the Kashihara Shrine and day after day displayed flashy campaign news of this in its news pages. The article that covered the ground breaking for the construction project by local middle schoolers on March 6, 1938 spoke of "glistening with perspiration—the shining spirit of the nation's founding," accompanied by a large photograph. On May 9, on the occasion of the cornerstone-laying ceremony, the paper reported: "Shrouded in a mist of purifying rain—the momentous first breaking of the ground on the holy precincts." Following the formation of the National Foundation

Figure 11   Nazi German youths helping with the construction work at Kashihara Shrine, October 1938.

Volunteer Labor Service Brigades on June 8, the paper introduced some of the group's members, from a "policeman from Korea" to a "masseur" and a "Tribal Chief from the South Seas." The paper also ran a report on how the German Nazi youth organization, "Hitler Jugend," on tour in Japan at the time to promote friendly relations between the two Axis countries, lent a helping hand in the construction works. Even when the Kansai region was struck by the Great Hanshin Flood, which claimed over 900 lives, on the second day of the disaster the *Asahi* gave more prominence to a report on the completion of the lodgings for the National Foundation Volunteer Labor Service Brigades, placing it before an article dealing with the flood that announced "More Rain Baptizes Reconstruction Works."[14] Moreover, the paper appealed to the public for a song memorializing the National Foundation Volunteer Labor Service Brigades, eventually crowning a piece entitled, "Under the Banner of the Three-legged Crow." The opening line read: "In Kashihara, so replete with greenery, the pillar of the Imperial Palace planted firmly."[15] Well-known composer Yamada Kōsaku created music for these lyrics and performances were subsequently held all over the country.

A collection of records entitled, "Kashihara Shrine and the National Foundation Volunteer Labor Service Brigades," documents the various projects. Through the work of more than 1.21 million volunteers, the grounds of the Kashihara Shrine grew to include a library center for research into the spirit of the nation's founding (*Kashihara bunko*), a judo training hall, "National Foundation Hall" (*Kenkoku kaikan*), and the Eight Corners of the World Dormitory (*Hakkōryō*), which housed lodgings and a training school. The frontispiece of this collection of records carries the calligraphy "Service to a sacred place" from the hand of *Asahi Newspaper* company president Ueno Seiichi. The address Ueno gave at the consecration ceremony was also included in the volume:

> Kashihara, this holy place surrounded by the green mountains where the divine soul of Emperor Jimmu rests [...] is a pure location, more suited than any other for building and training body and soul, so that individuals may follow the great spirit of eight corners of the world under one roof and energetically push forward the great enterprise of rising Asia.[16]

This creation of a national mythology was not just a phenomenon limited to Osaka; the Tokyo *Asahi* likewise saw its number of articles mentioning Kashihara Shrine increase yearly, from 34 articles in 1937 to no less than 259 in 1940.

Allegiance to Japan's national mythology

As 1940 dawned, heralding the 2,600th year of imperial rule according to the Japanese myth, *Asahi*'s New Year's Day edition was all geared toward the celebration. The front page of the Osaka *Asahi* carried a picture by artist Yokoyama Taikan showing the sun rising over ocean waves, alongside an article detailing trends within the imperial family and a headline that read, "Welcoming a Beautiful New Year of Construction and Development in Asia. Cherishing the Prosperity of Our Revered Imperial Household."

The Tokyo *Asahi* published a large photo of the imperial family, accompanied by the caption: "The Imperial Family Prospers Ever More." The editorial entitled, "Welcoming a New Year of Celebrations for the Founding Year of the Nation," was common to the Osaka and the Tokyo *Asahi* and read: "How must all 100 million Japanese citizens, high and low, have looked forward to this 2,600th year with noble and pure sentiments! How they must have eagerly awaited it with boundless joy and their extraordinary pride that is unrivalled in the world!" The *Asahi* column *Tensei jingo* (*Vox Populi, Vox Dei*) adopted a fairly assertive tone: "We should see this as a great opportunity to make the 27th century [Japan's calculation of its imperial reign] and the era beyond into an age when there is no longer talk of 'Japan in the world,' but rather of 'Japan's world.'"

The *Asahi* not only showed its allegiance to the Japanese mythological past in its pages but also through the company's actions. On February 1, executives from the company's head office split into several groups and visited the main shrines all over the country to pray for the prosperity of the nation and for the Imperial Army's success in war. On National Foundation Day (February 11), the Tokyo *Asahi* printed artist Nakamura Fusetsu's "Portrait of Emperor Jimmu" in the center of its front page. The shift in the paper's coverage from reporting news to eulogizing imperial mythology was clearly already underway. On that same day, the children's page ran an "account of a visit to Kashihara Shrine," while the culture page had a haiku poem by Iida Dakotsu entitled, "Celebrating the Nation's Founding." This ran alongside a *tanka* poem by Saitō Ryū called, "Celebrating National Foundation Day," complete with photos of Mount Unebi and Mount Takachiho under the caption: "The holy sites of the shining nation's founding."[17] In this way, approximately half the paper was stocked with articles connected to either the Imperial House or the Shinto religion.

On July 22, 1940, the second Konoe Cabinet was inaugurated. The Cabinet Information Office was upgraded to the Cabinet Information Bureau, and the regulation of media coverage became even more strict. The handbook for executives of the Cabinet Information Bureau provided instructions stating that internal guidance for interviews was absolutely necessary so as to have newspapers cooperate with national policies of their own accord. On October 11, a naval review took place at the port of Yokohama, during which the Emperor inspected the Imperial Fleet. Those journalists who had been granted permission to attend and report on the event received "Guidelines for the Reporters Accompanying the Inspection," which included items such as "dress code is morning coat and top hat," and instructions that "articles will be censored aboard the ship." The only choice journalists were left with was to compete using beautifully crafted pieces of writing that were devoid of any content. On October 12, the headlines reporting on the naval review in various newspapers all noted that the "Imperial Standard Sparkled in the Sea Breeze" (*Tokyo Nichinichi*), and "Everyone Touched by the Gracious Words of the Emperor" (*Yomiuri*). Meanwhile, *Asahi*'s text described how "the Imperial Standard stood out clearly against the deep azure sky and its golden coat of arms laced with deep crimson glittered and shimmered brightly in the morning sun." The choice not to write or not to publish no longer existed.

The Road to the Japan-US War

Approving the Anti-Comintern Pact

A little over a month after the Berlin Olympics had concluded, in September 1936, the head of the *Asahi* foreign correspondents office in Berlin, Hamada Tsunejirō, suspected he was being followed. During the Olympics Hamada had discovered that talks were moving forward between Germany and Japan concerning a possible Anti-Comintern Pact, which would establish cooperation between the two countries to counter the threat of communism. Hamada had communicated the gist of what he knew in a letter to those in charge at the *Asahi* offices in Osaka and Tokyo, asking them to investigate what would be the best way and time to turn this information into an article. *Asahi* sought confirmation about the report from the Ministry of Foreign Affairs and the Army's General Staff Office but both vehemently denied any knowledge. Following this incident, the Japanese Embassy in Germany issued a request to the local German authorities to investigate Hamada's movements and the German secret police went into action. This left Hamada in absolute fear, especially given that four foreign journalists had gone missing since the Nazis had come to power.[1]

In the fall of the same year, the government sought approval for the Anti-Comintern Pact from Yoshida Shigeru, Japanese Ambassador to Great Britain at the time (and postwar prime minister). Yoshida opposed the idea, reasoning that if the Axis Powers (Germany and Italy) started a war, Japan would find itself in the dilemma of having to fight both Great Britain and America.[2] The Home Ministry prohibited any news coverage of the pact and forestalled any debate about its potential pros and cons. This official silence meant that Hamada's potential breaking news never saw the light of day. It was not until November 25, the day the pact was signed in Berlin, that the ban was eventually lifted. In an editorial the next day, *Asahi* assured readers that "this pact with Germany by no means has any exclusive meaning," echoing the government's position. The editorials of all the other papers also followed suit. Only the *Yomiuri Newspaper* was critical of whether "it was necessary to explicitly enter into a pact" with Germany at a time when the country had fallen upon extremely hard times financially, as well as in its foreign relations.

Matsuoka Yōsuke, President of the South Manchuria Railway, and later Minister of Foreign Affairs, said in a public speech: "When we Japanese people enter into a partnership or an alliance we always push forward in a mutual embrace, with the clear determination to go to our final end together." He also expressed his "belief that, if Germany and Japan establish a close collaboration and courageously push forward together, other countries, starting with England, will definitely follow and show more understanding."[3] In July 1937, the Sino-Japanese War began and in November of that year Italy joined the Anti-Comintern Pact. In February of the following year, Hitler officially recognized "Manchukuo" as a state and *Asahi* in its editorial on February 22 was full of the "highest regard" for the "Führer's decision."

The Second World War begins

On April 20, 1939, a banquet was held in Berlin to celebrate Hitler's fiftieth birthday. After the party Shiratori Toshio, Japan's Ambassador to Italy, revealed to Ōshima Hiroshi, Japan's Ambassador to Germany, that "the German Minister of Foreign Affairs [Joachim von] Ribbentrop has threatened to make contact with the Soviet Union because Japan is not forthcoming enough in relations to Germany." At that time, Germany had plans to strengthen ties with Italy and Japan to turn the Anti-Comintern Pact into a military alliance so as to be able to compete with Great Britain, France, and the Soviet Union. Japan's Army was receptive to the suggestion but the Imperial Navy, including Navy Minister Yonai Mitsumasa and Deputy Navy Minister Yamamoto Isoroku, strongly opposed such a move because in their opinion the odds would be against Japan if it antagonized the United States and Great Britain. Japan found itself in a bind, unable to offer Germany a reply. In light of this, von Ribbentrop voiced his impatience with Japan at Hitler's birthday party, announcing that Germany was considering an alliance with the Soviet Union. Ten days later, on April 30, Yamamoto confided to Sugimoto Ken, the *Asahi* reporter assigned to the Navy Ministry: "This just doesn't make sense. The Germans are saying that if Japan does not make up its mind quickly, Germany might enter into a Treaty of Non-Aggression with the Soviet Union. What a completely absurd notion!"[4]

Four months later, on August 21, the German government announced the conclusion of a Treaty of Non-Aggression with the Soviet Union. This news that Germany formed an alliance with its supposed enemy, after having joined an anti-communist pact with Japan and Italy earlier, startled the world. *Asahi*'s report on the reception in Germany, from its special correspondent in Berlin, Moriyama Yoshio, read: "The streets of Berlin have returned to life and are bustling with energy. [...] It seems that the German people are overjoyed at the agreement with Moscow; the general feeling here is that the conclusion of such a treaty has averted the danger of war between Germany and the Soviet Union."[5]

On August 28, Prime Minister Hiranuma Kiichirō stepped down in reaction to the German-Soviet treaty and left with the parting words: "The universe that is Europe is complicated and inscrutable." On that day, the editor-in-chief of *Asahi*, Ogata Taketora, happened to be at the Navy Ministry and together with Yamamoto Isoroku and others met Navy Minister Yonai in the Minister's Office after the last Cabinet meeting. Ogata shook hands with Yonai, who had successfully seen through his opposition to a strengthening of the Anti-Comintern Pact. As

Asahi's editor-in-chief at that time recalled later, "[I was] so grateful in my heart that Yonai and Yamamoto had put up such a brave fight that tears unwittingly welled up in my eyes."[6]

Four days later, on September 1, Germany's invasion of Poland signaled the beginning of the Second World War in Europe. *Asahi* reported on the developments in several consecutive editorials but criticism of Germany was nowhere to be found in its coverage. An editorial from September 4 instead read: "We hope for the sake of civilization and the welfare of humankind that the experience of the First World War has made man a little wiser and has made its contribution, small as it may be, to preventing the calamity of war from spreading." In the very face of the enormous violence war entails, *Asahi*'s reports merely imparted its "hopes" to readers.

No opposition to the Tripartite Pact

In March and April 1940, German troops invaded Norway, Denmark, the Netherlands, and Belgium, and advanced into France. Meanwhile, novelist Nagai Kafū expressed his dissatisfaction with the pro-German news coverage in the Japanese press: "Of the news on the war in Europe in Japanese papers, I only read the news feed articles from the French and British. I never bother to look at reports from Germany or the Japanese take on events." He also avowed that he "continued to pray for France's victory day and night."[7] On June 14, 1940, Paris fell.

In the wake of these changes, the sense in Japan that it should not miss out on the opportunity to join forces with Germany heightened: "Germany is strong, France and Italy are weak – this was not only the opinion within the Japanese Army and the Navy but it eventually became the prevalent view within the Japanese population."[8] On July 13, the Tokyo *Asahi* argued that in light of Germany's crushing victories, it was Japan's "inevitable fate" to shake off its dependence on Great Britain and the United States in its foreign relations and instead form an alliance with Germany and Italy. On July 16, Army Minister Hata Shunroku handed in his resignation under pressure from the Army, which was aiming to forge a tripartite pact between Japan, Germany, and Italy. Yonai, who opposed the pact, stepped down and the second Konoe Cabinet was formed with Matsuoka Yōsuke as the new Minister of Foreign Affairs.

In mid-August, the *Asahi Newspaper* held an editorial meeting in Osaka, at which editor-in-chief Ogata Taketora said: "Germany and Italy have become major forces in international politics. [...] We cannot oppose an alliance, not least also due to the relations Japan has established with these two powers with the Anti-Comintern Pact." Without any views to the contrary, the new orientation of the paper's editorial slant was thus decided.[9] Yurugi Eiichirō, an alumnus of *Asahi*, looking back at these events, recalled how "the journalists never even discussed the pros and cons of the Tripartite Pact with each other." After the war, Ogata reflected: "Whatever the situation in the country at the time—how pitiful that not a single newspaper in Japan openly advocated opposition to the Tripartite Pact in its pages, despite being against it at heart." He added, "I have no one but myself to blame."[10]

Figure 12   People celebrating the Tripartite Pact with Germany and Italy at Yasukuni Shrine in Tokyo, October 13, 1940.

"It's going to be the people who bear the brunt of this decision!"

On September 27, 1940, Germany, Italy, and Japan signed the Tripartite Pact in Berlin. At 9:15 p.m. the head of the Foreign Ministry's Intelligence Office, Suma Yakichirō, entered the press conference room in Tokyo's Ministry of Foreign Affairs, with a beaming smile on his face: "We will now be announcing details concerning the agreement concluded today between the three countries of Japan, Germany, and Italy." Journalists received advanced copies of the treaty text and rushed to hand them to messengers waiting on motorbikes to deliver them to the news offices.[11] When asked by a reporter how Japan would effectively implement the treaty in view of the United States, Suma asserted: "the treaty was not expected to lead to a significant deterioration in relations between Japan and the United States."[12]

On the 27th, the Home Ministry informed newspapers that articles against the pact or showing conflicting opinions would be suppressed.[13] In its editorial of the 28th, *Asahi* welcomed the Tripartite Pact, expressing how "truly delighted" it was with the treaty. In a rather excited manner, the paper described the scenes unfolding at the Minister of Foreign Affairs' residence:

> Scenes of the historical night that saw the Tripartite Pact sealed! The men who were forging the history of Japan, Germany and Italy that night repeatedly shouted "Banzai!" and raised their cups in toasts, determination written all over their faces. This included the Minister of Foreign Affairs Matsuoka, with flushed cheeks, and

the German Ambassador Eugen Ott, who raised his right hand up high and shouted: "Nippon! Nippon!" [Japan! Japan!] [...] Such were the strong emotions of a night that will change the course of world history.[14]

Suzuki Bunshirō, *Asahi* special correspondent, received the news of the conclusion of the Tripartite Pact while in San Francisco. As Suzuki later described, the United States took a rather strident view on the pact:

> In the opinion of the American government Japan was rattling its sabre at the United States by entering the Tripartite Pact and the Americans confidently proclaimed that they were not daunted by such a threat. In the US view, Japan was unlikely to have the military power to fight America, having been completely sapped of strength by the crisis in China.[15]

The writer Nogami Yaeko noted in her diary on the 29th: "Instead of Great Britain and the United States, Germany and Italy have now become our lords and masters. What will this come to ten years from now? In the end, it's going to be us the people paying the price for this decision."[16]

On October 3, the *Asahi* printed a "special dispatch from New York" on its front page, which argued:

> There are concerns that Japan risks drifting toward a war with the United States—just as the scheming war-mongers would have it—if relations between the two countries are neglected. [...] Now the cards are on the table and hostile relations between the parties have been unequivocally defined. [...] Japan, Germany, and Italy are on one side while Great Britain and the United States remain on the other side. There is no doubt that the United States will intensify economic pressure on its enemy Japan, aiming to bring relations to a level that is but one step away from war.

In fact, this article turned out to be clairvoyant in its predictions concerning subsequent Japanese-American relations.

The unexpected: outbreak of war between Germany and the Soviet Union

In April 1941, at the residence of the Japanese Ambassador in Berlin, Minister of Foreign Affairs Matsuoka Yōsuke asked: "In Berlin many people are saying that there will be war between Germany and the Soviet Union. How do you journalists evaluate the situation?" Ejiri Susumu, head of the Berlin branch of the *Dōmei* News Agency, replied, "War is inevitable." A month earlier, Ejiri had reported to the *Dōmei* News Agency headquarters in Tokyo that war between Germany and the Soviet Union was imminent, basing his information on eyewitness reports that confirmed large movements of German troops toward the East. Matsuoka's rather snappy retort was:

"Even you people believe such an absurd thing?"[17] Afterwards, Matsuoka visited Moscow to sign the Soviet-Japanese Neutrality Pact, ultimately planning to fix relations between Japan and the United States by balancing it against the authority of a German-mediated alliance between Japan, Germany, the Soviet Union, and Italy to back things up. Great Britain and the United States were wary of the Japanese-Soviet Neutrality Pact, considering it merely a strategic first move that would put Japan in a position to invade Southeast Asia.

On Navy Memorial Day, May 27, 1941, Captain Hiraide Hideo from the Imperial Headquarters' Navy Press Division delivered a speech on the "Spirit of Naval Warfare." In his radio broadcast, Hiraide boasted: "if someone challenges Japan [. . .] we will annihilate our opponent with a single blow." The next day, a draft of the speech adorned the front pages of other papers' morning editions. Only *Asahi* did not print it and this absence elicited protests from the Naval General Staff. Sugimoto Ken, the journalist in charge of covering the Navy Ministry, countered its complaints: "The Navy Ministry has previously made clear that the Navy has 'no intention whatsoever to start a war,' and 'wish that the press follow the same line and be cautious in their reporting.' We are merely respecting this wish." At the time, this was a "fairly bold statement," as Sugimoto reminisces in his *A Showa History of the Navy*.[18] Standing by its judgment not to print proved difficult and *Asahi's* evening edition on that day included an article about Hiraide's speech.

On June 22, 1941, Germany invaded the Soviet Union in violation of its Treaty of Non-Aggression, resulting in the Soviet Union joining forces with the United States and Great Britain. Matsuoka's plans for an alliance between four countries—Japan, Germany, Italy, and the Soviet Union—had effectively come to naught. *Asahi* assumed an appearance of composure in the face of the outbreak of war between Germany and the Soviet Union, calling it "not completely unexpected" in its editorial on the 23rd. The opening of hostilities between Germany and the Soviet Union, breaching an existing treaty, would have been a prime opportunity for Japan to declare the Tripartite Pact void. Japan, unfortunately, let this opportunity pass. On the morning of the 23rd, then 26-year-old Muno Takeji from the *Asahi* visited Foreign Minister Matsuoka Yōsuke's residence.[19] The minister freely spoke his mind: "What, who's saying that I am surprised? Surprised by the opening of war between Germany and the Soviet Union you say? People who are surprised by it must be out of their minds."[20] In Washington, meanwhile, negotiations between Japan and the United States had begun.

Hedged in by censorship

In July 1939, the United States had already nullified its Treaty of Commerce and Navigation with Japan in protest against the Japanese invasion of China. A year later, when Japan joined sides with Germany and Italy, relations with the United States continued to deteriorate. As war between Japan and the United States increasingly became a real possibility, talks between the two countries commenced, aiming to close the rift that had opened. Japan appointed to the United States Ambassador Nomura Kichisaburō, a personal acquaintance of President Roosevelt, to lead negotiations for the Japanese side. In February 1941, *Asahi* quoted the president as saying after talks with Nomura that "it was still possible to avoid a conflict."[21] Unfortunately, as official negotiations between Nomura and US Secretary of State Cordell Hull officially began on April 16, articles about the proceedings disappeared from Japanese newspapers and neither the start of the talks nor their further development received any coverage. It was under these circumstances that on May 29 Arthur Sears Henning from the *Chicago Daily Tribune* launched an exclusive report on the contents of the negotiations. Under the headline "Roosevelt's New Jap Policy!" he wrote:

> President Roosevelt summoned the leading members of Congress and took them into his confidence concerning his policies to take a lenient line toward Japan and fully focus on the war against Germany instead. The President said that "in the Japanese financial and business world opposition to the policies of the military authorities is gaining strength, and the Tripartite Act will in all likelihood effectively come to naught."

Internal *Asahi* archives reveal, however, that this article was suppressed by the Japanese Cabinet Information Bureau and never appeared in the *Asahi*. The next day, on May 30, Foreign Minister Matsuoka Yōsuke publicly commented on the subject, emphasizing that Japan would adhere to the Tripartite Pact. An article in the *Asahi* relating to this matter proclaimed in its headline: "False Rumors in American Paper Crushed. Our Nation's Diplomatic Relations with the Axis Powers Resolute." Even though the report rather rashly concluded that the American article was spreading "false rumors," it offered no further insight into the matter. On August 29, 1941, other than the announcements made by the authorities, censorship officials banned newspapers from printing news about the talks between Nomura and Hull. Furthermore, officials ordered that even these articles could not exceed a certain length and were not to be treated as top stories.[22] Editorials were written blindly, without any knowledge concerning the true status of the negotiations, according to *Asahi*'s internal archives. Censorship policies at that time were implemented with two goals in mind: maintaining the Tripartite Pact and not provoking the United States during negotiations. On August 30, the internal review section of *Asahi*'s Tokyo main office received a phone call from the Cabinet Information Bureau, ordering the paper "to publish nothing about the talks between Nomura and Roosevelt for the time being, [...] not even facts such as 'they talked for so many minutes.'"[23]

Yokota Seiki, head of the internal review section at the Tokyo main office, remembered in the *Asahi Weekly* from May 1958:

> In a special dispatch about the negotiations between Japan and the United States, which started out as a fairly lengthy report, [...] anything touching upon the contents of the talks was removed. A remark like "the two representatives first of all shook hands" would be cut as it contained pro-American sentiment. The fact that the "talks went on for an hour" was also omitted because it implied tensions in the negotiations. A statement like "negotiations will probably continue" would be cut as mere speculation about future events. In this way, the original dispatch was reduced to two and a half lines, a fraction of its original length.

The rift only widens

Negotiations between the United States and Japan had begun in April 1941 to prevent war but showed little visible progress. By late July, Japan dispatched additional troops to the region around Saigon in the south of French Indochina (present-day Vietnam). This deployment of troops marked the beginning of Japan's "southward expansion," which aimed, in general, to secure natural resources. The decision to follow this course of action had been made in an Imperial Conference held in the presence of the Emperor on July 2 but news coverage on specifics had been suppressed.

Around July 10, the Tokyo *Asahi* main office received a phone call from Itō Seiichi, head of the newspaper's branch office in Manchuria, who asked his colleagues: "Do you know what happened at that meeting?" The vice-director of the East Asia division, Sonoda Jirō, wary that the line might be tapped, urged him not to discuss this subject on the phone. Itō then said he "would have a written note delivered to Tokyo by someone from the paper's local news division, who was in Manchuria as part of the Army Ministry's observation group." Sonoda was soon summoned by the military police and he promised that he would hand Itō's letter over to the authorities unopened, once it arrived. Keeping his word, Sonoda and managing editor, Nomura Hideo, later hand-delivered the note to the head of the military police. As it turned out, its contents ultimately differed from the real conclusions reached at the meeting with the Emperor, but Itō was nevertheless detained by the military.[24]

It was not until July 30 that *Asahi* finally reported on the Japanese advancement into Southeast Asia: "More of the Imperial Army's and Navy's Best Troops Dispatched to the South of French Indochina." On August 1, the evening edition related that additional units had disembarked, headed for Saigon. The United States reacted strongly to these developments, considering them the first steps toward Japan taking control of Southeast Asia. US Undersecretary of State Benjamin Sumner Welles informed the Japanese Ambassador to the United States, Nomura Kichisaburō, that there was no longer a basis for negotiations. The American government froze all Japanese assets in the US on July 25 and on August 1 imposed an embargo on petrol exports.

For the Japanese side, the reaction of the US was unexpected. As Satō Kenryō, head of the Military Affairs Section of the Army Ministry, noted later: "The stationing of troops is not an invasion nor a war. [. . .] We personally did not think it would lead to war between Japan and the United States."[25] *Asahi* criticized the United States in its evening edition on the 3rd, speaking of "outrageous US behavior in its breaking off economic relations." As the United States and Great Britain announced the Atlantic Charter, which expressly stipulated territorial non-aggrandizement as a goal, the *Asahi* commented: "Great Britain and the United States aim for world domination."[26] On November 26, Japan received the so-called "Hull Note," a US proposal for negotiations hand-delivered by Secretary of State Hull himself. The conditions included the withdrawal of Japanese troops from China and French Indochina, and the annulment of the Tripartite Pact. The Japanese side took this as a final warning, as Minister of Foreign Affairs Tōgō Shigenori later described, writing how he "was hit by a dizzying sense of despair" at that moment.[27] The *Asahi* evening edition on the 28th similarly expressed the opinion that the "climax of the talks" had been reached. In an editorial that day, entitled "Last Negotiations Between Japan and the United States," the paper wrote: "The die has been cast right in front of our eyes. We [...] are steadfast, ready to face this significant moment in history." The specific contents of the Hull Note were not reproduced in any fashion in the newspaper.

The scoop that never made it to press

In an Imperial Conference meeting held in the presence of the Emperor on December 1, 1941, Japan officially decided to end negotiations with the United States and enter into war with America, Great Britain, and the Netherlands. News coverage of the proceedings was once again banned, not only concerning the specifics of the Cabinet's decision, as was to be expected, but even the very occurrence of the meeting was kept a guarded secret.

On December 6, then 28-year-old Ohara Masao, a journalist with *Asahi*, was cycling across Phnom Penh in the southern part of French Indochina, in what is now Cambodia, looking for the headquarters of the Japanese Army's Third Flight Squadron. He had embarked on his search in the morning but when he finally found the unit dusk was already approaching. Using the stairs at the back entrance, he climbed up to the second floor. In the hallway several mimeographed sheets scattered on a desk caught his eye. He ventured a peek at them and had to catch his breath. "Operations Order Number One: At early dawn on the 8th units of light and heavy bombers will support the landing operations of the ground forces." It was an operations order that clearly stated the day the war would begin! Ohara could not take notes and if he leaked the contents he would have been executed for disclosing state secrets. He told himself to calm down. From June 1941, Ohara had been stationed as an embedded war

Figure 13 Japanese troops passing in front of the royal palace in Phnom Penh, Cambodia after the occupation of southern French Indochina, August 2, 1941.

correspondent in Nanjing, where the Third Flight Squadron had its headquarters. In late October, a lieutenant colonel from the headquarters had secretly tipped him off: "Come to Phnom Penh by December 5 and if you do you'll be there in time for the operation." Consequently, Ohara had made his way to Phnom Penh via Guangdong and Saigon.

On December 7, the day after he had made his discovery in Phnom Penh, Ohara arrived at *Asahi*'s news base in Saigon. There, in front of six *Asahi* journalists and with the aid of a world map, he explained the Japanese Army's planned operations. In the evening, Ohara directed his steps toward Saigon's Catina Street, which was lined with French-style houses, and treated himself to an ice cream at a café. Some ten French women in bright outfits and make-up were laughing and chatting light-heartedly— everything seemed like in a scene from a film. "These women have no idea what the world will come to tomorrow," he thought to himself and at that moment he was hit by the enormity of the information that had fallen into his hands.

The manuscript containing Ohara's exclusive news reached *Asahi*'s East Asia Division at the main office in Tokyo by telegram. The Shanghai branch office also informed Tokyo: "War starts on the 8th." *Asahi*, however, chose not to turn this news item into print. At that time, *Asahi* held meetings virtually every evening in the VIP visitors' room on the fourth floor of the main branch in Tokyo. On December 6 at around seven in the evening, executives of the editorial bureau, all the division chiefs and senior writers assembled around the table. Sugimoto Ken, the journalist assigned to the Navy Ministry, claimed: "war was a certainty." Others like Isono Kiyoshi, the journalist in charge of army coverage, squarely opposed this view and argued that "this was too hasty a conclusion because [. . .] hope still rested on the negotiations with the United States."

Final negotiations between Japan and the United States were just about to break down. On December 3, Secretary of State Hull revealed details of the talks to the press, declaring that the key would be whether Japan accepted the US proposal in the Hull Note.[28] *Asahi*'s editorial on that day commented pessimistically: "One cannot help but acutely feel the light of hope growing dimmer and dimmer." On the 7th, the paper introduced an article from *The New York Times*, which predicted that "some sort of understanding can probably be reached to continue negotiations."

Meanwhile, Japan's preparations for war were steadily progressing.

That day

December 7, 1941 was a Sunday morning in Japan and the Ministry of Foreign Affairs in Tokyo was completely quiet. Thirty-three-year-old Kasuya Terasu, an *Asahi* journalist assigned to the Ministry of Foreign Affairs, had nevertheless made his way there having been tipped off the previous day from someone in the Ministry's Intelligence Division that he should "try and come here early tomorrow morning." As Kasuya walked through the Ministry, he noticed something out of the ordinary. In front of the entrance to the America Division, empty bowls were scattered about the hallway and the Telegraph Division was abuzz with people shuffling around. There was no doubt that the message they were sending was intended for the Embassy of Japan in the United States but Kasuya felt that "the sheer quantity was too large for it to be just the usual day-to-day telegraphic instruction." Intending to get to the bottom of this matter, he visited the homes of the Intelligence Division's bosses—to no avail. He was "unable to put even a single line on paper for an article that day."

Harumi Shizuo, the deputy editor on duty in the politics and economics division that night, later looked back on the events in an *Asahi* internal bulletin:

> The relations between Japan and the United States had finally entered a decisive stage. For several days, rumors concerning the start of the war had been coming into the news desk, basically of two sorts. There were those theorists that believed the war would begin on the 8th or the 15th, and those that were set on a Monday (Sunday in the United States). Regardless, no conclusive evidence existed for any of these.

The morning after, on December 8, the *Tokyo Nichinichi Newspaper* published an exclusive report on the outbreak of war with the United States. Meanwhile, the top story on *Asahi*'s front page was an article about a conference beginning that day, which would bring together representatives from the government, prefectures, and work places to discuss how to raise the morale of the population. Nomura Hideo, managing editor, was woken up in the early hours of the morning by a phone call from the company. Later he remembered: "The *Tokyo Nichinichi* knew everything, *Asahi* knew nothing! This was what the front pages were telling us in black and white. It seems that even Ogata Taketora was completely blindsided as far as the Pacific War went. *Asahi* had more or less been left in the dark by the military." Yajima Yasuo, at the time head of copy-editing at *Asahi*'s Osaka main office, recounted: "The *Mainichi* absolutely crushed the *Asahi* and the disappointment I felt back then is still so fresh in my mind that even now I can picture the pages of the *Mainichi Newspaper*."[29] Isono Kiyoshi, *Asahi* political correspondent assigned to the Army Ministry, looked back on that time: "My instincts told me that something was brewing but a war against Great Britain and the United States—that was beyond my imagination. This was due to a great lack of awareness on my part but the general atmosphere prevailing at the *Asahi* at the time was that war with Great Britain and the US was absurd."

The talks between Japan and the US had been progressing but ultimately failed, while the population had largely been kept in the dark about events. An atmosphere of uncertainty pervaded Japan. In this context, writer Itō Sei described the outbreak of war in the February 1942 issue of the magazine *New Tide* (*Shinchō*), in an article entitled, "A Record of December 8." "It was wonderful—this joy of finally having a clear direction. My body felt so light, as if a great weight had been lifted off my shoulders," he wrote.

The Wartime Greater East Asia Conference

A gathering of Asia's heads of state

Perhaps few have heard of what should be called the Asia Summit, a gathering of international heads of state that was held in Japan during the Pacific War. Although it was an important event at the time, history books such as the *Showa History*, published by Iwanami, contain no information on it whatsoever. For the entire postwar period, the prevalent view has pictured the summit as a farce in which Japan gathered puppet leaders. However, we should once again reconsider "The Greater East Asia Conference" held in Tokyo in November 1943.

"The Greater East Asia Conference, held in the imperial capital today, brought together representatives from the six countries of Japan, China, Thailand, Manchukuo, the Philippines, and Burma" for "Discussions on How to Finish the War and Further Future Development." On November 5, 1943, the morning editions of the main newspapers devoted the majority of their front pages to articles on the conference. Newspapers were prohibited from reporting on the conference before it occurred but as the conference opened it was as though a dam had been breached and a flood of articles related to the event appeared. *Asahi* also increased the number of pages in its evening edition. After reams of solemn articles, such as the farewell parties for student soldiers leaving for the front, this conference was greeted as the first positive news in a long while. However, to guard against air raids, the fact that this conference was happening at the Imperial Diet building had to be kept secret until the closing ceremony. Those assembled included Prime Minister Tōjō Hideki, who served as the conference chairperson, as well as representatives from the Republic of China's Nanjing Government, Thailand, Manchukuo, the Philippines and Burma. A representative from the Provisional Government of Free India was also in attendance as an observer.

In August 1940, Minister of Foreign Affairs Matsuoka Yōsuke had made the first public announcement of the "Greater East Asia Co-Prosperity Sphere," a plan to liberate China and Southeast Asia from Western rule and to create a far-reaching economic sphere of co-existence and co-prosperity under Japanese leadership. In 1943, Japan regarded the occupied countries of Burma and the Philippines as "independent," even if only in name, while Thailand had maintained its independence throughout the war and signed a treaty of alliance with Japan. The Greater East Asia Conference was a meeting to further these countries' future cooperation in the war. Ba Maw, the prime minister of Burma, who spoke passionately at the conference, had an especially deep relationship with Japan. He became the leader of the Burmese Executive Administration following Japan's occupation. A well-known figure in Japan at that time, he repeatedly appeared in the pages of *Asahi*. On July 19, 1942, his tale of escaping from prison was printed in the evening edition under the title, "Escaping from Prison into the Arms of the Imperial Japanese Army." As a follow-up report, an interview with his wife who supported him while he was imprisoned was treated as a major story. At the November 6 closing ceremony for the conference, five principles were stipulated as the Greater East Asia Declaration: "Co-existence and co-prosperity, autonomous independence, cultural promotion, economic prosperity, and contribution to global advancement, such as the abolition of racial discrimination." *Asahi*'s editor-in-chief, Ogata Taketora, summed up the conference in an article with the headline, "A New Period in World History." He praised the Greater East Asia Declaration as "fundamental ideals for the establishment of world peace," being "morally upstanding and not arbitrary," and "based upon friendship, not coercion."[1]

The plans of Minister of Foreign Affairs Shigemitsu Mamoru

At the height of the Pacific War, when the Japanese government gathered heads of state from across Asia for the Greater East Asia Conference in Tokyo, Minister of Foreign Affairs Shigemitsu Mamoru thought this would be an opportunity to explicitly expound upon what Japanese ambitions for the war were. Up until this point, the government's explanation for the war with the United States and Great Britain was portrayed as a matter of standing up for "self-preservation and self-defense," detailing how instances such as the oil embargo put pressure on the economy. However, with Japan's occupation expanding to territories in Southeast Asia, in which countries were bestowed with "independence," "the imperial war of self-defense also serves to liberate the nations and peoples of East Asia," Shigemitsu said.[2] He believed such discourse had become necessary and that the war was being fought for the liberation of Asia.

In the summer of 1943, Shigemitsu established the "Research Group for War Objectives" within the Ministry of Foreign Affairs to prepare and refine the declaration for the Greater East Asia Conference. The Ministry of Greater East Asia, which was responsible for occupied areas, also drafted its own proposal. The Ministry of Foreign Affairs demanded that emphasis be placed on the independence and equality of the nations of Asia, downplaying the belief in Japanese leadership of the coalition. In contrast, the Ministry of Greater East Asia stressed the centrality of propaganda to bring the war to an end. In the end, the declaration as drafted by the Ministry of Foreign Affairs was adopted, with a preamble criticizing the British and Americans, written by the Ministry of Greater East Asia.[3] Shigemitsu intended the Greater East Asia Declaration to counter the Atlantic Charter, which American President Franklin D. Roosevelt and British Prime Minister Winston Churchill had previously announced. The Atlantic Charter expressed British and American war objectives in terms of internationalist ideals such as "no territorial changes that do not accord with the freely expressed wishes of the peoples concerned," and "the right of all peoples to choose the form of Government under which they will live."[4] Including such universal ideals in the Greater East Asia Declaration, Shigemitsu was hoping to find the "key to bringing about the end of the war." In short, he reasoned that the declaration would be a weapon in Japan's diplomatic arsenal in future negotiations for peace and a cessation of hostilities.

At the press conference following the Greater East Asia Conference, Shigemitsu explained: "The Greater East Asia Declaration is a doctrine and policy on international relations that connects past and present, East and West. If we rely on this principle not only for the continued existence of all countries but also for their future development, our future will surely be promising."[5] Shigemitsu was not optimistic about the future of the war. As the declaration advocated universalist ideals, it seems he secretly harbored the belief that "whether we win or lose, our cause is just." However, once the conference was over, popular estimation was that the Greater East Asia Declaration had been empty rhetoric that "could never have been actualized," an Asian hand of the Ministry of Foreign Affairs wrote in his diary.[6] The editorial headlined, "The Cries of One Billion People," in *Asahi* on November 7, 1943, placed particular importance on one of the pillars of the Greater East Asia Declaration, the abolition of racial discrimination. The newspaper had received guidance from the Cabinet Information Bureau, which was responsible for censorship. Bureau head Amō Eiji explained, "It would not be an overstatement to say that the value of this conference lies entirely in its propaganda."

Multiple layers of censorship

When the Greater East Asia Conference commenced in November 1943, *Asahi*'s deputy editor-in-chief, Kaji Ryūichi, wrote an article entitled "Mobilizing Public Weaponry in Total War: The Importance of Newspapers."

> While basing our news on accurate reporting to establish an attitude of certain victory in an unshakeable union between national policy and the hearts and minds of the people, at the same time, throughout all the countries and nations of East Asia, if we are to promote a fighting spirit which possesses an indivisible totality, it can be said that at least in the context of a propaganda war preparations have already been made to destroy the enemy.[7]

Media pundits asserted that accurate reporting would precisely enable Japan to win the propaganda war and by saying that, they tried to fend off the authorities' efforts to censor. We can see here how newspaper staff struggled during the war. Censorship was becoming more and more uncompromising. In later years, Kaji penned *A Man, His Heart and His Travels,* a memoir that recalled this period.[8] As can be seen in his book, even worse than receiving a summons from the Cabinet Information Bureau and the military police was when agents would surreptitiously be sent to the offices of the newspaper to check on those who were writing that day's editorial. However, "even more unpleasant was when the military police arrived and requested a meeting. Without even waiting for a reply, they would follow the receptionist into the offices and, after looking around the room, would ply the journalist with a variety of questions." Ōta Unosuke, a

China hand and *Asahi* journalist who resided in Beijing and Shanghai, wrote editorials for the newspaper. In his diary on January 9, 1943, he wrote: "They cut some insignificant bits out during the prepublication censorship. Good grief, the stupidity!"

At that time, *Asahi* had an internal review section. The newspaper self-censored its own work and in constant coordination with the Cabinet Information Bureau's Censorship Division, articles would pass the "internal reading." It seems that Ōta's prepublication comments referred to this "internal reading." On January 1, 1943, *Asahi* ran an article by Nakano Seigō entitled "On Wartime Prime Ministers." The incident led to a publication ban even though the article had passed the paper's internal censors. Prime Minister Tōjō Hideki was furious when he read the morning edition and viewed it as critical of his work. This was a special case in which Tōjō invoked his authority to prohibit publication. The Cabinet Information Bureau made secret reports to the Cabinet regarding the Greater East Asia Conference: "The importance of the Greater East Asia Conference and the Greater East Asia Declaration has been expressed in advance to the editorial management of each newspaper and news agency. We have thoroughly planned and amply prepared with internal guidance." The report added: "Furthermore, each agency's editorial committee has been instructed to produce numerous explanations about the objectives of the Greater East Asia Declaration." In addition to prepublication censorship by the newspaper and the Cabinet Information Bureau, newspapers were subject to "internal guidance" and government demands for "numerous references" to the objectives. We can assess that due to these multiple layers of censorship the content of reports on the Greater East Asia Conference tended to be eerily similar from paper to paper.

Figure 14   Articles on the Greater East Asia Conference took up the majority of the front page of *Asahi*'s November 5, 1943 edition.

Making use of the newspaper conference

After the Greater East Asia Conference in Tokyo on the 5th and 6th of November 1943, related events continued in the imperial capital. On the 17th, editors and newspaper teams from across Asia attended the Greater East Asia Newspaper Conference. In addition to the six countries that were represented in the Greater East Asia Conference, media staff from seven other regions including Hong Kong, Java, Sumatra, Borneo, and elsewhere participated. The Japan Newspaper Association hosted the conference. The once autonomous Japan Newspaper League had been reorganized as a group under the powerful influence of this official regulatory body and the government. On November 16, *Asahi* ran a prelude to the event with the title, "Expansion of a Vigorous War of Words." The article was actually confirming the link between propaganda for the Greater East Asia Declaration and East Asia's cooperation in the war. Propaganda guidelines, which outlined the government's plan for the Greater East Asia Conference, stipulated that the Japanese "leadership of Greater East Asia should not be directly expressed." Although the government refrained from stating such things during the Greater East Asia Conference, the idea of "Japanese leadership" of the alliance was frankly confessed in the speeches of those who attended the newspaper conference. The Malay representative explained: "The only hope of the Malay youth is to stand at the frontlines ourselves and volunteer to drive out the Anglo-American influence from Greater East Asia." The Sumatran representative stated: "We will sweep away the remaining American, British and Dutch influence, and strengthen our belief in the victory of Japan as the core of a new Asia." The representative from Seram (in present-day eastern Indonesia) noted: "We will cultivate a spirit of loyalty to the great Nippon government." The adoration displayed toward Japan was so extreme that it was painful to witness. The representative from Borneo said in a speech: "We journalists in Borneo have been liberated through the sacrifice of the precious lives of Great Nippon and must lead the natives of Borneo to self-consciousness about the establishment of the Greater East Asia Co-Prosperity Sphere." After returning home, the local newspaper carried an article about the representative's time in Japan and his praise of how the imperial capital functioned.

For the Japanese, the conference was a stage for propaganda. The day before the conference began, the organizers guided participants to the palace for "imperial worship" before visiting the Yasukuni and Meiji Shrines. On the final day of the conference, they called out: "Long Live His Majesty the Emperor!" After the conference ended, participants spent ten days continuing their tour of Japan. They visited the Army Officers Academy in Zama, Kanagawa Prefecture, the Navy Air Squadron of Tsuchiura, Ibaraki Prefecture, Mitsubishi Heavy Industries in Nagoya, the Ise Grand Shrine in Mie Prefecture, the Army Flight School in Akeno, Mie Prefecture, and passed through Nara and Kyoto before disbanding in Osaka. The intention to showcase the robustness of Japan's military strength and industrial power was evident. Although the Japanese government was eager to bolster the propaganda value of the Greater East Asia Conference, including the newspaper conference, there was little international response aside from those countries involved. According to reactions collected by the Ministry of Greater East Asia, Chiang Kai-shek's government broadcast its retort out of

Chongqing in a short critique: "This is merely Japan's loss of faith in its victory. Using this puppet conference to avert destruction is an impossibility. . . ." The dispatch from the Associated Press in New York only conveyed the fact that the meeting had taken place and identified the individuals in attendance.

Countdown to the War's End

"Mokusatsu" and the Potsdam Declaration

On July 26, 1945, the Allies announced the Potsdam Declaration. With the joint signatures of the United States, Great Britain, and China, they pressed Japan to surrender. A little after five in the morning in Japan on the 27th, the Japanese government learned of the declaration by short-wave radio. After they deliberated on a response, all agreed "not to declare our intent and [...] we will decide upon a policy once we have discerned the intentions of the Soviet Union." At a regularly scheduled meeting with the Chief Secretary to the Cabinet, Sakomizu Hisatsune, the reporters responsible for covering the Cabinet inquired into the government's reaction. According to the accounts of *Asahi* reporters in attendance, the following exchange occurred:

> Sakomizu: "The government is not able to take up a position of accepting the proclamation. [...] Therefore, we are likely going to end up not placing much importance on it, or you could say disregarding it...."
> Reporter: "Then, it will be *mokusatsu*?"[1]
> Sakomizu: "Disregarding it could be like *mokusatsu*. Please do not run a large headline saying 'Potsdam Declaration Ignored.' [...] Simply treat it as a minor issue."[2]

The *Dōmei* News Agency used the English term "ignore" as a translation of the term "*mokusatsu*" in its English language article, which it sent out at about 11.00 p.m. on the 27th. However, both the Associated Press and Reuters paraphrased the article, changing "ignore" to "reject." Hasegawa Saiji, who served as the foreign bureau director for *Dōmei* at the time, recalled this change in wording in his memoirs. The July 28 edition of *The New York Times* also carried the AP wire that used the expression "reject." Back in Japan, on July 28 *Asahi* ran a summary of the declaration and Japan's response. Under the heading "Government's *Mokusatsu*," the paper explained that "This is not a declaration of great value, so it will be disregarded [*mokusatsu*]." The *Mainichi Newspaper* and *Yomiuri Newspaper* (which at that time was called *Yomiuri Hōchi*) called the declaration "laughable." On the afternoon of July 28, Prime Minister Suzuki Kantarō spoke at a press conference. Afterwards, he wrote his reflections on this event:

"The newspapers as well [...] reported on the meaning of *mokusatsu*. [...] [But at the conference] I indicated that I believe that this declaration was not something we need to focus on."[3] The July 30 edition of *The New York Times* reported: "Premier Kantaro Suzuki of Japan has put the official Japanese stamp of rejection on the surrender ultimatum [...] declaring that 'so far as the Imperial Government of Japan is concerned it will take no notice of this proclamation.'"[4] While the government dealt with this issue in a rather ambiguous manner, media reports unilaterally moved from "*mokusatsu*" to "reject." The subsequent dropping of the atomic bomb and the Soviet Union's participation in the war both stemmed from Japan's rejection of the Potsdam Declaration.

Shipping stocks skyrocket

Early in the morning on July 27, 1945, the day of the Potsdam Declaration in Japan, stock prices for the shipping company Nippon Yūsen Kaisha (NYK) surged. According to the July 29 special edition of the *Journal of Anti-Government Trends* (*Shisō junpō*), in which the Ministry of Home Affairs gathered responses to the Potsdam Declaration from many sectors, the stock market was very active after the Allies' announcement. This swing was especially true for NYK, which went from a high of 90 sen on the 27th to a high of 2 yen and 30 sen on the 28th, a pronounced rise. The Ministry of Home Affairs analyzed the sudden movement: "We can consider this as representative of an emerging outlook on a market full of hope for an early end to the war." With the tightening of economic controls that accompanied the worsening conditions during the war, stock exchanges across Japan were unified and stock-trading rules became increasingly strict. Even so, markets for bartering among people who owned stock survived. On page two of the July 29 edition of *Asahi*, "Trade Shares Average Price" (for the 28th) presented a table of around 150 companies' stock values. With the newspaper amounting to a mere two sides of one piece of paper, articles on the war nearly filled it entirely but in one corner the detailed stock index continued. The appended, short, explanatory article pointed out: "There is a noticeable atmosphere of trust toward the reliability of the commercial base."

The fighting disrupted sea routes to the extent that continuing the war was economically impossible. As the Allies released the Potsdam Declaration in the midst of this situation, estimates that the end of the war was near were rampant and shipping stocks reacted in tandem. Beginning with the NYK shipping company, the shipping industry in general had suffered a serious blow during the war. According to the *General Investigation of Shipping Losses from the Pacific War*, allied attacks sank 651 warships and an additional 2,934 merchant ships, some of which had been requisitioned by the military. At the same time, while some were calling for "*ichioku gyokusai*," a slogan clamoring for one hundred million Japanese to die valiant deaths either by last-ditch charges or suicide, other Japanese were coolly and calculatingly thinking about their finances.

Actually, the increase in stock values had occurred before the Potsdam Declaration and it was not merely NYK stocks. At the beginning of 1945, anything not related to defense industry procurement was called "peace stocks" and garnered attention. In mid-April: "Those scrambling around for peacetime industry stocks mostly purchased stocks of shipping companies, the *zaibatsu,* and textiles, such as NYK, Mitsui, and Mitsubishi. Suddenly this market was pushed to a stronger high." The situation became so overheated that: "As people felt that the final stages of the war were approaching, popular sentiment reached a boiling point. The peace stocks outstripped the sluggish wartime stocks and were bought in a mad rush. In early August the NYK stock price resurged to a new high while the excitement then extended to entertainment company stocks such as Shōchiku and Tōhō." The stock markets understood the news that Japan had already lost the war but this was not the only issue. The stock prices for cement companies and related businesses also surged. This business focus reflects the fact that there were people looking beyond defeat and demonstrated that many keenly foresaw the coming need for reconstruction.

The bomb

At 8:15 a.m. on August 6, 1945, an atomic bomb was dropped on Hiroshima. That afternoon the managing editors of the newspapers gathered at the Cabinet Information Bureau for a meeting. Tokyo *Asahi* managing editor Hosokawa Takamoto attended the meeting. An attending army officer related the following: "Although this bomb appears to be quite unusual, [. . .] as intelligence is obtained the Imperial General Headquarters will announce the news. Until this has been done the bombing should be reported much the same as other small normal city bombings." On August 7, the first news on the atomic bomb appeared on the front page of *Asahi*: "At about 7:50 a.m. on the 6th, two B29s entered Hiroshima airspace carrying an incendiary bombing device to attack the city. Due to this it appears Hiroshima and nearby areas have suffered some damage." The article was very short, at only four lines. It was not an announcement from the Imperial General Headquarters but rather *Asahi*'s Osaka branch, which used the Headquarters' standard phrase: "some damage," perhaps with an eye to the censors. Readers, however, must have wondered what "an incendiary bombing device" referred to but it was the authorities' use of the words "normal city bombing" that concealed the true nature of the destruction and produced a strangely coined phrase. Also on the 7th, British Prime Minister Clement Attlee announced that it was an atomic bomb that had been dropped on Hiroshima. On the same day, American President Harry Truman announced similar news. Once again the managing editors assembled for a meeting. The military requested that the Imperial General Headquarters label the atomic bomb only "a new form of bomb" in the media. *Asahi* managing editor Hosokawa asked: "Why can we not say in our reports that it is an atomic bomb?" But the military would not change its position.

For its part, the Cabinet Information Bureau decided on a policy in which it would "announce that it is an atomic bomb, which would demand a new determination among the people concerning the execution of the war." The Ministry of Foreign Affairs supported this but the military were opposed on the grounds that "this may be an invention of enemy propaganda." In a compromise proposal, the Cabinet Information

Figure 15   An expanding mushroom cloud fills the sky over Hiroshima following the atomic bombing on August 6, 1945. Photograph by the United States military.

Bureau suggested: "the enemy has announced that this is called an atomic bomb." However, the military stood firm, stating: "It would be foolish to assist in the enemy's propaganda."[5] The lead story for newspapers on August 8 was the Imperial General Headquarters' press release. In line with its previous decision, the term "atomic bomb" was not used. Instead, editors opted for the term "a new bomb" or "a new form of bomb." In both the August 9 and 10 editions of the *Asahi*, the newspaper continued to use the phrase "a new form of bomb."

On August 11, this reporting changed. On the lower half of *Asahi*'s front page a headline from Zurich was printed: "The Atomic Bomb is a Display of Power, Says Truman in His Speech on the War with Japan." According to Hosokawa, the article on Truman's speech was "the first use of the term 'atomic bomb' in a Japanese newspaper." Regardless, this was only possible because "the term atomic bomb was allowed when commenting on foreign reports." Even then *Mainichi* was still cautious and changed the term in the speech to "a new form of bomb."

The origin of atomic bomb myths

August 7, 1945: "First Atomic Bomb Dropped on Japan; Missile is Equal to 20,000 Tons of TNT; Truman Warns Foe of a 'Rain of Ruin.'" The large headline leapt from the front page of *The New York Times*. Also lined up across the front page was the article "Steel Tower 'Vaporized in Trial of Mighty Bomb,'" and "New Age Ushered: Day of Atomic Energy Hailed by President, Revealing Weapon."[6] Other pages provided reports on the process of developing the atomic bomb, including detailed profiles of the scientists involved. Of its thirty-eight pages, eleven were replete with articles on the atomic bomb. The other pages included sports and real estate matters. The advertisement section was filled with illustrated ads of women's dresses and perfumes. By contrast, Japan was suffering from a severe lack of goods. On the same day, *Asahi* printed on two sides of a single sheet of paper and all news and society was colored by the war. The gap in national power could be expressed in this difference of "38 to 2," representing the ability of an American newspaper to publish a full issue of thirty-eight pages to Japan's measly two pages.

Behind *The New York Times*' abundant reporting on the atomic bombing in this special coverage was the full cooperation of the American military. On the fifth page was the article: "War Department Called *Times* Reporter to Explain Bomb's Intricacies to Public." When the bomb was dropped over Nagasaki, a *New York Times* reporter accompanied the crew and covered the event. Features on the atomic bomb were a product of collaboration between newspapers and the American military, which was eager to publicize its success in the development of the bomb to the American citizenry. As stories of success dominated the pages of *The New York Times*, an editorial opened with the following lines: "The bomb that dropped on Hiroshima was doubtless heard by human ears for hundreds of miles around, but morally it was heard around the world. Its implications for good or evil are so tremendous in so many directions that it will take months before our minds can really begin to envisage them." The paper added, "Civilization and humanity can now survive only if there is a revolution in mankind's political thinking."[7] One can detect ambiguity expressed in the face of the enormity of atomic power. In Japan, however, as a way to heighten Japanese citizens' enmity toward the US, and in line with Japanese military opinion, newspapers emphasized the inhumanity of the American decision to use the bomb. To do this the government employed media discussions from abroad. In the article entitled "Why was the Atomic Bomb Aimed at Urban Areas" on the front page of the August 13 edition, *Asahi* journalists wrote: "Numerous European newspapers have raised criticism" and "Priests too have voiced furious objections."

After the war, the United States claimed that the atomic bomb was a necessity to bring about an early end to the war and a great amount of lives were saved. This came to be known as the "myth of the atomic bomb." Hiroshima and Nagasaki still continue to appeal against the inhumanity of nuclear weapons. The gap that could not be bridged between the two countries concerning this issue began in the pages of the newspapers immediately following the atomic bombings. American President Barack Obama has stated: "as the only nuclear power to have used a nuclear weapon the United States has a moral responsibility to act."[8] The question remains: how should we get rid of these "atomic bomb myths"?

Failed expectations

On the evening of August 8, 1945, Satō Naotake, Japan's ambassador to the Soviet Union, went to the Kremlin to meet with the Soviet Minister of Foreign Affairs Vyacheslav Molotov. The meeting was proposed by the Japanese side with the Soviet request that it be held on the evening of the 8th. As Japan's war situation deteriorated, expectant calls for the Soviet Union to act as an intermediary to end the war grew increasingly more vocal. Actually, not long before the Potsdam Declaration the Japanese government made moves to send former Prime Minister Konoe Fumimaro to the Soviet Union as a special envoy. Satō's meeting with Molotov was arranged to hear the Soviet response to such a proposal. As Satō began greeting the minister in Russian, Molotov raised his hand to cut him short. Molotov informed Satō that he had an important message to convey. Offering Satō a chair, Molotov then read aloud from a Russian document:

> After the defeat and capitulation of Hitlerite Germany, Japan became the only great power that still stood for the continuation of the war. [...] The Soviet Government considers that this policy is the only means able to bring peace nearer, free the people from further sacrifice and suffering and give the Japanese people the possibility of avoiding the dangers and destruction suffered by Germany after her refusal to capitulate unconditionally. [...] In view of the above, the Soviet Government declares that from tomorrow, that is from August 9, the Soviet Government will consider itself to be at war with Japan.[9]

It was a declaration of war. "The minute I heard this I realized there was nothing more to be done. I knew that any prospects for some form of change in the situation was no longer tenable," Satō said.[10]

The war with the Soviet Union had an impact upon the Japanese news correspondents living in Moscow. Three officials paid a visit to Watanabe Mikio of the *Mainichi Newspaper* on the evening of the 8th: "You will be immediately detained. [...] We request you to make your way to the embassy," he was informed. Since the signing of the Soviet-Japanese Neutrality Pact in 1941, Japan had paid considerable attention to maintaining favorable relations with the Soviet Union. The "Guidelines for Editing Newspaper Articles," collated by the Cabinet Information Bureau in the same year, stipulated that: "It must be remembered that Japanese citizens' determination against the unjust oppression of Japan by the British and Americans is bursting with emotion." But the Soviet Union was treated differently: "We will refrain from blatant provocation of the Soviet Union." On the other hand, a deep-seated distrust of the Soviet Union remained strong.

On July 15, 1945, an *Asahi* editorial had expressed a heightening fear that the Soviet Union would enter the war: "America's greatest hope is for Soviet intervention in the war with Japan." A warning appeared in the column "Ode to the Divine Wind" on the 17th: "[The United States] is striving to find somehow or some way to get the [Soviet Union] to cooperate with them in the war effort. [...] There is a need for great care to be placed upon the orientation of the Potsdam Conference." Actually, at the February 1945 Yalta Conference, the Soviet Union had decided to enter the war with Japan two to three months after the fall of Germany. Japan's hopes vanished and its fears became a reality.

The lost report on the Soviet entry into the war

On August 9, 1945, Yamada Ichirō, a 25-year-old reporter for the *Manchukuo* News Agency, was living in a dormitory in the city of Xinjing (now the city of Changchun). Just after midnight he heard the sound of bombing and felt the dull reverberations of the earth below him. Hurrying to the scene he saw the burned and charred bodies of people in their homes. The police told him: "Everyone is saying that there was a red star on its wings." It was a Soviet airplane. Returning to the agency Yamada sent the first report to the *Dōmei* News Agency head office in Tokyo, exclaiming: "Soviet Plane Attacks Xinjing." Although technically an affiliate of *Dōmei*, the *Manchukuo* News Agency was really more of a branch office. *Dōmei* replied and asked Yamada to correct his report to: "Plane of Unknown Origin." After going to the Kwantung Army Headquarters, an acquaintance of his who was the officer in charge of reporting said nothing but handed him a top-secret telegram. It was an urgent report from the military headquarters at the Soviet-Manchukuo border and read: "Under fire from the Soviet Army." Confirmation had been made. Yamada raced back and sent off his report in line with the coverage guidelines for the outbreak of war with the Soviet Union, which was at-the-ready and stored in a safe: "Our Elite Kwantung Army Begins Resolute Counteroffensive." This was the historical first report of the Soviet Union's entry into the war, sent out around the break of dawn at four in the morning. A short while later, *Dōmei* issued orders for the entire article to be squelched. Hasegawa Saiji, the foreign bureau director for *Dōmei*, made a telephone call explaining that as the government was in the midst of beginning the top secret procedures for dealing with the Potsdam Declaration, he was worried that an article about a resolute counteroffensive would provoke the Soviet Union.

As the *Dōmei* News Agency was a state-sanctioned company, it served as the link and window between the Japanese government and the outside world. At the time, Hasegawa was in frequent contact with both Foreign Minister Tōgō Shigenori and Chief Cabinet Secretary Sakomizu Hisatsune. At four in the morning, the "Soviet Declaration of War" flew in on the wire from Moscow, landing in Hasegawa's hands. He immediately reported it to Sakomizu, who responded with: "Hasegawa, are you sure you haven't misread that telegram?" The Japanese government was eagerly anticipating a reply concerning their sending a special envoy to keep hopes alive of having the Soviet Union act as peace mediator. Unfortunately, the reply that came was a declaration of war on Japan. Yamada appears to have sent out his initial draft concerning the Soviet entry into the war at about the same time the report on the Soviet declaration of war from Moscow arrived. Sakomizu, Hasegawa and others consulted and rejected Yamada's report from Xinjing. At 7 a.m. on the 9th, Tōgō rushed over to the private residence of Prime Minister Suzuki Kantarō. Suzuki said to him: "So, the final blow has come."[11] At half past ten in the morning, the Prime Minister, the Ministers of War, the Navy and the other members of the "Big Six," held a meeting of the top war leaders. While they engaged in stern discussions on whether or not to accept the Potsdam Declaration, "the news of the second atomic bomb being dropped on Nagasaki arrived. [...] It had happened that very morning."[12] The article "Soviet Union Declares War on Japan" that finally appeared in *Asahi*'s August 10 edition was a report dispatched from Tokyo's Imperial General Headquarters at 5 p.m. on the 9th.

Reporters at ground zero

At 11:02 on the morning of August 9, 1945, an atomic bomb was dropped on Nagasaki. Ogawa Takeshi, a reporter at *Asahi*'s Nagasaki branch office, had been at the home of an acquaintance and rushed back to the office. Ripping the telephone out from the building as fire pressed in, he wrapped it in the company flag and escaped. All around him "bodies were burned and blistered beyond recognition and I could not tell if they were men or women," Ogawa remembered. As the trains were no longer running at Nagasaki Station, he walked three stations up the line where he entrusted his report on the disastrous situation to the train conductor. "Although there were support journalists and photographers actively engaged in covering the bombing, it was not until August 12 that the first report appeared in print.

The August 12 headline, "Nagasaki Also Hit by New Form of Bomb," was spread across two columns. However, the content of the article was only seven lines announced by the Army's Western Regional Command: "The Damage was Comparatively Minor." Although articles were subject to censorship, journalists also censored themselves. A Hiroshima *Asahi* branch employee recalled: "Normally we would write up long pieces, then rack our brains thinking if we should send them or not. But that was never really the case. We newspaper journalists were completely used to the fact that one did not write about things that were not in the official pronouncements. We were already far beyond being real journalists." Reporting by journalists from ground zero was published on the second page of the postwar August 22 western Japan edition. *Asahi* was scooped by the *Mainichi*'s August 15 edition in Tokyo, which was the first paper in Japan to truthfully report on the atomic bomb with its graphic second page article, headed by the large title: "The Atomic Bomb: A Barbarity Unprecedented in History: Passengers Burnt to Cinders in a Flash While Holding Overhead Hand Straps, Charred Black Skulls in Helmets." Watanabe Masaaki had been dispatched from Fukuoka to cover the scene in Nagasaki and although his mind is often a bit foggy, he remains in Kyushu and still strains to say a few words on his coverage: "I was angry and I wanted to write so much more."

As for Ogawa, after the war he turned to oil painting and left behind many of his works. Following the end of the war he immediately took up a brush to paint the atomic bomb but this was the only painting he could not finish before his death in 1989. His painting depicts the destroyed Urakami Cathedral in Nagasaki, which was virtually the epicenter of the bomb. In the frame a mother suckling her infant child leans against the stone steps and vacantly gazes up at the sky. Contrasted with the reddish body of the child, the mother is pale. From atop the stone steps, the statues of saints that had survived the blast gaze down upon mother and child. The company flag that Ogawa carried out from the office was splotched with blood and mud. Before his death he asked his family to cremate him with it; however, he never said what to do with the painting of the Cathedral. "'Only that painting defied me. I painted it and painted it but could never get it to come out as I wanted.' He was always saying this," his wife Sakae remarked. There was something about that moment that he could not communicate, the incommunicable that was left behind on the canvas.

Misleading inferences

On August 11, 1945, Japanese newspapers completely diverged, running two distinctly different statements. The head of the Cabinet Information Bureau, Shimomura Hiroshi, produced a statement: "[With the new form of bomb and the Soviet declaration of war] we cannot help but admit that we now find ourselves in the worst situation. [...] While the government is doing its utmost, we expect our 100 million citizens to overcome all difficulties and strive to preserve the national polity." General Anami Korechika issued a directive from the Army Ministry: "This holy war is being waged in order to resolutely defend the land of the Gods. [...] Have faith that our people can battle through this dire situation, even if we are prostrate on the field of battle, tasting the dirt in our mouths."

After reading the statement by the head of the Cabinet Information Bureau, the writer Takami Jun knowingly wrote in his diary: "Is this not a proposal to end the war?" He added, "Even so, just what was the Minister of Army's directive? [...] I just cannot tell what is going on from these newspaper articles."[13] Takami's instincts were correct. Beginning on the 9th, the government and the Army were embroiled in negotiations. The Emperor's judgment in the early dawn of August 10 was to accept the Potsdam Declaration under the condition of protecting the national polity. This proposal was submitted to the Allied Powers but the decision was not made public to the Japanese people. A decision was made to "gradually promote a change of direction toward an atmosphere of ending the war."[14] On the afternoon of the 10th, the statement from the head of the Cabinet Information Bureau was revealed. However, those in the military who thoroughly opposed ending the war also pressed newspapers to publish the Minister of Army's directive.

Asahi was aware of the true state of affairs. Some of the reporters insisted that the paper's decision to "now publish the Minister of the Army's directive after the government had decided to accept the Potsdam Declaration will mislead the public." However, Hasebe Tadasu, head of *Asahi*'s political section, would not relent: "The role of the newspapers is to bring a smooth transition to the end of the war. If the tone of the news suddenly changes it will likely present unanticipated provocations for the military and society. We should also release the Minister of Army's directive." In the end, Tokyo managing editor Hosokawa Takamoto supported Hasebe and directed: "Place Anami's statement and Shimomura's statement side-by-side with the same font size." On August 12, *Asahi* ran an editorial titled, "The Nation Should Remain Calm." The editorial appealed to people to overcome this "national ordeal." On the 13th, the *Mainichi Newspaper* editorial quoted from the Cabinet Information Bureau statement. Discussing possibilities for the revival of the nation and reflecting, the editorial exclaimed: "The government has clearly called this the most grievous of situations. However, we believe in the wisdom of the Japanese to be able to persevere." To many readers, the newspapers' attempts to lay the groundwork for coverage of the conclusion of the war was too oblique. "Inference persisted as inference right to the end."[15]

The Puzzle of the August 15 Edition

On the eve of the war's end

On the morning of August 14, 1945, the Emperor delivered the decision to his Cabinet Ministers to bring an end to the war. At the afternoon Cabinet meeting, leaders discussed how to inform the people of the surrender. Radio was by far the fastest and most effective means to get the message out. At noon on the 15th, a recording of Emperor Hirohito reading out the imperial decree would be broadcast by radio. Newspaper agencies were instructed to send out news of the war's end after the broadcast because only the Emperor's voice could bring an end to the war. The reasoning behind this decision was that those who wanted to fight to the bitter end might run amok if the news was delivered through the newspapers first. On the afternoon of the 14th, while the sun was still high in the sky, *Asahi*'s Osaka branch received a telephone call from the Tokyo head office. Picking up the receiver, the operator said: "Hello, this is Osaka." The response came in a loud shout. "We've surrendered! We've surrendered!" the voice said.

At the same time, about one hundred American B29 bombers attacked the arms factory and arsenal inside the grounds of Osaka Castle, resulting in approximately five hundred casualties. At four that afternoon, a draft of the imperial edict to surrender was presented at a Cabinet meeting and ministers argued over the precise wording of the document. That evening, the general news staff of *Asahi*'s Tokyo head office held a division meeting. Present at the meeting was 30-year-old employee Muno Takeji. He said: "Beginning tomorrow I will not be coming in. It is time for those who sent out mistaken newspapers to leave and for those who are capable of producing a new generation of newspaper to step forward." That evening at nine o'clock the radio announced: "At noon tomorrow, the 15th of August, a broadcast of extreme importance will be transmitted." At eleven o'clock on the 14th, the imperial decree to surrender was promulgated. At the underground bomb shelter of the Prime Minister's residence, the Chief Secretary to the Cabinet, Sakomizu Hisatsune, handed the imperial decree to the assembled journalists.

On August 15, around 1:30 or 2.00 a.m., *Asahi* employee Aragaki Hideo went by foot to the nearby Ginza area of Tokyo. Looking up at the sky free of American B29s, he thought: "Was the sky always such a beautiful thing?" Tears of sadness poured out with Japan's defeat. Takahara Shirō, local news reporter at the time, recalled another scene: just after four in the morning about ten journalists from *Mainichi*'s local news division went to the Imperial Palace Plaza. They had spent the entire night drinking sake and beer. The division head knelt down on the gravel and the other employees followed suit, silently with heads bowed.[1]

On the 15th, *Asahi* published in its morning edition an article describing the scene at the Imperial Palace Plaza.

"Tears of worship at the Imperial Palace"

On August 15, 1945, as the clock struck noon, the radio announced: "A broadcast of great importance will now begin. We ask all our listeners across the nation to please stand up." The national anthem played and the Emperor's voice sounded out:

> After deeply pondering the general trends of the world and the actual conditions present in our Empire today, we have decided to effect a settlement of the current situation by resorting to an extraordinary measure. . . .[2]

The staff of *Asahi*'s Tokyo head office listened to the "Imperial Rescript on Surrender" in the company's seventh-floor auditorium. Twenty-two-year-old Kitano Teruhi was working in the sales department at the time. After the broadcast, she and another female staff member went to the Imperial Palace Plaza, about a fifteen-minute walk from the head office in Yūrakuchō ward. They were there from about 1.00 until 2.00 p.m. Just

Figure 16 The August 15, 1945 Tokyo edition of the *Asahi* featured the "Tears of Worship" article on the second page. The newspaper had two pages, front and back.

in front of the Nijūbashi Bridge people were prostrating themselves to the Emperor, crying and apologizing for losing the war. Kitano also bowed her head and started to cry but at the same time she was thinking why must I apologize? On the second page of *Asahi* that afternoon, an article ran with the title: "Tightly Grasping Gravel in Their Hands, They Cry Tears of Worship at the Imperial Palace." One article in the paper said: "When my steps stopped at the palace I was no longer able to stand. The tears I had been holding back burst forth and ran down my cheeks. My knees buckled and I bowed down in the gravel. I cried with loud sobs." The author said: "I cried until I could cry no more and I sobbed as much as one could. Crying lonely wails on this sacred ground, unconsciously grasping the gravel in my hands, with clenched fists I shouted out: 'Your Majesty...' I managed to continue: 'forgive ...,' but I could get no more words to come out." This article's use of the first person was unusual and it was published without the author's name, only the subtitle, "The Humble Notes of a Journalist." Totaling 2,300 characters, it was quite long for a news article.

Twenty-nine years after the war, in 1974, the foreign affairs critic Kase Hideaki took an interest in this article. Kase had published a series of non-fiction articles, "The Imperial Family's War," concerning the imperial family from the final days of the war to the occupation period, in the popular magazine *The Weekly New Tide* (*Shūkan Shinchō*). Kase inquired into the story behind the construction of the August 15th morning edition through an acquaintance at *Asahi*. He was told that it was printed at noon and distributed after the "Imperial Rescript on Surrender" was broadcast. However, his friend had not been directly involved in the composition of the news on the day of surrender. In his serialized article in the October 10, 1974 edition of *The Weekly New Tide*, Kase points out: "That article was a piece that had been written up beforehand."[3] More recently, he has once again returned to the article, criticizing it as a "fabrication."[4] What was the real story?

Writing an article without witnessing the scene

In the spring of 1984, *Asahi* readers wrote in to the newspaper with questions such as "that article, 'Tears of Worship at the Imperial Palace,' which was on the second page of the morning edition on August 15, 1945, appears to have been written up after the 'Imperial Rescript on Surrender,' but when was it printed?" After listening to the stories of those who were responsible for editing the story, Sugiyama Katsumi, head of copyediting in the Tokyo office at the end of the war, learned the following. Suetsune Takurō, who worked at the local news desk, wrote the article. Suetsune explained: "At the very moment the Imperial Rescript on Surrender began broadcasting [...] I went down to the Imperial Palace to cover the scene." Although he then immediately returned to the office to write it up, "the depth of emotion that I felt made it difficult to put it into words." He continued, "The draft passed copy-reading at about 12:30 [...] and was brought to print and delivered around 3:00 p.m." However, the puzzle was far from solved.

From the head office in Yūrakuchō ward to the Imperial Palace Plaza it takes no more than five minutes by car. Even so, is it possible to be in front of the Palace around noon and have a very long article produced from scratch and handed in by 12:30 p.m.? Was the article based on a scene that Suetsune would have liked to have seen? Perhaps he wrote up the article beforehand? The journalist Muno Takeji, who worked for *Asahi* during the war, bitterly recalls the submission of "pre-written drafts." On June 5, 1943, the state funeral for Commander-in-Chief of the Combined Fleet, Admiral Yamamoto Isoroku, was held in Tokyo. According to the plan, Prime Minister Tōjō Hideki was to be the first to enter the hall and so that is the way it was written up. But before the scheduled time, Foreign Minister Shigemitsu Mamoru came in, leaning on his cane. Shigemitsu had lost a leg in a terrorist attack in China and because he could not keep pace, he entered the room first. Before the event had even started Muno was ordered to submit a draft to the editors based on the pre-fixed schedule. Ceremonies and events were carefully detailed in their schedules, so media reports could usually be written up beforehand to meet deadlines. The cliché-ridden pre-written draft would then become an article. Another newspaper, the *Yomiuri Hōchi*, reported live from the event and noted the simple fact: "Minister of Foreign Affairs Shigemitsu came into the empty pavilion alone." "I felt defeated," Muno said. Even today his regret lingers.

Tanaka Toku, the *Kyōdō News* journalist responsible for coverage of the Imperial Household from the war to the postwar period, witnessed such situations, writing: "[Until the end of the war, articles on the Imperial Household] even about things such as births and marriages, [...] were pre-publication reports and written based on our imagination of the scenes. [...] It was something entirely down to form." Those manufactured articles designed to promote a wartime spirit and praise Japan as the land of the gods could even be written up in the absence of having attended the real event and indeed they often were.

Suetsune Takurō's account of events

On March 18, 1945, the Emperor visited areas devastated by the Tokyo air raids. On the following day, *Asahi* reported on its front page: "With the empire in crisis, it is lamentable that our 100 million subjects do not maintain loyalty in their hearts at all times." The paper noted, "Under the guidance of the Emperor we must be victorious. [...] This is the only path for imperial subjects: to put sincere belief in our hearts and follow the Emperor's will." The article contained an apology to the Emperor for the "disloyalty" of allowing the "atrocities" committed by "vile enemy aircraft." At the bottom of the article was the signature "Suetsune Takurō, journalist." Suetsune also penned an article concerning the people's apology to the Emperor for losing the war on the day of surrender. The question is, when was it written? In 1974, Suetsune passed away at the age of 68. Even his surviving family members do not know the real situation surrounding the article.

After a thorough investigation of a massive volume of internal company documents, the reminiscences of one member of staff yielded the following few lines: "On the evening of August 14th, the day before the surrender, it was once again my turn to serve as the night watch. Before dawn on the 15th, 'S' journalist from the local news division came out of the gloomy [Tokyo main] editorial office with a bitter face, having just written an article on the end of the war. Seeing him tugged at my heartstrings." Was "S" Suetsune? The employee who had written the memo died in 2002, so we can no longer verify the situation. In July 2009, it came to light that Suetsune personally recalled the time of surrender in a newsletter of the *Asahi* retirees club. Suetsune made the following comments: "I was told on the 14th to go to the Imperial Palace and write about the scene for the next day's morning edition." "Then, to confirm the situation I walked back to the palace on the morning of the 15th and added to my earlier draft." In effect, Suetsune's article was a pre-written piece. One may surmise that perhaps the scene at the Imperial Palace Plaza never occurred in the way that Suetsune described it. Rather, before the unprecedented circumstances of losing the war, Suetsune tried to depict the "correct attitude" (the way of the imperial subject) that he believed "the people" should be taking and wrote this up as his article. They were not rushing to fight to the bitter end, nor questioning the responsibility of the emperor or the military, but only weeping and also apologizing for their disloyalty. "The only cries that were shouted out were: 'Our offenses to his majesty the Emperor are inexcusable. . .'." *Asahi* ran the article in the morning edition on the afternoon of the 15th, thinking that such a description should be published in the first newspaper to be released after the Imperial Rescript on Surrender. Such is the duty of newspapers because the next day would have been too late.

Tears but no photographs

On the afternoon of August 15, 1945, there were others who witnessed the scene at the Imperial Palace Plaza from atop the iron Nijūbashi Bridge. Enai Masahisa was 28 years old and serving in the second regiment of the Imperial Guard. Although he had joined *Asahi* in the spring of 1941, he was called into service while employed at the Kōchi city branch. He was transferred from the Shikoku regiment in the autumn of 1944. "As a newspaper journalist, I stood there for hours mesmerized while the historical scene etched itself into my mind," he said. Having heard the Imperial Rescript on Surrender, people filed into the plaza one after the other. There were those who fell to their knees on the ground, those that stood with heads bowed, those that shouted *"banzai,"* and those who cried out. The sound of the gravel crunching underfoot mixed with the sound of the people sobbing reverberated in Enai's ears. Early in the afternoon of the same day, a photographer from *Asahi* went to the Imperial Palace Plaza. However, he was unable to take a picture. "I could not take a single photograph. The viewfinder was all foggy with my tears," he said. Another cameraman also went to the scene alone but he too shortly returned with eyes red and full of tears, not having taken any photographs.

Kageyama Kōyō from the photography department also went to the plaza. "Everyone was sitting formally (*seiza*) or kneeling down in the gravel murmuring the national anthem," he recalled. He took one or two pictures and returned to the agency but did not process the film. It was not possible to take pictures and say "here they are," while more junior members in the office were unable to. Kojima Masaji, a 31-year-old *Asahi* photographer, heard the Imperial Rescript on Surrender while visiting the home of his wife's parents in Sawara, Chiba Prefecture. He returned to Tokyo and by the time he arrived at the office it was already evening. He remembers other staff members saying: "How could a photographer go to the scene and not take any pictures?" "Why not take any at all?"

Kojima recalls that staff criticized Kageyama and others. On the following day, August 16th, both *Mainichi* and *Yomiuri* ran photos of the Imperial Palace Plaza on their front pages. At an editorial meeting, *Asahi* editors came to the conclusion that "this was a complete failure for a newspaper reporting on the first day of the defeat." Kageyama handed in his letter of resignation the same day. A picture that Kageyama

Figure 17   The photograph in front of the Nijūbashi Bridge reproduced in *Asahi*'s Osaka edition, as well as other newspapers.

Figure 18   Another photograph of the Nijūbashi Bridge. The *Kyoto Shimbun* and a number of other print media outlets ran this photograph.

took on the day of surrender, entitled "Tears at the Imperial Palace Plaza," was later released as part of his photography collection.[5] Kageyama's son, Kageyama Tomohiro, said: "Even if they had been developed at that time, they probably would not have been published in the newspaper." This was because all the people in the photo had their backs turned to the Imperial Palace, and therefore, to the Emperor. On the afternoon of the 15th, the Tokyo edition of *Asahi* did not run a picture of people bowing at the Imperial Palace Plaza but the Osaka edition did. The question remains, where did this picture come from?

In front of the Imperial Palace on the day before surrender

The Japan Newspaper Museum (Newspark) in Yokohama investigated media at the time of the surrender and found that the same picture that was run in *Asahi*'s August 15 Osaka edition was printed on August 16 in the *Shinano Mainichi Newspaper* and the *Yamagata Newspaper*. The photo also appeared in the August 17 editions of both the *Shiniwate Daily* and the *Kōbe Newspaper*. Even stranger, a picture with people in remarkably similar arrangements appeared in the August 16 editions of the *Kyoto Newspaper* and the *Nishinihon Newspaper*, as well as the August 17 editions of the *Shimane Newspaper*, the *Tōō Nippō*, and the *Gōdō Newspaper* (now the *San'yō Newspaper*). It appears that some of those photographed in one picture also appeared in another. Due to the large number of newspapers carrying similar images, it causes one to wonder if they were distributed by the national news agency, *Dōmei*, rather than actually having been taken by individual journalists witnessing the scene for themselves. What was the truth behind the matter?

Kase Hideaki wrote in his 1974 article in *The New Weekly Tide* (*Shūkan Shinchō*) that the piece, "Tears of Worship at the Imperial Palace," which featured in the August 15, 1945 edition of *Asahi*, was a "pre-written draft." Having seen Kase's article, Hanada Shōzō of Aomori City sent in a letter. Hanada, a student at Yamagata Prefecture's Yonezawa Technical College during the late stages of the war, had been mobilized to work at a factory in Fukushima City. On August 14, the day before the surrender, he had come to Tokyo to commandeer some supply parts. After finishing his work in the vicinity of the palace, he made his way by foot to the area in front of Nijūbashi Bridge at the Imperial Palace Plaza. It was there that a photographer wearing an official armband asked him to prostrate himself on the ground to have his photograph taken. The photographer was wiping tears away with his arm. Kase talked more on the phone with Hanada and said, "Hanada was convinced that the photographer was from *Asahi*." Hanada's experiences were reported in the January 15, 1989 Aomori edition of the *Yomiuri*, as well as in the August 14, 2005 Aomori edition of the *Mainichi Newspaper*. These reports explained that Hanada first heard the Imperial Rescript on Surrender at a factory in the Shinagawa ward of Tokyo. Wanting to leave Tokyo immediately, he made for Ueno Station by tram. There on the tram he saw a picture of his own figure carried in the newspapers fellow passengers had opened and were reading. But what newspaper was it?

On the 15th, we know that *Asahi*'s Tokyo edition did not carry a photograph of the Imperial Palace Plaza. At the time there was only a morning edition. Both *Yomiuri* and *Mainichi* ran a photograph in their August 16 editions. The *Tokyo Newspaper* ran a photograph of four people bowing in the direction of the Nijūbashi Bridge and Ishii Kōnosuke, a photographer from the newspaper, recalled that he shot the picture on the afternoon of August 15. But the number of people does not correspond to the ten to twenty men and women that Hanada says were in the photo with him. Despite much research into photographs in other newspapers, this mystery remains unsolved. Today, those photographs taken on the day of surrender are held by *Kyōdō News*, which supplies photographs to newspapers and magazines. They assumed this responsibility from the *Dōmei* News Agency immediately after the war. For unknown reasons, the newspapers that carried those photographs from the time of surrender are nowhere to be found.

Real summer grass

Hanamori Yasuji, the editor-in-chief for the magazine *Notebook on Living* (*Kurashi no techō*), went to the Imperial Palace Plaza on the afternoon of the day the war ended. He went to observe what was happening at this most revered location. "When I went to see all was somber, but also it was just like the annual festival at the Yasukuni Shrine, as there were people everywhere," he wrote. The photographs of the Imperial Palace Plaza taken by the *Dōmei* News Agency photographers on August 15, 1945 are now preserved by *Kyōdō News*. The one where everyone is bowing and facing the Imperial Palace has been featured in numerous news briefs and magazines over the years. However, even after inspecting all the newspapers from the end of the war that are held in the National Diet Library, although there are newspapers carrying photographs that seem to be taken up until August 14, those newspapers that carried photographs taken on the 15th are nowhere to be found. What does this mean?

Agatsuma Seiji, chief of research for photography at *Kyōdō News*, explains: "It is not as it appears. It is quite likely that it was not possible to provide any photo because of the disorderly atmosphere in front of the Imperial Palace." Although certainly the people in front of the photographer were on their knees, people outside of the frame had their backs turned toward the palace. Everyone did not simply prostrate themselves at the same time. It was surely as uneven a scene as the annual festival at the Yasukuni Shrine. During the war, newspapers did not report on a scene "as it happened," but rather "as it should have happened." For instance, newspapers would report that the damage from air raids had been "insignificant." Whatever may have actually happened, the damage had to be "insignificant." The pictures in front of the Imperial Palace are of the same genre. The photographs taken beforehand were better suited for maintaining order than those of what actually happened, as the former showed what the people should have been doing. The article, "Tears of Worship at the Imperial Palace," in the *Asahi* on August 15, 1945, was also similar. It described people's feelings as many would have hoped would have been the case when the war was lost. It was an extreme form of "reporting in wartime" and it was a "masterpiece" article that should never be written again. Journalists had to think about portraying those attitudes as part of their personal responsibility.

At the end of the summer of 1945, Katō Shūichi, a doctor who later became a social critic, returned to Tokyo from Nagano Prefecture where he had evacuated. He saw that the burned-out ruins of Tokyo exposed the lies of wartime language such as "should the insurgent enemy planes reach the skies over the Imperial Palace, they will be downed by *Kamikaze* winds." He wrote, "The wide evening sky and the summer grass thriving among the rubble were not fake; and as long as they were genuine, even the charred ruins shone with greater splendor than a palace concocted of lies. At that time, my heart was filled with hope."[6]

From these charred ruins the postwar began.

The Fate of 6.6 Million Abroad

The road to repatriation

On August 15, 1945, the radio broadcast that transmitted Emperor Hirohito's surrender broadcast, announcing defeat to the Japanese people, was boosted to six times its average strength and also diffused by shortwave across Asia to Korea, China, Southeast Asia, and throughout the colonies and occupied territories where Japanese lived.[1] The number of Japanese military and civilians living abroad exceeded 6.6 million, close to a tenth of the total Japanese population at the time and the broadcast had to reach everyone.[2] On August 14, the Japanese government had sent an encoded message to its overseas missions with the following command: "Endeavor to have Japanese residents stay and live in their locales to the extent possible."

The Potsdam Declaration had been accepted and the sovereignty of Japan would now be restricted to the four main islands of Honshu, Hokkaido, Kyushu, and Shikoku, along with some surrounding satellite islands. The military had been ordered to disarm and return home. Already facing a crisis of dwindling food supplies in a smaller Japan, the country would have great problems with just the repatriation of its military personnel, numbering 3.5 million. Therefore, the government's directive "effectively abandoned Japanese civilians abroad."[3] Japan signed the Instrument of Surrender on September 2 and it was around this time that Japanese throughout the former empire were informed that if they could not repatriate swiftly, they faced a perilous situation. A brief look at the headlines in the *Asahi* reveals the situation: "Public Order Deteriorates in Korea and Manchuria" (September 10); "Manchurian Mobs Attack; Many Japanese Unable to Leave Home" (October 14); "Manchurian Thugs in Mukden; Looting and Arson; Women and Children Caught in Siege; Repatriation Encounters Difficulties" (October 17); "Hungry and Cold, Manchurian and Korean Compatriots; Bounties for Hunting Japanese" (November 10).

A tragedy was unfolding in Manchuria and Korea. American General Douglas MacArthur, Supreme Commander for the Allied Powers, issued General Order Number One on September 2. He stipulated that Japanese soldiers abroad should surrender to the respective Allied Command in each area and civilians were placed under this authority. Wherever one happened to be at that time determined the turning point for one's destiny. The ways in which the repatriated Japanese were handled varied considerably by country.[4] On November 24, 1945, *Asahi* ran the headline, "7 Million of our Compatriots Waiting for Ships Home." The article showcased anxiety about that "The Unbearable Pain of the 1.8 million Japanese in Northern Korea, Manchuria, Sakhalin and the Kuril Islands." At the same time, the paper anticipated repatriation: "With kindness, the Supreme Allied Command has offered a great number of landing ship tanks (LST)," thus "creating hope for a remarkably faster" repatriation. With defeat, Japan had lost its diplomatic authority. The Soviet Union, which occupied Manchuria and Northern Korea, refused to assure the safety of the Japanese, so MacArthur's "kindness" was the only guarantee the Japanese had. The era of occupation had begun.

Moving a people

A man "with the appearance of a ghost" shocked the staff at *Asahi*'s western office (in what is now Northern Kyushu City) on December 4, 1945. He was 26-year-old Ishiguro Masashi and he had been employed in the Chongjin (Ch'ŏngjin) city branch in the far north of Korea, not far from the border with the Soviet Union. There were about 30,000 Japanese living in Chongjin and on August 9, when the Soviet Union declared war on Japan, aerial and naval bombardment began.[5] After evacuating his family, Ishiguro fled as well. Once the Soviet occupation was in place, a People's Committee began investigating the Japanese refugees' ideological orientation. Ishiguro was questioned regarding the armband identifying him as "correspondent" found in his luggage. "This is getting dangerous," he assessed. Jumping at the opportunity to join fishermen he heard were heading south, without preparing anything in the way of provisions, Ishiguro made it back to Japan. "Escape from Death in Northern Korea" is a recollection that Ishiguro wrote and prepared as a piece for newspaper publication. It was rejected as "not authorized" by the General Headquarters (GHQ) of the Allied Command. Under the press code issued by GHQ on September 19, no "destructive criticism" of the Allied forces was allowed. *Asahi*'s internal review section chief at the time detailed: "For those who have fled from Manchuria and Northern Korea, talk of Soviet troops pillaging materials or assaulting Japanese women and children is not permitted." Once Ishiguro returned to Japan, the American-led repatriation efforts for the Japanese began to take on a more orderly progress.

On December 17, *Asahi* printed President Harry Truman's December 15 statement regarding American policy toward China: "The maintenance of peace in the Pacific may be jeopardized, if not frustrated, unless Japanese influence in China is wholly removed and unless China takes her place as a unified, democratic, and peaceful nation."[6] By 1946, the American military was lending about two hundred ships to Japan and by the end of the year more than five million Japanese had been repatriated in "the moving of this historically unprecedented large number of people."[7]

How did the newspapers cover this? In a February 20 *Asahi* editorial: "How Much Have Citizens at Home Helped in this Mass Repatriation?" The editorial lamented, "Our hands are already full with our own troubles and those of our families." It continued, "We wish to convey our gratitude" to the GHQ for the continued "good will of the Allied forces [in taking care of the Japanese abroad]." Was America showing nothing more than good will? Katō Kiyofumi, Assistant Professor of Japanese Modern and Contemporary History at the National Institute for Japanese Literature, explains the international situation at the time.

> Once its own soldiers had been repatriated, the American military had extra ships available. After the Soviet withdrawal from Manchuria and to curb the influence of the Chinese Communist Party, the Americans transported elements of the Chinese Nationalist Army to Manchuria from southern China. Once the boats were unloaded, they continued on to Japan. The responsibility of manning the vessels and paying for the costs fell to Japan.

Despite this, there were many who did not return home.

Internment in Siberia

After defeat in August 1945, the Japanese Army in Manchuria, Northern Korea, Sakhalin, and the Kuril Islands surrendered to the Soviet Union. On September 11, the Soviets announced that "approximately 594,000 people have been detained," but after that information ceased. Both communication and transportation routes were closed and the Soviet Union refrained from issuing further reports. It was not until the following year, 1946, that a foreign report was received announcing that Japanese had been sent to Siberian internment camps. Final confirmation arrived in May when Satō Naotake, Japan's former Ambassador to the Soviet Union, returned to Japan with Kiyokawa Yūkichi, *Asahi*'s former Moscow correspondent. They had both been detained by Soviet authorities after the outbreak of war between the two countries in August 1945, and were finally repatriated to Japan by the Trans-Siberian Railroad. On the way to Japan, they saw first-hand Japanese prisoners in Siberia. "From the window of the train we could see our captive compatriots [. . .] who looked healthy." This was the first report by Kiyokawa after his return and it was published in the June 2, 1946 edition of *Asahi*, helping to ease the worries of family members who were waiting for their loved ones. At the time, Bandō Munemitsu, a paymaster lieutenant who had been conscripted only one month after becoming a journalist for *Asahi*, was interned in a labor camp in the Northeast Siberian port of Magadan. Tricked by Soviet troops in the Northern Kuril Islands into believing he was to return home, he had been taken as a prisoner of war.

Kawamori Shōji, a former paymaster corporal from Sapporo and an acquaintance of Bandō's, underwent an experience in Magadan that differs quite dramatically from Kiyokawa's article. "We were forced to do construction, lumberjacking, and coal mining. During the first winter many died, and due to a lack of decent food many of us suffered from malnutrition." Acquiescing to strong requests from the Japanese government and the families of those still held abroad, occupation authorities put pressure on the Soviet Union to honor the Potsdam Declaration and return Japanese soldiers to their families. On December 19, a formal agreement was signed between the United States and the Soviet Union stipulating that the Japanese be repatriated at a rate of 50,000 a month. Repatriation ships filtered into the Japanese ports of Maizuru and

Hakodate one after another and interview teams surrounded the returning soldiers to report on the situation: "sanitary conditions were good and treatment of the sick was excellent" (*Asahi*, January 5, 1947); "detainees are all being treated well [...] and receiving better provisions than the Soviets" (*Asahi*, January 8, 1947).

For such words to make it to print, they had to pass through pre-publication censorship and permission was sometimes denied at the instruction of the occupation authorities. As a member of the Allies, the Soviet Union could not be criticized, yet such talk would slip in from time to time. "[Prisoners of war who labored as cargo handlers] "wore old and tattered clothing and shoes. Both mentally and physically they appeared completely drained," *Asahi* detailed in a September 7, 1947 article. On April 21, 1950, TASS, the official Soviet news agency, announced that all Japanese other than war criminals had been repatriated; however, there were still many at home waiting for their relatives. On April 23, this legacy of grief was given voice in the column *Vox Populi, Vox Dei*: "All forsaken in just a few dozen lines of an announcement."

Bandō Munemitsu, the *Asahi* journalist, also had yet to return.

Eleven years of life in detention

The problem for those in detention in Siberia was that they became fodder for mutual American-Soviet criticism in the Cold War. *Asahi* did its utmost to remain outside of this growing American-Soviet rift, calling for a peaceful resolution to the confrontation, but it was difficult. When the Soviet Union did not keep to its promised pace of 50,000 a month, American criticism intensified in the autumn of 1948. An October 27 *Asahi* editorial surmised that there must be mitigating circumstances in the USSR and refused to join in the criticism. When SCAP's consultative organ, the Allied Council for Japan, heatedly debated the internment issue, *Asahi* argued in its editorial that repatriation was not a matter of being "anti-Soviet or pro-Soviet" but rather expressed the "most humble wishes from relatives."[8] The resolution of the internment issue would not come until the normalization of Japan-Soviet relations on October 19, 1956. Only then were the remaining war criminals returned and the repatriation finally completed. *Asahi* then published a list of the 1,025 Japanese who were slated to return home at the end of the year. The list also contained the name of *Asahi* journalist Bandō Munemitsu. After Bandō returned to work, in the company's internal newsletter he explained the reasons behind his interminable eleven years of detention. In 1949, under Article 58 of the Soviet criminal code, which concerns crimes by counter-revolutionaries and others, Bandō, his superior Yamada Shirō, and two others were each sentenced to ten years. Each internment camp was slated to charge war criminals but as there were none at Magadan these unlucky four were "sacrificed" to fulfill the prosecutor's quota. According to Yamada's biography, *Black Snow*, quotas were also imposed on prisoner labor. Food was issued to prisoners in relation to the amount of work they finished on a scale of four different grades. When Bandō and others tried their best to ignore this and help all eat equally, they were accused of "hindering the progress of work." Although Bandō was critical of the blind faith in the Soviets' warped work quota policy, immediately after his return he never spoke of his internment experiences again, even to his family.

After having served as the head of the Yamagata branch office, he passed away in January 2009, at the age of 90. Following the normalization of Japan-Soviet relations, articles concerning the internment issue quickly faded from the pages of Japanese newspapers.

But why would the Soviet Union take 561,000 Japanese as prisoners? The number of dead reached approximately one-tenth of the total detained, about 53,000 people. These numbers are estimates calculated by the Ministry of Health, Labor and Welfare and do not include statistics for Mongolia. Incorporating the prisoners as "reconstruction work forces in war-torn areas" was one early explanation behind the Soviets decisions to detain. On November 12, 1947, *Asahi* pointed out: "The new Soviet Union five-year plan is being executed using prisoners from Japan and Germany and other places." On August 18, 1945, Truman had rejected Stalin's plan to occupy the northern area of Hokkaido, so some say that the Soviets were acting in revenge. Yokote Shinji, Professor of Russian Political and Diplomatic History at Keio University, has focused on Stalin's discourse in late 1945. According to Yokote, at a meeting with Chiang Kai-shek's son Chiang Ching-kuo, Stalin spoke of his fear of the resurgence of Japanese militarism: "In order to check such a rise, we need to detain 500,000 to 600,000 Japanese soldiers."

Fiancé on the Quay

The song *Mother on the Quay* was well known in Maizuru port, in the northern section of Kyoto Prefecture, where soldiers were returning from their internment in Siberia. On June 27, 1949, the *Takasagomaru* pulled into port carrying 2,000 Japanese from Nakhodka. The repatriation had resumed after a six-month hiatus and *Asahi* had prepared a robust interview team of thirty-five. However, "the returnees did not respond in the usual way to cries of 'Welcome Home.' Instead, they sang out revolutionary songs, put their shoulders together and stamped their feet, dancing the *sōran* dance, a traditional Japanese fisherman's dance." Having learned about Marxism while in the internment camps, they were led by inmates termed activists and began to be proactive in political movements. Known as the "red returnees," their numbers increased dramatically among the late repatriating Japanese. Disturbances were not uncommon. While onboard the ship, the former detainees denounced the ship's captain for serving dry bread that was infested with insects. The captain then charged all two thousand men for interfering with his duties.[9] One thousand three hundred detainees staged a hunger strike in which they made thirty demands, including such things as a special year-end allowance.[10]

Maizuru, where such disturbances were covered, was also the frontline for the American intelligence war against the Soviet Union. The Maizuru Local Repatriates Relief Bureau was the entry point for returnees, established by the Ministry of Health and Welfare. Within the Maizuru Reception Center's Taira Camp were American officers of Japanese descent serving in the Counter Intelligence Corps under the command of the occupation's Assistant Chief of Staff (G2). Spread out was a large map of Siberia marked with information gleaned on the locations, prisoner numbers, and work details of the internment camps. There were also Japanese staff members working at the camp, including Ueno Yōko. Ueno had a fiancé who had not yet returned and, thinking she might be able to get some news about him if she stayed in Maizuru, she had applied to work at the Counter Intelligence Corps and moved there alone from Hyogo Prefecture. Making use of the Russian she had learned while working in Manchuria, she translated the newspapers and documents that returnees brought back with them. Her supervisor, First Lieutenant Fujio Takagi, particularly desired data on the Soviet Union's nuclear weapons and transport networks. "Those returning from behind 'the Iron Curtain' offered a treasure trove of information," she said. Katō Kiyofumi explains: "The Americans and the Soviets were looking at Maizuru on their world maps, while Japan, including its media, lacked such an international perspective." Maizuru's role as a major port for repatriation ended in 1958, after having served as the re-entry point for more than 660,000 returnees. After learning of her fiancé's death, Ueno continued to live in Maizuru and eventually started a family there.

Escaping from the hell of starvation

In June 1946, civil war broke out between Chiang Kai-shek's Chinese Nationalist forces (KMT) and Mao Zedong's Communist Party (CCP) military. By the end of the year, 1.01 million Japanese had been repatriated from former Manchukuo but many remained behind. In the Nationalist-controlled city of Changchun alone there were 1,200 Japanese.[11] These individuals were often engineers or scientists hired by government organizations, factories, universities and such places, and they were known as "the retained" (*ryūyōsha*). There were also those that stayed behind of their own accord. According to the *Asahi* on January 5, 1948, "CCP Army Advances on Changchun." Reported as the "CCP Army," the Eighth Route Army of the Communist Party forces had encircled Changchun, cutting off food supplies and provisions to 100,000 Chinese Nationalist troops. Hundreds of thousands of Changchun residents were caught in the siege. An *Asahi* headline detailed on August 10, "Inside the City about 200 People Starving to Death Every Day." Japanese news correspondents had all been repatriated, resulting in a reliance on foreign press reports. The October 26 article, "150,000 Starve to Death," reporting the fall of Changchun, was also from a foreign dispatch and included no information on the Japanese in Changchun.

Chinese interpreter Kanzaki Tamiko is one who endured this hell of starvation. The second daughter of Yoshimura Jun, a "retained" professor of physical sciences at the Nationalist-established Changchun University, Kanzaki was only 13 years old at the time. "Once everything else was gone, we ate long grass and leaves from elm trees. We were all on death's door, suffering from malnutrition," she recalls. The only way to survive was to escape to Communist-controlled areas but to do so required having to first pass through the much-feared no-man's land. No-man's land was an area sandwiched between the barbed wire encircling the Nationalist-controlled city and the Communists' own fence line. It was a doughnut-shaped band that stretched to the width of one kilometer around the city. The Japanese formed small groups and escaped. On September 12, a group of about 50, with Yoshimura and other Changchun University professors at its core, left the Nationalists' gate and passed into the no-man's land. "The moment we entered we came under attack from the people inside. They snatched away the little food and water in canteens that we were carrying." The gate controlled by the Communists rarely opened and the corpses of those who had starved to death before they could escape were scattered around for all to see. The following day, just as they resigned themselves to their deaths, a Chinese soldier suddenly appeared before Yoshimura. Having heard of their escape, the Communist Party operative met with them hoping to have those "retained" work for their side. They were finally able to leave this "hell" on the third day. Unfortunately, Arakawa Yoshiko and her son could not continue on with the group. Yoshiko's husband, a research official at an agricultural research center, had starved to death. Having no use for a bereaved family without someone of technical ability, the Communist Party abandoned them. Luckily, after waiting for three days, the mother and son used the distraction of a melee at the gate and managed to slip through to safety. Ending with the surrender of Nationalist troops, the battle is still remembered as a "peaceful liberation" in Chinese military history.

"Retained" scholars

In 1953, five years after the "rebirth" of China under the Communist Party, a group of 26,000 remaining Japanese were repatriated to Japan. These men and some women had worked in government organizations, factories, hospitals, and the like. The October 14, 1953 evening *Asahi* reported on several notable "retained" who were among the 1,493 people who arrived in Maizuru aboard the *Takasagomaru*. One of those aboard was Yoshimura Jun. Yoshimura, a scientist known for his research on radioactive elements such as uranium and thorium, had moved to the Manchukuo research organization, Tairiku Science Institute, from Japan's Institute of Physical and Chemical Research (RIKEN) in 1937. According to Yoshimura's own records, in 1944 he was "responsible for research on the U element near Haicheng." "U" is chemistry shorthand for uranium, while Haicheng is a city in the southern part of former Manchukuo. It seems Yoshimura went to Manchuria at the request of his mentor Dr Iimori Satoyasu at RIKEN. Iimori had joined the atomic bomb development project headed by Dr Nishina Yoshio, a scientist entrusted by the Army with this task. Iimori was responsible for collecting the uranium necessary for the bomb. On August 6, 1945, when the atomic bomb was dropped on Yoshimura's hometown of Hiroshima, he said, "The Americans have beaten us to it. I won't be doing any more research. I want to teach young people." Yoshimura's words left an impression on his family but Yoshimura did not have the opportunity to repatriate and became a "retained" professor at Changchun University at the request of the Chinese Nationalists. The Communist Party did not overlook his talent either. The Communists helped Yoshimura escape from deprivation in Changchun during the civil war and he became a "retained" professor for one of the Communist Party's universities. Yoshimura successfully mentored countless young Chinese researchers and, at the behest of the nationalized petrochemical corporation, he also successfully developed the use of thorium as a catalyst for conducting mineral isolation experiments. The existence of the "retained" was soon forgotten by Japanese society when they repatriated but on October 16, 1964, while Japan was enthralled with the Tokyo Olympics, an event occurred that brought the issue of those "retained" back to the fore.

The Chinese government had announced the success of its first nuclear test. The world was shocked as "new" China had broken the American and Soviet monopoly on nuclear capabilities, developing the high level of technology needed to detonate a uranium-based atomic bomb. The November 7 *Asahi* ran a feature entitled, "The Story behind the Scientific Education Leading to China's Nuclear Test." The story pointed out that while China's technological development had only a short history, the use of engineers from Japan and the translation of Japanese textbooks was important. Although Yoshimura could not have remained indifferent to China's nuclear tests, he said nothing about the matter, not even to his family. Dean of the Faculty of Physical Sciences at Kyushu University in his later years, he passed away in 1975 at the age of 75.

The tragedy of the colonization brigades in Manchuria and Mongolia

Many of the victims of the Soviet attack on Manchuria that began on August 9, 1945 were colonial settlers sent by the Japanese government under the policy of colonizing Manchuria and Mongolia. Just before, a mobilization campaign had drafted 47,000 strong young men to the region but a majority of the remaining 223,000 were elderly, women and children.[12] Three months after the surrender three workers from a heavy industry plant in Manchuria held a press conference to talk about their desperate escape and to tell people about the terrible plight of the former colonizers. Covered on November 10 in the *Asahi*, the story tells of 170,000 refugees "close to freezing and starving to death" and, with only the clothes on their backs, the mass flowed into Harbin and Xinjing (now Changchun) from the hinterlands near the border with the Soviet Union.

Now living in Kiso, Nagano Prefecture, Saitō Satoshi was one of those refugees. Twenty years old at the time, Saitō and her 16-year-old sister were part of a colonization brigade near the Soviet border. Both were driven south by the encroaching Soviet Army and a month later they finally arrived at a refugee camp in Shenyang (Mukden). Throughout the harsh winter, Saitō slept on the floor and foraged for scraps in the piles of vegetable refuse before being stricken with typhus. Falling unconscious, she was almost taken in as the second wife of a local Chinese man but when her strength returned she escaped. When the chance presented itself, *Asahi* and other newspapers reported on the plight of the Japanese refugees. On March 15, 1946, *Asahi* printed a letter from Takasaki Tatsunosuke in his capacity as head of the All Manchuria Japanese Association, a group devoted to providing refugee relief: "This descent into an unnecessary level of misery is the result of soldiers and officials running away and leaving their countrymen behind." Children who lost their parents or had become separated from them during the post-surrender confusion were also written about. One repatriate said that "orphans numbered more than 10,000," half of whom were sold off by brokers.[13] It was not until the summer of 2009 that Saitō saw newspapers from that era for the first time. There were truthful reports about the situation that the former colonizers had faced, rendering Saitō's feelings of frustration all the more bitter. "If they knew what was happening there, why was there no relief effort?" There were various reasons why Japanese chose or were forced to stay behind but in Japan the perspective was more pessimistic: "More than 40,000 have given up on the idea of returning home and remain where life is so difficult."[14] "No one had given up on the idea of returning home," Saitō said. Saitō's younger sister was tricked into leaving the refugee camp and went missing. Saitō stayed in Shenyang to search for her sister, marrying a Chinese husband who promised that: "When the time comes that you can return to Japan, I will let you go." After the normalization of Japan-China relations in 1972, Saitō was finally able to return to Japan in 1979. She was 53 years old. The whereabouts of her sister remain unknown.

There were also many who could not return. In the end, approximately 72,000 settlers died and estimates calculate that 6,500 from the 11,000 of those whose fate remains unknown also perished.[15]

A record of separation

The repatriation of Japanese from China proceeded relatively smoothly but had its troubles nonetheless. By the end of 1958, the number of Japanese that had not been repatriated amounted to 21,287 and further communication with many of these people ceased. In March 1959, a special Japanese law was passed to deal with the legal issues of those who had not returned. For those who had not been heard from in more than seven years, their household registry could be deleted and they would be considered dead. In 1964, under this provision 16,976 were thus declared "wartime deceased." This "postwar processing" included orphans and women who wanted to return to Japan but could not and thus were considered dead by the Japanese government. Articles in *Asahi* shared little concern for those in this predicament. The Chinese government also devised policies to deal with the remaining Japanese. According to a confidential document dated January 21, 1955, the Chinese Ministries of Public Security, Foreign Affairs and the State Council agreed on a plan in which those Japanese orphans that had been raised by Chinese parents and had not yet reached 18 years of age by 1955 would receive Chinese citizenship. In 2005, Ōsawa Takeshi, Professor at Kumamoto Gakuen University, found these documents in the archives of China's Ministry of Foreign Affairs in Beijing. Although there were no documents verifying the implementation of this policy, Ōsawa believes that "there is a high possibility that those orphans became Chinese citizens." As "Chinese" it was impossible for them to search for their Japanese families or return to Japan. Other documents indicated that the Ministry of Public Security was aware of the existence of 1,898 Japanese orphans. Attention was once again paid to the non-returnees with the resumption of Japan-China diplomatic relations in 1972. Former settlers who had left children behind in Manchukuo immediately created the Japan-China Friends Joining Hands Association (*Nicchū yūkōte o tsunagukai*). On August 15, 1974, using the information gathered by this organization, *Asahi* carried a special feature on those seeking their relatives: "A Record of Those Separated." The association offered its data to all of the major newspapers but

Figure 19   On August 15, 1974, *Asahi* began running special articles on "A Record of Those Separated" in a campaign to reunite lost family members.

only *Asahi* took up the offer. This effort was due to Sakamoto Tatsuhiko, a reporter who grasped the great significance of this information. At the end of the war, Sakamoto was a first-year student at Harbin Middle School (7th grade). He witnessed first hand the plight of the refugees, as he was one of those repatriated. "I wanted information about the 5,000 people that were left in China to be known—mothers long separated from their children, siblings from siblings, and husbands from wives," he said.

In the beginning, *Asahi* had vocally supported dispatching colonial settlers to Manchukuo and the paper sponsored a June 7, 1939 farewell party for "The Manchuria Mongolia Colonizer Youth Volunteer Army." Thirty years later, the paper was starting to make amends and, in September and November 1974, it ran a series of feature stories that showcased the identities of orphans. In March 1975, under public pressure, Japan's Ministry of Health and Welfare Relief Bureau started to release all of the related documents in its possession. In the spring of 1981, groups of these orphans came to Japan for the first time in search of their families.

Newspapers Under the Occupation

The atmosphere immediately following defeat

What was it like in the newspaper offices immediately after defeat? On August 16, 1945, the headline of *Asahi*'s front-page top story read "Imperial Broadcast Provokes Sobbing and Wailing." This described well the response of those journalists who had listened to the radio transmission declaring Japan's surrender in the Tokyo main office at noon on the 15th. According to internal records, "Once it started, the tears just kept on flowing, as if a dam had burst. I wonder if there is any Japanese person alive who didn't cry on that day?" In the afternoon a division head meeting was convened in the editorial bureau, where managing editor Hosokawa Takamoto spoke:

> The way in which we have been writing articles until now, employing bombastic turns of phrase such as "one hundred million people, one mind," "a hundred million united," "honorable death," and "destroying the vile enemy" in a bid to move our readers, must now change completely. In this we have no choice. It will not do, however, to swing too far in the opposite direction, referring to as "saviors" today the people that we were only yesterday calling the "vile enemy." The way to go about things is to change a little at a time.

The company president, Murayama Nagataka, concurred.

However, as previously mentioned, local news journalist Muno Takeji resigned on the same day. Muno said to his colleagues:

> We gave our support to the war effort, both individually as journalists and together as a newspaper company. Even if for some that support was not an expression of our true feelings but rather a passive form of cooperation, things are not going to change overnight simply if we put the Stars and Stripes on our roof in place of the Rising Sun. Luckily, the majority of our facilities are now worth next to nothing due to depreciation anyway, so we should offer them up to the next generation of journalists, completely different from ourselves, and usher them into empty offices where they should start up a brand new newspaper.

Some of Muno's colleagues shared his sentiments but others expressed that they "need to provide for their wives and children," or that "your ideas are naïve and there is no possibility of their implementation." The deputy head of the Euro-American news division, Nakamura Shōgo, also left the paper on August 18 but did so for an entirely different reason. Nakamura was a trusted associate of Ogata Taketora, who had occupied the post of editor-in-chief at *Asahi* for many years. After his resignation in the wake of internal conflict, Ogata had become Minister of State in Koiso Kuniaki's Cabinet and chief of the Cabinet Information Bureau. Nakamura had served as Ogata's ministerial secretary. Now, with Ogata joining the postwar Cabinet led by Higashikuni Naruhiko, Nakamura reassumed this role. Once again Ogata was also fulfilling the role of chief of the Cabinet Information Bureau in addition to his ministerial duties and was therefore responsible for censorship. Thus, the stage was set for a major drama to unfold. As Ariyama Teruo, Professor at Tokyo Keizai University and expert in media history, comments: "It was because of its close ties with the Cabinet Information Bureau that *Asahi* became a target for the GHQ."

A new form of censorship

People who now look up the *Asahi* from September 1945 in reprinted editions are probably surprised that the issues from the 19th and 20th are absent. A front-page company statement on September 21 helps to unravel the mystery. "Publication was suspended between 4.00 p.m. on September 18th and 4.00 p.m. on September 20th owing to a violation of 'Article 1 of the SCAP Newspaper Article Regulations,' which states that 'untruthful information, or that which threatens peace and order, must not be printed.'" Hosokawa Takamoto, managing editor at the time, reveals in his book that he wrote that statement. He explains how he was summoned by Lieutenant Colonel Timothy J. Ryan from GHQ on September 17 (although this is possibly misremembered, as the date in question would seem to be September 18), who asked him why he had published "such an improper article," and stated: "the inclusion of elements slandering the victorious nations was inexcusable." The first problematic article was that on the 15th entitled "Plans for the Formation of a New Political Party," which contained a comment by Hatoyama Ichirō, who was later to become Prime Minister. Hatoyama exclaimed that, "A country like America, with its slogan 'justice is power,' cannot deny that acts such as the use of atomic bombs and the slaughter of innocent citizens are at least as much war crimes in contravention of international law as the bombing of hospital boats or the use of poison gas." Then there was the September 17 article, "Explanation Needed from Military." This was a response to a US military report published on September 16 concerning the "typical atrocities perpetrated by the Japanese Army" in the Philippines during the war. "Surely the reaction shared by practically every Japanese person who read the report was that of disbelief that this kind of violence had been committed," the article stated. The *Asahi* article continued, "There are those who voice doubt that there could be a connection between news reports about American acts of violence and GHQ's announcement concerning the misconduct of the Japanese troops." Mori Kyōzō, who would later become director of the editorial board, was responsible for producing both of these articles. He explains that the comment about the atomic bombs was something "he felt he had to say as a Japanese citizen." Regarding the comment on the violent acts of the American troops, he notes how "at that time, after all the regret I felt toward our own behavior during the war, I was determined not to adopt the attitude of blind agreement, regardless of the authority I was facing. I wanted to offer resistance, even if I was unable to champion this opinion in the end." On September 19, author Takami Jun wrote in his diary,

> *Asahi*, which during the war was disliked for being liberal and democratic, is now being punished for being patriotic. I find this most interesting. Since the arrival of the US troops newspapers that were previously printing crude pieces rallying support for the government are now publishing accommodating articles and are consequently not being subject to print bans.[1]

However, even *Asahi* was forced to pander after this point because on September 19 the occupation authorities issued the new Press Code. It comprised ten articles, making stipulations such as: "There shall be no false or destructive criticism of the Allied Powers." A new form of censorship, this time at the hands of the occupation powers, had taken over from that of the Japanese military and the Cabinet Information Bureau.

The mystery of the imperial meeting

On September 29, 1945, there was a rather unusual occurrence. Three newspapers—*Asahi*, *Mainichi*, and *Yomiuri*—received Japanese government orders to terminate printing; the orders were then immediately lifted again at SCAP's command. Each of the newspapers had published a photo of Emperor Hirohito standing alongside the Supreme Commander for the Allied Powers, General Douglas MacArthur. The picture was taken during the Emperor's visit to the headquarters of the occupation on September 27. Many sources have attributed the ban to the fact that the photograph was seen as "disrespectful," but was this really the reason? A September 30 *Asahi* article identified the impetus behind the ban as "an article the paper had published concerning the Emperor's visit and written by an American journalist." The *Asahi* company history, however, states that the ban was imposed on the grounds that both the article and the photograph "undermined the Emperor's dignity and jeopardized public safety," adding that the "official reason" was the article about the meeting. Media historian Ariyama Teruo explains that, "it is certain that the Home Ministry and the Cabinet Information Bureau felt uncomfortable about the photograph but they would not have imposed a ban on that basis alone. We must not ignore the article written by an American which also raised some problematic issues."

The article in question, published on September 29, concerned the September 25 meeting between the Emperor and *The New York Times* journalist, Frank L. Kluckhohn. This *Asahi* article was actually a translation of *The New York Times* article about this meeting under the headline, "Hirohito in Interview Puts Blame on Tojo in Sneak Raid;

Figure 20   The front page of the *Asahi*, September 29, 1945. Photograph of the
Japanese Emperor and MacArthur, with an American journalist's article about their
meeting on the left.

Says He Now Opposes War."[2] When the Emperor was asked whether, in issuing the
Imperial rescript declaring war, had he intended Prime Minister Tōjō Hideki to
orchestrate the attack of Pearl Harbor, he replied, "It was not my intention that the war
rescript should have been used as Tojo used it."[3] On September 29, *The New York Times*
published the Cabinet Information Bureau's reasons for banning the article. "It
is traditional, the spokesman said, that the Emperor never accuses any individual
personally." If the Japanese people think the Emperor himself accused Tōjō, "This
might have led to public disturbances," the Bureau suggested.[4] The Cabinet Information
Bureau also released a version of the Emperor's answer to the question which did not
contain any criticism of Tōjō. Which, then, was the real version? The mystery was
finally solved in 2006 when a record of the Emperor's answer was discovered in the
Imperial Household Agency archives and showed it to be just as Kluckhohn had
reported.

Why had the Emperor criticized Tōjō? At the time, the call from overseas to
investigate the Emperor's war responsibility was growing fiercer by the day and
American public opinion was very critical of the "sneak attack" on Pearl Harbor in
December 1941. Those close to the Emperor urged him to provide concrete evidence
to support the notion that he bore no war responsibility.[5] The diary of Lord Keeper of
the Privy Seal, Kido Kōichi, reveals that the Emperor's statement was in fact carefully
crafted. In Kido's journal we find entries such as "met with Chief Secretary Matsudaira,
to discuss US journalists' requests to meet with the Emperor." Another day it reads,
"met with Prince Konoe to discuss the growing US antagonism," and yet another,
"Emperor sent Grand Chamberlain to SCAP, discussed meeting with the American
journalist." On the same day September 29, SCAP rescinded all censorship laws such as
the Press Law and the National Mobilization Law. Occupation authorities also dissolved
the Cabinet Information Bureau at the end of 1945. The time had come for newspapers
to question their own war responsibility.

Revolution from below

Asahi launched the first salvo to broach the question of how to go about dealing with media responsibility of having fanned the flames of war. The catalyst for this was a plan for changes in the executive staff line-up, demanded without warning by *Asahi* company president Murayama Nagataka on October 15, 1945. Managing editor of the Tokyo office, Hosokawa Takamoto, and others were ousted from their posts and reputedly "pro-America" Suzuki Bunshirō appointed as editor-in-chief. There was also a plan to replace division heads. This "revolution from above" set ablaze a full-blown debate surrounding the hitherto smoldering issue of war responsibility. Hosokawa and his group met in a black-market restaurant in Tsukiji to discuss the matter and on October 17 also got together with company president Murayama to call for his resignation and that of the other newspaper executives. "It was nothing less than a coup d'état," said Hosokawa. Murayama resisted the demand but the movement spread through the entire company. The division heads' committee of the Tokyo editorial bureau supported Hosokawa and the others, forming a "representative committee" chaired by editorial committee member Kikunami Katsumi. On October 19, Murayama addressed employees in the auditorium, saying, "The end of the war has brought with it a sudden swing toward democratic thinking and I believe that this company's style of management will have to change and follow the lead in that direction. [. . .] However, what concerns me is that this will damage the paper's traditional, familial kind of pride." Hosokawa related how the employees jeered Murayama's speech. On October 22, Murayama renounced the proposed managerial reshuffle and resigned. At a special shareholders' meeting held in November, most executives announced their resignations, while Murayama and the chairman, Ueno Seiichi, handed over their positions to the new "company president," and they became "owners." The same month saw the establishment of an employees union and the following year, 1946, witnessed the first "open election" to select chief executives. And as a trial, a selection committee of company employees was formed to determine candidates for the chief executive position.

In the background of this series of changes, termed the "October Revolution," lay the powerful influence of the occupation authorities. On October 24, 1945, Ken R. Dyke, head of the Civil Information and Education Section (CI&E), responsible for directing educational and cultural affairs, summoned representatives from all the newspaper and broadcasting companies. His purpose in doing so was to "develop awareness of their responsibility for establishing free and independent reporting."[6] For the Allied Powers to guide reporting would have contravened both democratic principles in general and the Potsdam Treaty in particular. SCAP had no such intentions. Yet, there was still a lack of frank discussion in the Japanese newspapers on topics such as war crimes and freedom of thought and speech. The CI&E's stance in the first period of the occupation provided a tailwind for this "revolution from below" within the media industry. On October 24, 1945, *Asahi* announced the resignation of its managerial staff members with the headline, "War Responsibility Emerges." Alongside this was a short article stating that, "those at the *Yomiuri Newspaper* have decided to call for the resignation of their chief executive, deputy executive and other executives, as well as all bureau heads, to illuminate the paper's war responsibility." The stage was now set for the "*Yomiuri* Dispute" that was to rock the newspaper industry.

The winds of democratic change

Asahi's move to democratize affected other newspapers, and journalists' denunciation of *Yomiuri* company president Shōriki Matsutarō gathered strength after the *Yomiuri* general staff meeting on October 23, 1945. The *Yomiuri* (at the time called the *Yomiuri Hōchi*) editorial from October 25 entitled, "Condemning the Newspapers," took a virulent tone: "We must sweep away the heads of newspaper corporations and their subordinates, who have ridden the wave of totalitarianism, sacrificing the well-being of their employees and restricting freedom of expression, while they have lined their own pockets. [...] Our colleagues at *Asahi* are already undertaking this task...." Shōriki countered, calling it "an outrageous dispute, an attempt by people who are no more than employees to usurp the company's managerial rights without any legal grounds whatsoever to do so." He justified past actions with the statement: "In wartime, we were all entirely deprived of the right to free thinking [...] regarding the dissemination of information." One of the key members of the group raising the "dispute" was Suzuki Tōmin, who would later become *Yomiuri*'s managing editor. Suzuki joined the Osaka *Asahi* in 1923, travelling to Germany three years later for the Dentsū Company. After being exiled in connection with anti-Nazi reporting, he began working for *Yomiuri* in 1935. He was suspended from his position in 1944 in connection with the Yokohama Incident, but returned to his post after the war.[7]

Left-wing thinkers were not a rarity in the *Yomiuri*, as Shōriki had pursued a policy of employing talented and diligent staff regardless of their political inclinations. In the postwar, a number of veteran journalists along with Suzuki came together and formed a radical committee. They took over the editing bureau, claiming the editorial right to determine the paper's content. On December 3, SCAP ordered Shōriki's arrest as a suspected war criminal and the editorial management dispute was settled on December 11. Among other stipulations, agreement memoranda scripted that Shōriki would resign as chief executive and that a management committee made up of the new company executive and employee representatives would be established. In an editorial published on December 12, *Asahi* held up the *Yomiuri* dispute as "an exemplar of a firm's democratization." The paper stated that: "In the employees' battle to democratize the newspaper [...] the common objective lies in the establishment of newspapers as public organs by severing the links between capital and the managerial and editing departments." In November, the *Mainichi Newspaper* enjoyed its own democratization reform. In the end, an employee committee recommended candidates for executives who were then put up for a vote. On November 10, the paper published a front-page company announcement entitled, "A New Start for *Mainichi*! Toward Clarifying War Responsibility and Establishing a Democratic System." Another article on November 29, entitled "A New Departure for Our Company," detailed: "We shall purge the word 'executive' of every trace of undemocratic spirit. [...] As an organ of public opinion, the paper will be maintained as entirely free and independent." On November 7, *Asahi* published a front-page "declaration," entitled "We Shall Stand Alongside the People." It read: "Henceforth, *Asahi* will be managed through the consensus of all employees as its cornerstone. It will always stand alongside the Japanese citizens and we will make their voice our voice." This phrase, "the consensus of all employees," became something of a buzzword in the media at the time.

"Re-educating" the Japanese

On November 22, 1945, a meeting between the Planning Department of SCAP's CI&E section and *Kyōdō News* discussed plans for a long feature, the first installment of which was to be published by all newspapers as a two-page spread on December 8, the anniversary of the Japanese attack on Pearl Harbor. The remainder of the article was then to be serialized in subsequent editions. The article entitled, "The History of the Pacific War," was written under the auspices of the Planning Department, then translated and distributed by *Kyōdō News*. Looking at the December 8 *Asahi*, the usual two-page edition was now stretched to four, two pages of which were taken up by "The History of the Pacific War." The article offered a harsh critique of the wartime that Japanese citizens had never been informed about and of the responsible militarists. The story was published daily over a total of ten installments, concluding on December 17. The final installment dealt with the nuclear bombs, stating: "It was decided that such weapons should be used immediately to put an end to the conflict and to save the lives of thousands." The CI&E section, which originated the article, had been established in September 1945. One of its main functions was to secure the "understanding and cooperation" of newspapers, publishing companies, and broadcasting stations, to educate the Japanese about facts relating to the defeat, war crimes, responsibility of military individuals, and the goals of the Allied occupation.

"The History of the Pacific War" was also made into a radio drama titled *Now It Can Be Told* (*Shinsō wa kō da*) and broadcast in ten episodes. Hamada Kenji, who was responsible for the series at the NHK, recalled, "The stronger a person's militaristic tendencies, the more violent his or her reaction was to the program. As the drama continued to be broadcast, the number of threatening letters that we received grew."[8] The American scriptwriter for the program wrote in his diary, "The voices of those criticizing the program are forever ringing in my ears. [...] Even a close friend of mine pronounced it 'bad' [...] saying that it rubs the defeat in their faces. [...] But wasn't it constructive, in the sense that it made listeners think about what the facts were?"[9] Takeyama Akiko, former professor at Showa Women's University, explains: "The follow-up program, *Box of Truths* (*Shinsōbako*), was far more gentle in tone. As a result of the strong criticism its predecessor received, the Japanese reeducation program changed course, away from a punitive rejection of militarism toward establishing a more democratic mindset."

This is not to say that there was a total lack of *Asahi* internal investigations probing into matters surrounding the defeat. An article from August 25, 1945, bearing the headline "Financial Troubles Threaten Continuance of Organized Resistance Movement," analyzed the bankruptcy of economic power, while "Defeat in the Scientific War" on September 14 relayed the limits of Japan's technological strength. This was news content that could not have been published during the war. A special edition of the *Voices* (*Koe*) opinion column on January 19, 1946 brought together a collection of criticism focused on the radio. *Now It Can Be Told* was not mentioned specifically but the column stated that there had been ten letters of complaint. At the very least, this response showed a certain resistance to the pre-printing censorship that had been implemented by SCAP on October 9, 1945.

The state of censorship

Pre-publication censorship, where newspaper drafts were initially passed through SCAP's Civil Censorship Division (CCD), began on October 9, 1945. On July 15, 1948, the system changed to a post-production inspection, which came to an end with all censorship on October 24, 1949. How did the newspaper industry react to these developments and what effect did it have on the papers themselves? During the war the Tokyo, Osaka and Western *Asahi* offices each had their own internal review section, in response to the censorship imposed by the military and government. The number of review sections and staff were downgraded when the war ended but in March 1946 the internal review sections in the Tokyo and Osaka branches were once again elevated in status and staff re-hired. According to internal records, Negi Tatsugorō, head of the Tokyo internal review section after the war, lamented:

> It was problematic because the standards for the Allied Powers' censorship were unclear. The only guidance we had was the ten-article long Press Code. Setting aside the stipulation that "news must adhere strictly to the truth," there were articles that were incredibly abstract, like the one that banned "false or destructive criticism of the Allied Powers." [...] You could show the same article to two people and have it approved by one but turned down by another and even the same person might change his approach depending on his mood. It was very hard work.

Initially, it was just a "large print" of the entire paper that passed through censorship but then the policy of submitting "small prints" of each article was introduced to cut down the time that the censorship took. It was certainly an arduous process. The *Asahi* internal review section would release censorship reports roughly each month, encouraging caution within the company. In the first phase of censorship, the subjects most liable to be cut and therefore deserving special care were: SCAP policy, the tragic situation of the Japanese still stranded abroad, and the misbehavior of the occupation forces. Regarding the behavior of occupation forces, Negi related: "We couldn't write 'American soldiers,' so we would use phrases such as 'a number of large men did so-and-so.'" Knowing this, the January 9, 1946 article with the headline "Group of Three Large Men Steal 310 Yen" makes more sense. However, it soon became common knowledge that this phrase was code for "American soldiers" and journalists were no longer able to use it. The state of censorship also changed over time. From April 1946 onwards, the number of articles rejected increased. This was most likely due to an expansion in the number of cases where the CCD itself researched the claims made in articles, as they began to pay more attention to "truthful reporting."

It was now also no longer unusual for other branches of SCAP to issue orders concerning articles that had already passed through CCD censorship. An *Asahi* exclusive from June 24, 1946, featuring news about witness testimony in the Tokyo Trial (the International Military Tribunal for the Far East), infuriated CI&E Major (later Lieutenant Colonel) Daniel C. Imboden, who saw it as an "insult to the international court." The affair was put to a close when both *Asahi* and *Mainichi,* which had also featured an article covering the same story, produced apologetic editorials.

The *Asahi* editorial contrition appeared on July 7, under the title "Apology for Violating Orders." From this point onwards, all articles concerning the Tokyo Trial were subject to "double censorship," passing through the normal censorship department before being checked by Imboden himself.

Failure of the general strike

On May 28, 1946, *Asahi* published a short article entitled "Brigadier General Ken Dyke Returns to America." Kermit "Ken" Dyke, the CI&E chief, had been a "liberal" but his successor, Donald R. Nugent, was "a dyed-in-the-wool conservative."[10] This personnel change symbolized the swing that occupation policies took as the Cold War developed, dividing the east and west and heading in a direction that was increasingly anti-communist and anti-labor union. General MacArthur, Supreme Commander for the Allied Powers who had been responsible for the CI&E reshuffle, made an official statement on May 20 that "mob demonstrations will not be permitted." Meanwhile, CI&E chief Nugent announced that the time for nurturing Japan's newspapers had come to an end. The *Yomiuri* bore the brunt of the backlash. On June 5, Imboden from the CI&E newspaper section judged a *Yomiuri* article from the previous day as too subjective and issued a "severe warning." Company President Baba Tsunego, dissatisfied with the "left-wing paper" being produced by managing editor Suzuki Tōmin who had spearheaded the first "Yomiuri dispute" the previous year, gained SCAP support and fired Suzuki and five other staff members on June 14. These six, who were forced out of the company, occupied the editorial office, which led the police to arrest 53 members of staff. Under pressure from Imboden, Suzuki and the others accepted their dismissals. On June 25, at the high point of this second *Yomiuri* controversy, an *Asahi* editorial issued a plea: "However insurmountable the walls that surround us may appear, we must not despair." The incident at the *Yomiuri Newspaper* was not explicitly mentioned but the point was clear. "These were distressing and painful events, which probably gave the Japanese their first taste of despondence after the end of the war."[11]

Autumn came and the sense of antagonism between management and workers heightened, so workers decided on a "general newspaper strike" on October 5. They sought to push through the demands of the *Yomiuri* journalists who were fighting the dispute, among other measures. An *Asahi* editorial on October 3 opposed the move saying, "We believe it is necessary to make every effort possible to secure the quick resolution of the dispute and avoid the strike." On the other hand, the *Asahi* labor union wavered over the issue. Eventually, after discussions that lasted two days and nights, journalists decided not to participate in the strike. Mark Gayn, a foreign journalist who covered the meeting for the *Chicago Sun*, relayed how "When the decision not to strike was finally announced there was a period of silence. The only sound audible in the room was men sobbing—both the victors and the losers. Even the men who opposed the strike said fear was their only counsel."[12] The general strike was a failure; thirty-seven members of the *Yomiuri* staff left the paper and the controversy at the newspaper company fizzled out. One of those who left, former employee of the politics and economics division Ōnuma Naoshi, returned to his home in Miyagi

Prefecture and set up a regional paper, the *Senboku*. His eldest daughter Wakasugi Naomi, a professor at Waseda University, remembers hearing from her father as a child that he "fought against the control that SCAP was trying to exert over newspaper reporting."

A censor turned journalist

The life story of Watanabe Makio is a rather curious one. His father had been killed by anti-Japanese guerillas in Manchuria when Watanabe was aged 9. Having returned to Japan after surviving a direct torpedo hit while in the Navy, after the war Watanabe worked as a mail inspector for SCAP. He then moved over to the *Asahi Newspaper*, which itself was being censored. In June 1946, repatriated from the Malay Peninsula, his mother experienced a hard life alone as best as she could. Watanabe's friend, who was working for the CCD inspecting letters to earn his college fees, told him that the job was well paid and suggested that he join. Although Watanabe had misgivings about working as the front man for the American troops who had previously been the enemy, he finally agreed to take the position at the end of the year after mulling it over. He told himself that the salary came from the Japanese government after all, so he would not be receiving any money from the enemy. He was employed at the Central Tokyo Post Office in front of Tokyo Station. Tasks were divided among around eight hundred employees who opened about one in every ten letters and read the contents. If the missive contained criticism of the Allied Powers or militaristic statements, the inspector would translate the content into English. Clues to understanding the hearts and minds of the people were also considered important. Prices, for example, were significant. If a letter contained facts stating how much something cost in a particular month it was selected for translation. Watanabe recalled:

> I think that SCAP was trying to feel out what the Japanese citizens were thinking, with great trepidation. In the battle of Okinawa, for instance, American soldiers thought that they had done in the Japanese only for them to emerge from a different hiding place. The Japanese soldiers attacked, fully accepting their own deaths. The Americans must have been frightened about what the Japanese were thinking and probably found it eerie how they had abruptly fallen silent after the Imperial Broadcast announcing the defeat.

Many of the letters deeply touched Watanabe. There was the gravely ill teacher appealing to his/her elder brother to take care of the children and a daughter lamenting how her father would not have turned violent if it had not been for the war. "The sense of guilt at having pried into other people's private correspondence still haunts me. I decided to become a journalist to utilize that experience of coming into contact with people's real-life situations," he said. Watanabe used the money he earned at the CCD to attend Keio University and, after graduating in the spring of 1949, he went to work at the local branch of *Asahi* in Saitama Prefecture. Watanabe still remembers the dismay of the more experienced journalists at being "had again" by the censorship office. He himself wrote an article on the American soldiers' violent acts, which was refused a number of times before eventual publication. He recalls that SCAP still caused problems, even after the abolition of censorship in October 1949. Ohara Masao was a journalist in the local news division at the time. Just before he passed away in 2009 at the age of 96, he explained that, "It's better not to publish newspapers under an occupation." It was much like a final will and testament—strict censorship featured under the occupation of both Japanese and American troops, a fact he had also become painfully aware of during his time in the imperial armed forces. Yet Ohara also explained, "there were positive aspects to the SCAP orders. Take the phrase, 'according to,' for example. That was something that that we thought up in the *Asahi*, after being ordered to be more objective."

Suspicion runs wild

Back on October 18, 1945, when the movement to question their executives' war responsibility was still a hot topic at the *Asahi*, two journalists from the newspaper went to visit the CI&E section. According to the *CI&E Daily Report*, the two volunteered their assessment of the situation at the company "without having been asked to," that the *Asahi* was split in two. Members of the editorial staff who had coalesced to oppose those at the top of the company held that staff with the taint of war responsibility should resign. On the same day, a CI&E official met with a different member of the *Asahi* staff. That employee outlined the complex situation of *Asahi*'s executive staff, claiming that among them were five "bad guys," who had entertained close ties to the military during the war and that the employees had asked the company president for advice. These two events illustrate how various individuals within *Asahi* attempted to cozy up to GHQ for different reasons.

In 1947, General MacArthur ordered the cancellation of the February 1 general strike scheduled by the Japanese Workers' Association. In a meeting with journalists, Imboden, from the CI&E newspaper section, criticized an *Asahi* editorial that blamed the government. Three months later Imboden enigmatically asked *Asahi* chief executive Hasebe Tadasu if he knew about a list of communist sympathizers at the paper. Imboden then read out the list of nineteen names, saying that he had obtained the information from "someone on the editing team," who was also a keen union member. This query was the prelude to an event that would rock not only the *Asahi* but also the entire media world. Three years later, in June 1950, the Korean War exploded and SCAP ordered the Communist Party newspaper, *Red Flag* (*Akahata*), to cease operations. In July, Colonel Jack Napier of SCAP's government section summoned Hasebe. Napier explained, "There will be no problem in expelling the communist element from *Asahi* using MacArthur's letter." The "correspondence" referred to was addressed to Prime Minister Yoshida Shigeru and ordered the cessation of *Red Flag*; it made no reference to general newspapers. According to his diary, Hasebe replied to Napier that he would need new instructions, to which Napier responded, "General MacArthur's general principle was to leave the responsibility of sorting out Japanese problems to the Japanese themselves."[13] Thus began the "red purge" of the Japanese media world on July

28, 1950. By August, *Asahi* had turned out 104 staff members, second only to the public radio station, NHK, where the number reached 119. Kitano Teruhi, who was 27 at the time and employed in *Asahi*'s business administration bureau, received notice of her dismissal on the first day of the purge. She became unemployed with a young family and sick child to support. "Among the remaining employees an atmosphere of great suspicion arose of people believing they might be betrayed at any time." The story was covered in the *Asahi* in a minor article on July 29, entitled "The News World's 'Red' Purge."

A suffering journalist

Ohara Masao worked as an *Asahi* war correspondent during the Second World War, traveling to many battle zones. After the war ended, his reporting focused mainly on labor issues and in his role as a local news journalist he became a living witness to the turbulent years of the Showa (1926–1989) era. His story must not remain untold when discussing the red purge at *Asahi*. In August 1950, he was summoned to speak with managing editor Shinobu Kan'ichirō. "I have taken the necessary measures to process your dismissal from the company," Shinobu said with trembling hands. "I cannot agree with this decision," Ohara replied. Refusing to accept his redundancy payment, Ohara returned to the local news division, collected his books and belongings, went outside, crossed the street from the offices and stared up at the *Asahi* building. Customarily, doing so was enough to fill him with excitement but this time the building appeared unapproachable. He knew that in the future this enormous newspaper company would become his nemesis.

The target of the purges were members of the Communist Party and their supporters. "Some of the students at my university joined the party," Ohara said, "but I did not in the end." Yet, he was not completely clueless as to why he had been dismissed. At that time, anyone was suspect merely for being a "workers' journalist" and on top of that Ohara had been a member of the *Asahi* Third Workers' Union that had adopted a confrontational stance toward management. The main reason for his discharge stemmed from a dispute that had arisen a year and a half earlier, following the purge of workers from the *Kaizō* Publishing Company. Submissions to the magazine *Reconstruction* (*Kaizō*) from labor union sympathizers were rejected, which led to problems with the publication of the magazine's new year's edition. Ohara, who was sent to report on those developments, grilled *Kaizō*'s executives, and SCAP was apparently informed. Ohara was subsequently called in for questioning by Imboden, from the CI&E newspaper section, but the affair was settled when an *Asahi* editorial bureau executive offered an explanation. Ohara nevertheless believes that this was the episode that led to his eventual dismissal. In July 1951, the Central Labor Committee that Ohara had formerly liaised with as part of his job issued a demand that Ohara and another worker be reinstated. However, even when Ohara returned to the office, his superiors would not give him any work and he was left to answer the phone all day. In court, he called upon his colleagues and superiors as witnesses. "The people who gave evidence were truly courageous," he proclaimed. The Supreme Court ruled in his favor and Ohara finally returned to the local news division of the *Asahi Newspaper* in 1958, eight years after his initial dismissal. In the years that followed, Ohara heard from a former *Asahi* executive that the Executive Board had been split on whether Ohara should be let go but the opinion of one particular individual had sealed the matter. His colleagues had helped him but they had also betrayed him. As he told this story, Ohara's voice sank. "There is no value to newspapers if they do not criticize those in power," he declared. This was the moral that Ohara drew from witnessing first-hand the dramatic changes of the times.

The *Asahi Review*

Asahi Review (*Asahi Hyōron*), a monthly periodical published by the *Asahi* Newspaper Company, has a missing edition. The August 1950 issue was recalled before it went on sale and never reached readers. The *Review* was established in March 1946 and its first editor, Iijima Tamotsu, wrote in the back of that issue that "as well as airing the fervor of revolutionary Japan, we would like to provide, in some sense, a space for reflection and calm contemplation." At the peak of its popularity in 1949 the magazine sold 52,000 copies. But why was the August 1950 edition recalled? The July issue had featured a piece entitled "Japan and the Cold War" by Tanaka Shinjirō, head of the research department at the *Asahi Newspaper*. "If we appeal to America for 'support'," the article said, "we should ask for something greater than dollars, namely 'world peace.'" The article went on to state, "it is facile to take the view that the race for military expansion can maintain America's domination in foreign policy." According to the *Asahi Newspaper* publishing bureau records, Imboden, head of the CI&E newspaper section, warned editor Kawamura Takeshi that Tanaka's article constituted a violation of the Press Code. "Ban the production of the *Asahi Review* and fire the head of the editing department. [...] We have to decide what measures to take against the *Asahi Newspaper*," Imboden said. He conceded, however, that: "This time they would make an exception and refrain from taking action." Kawamura judged that the August issue was also risky; it contained an article by Shimizu Ikutarō, which stated: "if public discussion of Marxism becomes impossible it will constitute the final straw for the social sciences." Another selection by Kainō Michitaka critiqued the view that the Communist Party fueled the emergence of a radical left faction among students. Matsuura Sōzō, editor of *Reconstruction* magazine at the time, recollected in an April 17, 1967 article in *The Weekly Reader* (*Shūkan Dokushojin*), that "Before the start of the Korean War articles were not subject to so much scrutiny unless the authors were actual members of the Japanese Communist Party. 'Now, even the liberals are getting their due' became a standard refrain," Matsuura said. Ikejima Shinpei, editor of *Literary Annals* (*Bungei Shunjū*), recalls: "the Japanese military simply commanded one to stop but the Americans were extremely clever in their tactics." This meant that "the newspaper companies were a constant target of criticism and were kept very busy defending themselves."

Kawamura wrote in the joint August/September issue that the recall of the August edition was "a decision taken entirely by the company itself." Publication of the *Asahi*

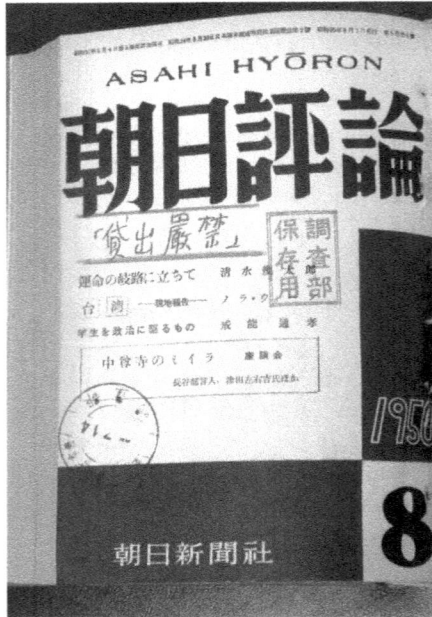

Figure 21　The August 1950 edition of the *Asahi Review* that was recalled and never published. The copy kept at *Asahi* for internal reference is marked "Borrowing Strictly Prohibited."

Review was suspended as of December, which for all intents and purposes meant its journey had ended. The magazine's "Notes on the Suspension" stated: "taking into account the ground-breaking success of the *Asahi Weekly*, we have judged it will be difficult to take the *Asahi Review* to further heights." It was a full thirty years later before Tanaka Shinjirō revealed the truth of the matter in his book, *Scrapbook* (*Hashikurechō*). "Modern readers would be appalled to learn that a magazine had been forced to suspend its publication merely because it printed some unremarkable essay. But in occupied Japan, such a thing was fully possible."

13

Layers of Responsibility

Tōjō's attempted suicide

It happened in the afternoon on September 11, 1945, close to one month after the end of the war. "I'm coming out, just hold on a moment," said former Prime Minister Tōjō Hideki, showing his face at the drawing room window of his house in Yōga, Tokyo. Outside, the American Army military policemen who had come to arrest him on charges of war crimes waited. Hasegawa Yukio from the *Asahi* publications general office happened to be at the scene at exactly that time, having come to Tōjō's house to request an interview. Hasegawa heard a gunshot and his first intuition was that Tōjō had committed suicide. He followed the military policemen inside the house and saw that Tōjō was wounded in the left side of his stomach. The general's face was twisted in pain and he was moaning. In response to Hasegawa's question if there was anything that he wished to say, Tōjō murmured, "I wanted to die with a single shot," but the bullet had failed to hit his vital organs.[1] The Japanese people looked coldly on the attempted suicide of the man who had once, as prime minister, ordered soldiers to "never live to endure the humiliation of being taken as a prisoner." The populace felt that using a gun, as if he was unable to summon the courage to commit *hara-kiri*, was disgraceful; such behavior rendered anything Tōjō might have had to say in the courtroom after his recovery even more deplorable. When the police collected the general public's response to the incident, they found "each and every one extremely critical."[2]

On September 12, Prime Minister Higashikuni Naruhiko's Cabinet decided to make a request to the Allied Powers that Japan be permitted to conduct trials of its war criminals. The Emperor was informed of this move and said to Higashikuni that "to punish in the Emperor's name those war criminals, particularly those in positions of great responsibility, who were once viewed as earnestly carrying out their duty with loyalty," was unbearable. The Emperor asked if there was not some "room for reconsideration."[3] In the end, the Allied Powers refused the Cabinet's request to stage independent trials but it was around this time that the Emperor expressed to the Lord Keeper of the Privy Seal, Kido Kōichi, "It is truly a matter of the greatest distress to me to hand those responsible for the war to the Allied Powers but would it end the matter if I were to take the responsibility upon myself and abdicate?"

Kido responded that the abdication of the Emperor might spark calls to turn Japan into a republic and that this matter required careful consideration. On September 17,

Asahi published an editorial under the headline "The Offences of the Tōjō Military Regime," asserting that "Now is the time to carry out a thorough investigation into the question of war responsibility that will ground the issue in facts." This article marked a breakaway from the so-called "repentance of the one hundred million" attitude the paper had adopted when the war had ended, which held that all Japanese citizens needed to reflect on their role in the war and share a portion of the blame.

What to do with the Emperor?

In 1943, around the time the war situation was starting to look perilous for Japan, some were pondering the question of what the Emperor would do if Japan lost the war. In April 1944, former Prime Minister Konoe Fumimaro spoke to Higashikuni Naruhiko, uncle of the emperor, saying "[the Japanese Prime Minister] Tōjō has been an object of hatred for the rest of the world, much like Hitler, so I believe it would be best to place all responsibility at his feet." Konoe believed that, in the worst scenario, the Emperor would abdicate and enter a Buddhist monastery, and that the Allied Powers would then leave him alone.

In America, public opinion was strongly opposed to Emperor Hirohito. In a study carried out in August 1945, 66 percent of people said that the imperial system should be abolished after Japan's surrender, while 26 percent said that the decision should be "left to the Japanese."[4] As reported in *Asahi* on September 16, Higashikuni, who became prime minister directly after the end of the war, responded to an American journalist in writing. "American citizens can you not somehow forget about Pearl Harbor? We Japanese shall also forget about the tragedy caused by the atomic bombs."[5] On September 18, a group of foreign journalists interviewed Higashikuni and questions centered on the issue of the Emperor's responsibility for the war. "Did the surprise attack on Pearl Harbor take place with the Emperor's consent?" The prime minister was unable to provide a clear answer, saying, "Things at that time were top secret and not announced. I do not know."[6] The Japanese political and financial worlds' verdict on the interview was harsh: "Only diffident answers were offered, which is very worrisome," they reflected.[7] The *Asahi* editorial of September 21 went to press with the headline "The Responsibility of Senior Statesmen," and launched into a scathing criticism of former Prime Minister Konoe Fumimaro. "If not with Konoe, where else does the responsibility lie for making abusive public announcements in the government's name that turned fellow countrymen's faces red with shame, such as his refusal to negotiate with Chiang Kai-shek?" An editorial on the following day, the 22nd, entitled "Where Does Responsibility for the War Really Lie?," emphasized this point. The article discussed that "this time, the responsibility of those who led the war effort must be thoroughly examined."

Putting others on trial

On October 4, 1945, SCAP released a memo requesting a guarantee from the Japanese government that they would openly debate the issue of the Emperor and the Imperial

Household. On October 24, the occupation authorities ordered broadcasting organizations to discuss freely issues like war crimes and the imperial system. On November 11, the *Voices* column of the *Asahi* entitled "Discussing the Imperial System" opined, "Of course, the Emperor must take on responsibility for the imperial system being misused by militarists. [. . .] However, if we rid ourselves too hastily and carelessly of the imperial system, the people of Japan will come to know even greater depths of unhappiness and darkness." That autumn *Asahi* worked hard to investigate its own responsibility for the war. On October 24, the paper ran an article announcing the resignation of the executive staff, including the company president. An editorial of the same day stated, "If we are going to adjudicate others, we must first try ourselves." Furthermore, on November 7, *Asahi* printed a front-page declaration: "We Shall Stand Alongside the Japanese Citizens." Here, the paper apologized for its "failure to live up to the important responsibility to provide truthful coverage and serious criticism" during the war and for its "guilt in letting Japan sink into its current predicament." The editorial from the same day's issue entitled "The Newspaper's New Mission" voiced the opinion that "the newspaper's mission and role from now on was to stand at the frontlines of civilian democracy." It was the duty of newspapers to advance beyond merely examining war responsibility, by making a contribution to expunging militarism and establishing democracy. With hindsight, however, we should acknowledge what accompanied this contribution to democracy should have been a review of the media's own actions and the content of its reporting from the beginning of the entire Showa era in 1926.

On November 15, 1945, *Asahi* featured an interview with Army General Masaki Jinzaburō, one of the leading members of the imperial faction that had been responsible for the February 26, 1936 attempted coup. Masaki stated, "Everybody knows the truth about the explosion on the South Manchurian Railway which sparked the Manchurian Incident [in 1931]. It was a Japanese plot and I find that sort of backhanded way of

Figure 22 Children taking classes outside, having lost their school in the air raids. Shinagawa Ward, Tokyo, November 1945.

doing things absolutely detestable." However, although there may have been rumors that the event was the handiwork of the Japanese Army, at that time it was hardly something "everybody" knew. It was not until the start of the Tokyo Trial in 1946 that the facts of the matter became clear.

Why did newspapers not more aggressively take the initiative to investigate the details of Japan's invasion of Asia? Digging up, analyzing, and publicizing facts that they had not reported at the time could have clarified the responsibility of the newspapers, which had been wielding warmongering rhetoric all along. Instead, newspapers set off down the path toward a new postwar identity without engaging in this important task.

Konoe's memoranda

"I believe that there are two people today who share a fundamental responsibility for the war, namely General Tōjō Hideki and Prince Konoe Fumimaro," pronounced Saitō Takao in a speech to the Lower House of the Diet on November 28, 1945. As a politician, Saitō was something of a rebel and had been ousted from parliament after criticizing the military during the Sino-Japanese war. He ruthlessly pursued the subject of Konoe's war responsibility. The former prime minister had been unable to contain the expansion of the war, which eventually resulted in Japan signing the Tripartite Pact with Germany and Italy. "Konoe has recently been showing signs of trying to evade his war responsibility by flagging up his efforts in American-Japanese negotiations but these negotiations took place as a result of Japan's invasion of China. Does it make any sense that he denies his responsibility, while he is the one who actually started this raging conflagration?," Saitō said. Konoe had been staying at his holiday home in Karuizawa since the day before Saitō's speech. Kosaka Tokusaburō, an *Asahi* journalist who would later become a member of parliament, visited Konoe for interviews, traveling back and forth to his house for three days in a row. On December 6, Kosaka again went to Karuizawa to show Konoe the draft he had prepared and Konoe said, "I leave it all up to you." While Kosaka was still there, the telephone rang and he picked it up. On the line was an American news agency announcing that a warrant had been issued for Konoe's arrest and asked if he was there. Kosaka answered that the former prime minister was out. That day GHQ issued warrants for the arrest of nine individuals suspected of war crimes, including Konoe as well as Kido Kōichi who had served as Lord Keeper of the Privy Seal. Konoe returned to Tokyo and poisoned himself in his own house before dawn on December 16, the day that he was supposed to turn himself in. He was 54. In his suicide note he wrote that he found "the idea of being tried as a war criminal in an American court unbearable." An editorial in *Asahi* on December 17 stated: "It is a fact that the weakness of Konoe's personality facilitated the slide toward the outbreak of war. [. . .] It is certainly impossible to deny the great responsibility he held as a public figure, both politically and morally."

On December 20, *Asahi* published the first installment of the serialization of "Konoe's Records of the US-Japanese Negotiations," written by Kosaka. The last of the eleven installments, published on December 30, included the explanation:

The problem of the supreme command is that the government has no authority to say anything. Only the Emperor had the ability to dominate both government and military authorities. It is fine for the Emperor to remain impassive when times are peaceful but it is not inconceivable that there could be damage done by an Emperor who remains immobile as he stands at the border between the life and death of the nation, as when deciding between war and peace.

According to Konoe's interpretation, only the Emperor could have prevented war between Japan and America yet he failed to do so. Konoe's account called the Emperor's responsibility into question and after reading the article the Emperor remarked to his advisers, "Konoe is just saying whatever is most convenient for himself."[8]

A transformed emperor

On the morning of December 22, 1945, seventeen journalists assigned to the Imperial Household Agency were standing in a line outside the Sōkintei Teahouse in the inner garden of the Imperial Palace. The Emperor, who was heading to his biology laboratory on the palace grounds, came face to face with the group in a set up that was made to look as if it happened by chance. When the journalists all bowed to him, the Emperor removed his hat and politely returned the greeting. "I hear that the food supply is tight. How are you all getting on?," the Emperor asked. "It is extremely difficult but we are doing all we can and managing to get by," the journalists responded.

Emperor Hirohito's first ever meeting with Japanese journalists consisted of this short exchange, which lasted a mere ten minutes. Articles recording the event were printed in the 1946 new year's day editions of the newspapers. The *Asahi* article painted an image of the Emperor as having "a certain refinement embedded within a feminine sort of gentleness. [. . .] From a glance at his mild and trusting disposition one cannot but sense a bit of frailty." The figure of the Emperor as presented in the media underwent a dramatic change in the postwar period—from a "sacred and inviolable" living god and supreme commander of the imperial armed forces to a "human emperor" with a "feminine gentleness" and "frailty." One reason for this transformation lay with that day's front-page story, which bore the headline "Imperial Rescript Full of Hope for National Restoration." The article reported the promulgation of the imperial rescript known as the "Humanity Declaration," which denied the Emperor's divinity. One part of the statement read:

The ties between Us and Our people have always stood upon mutual trust and affection. They do not depend upon mere legends and myths. They are not predicated on the false conception that the Emperor is divine, and that the Japanese people are superior to other races and fated to rule the world.

The draft of the document denied that the Emperor emanated from the "line of gods." However, this was then altered at the insistence of the Emperor himself, so that it was rather the idea of the Emperor as a "living manifestation of a god" that was abandoned as an idea.

On January 25, 1946, General MacArthur sent a secret telegram to Chief of Staff of the US Army, Dwight D. Eisenhower, stating that there would be a great outrage in Japan if the Emperor were indicted as a war criminal and "a million troops would probably be necessary." On January 30, Minoda Muneki, a passionate nationalist who had denounced the idea of the Emperor as an organ of the state, committed suicide in his birthplace of Kumamoto at the age of 52. February 11 was National Foundation Day, the anniversary of the day that the first legendary Japanese Emperor Jimmu ascended to the throne. In commemoration, *Asahi* ran a photograph of the Emperor together with his son. In the picture, the pair are reading the American military newspaper, *Stars and Stripes*, which had been printed by Asahi Publications starting in October 1945. (This is the image on the front cover of this book.)

Democratic rights go undefended

On February 1, 1946, the *Mainichi Newspaper* scooped its competition with a draft of the proposed constitutional amendments from the government's Constitution Investigation Committee, chaired by Matsumoto Jōji. Proposed articles were as follows:

Article 1. The Japanese nation shall be a monarchy
Article 2. The Emperor shall be the monarch of the Japanese nation and possess
            the right to govern the nation according to the stipulations of this
            constitution.

The proposed amended constitution, which preserved the sovereignty of the Emperor much as in the previous Meiji Constitution, was judged by the *Mainichi* as "incredibly conservative. [...] Few will not be disappointed." *Asahi* did not follow the *Mainichi* in picking up the story. Yurugi Eiichirō, a political journalist at the time, comments that the draft was "just one of many. It was not the definitive government draft." One party who was shocked by the *Mainichi* story was SCAP. On February 3, General MacArthur presented to his government section three basic principles to include in the Japanese constitutional revision, declaring that this was a matter that could not be left to the Japanese government. These principles were: the continuation of the imperial system, a renunciation of war, and the abolition of the feudal system. SCAP began to work on drafts of a new Japanese constitution. Meanwhile, Hasebe Tadasu, deputy managing editor of the *Asahi* Tokyo headquarters, announced in a department meeting that he wanted each division to discuss what Japan should do with its emperor system. Following this, he explained, he would discuss the matter with the editorial committee and determine the paper's editorial stance. In the meeting, Yurugi answered that he felt a system like the British one, "where the monarch reigned but did not govern," would be best. Several days later, Hasebe told Yurugi that after discussing the matter the editorial staff had decided to go with his suggestion. However, *Asahi* never made its views about the imperial system clear in its editorials, nor did it assert the view that the governing rights of the Emperor should be handed over to the citizens. While championing for the democratization of Japan, *Asahi* got cold feet when it came to expressing its own views to the public.

On February 13, SCAP handed the Japanese government its draft for a new constitution, which was to serve as a model for the final version. Around this time, the Emperor had expressed his own thoughts to his Grand Chamberlain, Fujita Hisanori. The Emperor reasoned that ministers, who were in charge according to the constitution, had sought his permission to declare war after thorough discussion. Therefore, the only choice he had as a constitutional monarch was to grant them authorization.[9] On February 27, the *Yomiuri Hōchi Newspaper* ran a front-page story entitled "Emperor Considers Abdication." This move put General MacArthur, who envisaged using the Emperor as a tool in the occupation, into a panic. MacArthur ordered the Japanese government to speed up the creation of the new constitution so that the revised imperial system could be made public. On March 6, the Japanese government published the "Draft of the Revised Constitution," which defined the Emperor as the "symbol of the State and of the unity of the People" and firmly established the sovereignty of the people. In its editorials, *Asahi* wholeheartedly supported the constitution but the Tokyo Trial was also drawing near.

The Tokyo Trial begins

The Tokyo Trial, officially known as The International Military Tribunal for the Far East, opened on May 3, 1946. The following day *Asahi* reported that, while sitting in the defendant's seat Tōjō Hideki spat noisily into his handkerchief. He removed his glasses in order to leaf through the Japanese copy of the indictment in his right hand, frowning each time he heard the phrase "war of aggression."[10] Looking at the courtroom bathed in electric light, Nomura Masao, leader of the *Asahi* journalist team covering the trial, thought about the "path that the nation had journeyed through since the Meiji era."[11] It seemed to him that not only were the war criminals on trial but so also was Japan's past since the Meiji era. Nomura, who was argumentative by nature and who disliked any perversion of the truth, would come to be known by those around him as "Nomura Keenan," a play on the name of Joseph Keenan, chief prosecutor at the Tokyo Trial.

At the start of June 1946, the prosecution began airing the details of various events one after another: the Zhang Zuolin Assassination Incident of 1928, the Manchurian Incident of 1931, the events of the Sino-Japanese war from 1937 to 1945, the beginning of the war between Japan and America in December 1941. At this time, as reported in *Asahi* on June 20, Keenan announced in America that, "the Emperor will not be tried as a war criminal." In July, the prosecution turned to examining the Nanjing Massacre and doctors from Nanjing hospitals were called in to give evidence. *Asahi* reported the substance of the testimony on July 27, under the headline, "Three Months of Relentless Violence—Nanjing Massacre is Tragedy for Humanity." On the same day, the *Vox Populi, Vox Dei* column explained how "journalists we know who witnessed the atrocities at Nanjing, were overcome by despair that 'With this massacre Japan will lose the war.' Actually, it was only articles about acts of great courage that were printed and not a single article reported the truth of the situation." Defendant Matsui Iwane, who led the Nanjing invasion as military commander of central China, later testified in the courtroom that the legal duty to uphold military discipline lay with his subordinates and not with him.

The Emperor inspects the nation

On February 19, 1946, the Emperor paid a visit to a housing block in Kanagawa Prefecture where 103 people from twenty-three households who had lost everything during the war had taken refuge. Making his way down the narrow corridors, stopping at each room and standing at the doorway, the Emperor made comments such as "It must have been really awful for you." At some point, *Asahi* photographer Yoshioka Senzō, who was covering the Emperor's visit, pushed aside one of the Emperor's assistants, slipped past the Emperor and dove into a room two or three doors ahead. He set up his camera inside the room and when the Emperor appeared at the entrance Yoshioka took the shot. Until the end of the war it was forbidden to take close-up

Figure 23   The Emperor on his visit to a residential building in Yokohama City (*Asahi*, February 19, 1946).

photographs of the Emperor and slipping past the Emperor in the way Yoshioka had would have been unthinkable. Just over a month had passed since the "Humanity Declaration," negating the Emperor's divinity, and the Emperor's tour of the country started with a stop in Kanagawa Prefecture. *Asahi*'s *Vox Populi, Vox Dei* column from March 3 stated: "It is the heartfelt wish of the majority of Japanese citizens to crowd around the imperial car, draw in close to the windows and shout 'Banzai!'" *Asahi* employees welcomed the Emperor as he stepped out onto the street, yet Ōgane Masujirō, who accompanied the Emperor on his tour in his role as Grand Chamberlain, apparently found the behavior of journalists covering the event insufferable. "Inconsiderate and apparently having no sincere sense of grief, the journalists showered rough questions on those war victims and their relatives whose faces were streaming with tears after receiving the Emperor's comforting words."[12]

On June 9, the Emperor visited a residence for war victims and repatriates in Wakayama City. An Indonesian woman with a child in her arms jumped the queue and addressed the Emperor in fragmented Japanese: "Your Majesty I came from Java." The woman was a former singer, who had worked as an entertainer for the Japanese troops when they landed in Java. She married a man with a Japanese father and had arrived in Japan the previous year. The team of *Asahi* reporters had arranged with the woman beforehand to hear her impression of the Emperor after the visit but they had not anticipated that she would behave in such a way.[13] As the Osaka *Asahi* reported on June 10, the woman told the reporters, "I wonder why the Japanese went to war when they have such a kind Emperor?"

Tōjō Hideki: popularity and indifference

"The Emperor bears no responsibility for the war," declared Class A war criminal Tōjō Hideki in the affidavit he submitted to the court on December 26, 1947. As the evidence was read aloud, Tōjō stared up at the ceiling from the witness stand. "I assert that this war was waged in self-defense and that it did not breach the international laws to which we adhered at that time. [...] Responsibility for the defeat in the war belongs with me as Prime Minister at the time." By contrast, according to a December 28 *Asahi* editorial, the other defendants had "all just passively defended themselves," but Tōjō personally took responsibility for defeat, while also trying to justify Japan's position. Yet, during his cross-examination that began on December 31, Tōjō uttered the statement, "it is unthinkable that Japanese imperial subjects would contravene the Emperor's wishes in order to do this or that." It therefore stood to reason that it would have been impossible to begin a war against the wishes of the Emperor. Stating the matter as Tōjō had served to extend responsibility for the war to the Emperor. Perhaps not realizing the importance of the statement, *Asahi* did not report Tōjō's words. Chief Prosecutor Joseph Keenan, who had adopted the stance that the Emperor bore no responsibility, had to make Tōjō retract his statement. He secretly used prosecution witnesses such as former army officer, Tanaka Ryūkichi, to guide Tōjō in this direction.

On January 6, 1948, Tōjō testified in the courtroom, amending his previous statement to say that the Emperor reluctantly agreed to wage war at Tōjō's initiative.

The tide of public opinion toward Tōjō, whose attempted suicide at the time of his arrest had enraged people, was turning. On January 8, *Vox Populi, Vox Dei* recorded this shift, describing how "You overhear people on the train and so forth saying things like 'Tōjō's regained his popularity, hasn't he?' At the main office, we sometimes receive readers' letters praising Tōjō. [. . .] We cannot ignore the fact that we are now seeing glimpses of feelings of sympathy for him." Yet regarding the trial itself, the public seemed relatively indifferent. As one magazine put it, "When those war advocates now called 'war criminals' first appeared on the stage, we welcomed them with loud applause," the popular monthly lamented. When they fell, we followed along and spat on them. And now we have virtually forgotten about them."[14] The Tokyo Trial ended in April 1948 and that summer a certain rumor circulated in Tokyo that when the verdicts were delivered the Emperor would abdicate.[15]

Talk of abdication spreads

At an *Asahi Weekly* roundtable in May 1948, one month after the conclusion of the Tokyo Trial, Supreme Court Chief Judge Mibuchi Tadahiko said, "It was a matter of great disappointment to us that the Emperor did not issue an imperial rescript at the close of the war stating his own responsibility." This statement was picked up by foreign news agencies, and broadcast around the world. Reuters reported, "Rumors Spread in Tokyo of Emperor's Abdication on August 15." The May 29 *Asahi* recorded Mibuchi's claim that such reports were a "total misrepresentation" of his words. As the announcement of the Tokyo Trial verdicts drew nearer, discussion of the Emperor's abdication spread, both within Japan and overseas. On June 12, *Asahi* published a foreign news story that the Emperor "would like to abdicate" but worried that his abdication would cause social instability because the crown prince was still young and there was no suitable regent. The following day, *Asahi* printed a statement from the president of the University of Tokyo, Nanbara Shigeru: "I believe the Emperor should abdicate." A fervent supporter of the imperial system, Nanbara believed that to make the system "the spiritual cornerstone of our sacred nation's restoration," the Emperor needed to accept his moral responsibility.[16] Public opinion polls featured in the *Yomiuri* on August 15, 1948 put support for the continuation of the imperial system at 90.3 percent, support for the emperor at 68.5 percent, support for the imperial baton being passed to the Prince at 18.4 percent, and support for abolition of the imperial system in general at 4.0 percent. The majority of Japanese citizens supported the Emperor and the imperial system. A signature campaign to preserve the Emperor began and petitions formed piles on the general affairs section desk at the Imperial Household Agency.[17]

The August 26 *Yomiuri* published a pro-abdication statement from Yokota Kisaburō, a professor at the University of Tokyo and later Supreme Court Chief Judge. "How can we build a truly democratic nation if the individual who held the highest level of responsibility in the past does not try to claim that responsibility and the citizens do not attempt to make him to claim it, both sides burying the matter in obscurity?" The September 11 *Asahi*, on the other hand, divulged statements from the director of

United Press that the "highest in command" had stated "the Emperor's abdication was not being considered at all." *Asahi* dealt with the subject of abdication in its news but stated no opinion on the matter in its editorials.

Starting on November 4, the Tokyo Trial verdicts were read in court. In an editorial the next day, *Asahi* pointed the finger of blame at the nation's citizens, saying "the despotic control by the military" would not have been possible without the support of the people. On November 12, the court announced the sentences for Tōjō Hideki and the twenty-four other defendants.

The quest to save Tōjō

"Death by hanging." The voice of William Webb, Chief Judge at the Tokyo Trial, echoed through the courtroom. On November 12, 1948, General Tōjō Hideki and six others were handed the death penalty and eighteen others, including the ex-Lord Keeper of the Privy Seal, Kido Kōichi, were given various sentences. Author Osaragi Jirō witnessed the event from one of the journalists' seats and said it "felt strange that not one person admitted they were in the wrong."[18] Not one of the defendants apologized for the invasion of Asia. On that day, Tajima Michiji, head of the forerunner of the Imperial Household Agency, passed on to General MacArthur words from the Emperor: "I have determined to do my very utmost to add my own power to that of the citizens to overcome all the difficulties with the greatest resolve and see to the restoration of the Japanese nation as quickly as possible." The message was clear—the Emperor did not plan to abdicate. In a contribution to the November 28 *Asahi Weekly*, submitted directly after the verdicts were delivered, the head of the Tokyo branch of the Associated Press stated: "It became clear that the defendants expected Tōjō to claim responsibility and they would be saved. Many of the Japanese public shared this expectation. [...] The Japanese refuse to take responsibility until it is forced upon them." After Tōjō and the others were sentenced, French literature scholar Watanabe Kazuo heard a story from an acquaintance about an American soldier who was surrounded by a group of five or six drunk Japanese in a train carriage one night. The Japanese were saying things like, "Save Prime Minister Tōjō!" and "The sentences are too harsh!" but, not understanding the Japanese language, the American soldier just blankly stared at them. Then someone shouted, "Tōjō is a worldwide hero!" The other people in the carriage all began to chime in with agreement. The American soldier got off the train shortly afterwards and the people remaining in the carriage began shouting "Banzai!" in great elation. "Any ideology that looks to reform society that does not take into account this kind of reality risks being out of touch," thought Watanabe.[19]

Tōjō Hideki and the six other defendants were put to death before dawn on December 23, 1949. The *Asahi* editorial from that day, "A Prayer for Peace," stated: "If we do not take this opportunity to reflect on the weakness of character and moral responsibility of the citizens who allowed the fires of war to rage, then the execution of these seven defendants, and the Tokyo Trial itself, will lose much of its meaning." On the following day, SCAP announced the release of seventeen class A war criminal suspects, including Kishi Nobusuke, who would later become prime minister.

A lingering feeling

"I'm terribly sorry that you were injured, I wish you luck in the future and remain strong." These were the Emperor's words of encouragement to an ex-soldier who had been blinded in the war, during the imperial visit to Aichi Prefecture in March 1950. Tears "streamed" down the veteran's face.[20] The Emperor felt that he wanted to "console as far as possible the victims of the war" during his tour of the country. This desire originated from the Emperor's feeling of having done wrong and wishing to apologize, claimed Grand Chamberlain Ōgane Masujirō.[21] Yet Emperor Hirohito never apologized directly to the relatives of the war dead themselves. The Japanese people greeted their Emperor with tears and cries of "Banzai!" One of those who met the Emperor commented, "My son died in the war, so having the chance to lay my eyes on the Emperor's face has filled my heart with joy." Another divulged, "I lost my only son in the war in Manila so I joined the line of the bereaved and met the Emperor face to face. He asked me 'Are you well?' and I was so grateful. I shall carry those words of his with me to the grave." The Emperor apologized in his heart and the Japanese tearfully forgave him. For both parties concerned this process provided comfort for the tragedy brought about by the war. In 1971, the Emperor travelled to Europe, visiting Britain and France, but there the silent apology and forgiveness ritual did not work. The cedar tree that the Emperor planted was cut down and bottles were thrown at his car. "The past that the Japanese so readily dismissed remains vividly alive over there," explained an *Asahi* editorial on October 14. When questioned about his war responsibility at a press conference in 1975 the Emperor responded, "I am not very well studied in the field of the literary arts so these kinds of linguistic flourishes do not really make sense to me." Was the Emperor really now referring to the silent apology and forgiveness from the past as "linguistic flourishes" and "literature?" An *Asahi* editorial on November 3 asked, "Why did the newspapers not do more to delve into the nature of the connection between the Emperor and the war?" In 1951, former Lord Keeper of the Privy Seal Kido Kōichi, who was at the time imprisoned as a war criminal, conveyed to an executive from the Imperial Household Agency that the Emperor should abdicate at the time of the peace treaty. If he did not, Kido said, it would mean that only the Imperial Household had failed to shoulder responsibility, which would leave a "lingering feeling" and become a "source of eternal trouble." Has this "lingering feeling" of which Kido spoke ever been eradicated? After the Emperor's death the following line appeared in a reader's letter printed in the February 11, 1989 *Asahi*: "Isn't it because the Emperor never apologized that the Japanese citizens never felt the need to?"

14

The Korean War and Peace Treaties

The Kokura Incident

In July 1950, the streets of Kokura City (Fukuoka Prefecture) were bustling with people and the powerful beat of the *gion-daiko*, the *taiko* drum peculiar to the region, resounded all around and enveloped the town in a festival atmosphere. The previous month war had broken out on the Korean peninsula, just across the Straits of Japan from Kokura. The North Korean Army advanced quickly on the continent and in Kokura a blackout was enforced on June 29 following reports of the approach of a craft of unspecified origin. For many of the city's citizens, however, the events lacked any sense of clear and present danger.

Sugi Naohiko was covering the Kokura police department as a journalist. Sugi does not remember exactly what time it was when the commotion suddenly broke out but shortly afterwards he gathered that some American soldiers in the town were running riot. On July 11, a number of African-American soldiers went AWOL from the Jōno camp in Kokura; they were to be deployed to Korea where the war situation was rapidly deteriorating. According to an article published twenty-five years later by the Western *Asahi* in a "re-reporting" special edition, the soldiers stole wine and a large bottle of sake from a liquor store. They then started to target women in the surrounding houses, saying "Hey *mama-san*, are there any girls in here?" The soldiers entered homes without removing their shoes and even opened closets in their hunt for girls. If the search proved futile they would leave. Testimony revealed in the July 1975 Fukuoka Prefectural edition of the *Asahi* suggests that some women were sexually assaulted in front of their husbands.

At that time, SCAP had ceased censoring newspapers but the media still had to be careful when reporting the crimes of American soldiers. "The occupation troops are special beings. We should not go sticking our noses into their affairs. That was the general mood," Sugi said. He suggested that they use the *Asahi* news car to travel the area, issuing warnings to its citizens. In the end, the Western *Asahi* news car drove around the streets of Kokura that night using a loudspeaker to advise people not to leave their homes but they made no mention of the American soldiers. No news about the event was printed in the *Asahi* the following day. The commander of the military police force made a request for information about the incident on July 15 and this was covered in a July 18 article entitled "American Forces Express Regret." However, only the US announcement was mentioned, and no details were given of harm to any Japanese citizens. Author Matsumoto Seichō, who was working at the time in the *Asahi* advertising section, caused a stir when he published his novel *Tattoo on the Black Soldier's Breast* (*Kuroji no e*) based on this event.

Obstacle-ridden reporting

In the early hours of June 25, 1950, North Korean forces crossed the 38th parallel and invaded South Korea—the Korean War had begun. On the following day, *Asahi* announced the news with a large front-page headline that read, "Crisis Threatens Seoul as North Korea Declares War on South Korea." The report of the declaration of war was an erroneous one that came from a foreign news agency. Japan had no diplomatic relations with Korea and there were no Japanese journalists stationed in South Korea. According to *Asahi* internal records, "Because we had to rely on foreign reports of all events that took place in such close proximity to Japan, we often had problems judging how accurate the reports were." Given these constraints, Japanese journalists came to rely extensively on international telephone calls. Those in the *Asahi* Fukuoka general office put an international call into the Korean Army Press Division in Seoul. The June 26 *Asahi* reported how the man on the other end of the phone, clearly struggling to maintain his composure, raised his voice and started to speak more quickly, repeatedly shouting, "We'll strike back by the morning of the 26th!" The tense situation on the other end of the line was palpable all the way in Japan.

Directly after the war commenced, the Fukuoka general office sent journalists to Tsushima Island, which lies around fifty kilometers from Pusan in South Korea. Photojournalist Fujii Kinji remembers boarding the boat and making the journey along with journalists from other newspapers. "A large group of American planes headed toward Korea, making a tremendous noise. Our war had finally ended and yet here we were with war once more. What would we do if we were sent to the front line? It was a time of great anxiety." On the island, the police were keeping a close eye out for stowaways from Korea.

How should Japan have responded to the Korean War? "Korea's War Chaos, Japan's Attitude," an *Asahi* editorial from July 1 stated: "The fires of war are close, yet this is not something that Japan can involve itself with at the present time. We must remain calm, we must not lose our composure." The article advocated a prudent stance, pointing out that the peace treaty with the Allied Powers had not yet been concluded, so "we have no standing to interfere in the disputes of foreign nations." Save for Red Cross aid, the paper provided no concrete suggestions for assistance. Finally, in July 1951, when the cease-fire conference began, an *Asahi* journalist was dispatched to the Korean peninsula. Suzukawa Isami accompanied the UN forces as a military journalist and reported on what was happening in Seoul, which now lay in ruins. He recollects that, under the supervision of the military authorities, "free reporting was impossible."

Subsequently, other journalists were sent to Korea on rotation. Nakamura Mitsugu, who went over in August 1952 shortly after Japan achieved independence, spent a year there, wearing an American military uniform when going about his job. "The controls and the censorship were very strict but the military authorities took care of everything, from telegraphs and phone calls for journalists down to transport, accommodation and food," he wrote in an internal memo.

Switzerland of the Pacific

Before the outbreak of the Korean War, discussion raged in Japan about the peace treaty. Would Japan conclude an overall peace treaty with all of the Allied Powers, including the Soviet Union and China, or separate peace treaties with only some, mainly, western nations, including the US. As the Cold War conflict between the Soviet Union and the US escalated, Japan, a nation that had now emerged from its tenure under American occupation, was questioning how it should make its return to the international arena. *Asahi* supported an overall peace treaty. For three consecutive days from May 20, 1950 onwards, it published a serialized editorial entitled "Attitudes to Peace," written by the director of the editorial board, Ryū Shintarō. "Japan, which surrendered to all the Allied Powers, is now in no place to be making casual pronouncements concerning how separate peace treaties would be better," the piece argued. The editorial advocated that Japan take a position of unarmed neutrality after the conclusion of the treaty, demanding that "the United Nations and other countries agreeing to peace with Japan, or rather any country which shows total agreement with the new Japanese constitution, [. . .] will set a new international agreement securing the safety of this disarmed country." As "the presence of bases for a single nation's military forces within this territory would make the discussion of such measures impossible," the newspaper opposed the presence of a foreign military on Japanese territory.

An overall peace treaty had been advocated by the Peace Problem Discussion Board, to which various intellectuals such as philosopher Abe Yoshishige contributed. The Board's verdict on the peace treaty issue had been announced in January and published in the March edition of the Iwanami Publishing journal *The World* (*Sekai*). Ryū praised the outcome in the April edition of the magazine, commenting that, "it was beyond reasonable that such an opinion had been voiced." During the Second World War, Ryū had worked as a special correspondent in the neutral country of Switzerland. On his journey back to Japan by boat in 1948, he read the new Japanese Constitution in English. "The new Japanese constitution and the diplomacy of Switzerland, the small country that I had spent almost four years in, were definitely linked somehow in my mind," he wrote. This link had formed the starting point for Ryū's stance in favor of an overall peace treaty, and from February 1949 onwards Ryū began to advocate Japanese neutrality in his editorials. As reported in the *Asahi* on March 3, General MacArthur also expressed his support for Japanese neutrality in an interview with a British newspaper, stating: "the role of Japan was to become the Switzerland of the Pacific."

The overall peace treaty movement garnered most of its support from intellectuals, students and workers. There was no shortage of backers within the *Asahi* offices either. Muneta Fumitaka, at the time a new journalist at the Shizuoka branch, was one of them. "Peace was precious and had come at the price of many sacrifices we made during the war. Everybody was fed up with war. It seemed to me that, with its constitution pledging peace, Japan should adopt a foreign policy that would help ease the conflict between America and the Soviet Union, not side with America," he said. Toward the end of the Pacific War, Muneta had served as leader of a platoon of probationary officers, with fifty subordinates. In preparation for the arrival of the American troops, he and his men had dug trenches on the Chiba Prefecture coastline and prepared themselves for death. His strong desire for peace was thus understandable.

"Get rid of Ryū!"

Hasebe Tadasu, *Asahi* company president during the occupation, was summoned to the Allied headquarters on several occasions in connection with editorials dealing with the Korean War. A particularly troublesome one was that of July 4, 1950, entitled "Rash Action will be Admonished." "The Japanese should follow orders of the occupation forces and remain faithful to the occupation administration," the editorial stated, "but a clear line must be drawn, as a matter of principle, between this and cooperating with US military action." The piece criticized the Japanese government that was proposing to offer support to the US military in the Korean War. Imboden, head of the SCAP newspaper section, immediately issued a warning to the Japanese. Hasebe later described America's position on the matter in the memorial collection, *Reminisces of Ryū Shintarō*: "What America did was absolutely right and what North Korea did was absolutely wrong. There was no space for any middle position on the matter. The fact that *Asahi* editorials took the middle position the Americans found inexcusable."[1] Hasebe warned those in the company that the occupation troops were becoming more sensitive. He spoke with the heads of the editing and editorial sections several times about the Korean War, confirming that they understood the following facts. First, the North Korean forces had committed an act of invasion; second, the UN decision to respond had been unavoidable; and third, it stood to reason that America would take military action based on the UN resolution. In conclusion, all editorials had to be written with these guidelines in mind.[2] On July 24, 1950, SCAP ordered the so-called "red purge" to expel Communist Party members and their sympathizers from public office. *Asahi* made 104 of its employees redundant and, around this time SCAP ordered Ryū Shintarō, director of the editorial board, to step down. Suzuki Kenzō, who worked as Hasebe's interpreter at the time, claimed that Imboden slammed his fist on the desk, exclaiming violently to Hasebe, "Fire Ryū, get rid of him!" Hasebe, who was very anguished over this, visited Imboden's house on July 29. According to Tokyo Keizai University professor and media history expert Ariyama Teruo, who has studied Hasebe's diary, Hasebe explained how *Asahi*'s position was "uncomplicatedly in favor of overall peace, permanent neutrality, and against military bases. [...] But it was not actually so simple," he claimed. After Hasebe had obtained Imboden's understanding, the two shook hands and parted. It is not clear, however, how Hasebe managed to convince the normally uncompromising Imboden. The *Asahi* company history states that Hasebe told Imboden that if he wanted to fire Ryū, he would have to fire him first, which Imboden refused to do. With that closure, the issue of Ryū's potential dismissal remained cloaked in obscurity.

Asahi had already decided to support the American side in the Korean War, which made the Soviet Union and the other nations within the Communist sphere the enemy. On the other hand, overall peace would have meant concluding treaties with all of the Allied Powers including the Soviet Union, preserving neutrality after independence, and refusing to accept the presence of American military bases in Japan. The two positions were not compatible and Hasebe began the process of amending *Asahi's* editorial position.

An unexplained change of heart

Asahi company president, Hasebe Tadasu, had come to the decision to drop *Asahi* support for the overall peace plan, which would have entailed concluding peace treaties with all the Allied Powers, including the Soviet Union. A new editorial stance was therefore necessary. At the beginning of August 1950, according to Ariyama Teruo, Hasebe produced a set of thirty-six guidelines and circulated them around the company. In summary, the guidelines read:

1. *Asahi* must clearly state its anti-communist position.
2. Owing to the Korean War, there is no hope for an overall peace plan unless US-Soviet relations undergo a sudden turnaround.
3. Support for the overall peace plan is liable to be mixed with what communism advocates and is inappropriate as the position of a responsible newspaper.
4. Permanent neutrality is unrealistic.
5. Japan can only look to America to guarantee national security.

On August 19, the intelligence division of the Ministry of Foreign Affairs published a memo, "The Korean Disturbance and the Japanese Position." The report criticized the overall peace plan, stating that "the wish to stand midway between two entirely opposed worlds and win the affection of both sides is an utterly selfish demand" and it asserted: "indecisive behavior would [. . .] fuel communism." Yoshino Bunroku, who had worked as the head of the American Bureau in the Ministry of Foreign Affairs immediately after the war and researched the peace treaty issue, stated: "Five years after the war ended the foundation for democracy was in place. The people in government were eager for Japan to become independent and to recover economically and they believed that if they waited for the Soviet Union they would not be able to come to a peace agreement." In its editorial of August 28, "Listen to the Voiceless," *Asahi* criticized the Ministry of Foreign Affairs' memo. The paper questioned "the attitude and tone of officials who place themselves above the citizens, lecturing, admonishing, and guiding their own people," stigmatizing their attitude as "the return of bureaucratic cronyism." However, *Asahi* avoided a straightforward discussion of problems surrounding the issue of peace plans.

The following month, hearing that the American government had begun to make preparations for concluding a peace treaty, *Asahi* published an editorial on September 16 entitled, "First Steps Toward Peace with Japan." The article acknowledged that while an "overall peace plan was what many Japanese people wished for," it said that "the proponents of separate treaties [...] are merely taking into account the possibility that the Soviet Union might not cooperate, not expressing the intention to exclude the Soviet Union. So, in essence, the two viewpoints are not fundamentally opposed at base." But in fact the paper advocated separate peace treaties. In an *Asahi* public opinion poll conducted in September 1950 and published on November 15, the 45.6 percent of people in favor of separate peace treaties vastly exceeded the 21.4 percent supportive of an overall peace treaty. As Ariyama explained, "There will be times when newspapers change their positions according to the international situation, yet it is their responsibility to provide readers with a proper explanation behind their reasons for doing so." The *Asahi* editorial provided no explanations for its change of heart.

Losing out to the facts

Ryū Shintarō, who had spearheaded *Asahi*'s support of overall peace as director of the editorial board, remained the "face of the editorial" even after the company had changed its stance to favor separate peace treaties. In the book he wrote in 1965 after leaving his post, *The State of Japan Twenty Years After the War*, Ryū looked back at the dispute fifteen years earlier, reflecting on how "the argument in favor of overall peace dissolved in the face of the facts."[3] At the time of writing, Ryū had only recently discovered that the US had already initiated "preliminary preparations for a Security Treaty" before the start of the Korean War. This made him "realize how painfully credulous he was to repeatedly speak out in favor of an overall peace treaty," and he admitted frankly how exasperating it was to appreciate the naivety of his perceptions at the time. It is hard to deny that Ryū's analysis of the state of affairs at that time was insufficient. MacArthur's advocacy of Japanese neutrality in the spring of 1949 had in fact lent much support to the argument in favor of an overall peace treaty. However, according to Kusunoki Ayako, author of *Yoshida Shigeru and the Formation of the Security Policy*, MacArthur's idea of "turning Japan into Switzerland" was already obsolete by the fall of 1949, following the success of the Soviet Union's nuclear test in August 1949 and Communist China's victory in October.[4]

In a speech at the start of 1950, MacArthur stated that the Japanese constitution did not deprive Japan of the right to self-defense in case of attack. On June 12, before a visit of top officials from the US State Department and high-ranking military figures, *Asahi* published a front-page spread assembled by its Washington special correspondents about the US government's peace policy toward Japan. As far as the presence of US troops in Japan after the peace agreement was concerned, US policy asserted that "leaving Japan suddenly in a 'powerless state between the US and Soviet Union' would leave it vulnerable to 'threats' from the Soviet Union," hinting at the possibility that US troops would continue to be stationed for there for a while. America also believed that the "neutrality" of any country was unthinkable so long as the Cold War endured. The prospect of an overall peace agreement had suddenly become more remote. Yet, an editorial in the *Asahi Newspaper* on June 25 renewed the argument that an international agreement could ensure the safety of a demilitarized Japan. It was on that very same day that the Korean War began.

Ryū believed strongly that the attitude newspapers should adopt toward the peace problem was not one of "supporting whichever approach seemed the most likely to come about" but rather one of "making demands based on some kind of ideals about what kind of future we want to build for Japan [. . .] and ideals of our own making." The Peace Treaty was signed in San Francisco on September 8, 1951 by forty-nine countries, including the United States. The communist nations—the Soviet Union, Czechoslovakia, and Poland—did not sign the treaty. The September 10 *Asahi* editorial accepted the existence of the US-Japan Security Treaty, which was signed at the same time, but also stressed its strict application, pointing out that the treaty's sole purpose was to protect Japan from foreign military attacks. With the Korean War and the remilitarization of Japan steadily advancing in response, Ryū's "ideals" were becoming increasingly irrelevant.

The road to remilitarization

"It is remarkable how many wars in recent years have been waged in the name of the right to national self-defense. [. . .] I believe that your argument is harmful and without benefit," said Yoshida Shigeru during a June 28, 1946 Lower House representatives debate over the drafting for the new constitution. His remarks met with a round of applause. Yoshida was responding to Nosaka Sanzō, an elite member of Japan's Communist Party, who had called into question the clause on the subject of abandoning war, stating that "I think we would not have any objections to calling a war just if it was fought in self-defense by a country that had been invaded." Looking at the situation now, it seems that the "conservative" and "revolution" parties espoused statements normally ascribed to their opponents. The Japanese constitution, which relinquished military force, was made public in November. The Korean War that took place four years later changed people's thinking on the matter. On July 8, 1950, General MacArthur ordered the Japanese government to strengthen its police force. He "permitted" the establishment of a 75,000-strong National Police Reserve and the expansion of the Japan Coast Guard by 8,000 troops. An *Asahi* editorial from the following day endorsed the founding of the National Police Reserve, which would become the basis of the Self-Defense Forces, as a simple reinforcement of the police. "It is a question of strengthening the police force from the perspective of what is necessary for public safety."

In a press conference held on April 28, 1952, Yoshida announced that the country would not be militarized before the nation had regained its power. "This is the reason why we have provisionally secured the safety of the Japanese nation with the Security Treaty," Yoshida proclaimed. He added, "The constitution will not be amended."[5] Yet even the Americans were aware of the contradictions with the Japanese constitution that this move entailed. Frank Kowalski, who was involved in the formation of the National Police Reserve, later wrote that the Japanese "turned their back on their noble burden, bringing disrespect to their constitution and stepping forward instead into a chaotic future." Hasebe Tadasu, the *Asahi* company president, revealed his true feelings on the matter in a memo dated 1950: "However we dress it up the National Police Reserve is nothing other than an army. The law that Article 9 sets out in the constitution, renouncing militarization, has already been infringed," he opined. An editorial on April 30, 1952 expressed concern about how the National Police Reserve seemed more like a military force but at the same time positively assessed Yoshida's denial of Japan's remilitarization as "logically consistent behavior for the person responsible for concluding the Security Treaty with America." In the same year, the National Police Reserve became the "National Safety Forces." An *Asahi* editorial from October 16 "felt that this was nothing more than a play on words to avoid criticism that this was a violation of the constitution," but the paper still attempted to draw a line between the two. "One of the main factors that distinguishes the army from the police, regardless of the pretext under which this is done, hangs on whether the force is sent overseas." Shimada Junkō, who covered politics for the *Asahi* newspaper at the time, viewed the National Police Reserve as "a step toward remilitarization but the thought caused no real discomfort." In this manner, Japanese militarization progressed.

The self-defense forces and the constitution

The power of the National Police Reserve continued to grow and in 1954 it began a new life as the Self-Defense Forces. In response to this change, a lengthy debate began about whether such a shift was constitutional. Answering questions in parliament in November 1953, Prime Minister Yoshida Shigeru stated, "the Self-Defense Forces might be military but they possess no military force and are therefore within the bounds of the Constitution." The phrase "armed forces without military power" was thus introduced into the lexicon.

Asahi showed a critical attitude in its November 5 editorial but its position was ultimately unclear: "It is regrettable that the nation is split over the defense question. While protecting our peaceful constitution [...] we cannot but hope that the factions of each party come together and pool their knowledge in a non-partisan fashion [...] to discover a solution for the nation which leaves space for us to defend ourselves." The director of the editorial board at the time was still Ryū Shintarō. An editorial on December 16 expressed an opinion on the nation's right to self-defense: "The majority of Japanese citizens are of the mind that the power to defend ourselves effectively is necessary. We agree with this." Yet, after this pronouncement *Asahi* continued to criticize the state of the Self-Defense Forces, for example pointing out its connections with old members of the Japanese military. An article on March 6, 1954 commented: "There is a grave danger that we will veer away from the constitution. [...] Why is this matter pushed so rashly, without garnering public support?" Another piece on March 13 stated: "There is concern that what began 'for the purposes of self-defense' will be turned into 'a means for solving international disputes' and then 'for invasion.'"

In December 1954, Hatoyama Ichirō became prime minister and expressed his opinion that the existence of those forces "on a scale necessary for self-defense" was within the bounds of the constitution. An *Asahi* editorial from May 3, 1964 stated: "we cannot but approve of the minimum of Self-Defense Forces based on the right to self-defense. The question today is how we, as Japanese citizens, should control the ceaseless expansion of our military forces." An editorial two years later, on May 3, 1966, touched on the results of a survey that found that while most Japanese citizens regarded the Self-Defense Forces as necessary, they were opposed to revising Article 9 of the Constitution. The editorial called the attitude of unarmed neutrality "the most desirable position," but stated that, "as general public support of this stance is not in evidence at present, it would be practically speaking nigh on impossible to realize." What was the crux of *Asahi*'s arguments concerning the peace, remilitarization, and the constitution? The editorial, entitled "A Split in National Opinion," from December 13, 1951, after the overall peace treaty option had failed, opined that "democracy has clearly not arrived" and demanded that efforts be made so as to reach unity of opinion. Amid the growing antagonism between East and West on the international stage, and a divided Japan, what *Asahi* viewed as most necessary was seemingly the "consensus" of the people.

15

The Bandung Conference

No longer "Asia's orphan"

On April 18, 1955, a great crowd had assembled in the center of Bandung, an Indonesian city about one hundred and twenty kilometers away from the capital Jakarta. The masses had come to catch a glimpse of Indian Prime Minister Jawaharlal Nehru, the Premier of the People's Republic of China (PRC) Zhou Enlai, the Egyptian Prime Minister Gamal Abdel Nasser, and the President of Indonesia, Sukarno. This was the opening of the Bandung Conference, the world's first Asia-Africa Conference, which had brought twenty-nine non-Western countries to assemble in the host nation, Indonesia. *Asahi* had first covered the conference half a year previously in September 1954. Asked whether Japan would be invited, the Indonesian President replied that there would be "no discrimination against any country" though in fact Japan's participation was still an unknown by that point. In December 1954, Hatoyama Ichirō became Japan's prime minister after the fall of Yoshida Shigeru. In contrast to Yoshida's pro-US stance, Hatoyama's Cabinet favored an autonomous direction in its foreign policy and proposed looking into improving relations with Communist China and the Soviet Union. The conference was a chance to make a good impression for the new Japanese government. A month before the conference opened on March 15, 1955, *Asahi* published behind-the-scenes details about Japan's participation. In discussing the government's motivation to attend, the paper suggested that Japan, which had grown estranged from the rest of Asia since its loss in the Second World War, was looking for "the chance to become 'friends' with the other Asian countries and leave behind its status as 'Asia's orphan.'" Furthermore, the conference would provide the opportunity for Japan "to affirm its non-aggression stance and its desire to actively cooperate with the other members." In order to attend, Japan first needed to garner America's approval. American Assistant Secretary of State for Far Eastern Affairs, Walter S. Robertson, had warned of the Chinese communist threat and opposed Japan's participation in the conference. Secretary of State John Foster Dulles, however, believed that it was better for pro-American nations such as Japan to attend the conference and "neutralize" the arguments of nations such as China and India. The Japanese Ambassador in America, Iguchi Sadao, sent a telegram to Japanese Foreign Minister Shigemitsu Mamoru on February 3, reporting: "the American side is strongly in favor of the active participation of free nations, as intimated by Dulles." Eventually, the US agreed to Japanese participation.

Figure 24   (From right) Japanese representative Takasaki Tatsunosuke, interpreter Okada Akira and Chinese Prime Minister Zhou Enlai talking in the hotel lobby, April 1955.

A secondary problem was the question of whom Japan would send as its representative because the political situation was in flux. Foreign Minister Shigemitsu could not leave Japan while parliament was in session. He planned to send his trusted ally Tani Masayuki, an adviser at the Foreign Ministry, but was told by Indonesia to send somebody who was at least a member of the Cabinet. It was not until April 1, when the conference's start date was rapidly approaching, that the government decided to send Takasaki Tatsunosuke. At the time Takasaki was head of the Economic Council Agency (the predecessor of the Economic Planning Agency). The *Vox Populi, Vox Dei* column on April 2 cast doubt on the decision to send him with the comment: "The head of the Economic Council Agency, Takasaki, is not exactly a minor player but surely a figure like the Foreign Minister would be able to make better use of a historic conference like this one?" After all, who was Takasaki Tatsunosuke anyway?

The "cowboy" representative

The 70-year-old Japanese representative at the Bandung Conference, Takasaki, had started his career in the world of finance before becoming head of the Economic Council Agency. As such, he was somewhat unique in the world of politicians. Born in Osaka, Takasaki graduated from a fisheries college before doing an apprenticeship in the canned goods industry in the US and Mexico. It was at this time that he forged a relationship with Herbert Hoover, who was later to become a US President. After returning to Japan, Takasaki founded his own canned goods company. During the war he became the director of the Manchurian Industrial Development Company. After defeat he was head of the Japanese Citizen's Association abroad and worked hard to secure the return of Japanese from overseas territories. Takasaki later became the first president of the Electric Power Development Company and was involved with the construction of Sakuma Dam, cited as the largest in Japan. When Takasaki joined the Cabinet, *Asahi* on December 11, 1954, introduced him as "an innovative businessman" who was capable of "talking big like a cowboy," but also "was often criticized as being nothing more than an international-scale bluffer." Former *Asahi* journalist Hatano Kōichi, who came to know Takasaki, reflects that he was "a man with a straight-talking and frank nature, who was able to put things in perspective."

At the time when the selection of the Japanese representative was being hotly debated, Takasaki was demonstrating his ability as the chairperson at the meeting of the UN Economic Commission for Asia and the Far East (ECAFE) held in Tokyo. With the parliament aiming to prioritize economic affairs at the upcoming Bandung Conference, Prime Minister Hatoyama's gaze ultimately settled upon the trustworthy Takasaki as someone internationally inclined and well versed in economic matters. Takasaki straightaway put in a request to the Foreign Ministry to be provided with a Chinese interpreter and it was agreed that Okada Akira, a China affairs specialist from the Ministry, would accompany him to translate. Okada subsequently worked at the Japanese Consulate General in Hong Kong and as Japanese Ambassador to Switzerland. Many of his career-specific memories have faded but he says that the Bandung meeting left a particularly strong impression. The conference was to be mainly carried out in English and a Chinese interpreter would probably not have been necessary. Okada recalls the incident with a frown. "Before he went, Takasaki intended to meet Premier Zhou Enlai and my bosses in the Foreign Ministry were not too pleased at Takasaki dragging me along," he said.

There was already conflict between the two "Chinese" states: the People's Republic of China on the mainland and the Republic of China on the island now better known as Taiwan. Japan had diplomatic relations with the latter but it was the former that was invited to the Bandung Conference. There was the danger that the debate over Taiwan would erupt into a US-supported military collision and much attention was paid to understanding how China was positioning itself. Under such circumstances, Japan's Foreign Ministry, which prioritized relations with the US, was concerned with how Takasaki would behave as the "cowboy" and sent a selection of Foreign Minister Shigemitsu's trusted advisors, including Tani Masayuki and Kase Toshikazu, to serve as "spies" of Takasaki. The two had the task of supervising Takasaki's "amateur foreign policy." Takasaki, however, was not the kind of man to go along the path set out by the Foreign Ministry.

Secret meetings between Japan and China

As the People's Republic of China had only recently been established, Premier Zhou Enlai wished to focus on internal policy and his approach to foreign policy at the Bandung Conference was therefore one of "smiling diplomacy." To facilitate discussions aimed at ameliorating relations with Japan as well, Zhou had brought Liao Chengzhi as an interpreter. Liao had been born and raised in Japan and spoke with a Tokyo accent.

On the evening of the first day of the conference, April 18, 1955, Takasaki sent a telegram to Foreign Minister Shigemitsu Mamoru describing the events of that morning: "Ahead of the opening ceremony that morning, the representatives from each nation were waiting in the hotel lobby to greet the arrival of the Indonesian President. Coincidentally, I happened to be sitting next the Chinese representative and the two of us exchanged greetings. This caught the attention of the press and journalists provided exaggerated reports of it." Okada, however, asserts, "It was not a coincidence. Zhou Enlai's interpreter Liao and I met before the event and arranged it." Takasaki and Zhou, understanding that Liao and Okada were old friends, left it to the two interpreters to set up a meeting for them. Early on the morning of April 22, Liao came to collect Takasaki at his hotel. Aware that there was a chance they would be followed by journalists, they changed cars midway through the journey before arriving at Zhou's lodgings. The windows were shut tight and the secret meeting began. Although it was not an official meeting, it marked the first time the two countries had come together for talks since the end of the Second World War. With the aim of improving relations, the two spoke for an hour and twenty-five minutes about issues that would lead to improving relations such as how to expand commerce and the possibility of establishing some form of governmental representation in each other's country.

The first time *Asahi* reported the secret meeting was in the April 23 morning edition, when it printed a transcript of an Associated Press wire report. The April 24 evening edition of the newspaper published a more detailed report from special correspondent Ueyama Masaji entitled, "Prime Minister Zhou's Revelations to Takasaki—Restore Diplomatic Relations Quickly—China Will Help with Return of Japanese War Criminals." The meeting became public knowledge immediately but there are details that stayed hidden for almost thirty years. These were finally revealed in Okada's memoir, published only after he left his post in 1983.[1] Okada relates how the following exchange took place as part of the secret meeting. When the meeting was drawing to a close, Takasaki abruptly asked Zhou, "Are you not going to unify with Taiwan?" The atmosphere suddenly grew tense. Zhou stiffened and the silence continued for a while before he replied that he would like to say more on the matter and suggested that they speak about it at a later date. Upon returning to the hotel, Okada reported the events to his superiors at the Foreign Ministry who were furious, shouting: "Don't push your luck! You're not supposed to talk about Taiwan!" The Japanese cancelled the next meeting and it never took place. The trusting relationship between Zhou and Takasaki established at the Bandung Conference, however, did leave its mark, with Liao's and Takasaki's initials used to name the "LT," a quasi-government trade arrangement established at a later date.

A pink flag

The star of the Bandung Conference was without a doubt the PRC's Premier Zhou Enlai. He had made his international debut the previous year at the Geneva Conference that had put an end to the First Indochina War between Vietnam and France. US Assistant Secretary of State Walter Robertson, who witnessed Zhou's agility first hand at the time, advised the Japanese Ambassador to the US, Iguchi Sadao, that Zhou was "a pretty shrewd and astute man whom they should keep an eye on." Iguchi reported this by telegram to the Japanese Foreign Minister, Shigemitsu Mamoru. Attending the Bandung Conference had nearly cost Zhou his life because the plane he was scheduled to fly crashed into the sea close to Borneo. In fact, Zhou was not on board but the crash killed the journalists and members of the Chinese representative team who had boarded. It is believed that a secret agent from the KMT, the Chinese Nationalist Party, planted a bomb on the plane in Hong Kong, but allegedly the Chinese did nothing to prevent or delay the flight, even though they suspected sabotage.[2] Until the conference began on April 18, Western nations had misgivings about Zhou. They thought it likely that he would be outspoken in his advocacy of Communism and his criticism of Europe and America. In his much-scrutinized conference speech, Zhou defied expectations and spoke with reserve. "The Chinese representative team has attended this conference out of a hope for solidarity and does not wish to argue with other nations," he announced. *Asahi* commented in its April 21 edition that Zhou had waved "a pink flag in place of a red one." On April 23, *Asahi* quoted an article from *The New York Times*, stating that Zhou had amended his speech by hand directly before presenting it. The paper asserted that, "he was aspiring to form friendly relations with the peoples of all nations except America, and hoped for solidarity."

At his first meeting with the Japanese representative Takasaki Tatsunosuke, Zhou Enlai proposed that, "the two nations arrive at a joint consensus for a simplified writing system of Chinese characters, passing this down as a cultural heritage for Japanese and Chinese citizens for a hundred or a thousand years to come." Japan and China discussed the proposal on several subsequent occasions and the issue was actively debated in *Asahi*'s letters to the editor section. The suggestion would have been hard to put into practice but it was a thought-provoking idea. Rosihan Anwar, a prominent Indonesian journalist who covered the Bandung Conference, notes that although Zhou's speech and behavior at the conference were memorable, it was the reception in the Chinese Embassy that left the deepest impression. Abandoning the Chinese Mao suit that he had worn to the official meetings, Zhou came dressed in a light blue Western suit. His entourage kept their Mao suits. "This conveyed the message that he was no longer serving as the representative of his nation and that he wanted to speak freely with the people around him, regardless of questions of nationality," Rosihan said.

Given that the UN had adopted a critical resolution against mainland China for its role in the Korean War as an "aggressor," the prevalent picture of China at the time was that of an "ominous Communist nation." However, Zhou was able to turn that image around instantaneously. By contrast, what was the general impression of "Asia's orphan," Japan?

Deference and discretion

In her home in an exclusive neighborhood in Jakarta, Herawati Diah searches her memory from a half-century ago. In the 1930s, Diah studied in Japan at the "High School" in Meguro and then continued on to Barnard College in New York. After the

Pacific War she and her husband returned to Indonesia to start a newspaper. As a trailblazing female journalist, she covered the 1955 Bandung Conference but she does not remember the name of Takasaki Tatsunosuke from the Japanese delegation. "Takasaki? I don't remember. The Japanese delegation wasn't very noticeable and I didn't cover them," she added. "The Bandung Conference was held only about ten years after Japanese rule ended, and along with Japanese words like *kempeitai* (military police) and *rōmusha* (physical or forced laborers), a negative image of Japan pervaded."

The conference was held in a Dutch colonial era building that had been renamed the "Greater East Asia Assembly Hall" during the Japanese occupation. One of the Japanese delegates was foreign affairs bureaucrat Kase Toshikazu. During the war Kase had been among those to draft the "Greater East Asia Manifesto" at the 1943 Greater East Asia Conference, which brought together the leaders of the Asian countries under Japan's influence. Wan Waithayakon, who had represented Thailand at the 1943 conference, came to Bandung in his new role as the Thai Foreign Minister. Journalist Rosihan Anwar describes how "the Japanese delegation was quiet and wary of its surroundings. Even at the meeting they never spoke. They gave the impression they didn't want to draw attention to themselves," he said. Japanese delegate Takasaki Tatsunosuke recalled, "because the political issues were extremely delicate, the policy was to keep silent."[3] Instead, the Japanese delegates put their efforts into fostering relations in the business world. They presented delegates of emerging countries in Africa with Japanese-made watches and cameras, appealing to them with Japanese technology.

The May 2, 1955 issue of *Asahi* published French journalist Robert Guillain's long article for *Le Monde* describing how "Japan's delegation came to the conference quietly, entering on tiptoes." This is the way the "Japanese at Bandung" were painted. The various Asian countries gathered at the conference had been used under the Japanese military occupation as servants, but now peaceful Japan did not even hint at putting on airs. In a complete transformation, the nation now appeared to be a thoroughly "unknown guest." Yesterday's "Great Japan" was now meek Japan. At this meeting, Japan observed postwar Asia and while other countries gave speeches and had discussions, Japan prepared to expand its commerce and trade. Guillain's article closed with: "To conclude, such 'deference' by Japan was in the end likely 'discretion.'" In the art of political maneuvering, what Guillain describes as "meekness" and "discretion" were Japan's tentative first steps of re-entering the Asian stage.

The point of departure for Asian diplomacy

The question at hand was how should Japan interact with Asia? On April 18, 1955, the opening day of the Bandung Conference, which was a starting point for Japan's post-war Asian foreign policy, *Asahi* published an editorial entitled, "Hopes for the Bandung Conference." The article stated, "there is a deep sense of responsibility for acts perpetrated against Asian countries by Japan in the past." It went on to request that Japan "make clear what contribution it was capable of making, whether that be with skills or with capital [. . .] and that Japan should thoroughly discuss with others how it is truly rebuilding itself as a peaceful nation so that it can gain acceptance." Japanese delegate Takasaki Tatsunosuke's address overlapped on many points with the *Asahi* editorial and in his speech on the second day of the conference Takasaki admitted that Japan had "inflicted war on its close Asian neighbors." He also pointed out, from Japan's singular position as the only nation ever to have experienced a nuclear bomb, that to resolve international disputes by force invited frightening disaster. Japan, Takasaki closed his speech by saying, "wants to progressively promote economic cooperation with each nation." *Asahi*'s special correspondent at Bandung, Ueyama Masaji, reported: "Japan is for the most part playing the leading role on the economic stage."[4] However, at the conference Japan played a minor role. An article on April 25, following the close of the conference, recapped: "Japan's political opinions were not given serious consideration and attention was limited to only its economic position." The evening edition of the *Asahi* on the 26th reprinted an article from the German paper, *Frankfurter Allgemeine*, that was even more pointed: "Japan was able to do little more than act as an observer. [...] Japan can be seen as the violet that blossomed on an isolated island protected by the United States of America."

In April 2005, heads of state met in Jakarta to mark the 50th anniversary of the Bandung Conference. Prime Minister Koizumi Junichirō again announced "feelings of deep remorse and a heartfelt apology" for Japan's past aggression. The prime minister expressed "Japan's determination to be a peaceful nation" and proposed measures to support economic development. Japan had become an economic superpower and, for a time, suffered criticism for being an "economic imperialist" but the country was no longer a shrinking violet. The April 12, 2005 editorial of the *Asahi* pointed to this "modest approach" as the "necessary realism of diplomacy" for Japan to be accepted by its close neighboring countries. This move echoed French journalist Guillain's observation decades earlier of Japan's "deference" and "discretion" at Bandung. Now, it was said, Japan's "remorse and apology" was made in consideration of the cooling off of Sino-Japanese relations over the "history problem." The discussions between Zhou Enlai and Takasaki at Bandung had helped pave the way for postwar Sino-Japanese relations. Relations with China were as central to Japan's relationship with Asia fifty years ago as they are today.

Restoring Japanese-Soviet Relations and Joining the United Nations

The Hatoyama boom

Japanese-Soviet relations, severed as a consequence of the Second World War, were restored in October 1956. The change of Japan's administration to the Democratic Party set the stage for the resumption. In December 1954, Hatoyama Ichirō of the Democratic Party became prime minister after a mass resignation by Yoshida Shigeru's Cabinet under the Jiyūtō Party and the following January Hatoyama dissolved the Lower House of the Diet. Hatoyama made his pet project normalization of Japanese-Soviet diplomatic relations, a campaign platform promise in the general election. During his first speech in Sendai, in front of an audience of about seven thousand, he proclaimed, "in the spirit of fraternity we will even restore diplomatic relations with the communist nation."

Hatoyama was so popular that he was surrounded by mobs of people everywhere he went during his election campaign. An article in the evening *Asahi* on February 16, 1956, entitled "Hatoyama Boom is Something to be Seen Rather than Heard," reported that "Prime Minister Hatoyama's 'hook' to beat out former Prime Minister Yoshida was to use language couched in the subtleties of kindness and to foster a mood of optimism." Hatakeyama Takeshi, a former political correspondent for *Asahi*, remembers: "in comparison to Yoshida who wouldn't let journalists near, Hatoyama was open. There was free access to Hatoyama at his Otowa Mansion and it was like a breath of fresh air." However, the evening edition of *Asahi* on January 20 also published a somewhat cooler assessment of the situation saying, "the Democratic Party boom is skillfully riding the wave of dissatisfaction with, and unpopularity of, Yoshida's Cabinet and Yoshida himself as prime minister." Strong antagonism to Yoshida and his "complete alignment with the United States" was behind Hatoyama's support of opening diplomatic relations with the Soviets. Hatoyama stated, "I have never been disrespectful in how I address others such as not using their titles properly, but with Yoshida, if I feel I have to or somehow I just don't feel like I am on his level [. . .] as he is so very pretentious."[1] With a strong foothold from the support of public opinion, Hatoyama pushed on with the restoration of Japanese-Soviet diplomatic relations. Hatakeyama said that Hatoyama's long time acquaintance, Ogata Taketora, once commented, "Hatoyama is turning into Kerensky." Alexander Kerensky was a revolutionary who rose to rule the Russian provisional government following the February Soviet Revolution of 1917 but was

Figure 25   Prime Minister Hatoyama Ichirō, on the left, arrives in Moscow. In the center is Agricultural Minister Kōno Ichirō and the negotiation delegation. Between the two, holding his hat, is the Prime Minister's secretary, Wakamiya Kotarō.

then driven out by Lenin in the October Revolution. Ogata was also concerned about the precariousness of Hatoyama's negotiations with the Soviet Union.

In the late summer of 1955 Hatoyama, who was on retreat at his cottage in Karuizawa in Nagano Prefecture, told reporters: "I am going to have a look at my grandchildren"— the move being a smokescreen to confuse reporters while Hatoyama disappeared into his son Iichirō's cottage next door. Hatoyama's grandson Kunio, who was six at the time, remembers thinking it was strange being told by his mother to "go outside and play" with Yukio who was eight. Then a car arrived; it was Chairman of the Socialist Party Suzuki Mosaburō. The secret meeting lasted for about an hour. In his memoirs Hatoyama wrote: "in negotiations with the Soviets we put territorial problems on the backburner as we first had to find a way to gain the return of Japanese 'detainees' and to be allowed to join the UN. [...] We candidly asked the Socialist Party for indirect assistance."[2] Nonetheless, resistance remained among his own party members.

Territorial negotiations

Negotiations to restore Japanese-Soviet diplomatic relations began in London in June 1955 and the main focus was the issue of the Northern Territories. The question was: should Japan insist on the return of all four islands, including Kunashiri and Etorofu, or initially narrow it down to the two islands of Habomai and Shikotan? Even within the government and ruling party the argument between those who pushed for the return of all four islands and those prioritizing two islands was complicated and even more polarized than it is today. In the midst of this, a September 17 editorial in the *Asahi* immediately hammered out support for the all-four-islands argument. The editorial declared that as Habomai and Shikotan were not subject to Japan's renunciation of the Kuril Islands under the San Francisco Peace Treaty, "there is absolutely no legal basis for the Soviet Union to continue its occupation." The editorial claimed that Kunashiri and Etorofu were "pure Japanese territories that had not been the site of immigration by other peoples" and therefore, based on this history and national sentiment, they should be returned to Japan. However, there was more to Japanese-Soviet negotiations than just the barriers of the territorial problems. The *Asahi* editorial did not present a comprehensive analysis of the reality that unless Japan restored diplomatic relations with the USSR, Japanese detainees in Siberia would not be returned. To get the Japanese detainees repatriated as quickly as possible, the paper did not question whether it would be acceptable to compromise on the territory problem but *Asahi* did report on popular support for the two-island argument.

In October 1955, the front page of *Asahi* ran four separate installments that detailed the responses of thirty-one intellectuals, including renowned journalist Ōya Sōichi. They all answered the question: "What do you think of Japanese-Soviet negotiations?" Responses in favor of the four-island plan and those who were not wedded to this specific plan were almost equal in number. A November 1955 public opinion poll surveyed respondents on the question: "Is it enough effort to secure the return of Habomai and Shikotan and abandon attempts to return Kunashiri and Etorofu to restore diplomatic relations with the Soviet Union?" The results showed that 27 percent of respondents agreed, 29 percent disagreed, and 44 percent had no opinion. In August of the following year, the responses to a poll on what was seen as the government's plan to postpone discussion of Kunashiri and Etorofu and delay the territorial problem in favor of restoring diplomatic relations first, showed that 46 percent supported the plan, 23 percent were against it, and 31 percent did not respond or answered "other."

Prime Minister Hatoyama Ichirō explained the Kunashiri/Etorofu situation, stating: "We do not think it is possible to immediately make these islands Japanese territory. We will push for such a policy because it's what the public keenly desire but if we cannot see eye to eye with the Soviets, then we have to consider the next best formula."[3] However, those advocating the all-four-islands prudent position toward negotiations grew in strength. Hatoyama, who had his eye on reaching a settlement quickly, found he was met with strong resistance from three sides: Yoshida Shigeru's Diet followers who were anti-Soviet; members of the diplomatic corps who were close to Yoshida; and the Americans who cautioned against rapprochement of Japanese-Soviet relations. The opposition party also took a hard line on the territory issue. Hatoyama would later speak bluntly about the problem in his memoirs writing, "I knew there were people saying things such as 'we absolutely cannot restore Japanese-Soviet relations without taking back Etorofu and Kunashiri,' but that was an unrealistic way of thinking which did not take the Japanese detainees in Siberia into consideration."[4]

Leaking news to the *Asahi*

The front-page headline scoop on August 20, 1955 proclaimed a change in the Japanese government's policy toward Japanese-Soviet negotiations: "Government Establishes

Policy on the Territorial Problems." The paper's headlines claimed the government's plan was to relinquish claims over the North Kuril Islands and Sakhalin but not to cede on the South Kuril islands, saying that Habomai and Shikotan were always Japanese territory.[5] The article announced that Japan considered the Northern Kurils to be anything north of Etorofu island, which essentially meant that all four islands— Habomai, Shikotan, Kunashiri and Etorofu—were considered "Southern Kurils" and Japan wanted them all returned.

In fact, when Japan's Ministry of Foreign Affairs began negotiations in London two months earlier in June, all delegates had been sent a directive. Even now, the Ministry of Foreign Affairs will not confirm the existence of this directive but there are many reports and memoirs from the 1970s and 1980s that speak of "the highest priority is to get Habomai and Shikotan returned." Waseda University professor Tanaka Takahiko has verified the credibility of such reports in the American archive, saying, "they were ordered to at the very least secure the return of Habomai and Shikotan." If this is indeed what happened, it means the Ministry of Foreign Affairs had already prepared for the option of bargaining for the return of only the two islands as a priority measure even before the start of negotiations. At the beginning of August the Soviet Union had, in fact, also proposed the concession of offering the return of Habomai and Shikotan, a posture that coincidentally corresponded to Japan's minimum conditional position.

Figure 26　The front page of the *Asahi Newspaper* on August 20, 1955 with the news banner announcing the Japanese government's plans for negotiations of the Northern Territories.

Strangely, just when it looked like there might be a negotiated settlement, the Japanese Ministry of Foreign Affairs completely reversed its position and sent out instructions to the delegation in London to demand all four islands as *Asahi* reported on its August 20 front page. The Soviet side balked in response to the four-island demand and negotiations broke down.

Tokyo University professor emeritus Wada Haruki took up the *Asahi* article in his own book and wrote: "when the Soviets put forth an unexpected concession suddenly it seemed like an agreement would be reached. Therefore, the Japanese faction opposed to the restoration of diplomatic relations hastily mobilized the four-island argument as a means to bog down the settlement process." Shigemitsu Mamoru, foreign minister at the time, wanted to reach a conclusion of sorts, but the foreign affairs bureaucracy was dominated by those connected to Prime Minister Yoshida Shigeru, who opposed the restoration of Japanese-Soviet relations. It is possible that the anti-diplomatic restoration faction leaked to the *Asahi* the demand for all four islands to make it a *fait accompli*. The *Asahi* article argued, "compared to the Japanese government's initial negotiating position in which they demanded the return of the 'southern part of Sakhalin Island and the Kurils,' their subsequent position was much more easily acceptable to the Soviets." However, the notion that the Soviets would accept the return of all four islands was overly optimistic. From the outset the Soviets said the return of South Sakhalin and the Northern Kurils was out of the question, and they firmly rejected returning Etorofu and Kunashiri. On January 1, 1956, *Asahi* political affairs section chief Nakamura Shōgo explained to readers the Ministry of Foreign Affairs' view that, "it is extremely unlikely that the Soviets would concede that any islands other than Habomai and Shikotan belong to Japan." The *Asahi* scoop had likely been taken in by speculation emanating from the faction opposing the restoration of diplomatic relations.

Caught between the United States and the Soviet Union

In February 1945, in the midst of the Pacific War, the United States, Great Britain and the Soviet Union signed the Yalta Agreement: a secret deal that if the Soviet Union agreed to join the war against Japan, it would be rewarded with the Kuril Islands. This accord was part of the basis for the Soviet Union's justification of its territorial possession of the islands. On September 13, 1956, the Japanese Ministry of Foreign Affairs made public the contents of a US State Department memo about the Yalta Agreement. The memo read: "the result of the Yalta agreement is not a legal territorial transfer" and "Kunashiri and Etorofu must be recognized as Japanese territory." The Soviet Union strongly refused to return Kunashiri and Etorofu while the United States was essentially giving Japan the green light to take a hard line on territorial negotiations. This stance was predicated on an American assumption that, "if the problem of the Northern Territories is resolved, the dissatisfaction of the Japanese over territories will then concentrate on the [American occupied] Ryukyu and Bonin Islands, and it would be unavoidable that Japanese popular sentiment might turn pro-Soviet and anti-American."

Meanwhile, the Soviet Union was counting on Prime Minister Hatoyama Ichirō to drive a wedge between US-Japanese relations. Hosei University professor Shimotomai Nobuo discovered an October 8, 1956 classified document from the Soviet Ministry of Foreign Affairs Intelligence Bureau, which stated: "according to Nosaka Sanzō, first secretary of the Japanese Communist Party, Hatoyama is different from other leaders of the Liberal Democratic Party. He sincerely seeks to achieve expedited normalization and consequently his Moscow visit is promising for the normalization of Japanese-Soviet relations [...] and the signing of a treaty is possible."

The US and Soviet Union locked horns in particular over the Northern Territories, which were seen as geographically and militarily essential. For example, the peace treaty draft that the Soviet Union showed Japan contained a clause stating that warships from countries other than those adjacent to the Sea of Japan could not navigate through it. Meanwhile, the United States was also uneasy about Japanese-Soviet diplomatic relations and the Americans made a move that could be construed as intervention: in August 1956, anti-Soviet hardliner Secretary of State John Foster Dulles remarked to Foreign Minister Shigemitsu Mamoru that if Japan turned over Kunashiri and Etorofu to the Soviets, then the United States could claim territorial possession of Okinawa. This came to be known as "Dulles' threat," and there was also concern raised within the American government as to whether this move might instigate anti-American sentiment by the Japanese. *Asahi* quoted Dulles' threat in large print on the front page of the August 30 edition but followed with the subheading "misunderstanding in Shigemitsu and Dulles talks." The report from Washington tried to play down the incident detailing, "Dulles was only saying that [America] has the right to demand [Okinawa]." A different front-page article asked: "Is their aim to support the Japanese side of the diplomatic relations or rather are they trying to break down Japanese-Soviet negotiations? [...] [The Japanese government] could not grasp the true intentions of the American side." In the end, Dulles' remarks proved to bolster the anti-Soviet hardliners within Japan and the plan to demand all four islands became all the more resolute.

The prime minister visits the Soviet Union to finalize the settlement

As he left for Moscow from Haneda Airport on October 7, 1956, Hatoyama's departing words were: "I firmly believe that sincerity is the path to success." Ill enough that he needed to rely on a wheelchair and a cane, Hatoyama attended the final round of negotiations in person to restore Japanese-Soviet diplomatic relations but the actual leader of the negotiations was Agricultural Minister Kōno Ichirō. On the 19th, after more than ten rounds of discussions, Kōno signed a joint declaration. The declaration made clear that after the conclusion of a peace treaty Habomai and Shikotan would be returned to Japan by the Soviet Union but the settlement of Etorofu and Kunashiri remained equivocal. The first draft of the Soviet's declaration contained an article that read: "The resolution of the territorial problems will be included in ongoing peace treaty negotiations." However, at the eleventh hour the Soviet Union demanded deletion of the clause "territorial problems" as it wanted to avoid further discussion on Kunashiri and Etorofu. Japan gave into the deletion while at the same time making public a separate correspondence between Japan and the Soviets, which said, "we will include territorial issues as part of future peace treaty negotiations." However, on this point criticism was raised that "Japan made concessions to the Soviet Union."

Kyōdō News reporter Sakai Shinji, who accompanied the Japanese delegation, explained, "the Japanese government was concerned that the joint declaration would be reported according to the Soviet interpretation." Sakai met with the *Yomiuri Newspaper*'s Togawa Isamu and the prime minister's secretary, Wakamiya Kotarō, where they exchanged information in something akin to a secret press conference. Wakamiya asked the two journalists their opinions concerning what the media and public opinion response to the settlement would be and at the end he said, "We will announce our own interpretation." An *Asahi* commentary on October 19 voiced the positive opinion that the overall result of the negotiations meant, "The pending issue of 'reconciliation on all fronts' will be substantially realized." However, an editorial the following day on the territorial problem was scathing: "The return of Habomai and Shikotan has been pushed back into the distant future. [...] What was already a heavy burden is being left as work for future governments." From the available archives we can ascertain that the Kōno delegation really worked hard on the negotiations. According to the Japanese translation of a detailed negotiation memo made public by Kōno's former secretary Ishikawa Tatsuo in the 2005 bulletin of the Political Journalists Alumnae Association, First Secretary of the Communist Party, Nikita Khrushchev, remarked that "the Japanese people are so stubborn." Khrushchev stated to Kōno that the return of Habomai and Shikotan would be contingent on America first handing back Okinawa, which Kōno fiercely opposed.

On the day of the signing, the local news page of the *Asahi* evening edition introduced the voices of fishermen with quotes both from those who were pleased and dissatisfied with the situation: "Deliberations over Kunashiri and Etorofu continue, so we hope that it can be resolved after diplomatic relations have returned to normal;" and "Kunashiri is our lifeline, the drawing of a national boundary in the middle means death." The November 28 edition printed a picture of Hatoyama shedding a tear during a visit to the Chairman of the Socialist Party Suzuki Mosaburō. After having achieved restoration of Japanese-Soviet relations as their swan song, Hatoyama's Cabinet resigned en masse on December 20.

The power of the "right of veto"

The Japanese government's efforts to restore diplomatic relations with the Soviet Union were grounded in its desire to join the United Nations. Japan applied to the UN as soon as possible on June 23, 1952—just two months after the San Francisco Peace treaty came into effect. The Soviet Union, which had not been a part of the peace treaty, looked certain to veto the move. According to the *Asahi* on June 24, which reported Japan's application to the UN, the Ministry of Foreign Affairs assessed that, "The Soviet Union will likely take the position that the treaty was unlawful, meaning that Japan is unqualified to join the United Nations as an independent nation" and "that the reason Japan is nonetheless going ahead with an application is to make good on its intention to join the UN as declared in the preamble of the treaty [...] regardless of whether or not it is realistic. The main objective is to convey that intention to the UN." The Ministry of Foreign Affairs' forecast was correct and when the UN Security Council voted on the Japanese application on September 18, the Japanese application garnered a 10 to 1 vote in which the Soviet Union defeated the motion by exercising its power of veto.

Japan's break came three years later in December 1955 when Japan joined eighteen countries including the Soviet ally, Mongolia, and submitted a joint application proposal to the Security Council. The Soviet UN delegate Arkady Sobolev backed this proposal. However, there was a sudden reversal and this time the Republic of China (Taiwan) exercised its veto, claiming: "Mongolia was usurped by the Soviets from China [...] and it cannot be considered an independent nation." The Soviets then made a complete about face and opposed the Japanese application. In the end, the application from the eighteen nations fell apart. An article on the December 14, 1955 front page of the evening *Asahi* read: "Japan's UN Application Unsuccessful." Miyachi Kenjirō, the New York special correspondent who wrote the article, recalled: "it didn't surprise me." He added, "At that time Japan was still saddled with the image of being a defeated nation. Japan thought it might escape such a stigma if it could join the UN, but due to the antagonistic situation between the United States and the Soviet Union it seemed as if Japan would not be admitted." A statement by Prime Minister Hatoyama, printed on the same page, was critical of the Ministry of Foreign Affairs. "The Ministry of Foreign Affairs was too rosy in its observations. [...] I would like to advance the problem of Japan's UN participation as part of the next negotiations between Japan and the Soviet Union." On December 14, the Security Council passed an application from sixteen countries, which excluded Japan and Mongolia. The Soviet diplomat Yakov Malik confided in Japan's ambassador to the UN, Kase Toshikazu: "In the end, the conclusion was that we should strike where it would hurt America the most. [...] It's not personal."[6] The *Asahi* editorial on the 17th, entitled "Japan: Left Behind," made the case that "the problem of Japan's participation in the UN is now being used as a tool in the power struggle between the two super powers of East and West. [...] We are adamantly against using the issue of joining the UN as a tool in the business of Japanese-Soviet negotiations." There was nothing more to be done to join the UN until Japanese-Soviet relations had been completely resolved.

The promotion of "impartiality"

The October 19, 1956 joint declaration signed by Japan and the Soviets included a clause concerned with Japan's UN participation: "The Soviet Union supports the application of Japan to join the United Nations." At a meeting of the Security Council on December 12, the Soviet Union, as promised, did not exercise its veto. At the general assembly meeting on the 18th, Japan's acceptance was officially decided. With seventy-seven votes for, none against, and two countries absent, the vote was unanimous. Foreign Minister Shigemitsu Mamoru, the Japanese representative, addressed the

General Assembly: "The substance of the current government, economy and culture of our country is the product of the fusion of both Western and Asian civilizations over the last century. In some ways Japan can serve as a bridge between East and West." On the 19th, *Asahi* wrote: "the figure of the Foreign Minister with his cane in hand is reminiscent of when he signed the Japanese Instrument of Surrender to the Allies aboard the *USS Missouri* on September 2, 1945. This time, however, Foreign Minister Shigemitsu was probably feeling radiant."

Among those listening to Shigemitsu's address at the UN headquarters was 25-year-old Akashi Yasushi. Akashi, who would later hold key positions at the UN, was in the United States studying at the Fletcher School of Law and Diplomacy at Tufts University. He had gone that day, by chance, to see the UN with his classmates. Even now, Akashi still clearly recalls the scene of the General Assembly. "The assembly hall was full of a warm mood welcoming Japan. Shigemitsu's speech gave off a joyous and frisson of excitement." The phrase Shigemitsu used, "a bridge between East and West," left a mark on Akashi. "I thought that 'East and West' conveyed both the dichotomy of Asia and the West as well as America and the Soviet Union. And to me the choice of the term the 'bridge' denoted the vulnerability of not being aligned with either. At the time I vaguely thought that Japan would in the future come up against the difficulty of 'choosing' on individual issues," he said. The editorial in *Asahi* on the 19th was not only celebratory but also pushed the idea that "we should be cautious of all this fuss like being drunk with happiness." The paper then reconfirmed the sentiment that "one could not help but feel that one day Japan would be added as a permanent member to the Security Council or the Economic and Social Council, which were at the heart of the UN. [...] This would clearly see Japan's responsibility increase." The editorial further advocated that "what is extremely important for Japan's foreign relations when we look at the current state of international affairs" from this point on was that "Japan's attitude be such that it 'takes no sides.' " Akashi pointed out, "in the UN Japan was eager to find a new foothold in diplomacy. For that reason alone the entire nation had a tendency to somewhat over-idealize and glamorize the UN. That is likely connected to today's polarized outlook on the UN in which people either have 'excessive expectations' or 'none at all.' "

The disappearance of UN-centered diplomacy

The day following Japan's entry into the UN, December 19, 1956, the *Asahi* editorial declared: "We promise to the world that we will live by UN-centered diplomacy to the utmost and cooperate in UN activities." But what is "UN-centered diplomacy?" The editorial explained the policy as "aiming to realize an essential national policy appropriate for Japan while following the public opinion [...] of the world." This was a problem: how should Japan respond in the event that UN forces requested Japan to deploy troops in light of Article 9 of the Constitution? The UN maintained a "police force" which was at the time set to guard the ceasefire in the second Middle East conflict in 1956. The problem of Japan's participation in UN military operations was of immediate concern but this editorial treated it optimistically, explaining that: "If we can get every country to grasp the current spirit in which we are trying to uphold our constitution, an appropriate result will sort itself out." Japan was soon put to the test in its second year of UN participation. In October 1957, the nation joined the ranks as a non-permanent council member of the Security Council. The *Vox Populi, Vox Dei* column on October 3 wrote cynically: "Well, it's true we are 'moving up quickly' [...] but this resembles Prime Minister Kishi Nobusuke's 'thinking like a super power', hurriedly running around to join the club of one of the great powers."

The subject of the general assembly meeting that year was arms reduction and Japan proposed a ban on nuclear weapons testing. However, France said the plan was the same as the Soviet Union's and the Soviet Union said its plan was identical to that of Western Europe. *Asahi* noted that actually Japan was "in a bind between east and west and isolated."[7] In addition, the arms reduction debate was gridlocked by the Soviet Union's withdrawal and Japan's proposal was buried. Kimura Tadao, bureau chief of *Asahi*'s New York office, pointed out that "this is where the limits of Japan's national power were visible."[8] The editorial on the 17th stated: "The increasing conflict [between East and West] created the UN's most striking tragedy." At first, the Ministry of Foreign Affairs also supported UN-centered diplomacy. The annual Foreign Affairs Blue Papers, which began to be produced in 1957, for two consecutive years specified the three principles of Japanese diplomacy as: "United Nations-centered," "cooperating with the countries of the free world," and "strongly upholding its position as a member of Asia." However, this "United Nations-centered" pillar disappeared in the 1959 Blue Paper. The reason given for the deletion was "at the present time to entrust the safety of all countries and world peace solely to the UN would be to ignore the limitations of the UN's capabilities and the actual international circumstances." In contrast, the story did not change in the *Asahi*. Mori Kyōzō, vice-director of the editorial board, wrote in a December 20, 1959 commentary: "For Japan there is no other way to make the best of the peace constitution than to strengthen the UN. [...] The hammering out of a real UN-centered diplomacy is the task of Japanese foreign diplomacy." However, with the escalation of the Cold War with the Cuban Missile Crisis in 1962, the phrase "UN-centered diplomacy" gradually disappeared even from *Asahi*.

The 1960 Security Treaty

A mysterious crash landing

"It's going to crash!" On the afternoon of September 24, 1959, a black jet was rapidly losing altitude above Fujisawa Airfield in Kanagawa Prefecture. "It looks like it's going to blow, everyone hit the ground!" yelled Takahashi Jun, the head of the Japan Flying Association and there to practice glider flying. The plane belly flopped just fifty meters in front of them. There were no markings on the airplane identifying its origin and it had two long wings like a glider. The pilot was helped from the plane but there was also nothing on his jumpsuit to identify his affiliation or rank. Not long afterwards, five or six US Army helicopters arrived and one whisked the pilot away. With pistols at their side, men in civilian clothes surrounded the crashed plane, preventing anyone from taking pictures and removing film from cameras. Japanese police who rushed to the scene were told not to approach and were not allowed to interfere.

In the course of the previous year, Takahashi had repeatedly observed the plane landing at the nearby Atsugi Naval Air Force Base. He had also heard that it was a spy plane called the U2, which could supposedly avoid radar detection and enter Soviet or other territory by flying at very high altitudes. It was rumored the plane could glide with the engines cut and gather intelligence before returning home. The crash landing of the U2 drove home the reality of the Soviet-US cold war but the *Asahi, Mainichi*, and *Yomiuri* newspapers did not run the story probably because police most likely did not even announce it. Only the *Kanagawa Newspaper* ran a short one-paragraph article in the local news section. The November 29 issue of the *Youth Weekly Sunday* (*Shūkan Shōnen Sandē*) reported the crash landing of the U2 plane in a five-page feature entitled "Strange but True, Mysterious Plane Flying Skies over Japan." It included first-hand accounts and pictures of the site that had not been confiscated. The headline of the *Asahi* the day of the U2 crash landing in September was "Prime Minister Resolves to Revise the US-Japan Security Treaty." The article described the way in which Prime Minister Kishi Nobusuke spoke about the revision of the Treaty of Mutual Cooperation and Security between Japan and the United States at a Liberal Democratic Party Foreign Policy Deliberation Committee. According to Kishi, "those opposed to the treaty revision are plotting to pull Japan into an anti-American, neutral position." "There is no need to dissolve the Lower House over the ratification of the US-Japan Security Treaty. [...] [In the event that the Socialist Party abandons the deliberations]

Figure 27   On June 15, 1960, student demonstrators clash with police inside the Diet grounds.

we can continue the process."¹ Kishi had already decided on the idea of unilateral deliberations and was now making his stance public. On January 19, 1960, Japan and the US signed the new US-Japan Security Treaty. In February, a debate on the treaty's ratification began in the National Diet, while American President Eisenhower's visit to Japan was slated for around June 20.

Soviets shoot down a U2 plane

The US-Japan Security Treaty had been concluded at the same time as the San Francisco Peace Treaty in September 1951 but did not stipulate that America was responsible for the defense of Japan. The treaty allowed for American forces in Japan to deploy outside of Japan as they saw fit and included items that were almost an extension of the American occupation, in that American forces could also be employed for domestic disturbances within Japan. A journalist in the political section of *Asahi* at the time, Hatakeyama Takeshi, claimed that Prime Minister Kishi Nobusuke expressed his dissatisfaction with the security treaty by saying, "This is exactly like 'Manshūkoku,'" in reference to Japan's imperial puppet state in Northern China where Kishi himself had served as a bureaucrat and participated in such rule and governance. In addition to clarifying America's duty to defend Japan, the new US-Japan Security Treaty, which Kishi signed in January 1960, stipulated that prior consultation between Japan and the United States be held in cases where American forces were deployed from bases in Japan on combat operations. The new agreement was deliberated in the Diet in May 1960 and director of the editorial board of the newspaper, Ryū Shintarō, described it as follows in the June issue of the magazine *Literary Annals*: "It's one thing to say that compared to the current security treaty the revised treaty is substantially better. [...]

However, I wouldn't go so far as to say it's a complete improvement." Ryū argued that the new security treaty must be revised and this was *Asahi*'s consistent assertion. At the same time, the *Asahi* editorial repeated the same demands which centered on three issues: (1) modify "prior consultation" to "prior agreement;" (2) restrict the treaty's purpose to protect Japan and not permit American forces to be deployed on combat missions from Japanese soil; and (3) shorten the ten-year term of the treaty.

On May 5, grave news emerged when Soviet Premier Nikita Khrushchev announced that an American military plane, which had violated Soviet airspace, had been shot down over the Urals region. The downed craft was a U2, the same type of spy plane that had crashed at the Fujisawa Airfield in Kanagawa Prefecture the previous autumn. This affair dispelled the sense of détente that had arisen from Khrushchev's visit to the United States the previous year. Khrushchev made the following public statement:

> If someone intends to fly over our territory, reconnoitering objectives and gleaning state secrets, we shall bring down such planes, just bring them down. [...] Those countries that have bases on their territories should note most carefully the following: if they allow others to fly from their bases to our territory we shall hit at those bases. Because we assess such actions as provocations against our country.[2]

With a host of American bases, Japan was in danger of becoming a Soviet target. Some feared that Japan's ties to America meant it would be drawn into a war while others thought that Japan must be tied to the United States to oppose the threat from the Soviet Union.

The end of the Diet session (May 26) was approaching and on May 19 the *Asahi* editorial, "Extension of the Diet Session Devoted to Completing Deliberations," warned that: "if the Liberal Democratic Party used an extension of the Diet as a tool to push through the new security treaty, it would demonstrate abhorrent behavior." On the evening of the 19th, the Chairman of the Lower House requested that a police squad be dispatched to the Diet.

Forced passage of the new security treaty

A squad of 500 policemen in gray uniforms and caps silently entered the National Diet on May 19, 1960 at 11:05 p.m. The police forcibly removed the members of the Socialist Party, who had planted themselves in front of the Lower House chairman's office in an attempt to block the vote on the extension of the parliament session. People wearing administrative badges of the Liberal Democratic Party jeered the socialists, calling them "hack members of parliament" and sneering, "shall we handcuff them?"[3]

At 11:48 p.m., the Speaker of the House, Kiyose Ichirō, returned to his seat in the Diet surrounded and assisted by Liberal Democratic Members (LDP) of the Diet and guards who were almost carrying him. At 12:06 a.m. on May 20, after a fifty-day extension of the Diet session was passed by only the members of the LDP, the new security treaty was voted in with calls of "banzai" and applause. Up until right before the forced vote, only a few of the LDP party members knew that it was to take place.

Twenty-seven members, including former prime ministers Ishibashi Tanzan and Miki Takeo, were absent. When *Asahi* director of the editorial board Ryū Shintarō heard about the news on the new security treaty he told vice-director Danno Nobuo, "Danno, write it up!" Danno hastily wrote the editorial, "Government Ruling Party's Undemocratic Behavior."[4] The paper resolutely pressed Kishi to do some serious reflection on what *Asahi* called "A forced measure not born of a democratic country." Most people first became aware of the extreme measures to pass the treaty on the morning of May 20 from the radio or the newspaper. The same day, Kishi canceled a press conference scheduled for the following morning with the excuse that "the political situation is delicate." Ryū wrote his own editorial: "I believe we are presently at a crossroads in which our parliamentary democracy will either survive or perish." This editorial, titled "Demand Kishi's Resignation and Call for General Election," was printed at the top of the front page on May 21, 1960. On the same page, the column *Vox Populi, Vox Dei* stated, "the Prime Minister Kishi we see on television is laughing and smiling smugly. [...] What you see there is that Kishi Nobusuke has a face for political power and party politics but unfortunately he does not even have a trace of the dignity of a democratic statesman. His time has come to resign." All the newspapers simultaneously criticized Kishi's strong stance. According to a Japan Newspaper Association analysis, of the fifty-nine papers with editorial columns that were part of the association, forty-seven advocated settling the present situation through actions such as the en masse resignation of the Cabinet or the dissolution of the Lower House of the Diet. The front pages of the papers published strong statements, such as "apologize to the people!" and "take responsibility!"

With the forced vote, "anti-Kishi" sentiment rose sharply and radically charged the anti-security treaty movement. May 26 saw what was claimed to be an unprecedented demonstration of 175,000 people surrounding the National Diet for the *People's Congress to Stop the Revision of the Security Treaty*'s "National Day of United Action," organized by groups such as the Socialist Party and the General Council of Trade Unions of Japan (*Sōhyō*). On May 28, Kishi addressed a press conference saying, "there is more to public opinion than just newspapers."

Listen to the silent majority

On the morning of May 28, 1960, one week after the forced vote on the New Security Treaty, Prime Minister Kishi addressed a press conference: "The newspapers fail to be objective and take up only the side of the opposition's argument. [...] Every day we are visited and supported by groups and we receive many such letters addressed to myself and the LDP." Kishi continued, "If we yield to these demonstrations it puts Japan in serious danger. [...] I believe we also must lend our ears to the 'silent majority.' At the moment all that can be heard are the loud voices." Kishi did not bend toward such public opinion. On June 3, *Asahi* printed the results of its public opinion poll, "What do you think of Kishi's Cabinet?" Twelve percent of respondents thought it "should continue on as is," while 58 percent thought "the Cabinet should be changed." This was the "voice" of the people.

On June 2, Kobayashi Tomi, a 30-year-old art teacher, made banners to use at the demonstrations. She wrote, "Hold a General Election!!" and "Send Back the U2 Planes!" in large letters. She turned the tables on Kishi, rearranged his own words and wrote: "Anyone can join the silent majority group." On the People's Congress to Stop the Revision of the Security Treaty's June 4 "Day of United Action," Kobayashi and two friends began walking in the demonstration. As they approached the National Diet building, they looked behind them and there were about thirty people. When Kobayashi and her friends called out "Why don't you join us?," businessmen and housewives joined the line from the sidewalk. "Where is this demonstration from?," they asked. Kobayashi's group replied, "It's not from anywhere. We just came together a moment ago."[5] That day the National Railways Labor Union went on a limited strike from the first morning train until 7.00 a.m. but it was not chaotic. The government declared that in its opinion "the failure of the strike to gather steam demonstrated that the tendency of public opinion was [dismissive of the anti-Security Treaty movement]."

On the one hand, the *Asahi* on June 5 explained that the reason people were calm was that they "could understand" the motivation for the strike, and if the government ignored the "silent majority" this would be "inviting a chaotic state of affairs." Printed on the same page as this editorial was a contribution by civil law scholar Wagatsuma Sakae (who had competed for valedictorian with Prime Minister Kishi at Tokyo Imperial University) titled "To my friend Kishi Nobusuke." It read: "Kishi there is only one path left open to you. Retire from the world of politics immediately and spend your days fishing. [...] If you do this, the people's opposition movement, I dare say, will not derail from the path of democracy."

An appeal to newspaper companies for support

On the afternoon of June 7, 1960, Prime Minister Kishi Nobusuke invited the heads of each media company to his official residence and appealed to them to support the upcoming visit of US President Dwight Eisenhower to Japan on June 19. "When President Eisenhower comes to Japan we would like to give him a festive national welcome that is divorced from our current domestic political problems." Those invited were the highest management from the *Yomiuri, Sankei, Mainichi, Tokyo Shimbun*, as well as the Japanese Broadcasting Corporation (NHK). The following day, on the 8th, Kishi requested the cooperation of representatives from *Kyōdō News, Jiji Press, Chūnichi, Hokkaidō, Nishi Nihon, Nikkei*, and commercial broadcasters. On the 9th, he invited *Asahi*.[6] On June 7, US Ambassador Douglas MacArthur II had also met informally for consultation with the editorial section heads from each newspaper and news company. Hirooka Tomoo (who later became company president) from *Asahi* attended. Years later, Hirooka reminisced about the events with Sophia University professor emeritus, Haruhara Akihiko: "The ambassador hit us with a one-sided speech that went something like, 'we have to drive out the forces that obstruct the presidential visit to Japan.' When I strongly objected and said 'right now if he insists on coming, it will only worsen Japan-American relations. It is better to call it off,' the discussion turned acrimonious."

Many estimate that Kishi forced through the vote on the new Security Treaty on May 20, 1960 so that it could be the icing on the cake for the American presidential visit. Once the treaty passed the Lower House thirty days later (in other words, on the date of the planned presidential visit of June 19), even without a vote by the Upper House, it would by default become law. Kishi anticipated the problems so he held the vote with just the ruling party present in the Diet. Anti-Security Treaty demonstrators shouted "Prevent Ike's visit!" *Asahi* wrote that in the interest of security it was possible "the president could be inconvenienced" and called in its June 1 editorial for the American government to delay his visit to Japan. More than twenty regional papers also published arguments in favor of postponing the visit.

On the afternoon of the 10th, the president's press secretary, James Hagerty, landed at Haneda Airport. Not far from the airport demonstrators surrounded the car carrying Hagerty and Ambassador MacArthur, who had come to greet Hagerty. Demonstrators threw rocks at the car, cracking the windows and leaving the car riddled with dents. Eventually, Hagerty and MacArthur had to be rescued by an American Army helicopter. On the evening of the same day, the deputy director of the Japan Newspaper Publishers and Editors Association (*Nihon Shimbun Kyōkai*), Ejiri Susumu, received a phone call from the head of a regional newspaper suggesting, "In such a time of need as this shouldn't the newspapers also be cooperating to help calm down the situation?"

The death of Kanba Michiko

On June 15, 1960, just after 3.00 p.m. in front of the main gates of the National Diet building, a reporter from the women's magazine *Mademoiselle* asked one of the female university student protestors taking part in the zigzag demonstration, "Do you think that by seeking the dissolution of the Diet you can stop the Security Treaty from being ratified?" Kanba Michiko, a 22-year-old Tokyo University student answered, "Yes, I do. My actions are based on my convictions," before disappearing back into the maelstrom of the demonstration.[7] After 5.00 p.m., right-wing thugs brandishing batons with nails attacked the line of demonstrators as they passed the second side gate of the Upper House and drove a large truck into the crowd, injuring many. At 7.00 p.m., students entered the Diet premises through the south side gate and the police force pulled back to the rear but students continued to stream in from the outside. The police attacked and from the back the students threw stones. Morita Hatsuaki, an *Asahi* cameraman who was hit, heard "a strange shriek somewhere between 'gya!' and 'un,'" and saw "illuminated by the light, face after face after face covered in blood." After 7:30 p.m., news started to circulate that a female university student had been killed. It was Kanba Michiko.

That day *Asahi* local news reporter Saeki Susumu, after having looked around the Diet, returned to the office at about 6.00 p.m. At about 8.00 p.m., the news filtered in that a female university student had died. How had the situation deteriorated to this point? Reporters who had witnessed the attack by the right-wingers believed that such action had incited the students to rush the Diet. There were also police reports that before the attack student leaders had been calling for a push on the Diet. Saeki compiled the differing reports. There were even reporters who speculated that Kanba was likely killed by police violence. The head of the local news section, Tashiro Kikuo, said: "don't report anything that you didn't see with your own eyes." (The Tokyo District Prosecutor's office later announced that Kanba was "crushed to death.") Late that night Saeki, accompanied by Tashiro, went to explain the situation to the director of the editorial board Ryū Shintarō. Ryū, face flushed, was busy correcting proofs. He nodded yes, yes and went back to his work, his hair completely disheveled.

In the early hours of the morning of the 16th, Kantō Radio broadcast a live report on the situation in front of the south side gate: "Right in front of us the police forces are swinging their batons and cursing [at the demonstrators]. [...] The police [...] the police forces are very violent. This is extreme violence by the police."[8] The students then set fire to a dozen police trucks. Around the same time the government released a statement concluding that the students' actions were "deliberate behavior manipulated by an international communist plot." *Yomiuri Newspaper* political section journalist Watanabe Tsuneo was asked by the chief Cabinet secretary to write the statement.[9]

Figure 28   People praying in front of an altar set up on the site of Kanba Michiko's death, June 16, 1960, in front of the southern side gate of the National Diet compound.

"Don't use adjectives!"

On June 15, 1960, the day Tokyo University student Kanba Michiko died inside the National Diet compound, Aoki Akira from the *Sankei Newspaper* local news desk took command of the headquarters in front of the Diet. Late that night Aoki advised the section chief, "what the newspaper must do [...] is admonish the violence of the police who are the representatives of authority." Aoki thought that this was basic to the concept that media should be critical of authority. *Sankei* settled on the headline for its local news page the following day: "Kanba's Death." An editorial in *Asahi* on the same day stated: "the rushing of the south entrance [...] is thought to have been a planned mobilization" and the paper urged the students to reflect on their actions. Aoki felt that if one had actually witnessed the events in person, "[editorials like *Asahi*'s] would probably not be published."[10] On the 15th, Yoshino Masahiro of the *Mainichi Newspaper* local news section witnessed police mercilessly attacking fleeing students with truncheons. When he sent in his report, the editorial desk said, "it is too subjective." Yoshino had no intention of writing it other than objectively but had to rewrite it many times. He gave it some thought and assessed that it was a mistake to use violence to barge into the Diet. However, if security guards gang up on a thief who has trespassed and in the ensuing melee someone in the neighborhood is killed and much blood is spilled, he surmised that "normally the important point to the news would be 'security guards go berserk' more so than focusing on 'the home intrusion.'"

The June 16 front page of *Asahi* only took up the matter of police brutality in a fragmented way. Head of the editing bureau Hirooka Tomoo directed reporters beforehand "definitely not to use any adjectives." Kobayashi Riki, a reporter at the time for the local news section who covered the events around the Diet during those days, recalls: "although I wrote the graphic story of what was happening, it wasn't printed." The August 1960 issue of *Literary Annals* (*Bungei Shunjū*), in its newspaper criticism column, pilloried the June 16 *Asahi* article of the death of Kanba, saying it was "cooler than any others" and the local news column turned out "prose that was curt and without flavor" and which only "followed the course of events."

The American president's arrival in Japan on June 19 was imminent. Matsuyama Yukio of the *Asahi* political section, while researching the story, heard police chief Kashiwara Nobuo tell Prime Minister Kishi Nobusuke directly, "the student leaders are resolute and the demonstration's support is wide. It really can't be properly policed. The only thing that can be done is for you, the prime minister, to correct your stance from that of ignoring the voice of the people." Kishi replied, "I will call in the self-defense forces." However, the Chief of the Japan Defense Agency, Akagi Munenori, opposed Kishi's decision and deployment was avoided. Early on the morning of the 16th, the vice-president of the Japan Newspaper Association, Ejiri Susumu, received phone calls at home from two regional newspaper managers who recommended: "At such a time, the newspaper world should act collectively." Ejiri then spoke to the management of the *Mainichi*, the *Yomiuri*, and the *Asahi* and expressed the opinion that they should make a collective statement.

The seven newspaper companies' collective declaration

At 1:30 p.m. on June 16, 1960, the day after Tokyo University student Kanba Michiko died, Ejiri Susumu called the director of *Asahi*'s editorial board, Ryū Shintarō and told him, "there are those who are calling for a unified statement." Ryū immediately approved the idea. In late May, Ryū had already conveyed to the director of *Mainichi*'s editorial board, Ikematsu Fumio, that "to ensure that social unrest does not get further out of control we should make a joint statement," so Ryū saw no reason to disagree.[11] Ejiri wrote the draft of the statement and it reached Ryū at 5.00 p.m. on June 16. Meanwhile, it seems Ryū had been formulating his own draft. The vice-director of *Yomiuri*'s editorial board, Aikawa Shigeyoshi, along with Ikematsu, Ejiri, and Ryū, gathered in the editorial office at *Asahi* and finalized the wording. When they finally agreed on the declaration, it was after 9:00 p.m. Late that night, a proof of the front page of the following day's morning edition was sent to each of *Asahi*'s editorial bureau sections.

The top story was "President Eisenhower's Japan Visit Postponed." The collective statement, "Reject Violence, Protect Parliamentary Democracy" was printed in the middle of the front page. It began: "the bloody incident which occurred in and around the Diet on the evening of June 15, putting aside the causes, is a regretful event which plunged our parliamentary democracy into crisis." The statement concluded: "At this time we believe that the people's desire is for both the socialist and democratic parties to put aside for a while their points of contention and take the initiative to return to the Diet and cooperate to take control of the situation through this process of normalization." There was no criticism directed at Prime Minister Kishi Nobusuke who had forced through the Security Treaty or calls for his resignation. Altogether seven companies, including the *Sankei Newspaper*, *Tokyo Newspaper*, *Tokyo Times*, and *Nikkei* signed their names to the declaration. That day Tokyo University president Kaya Seiji also released a statement: "We must fully understand what transpired to bring about such large and direct action by innocent students." He continued, "if parliamentarianism had returned to normal through such means as the dissolution of the Diet, then the students would likely not have taken the path they did. [...] There can be no resolution to the problem other than a return to democratically responsible government."[12] The newspapers tried to keep the reasons that led to the events separate, while Kaya appealed for a "full understanding about what brought about the events." The newspapers carrying the declaration were distributed on the 17th and forty-one regional papers synchronized their efforts to print the same statement. In response, criticism against the declaration erupted.

Approval by default

In answer to the June 17 "Seven Company Collective Declaration" call to "reject violence and protect parliamentary democracy," *Asahi* received a long critical commentary from intellectual pundit Nakano Yoshio. Nakano's submission was printed in the *Voices* column in the June 18 evening edition: "To not even touch on the 'lawful violence' of the forced vote (which is what set off the student violence) seems to be concealing some of the news." Nakano concluded, "Democracy cannot ride on the broken vehicle of parliamentary democracy. The first priority is to repair the broken car." Kanba Toshio, sociologist and father of Kanba Michiko the student killed in the riots in front of the Diet, also argued: "it was absurd that the papers did not bring into question the ruling government party's undemocratic behavior." Even within *Asahi* criticism existed. Editorial committee member Mori Kyōzō, convalescing from an illness, felt that for the newspaper to join hands with other papers and hammer out an opinion was "cowardly" and "lacked confidence."[13] Why did the collective statement go so far as to say "... put aside for a while their points of contention"? Honda Chikao, head of the Japan Newspaper Association and the president of the *Mainichi Newspaper* at the time, explained at a general meeting that the aim of the statement was "at the present, to quell the agitation and antagonism between the two opposing sides." Ryū Shintarō, *Asahi*'s director of the editorial board who had taken leadership over forming the statement, detailed to the vice-director, Danno Nobuo: "I had wanted to demand a general election of the Liberal Democratic Party government but the other companies had their own opinions and it was difficult to reconcile."[14] According to Danno, Ryū repeatedly lamented that, "violence begets violence. And then that will be the end of the postwar democracy we finally obtained."[15]

On the 18th, a demonstration of unprecedented size filled the area surrounding the Diet. According to the People's Congress to Stop the Revision of the Security Treaty,

Figure 29   At midnight on June 19, 1960, the new Security Treaty was "approved by default." Demonstrators continued to protest in front of the Diet main gate.

330,000 people gathered and even the police estimated 130,000. At midnight on the 19th, without a vote in the Upper House, the new Security Treaty passed into law by default. *Asahi* reported that "the students who were seated around the Diet did not move [...] there was no shouting, nor singing, nor voices raised in chorus, [...] the demonstration teams fell completely silent."[16] Former *Asahi* president Hasebe Tadasu took the issue head on in the *Asahi* on the 19th. "We repudiate all violence and reject it. [...] The attitude of Kishi's government which did not listen one iota to even orderly displays of public opinion must be thoroughly condemned."[17]

It was on this day that American President Eisenhower, on a tour of the Far East, arrived in Okinawa, which was still under US military control.

The American president goes to Okinawa

On June 19, 1960, a Japanese flag on the right and a stars and stripes on the left adorned the front page of the *Ryukyu Newspaper* (*Ryūkyū Shimpō*) to welcome US President Eisenhower on his visit. The news that at midnight the new Security Treaty had been passed into law by default was printed on the second page. At that time Okinawa was under American administrative authority. The president, who had canceled his visit to mainland Japan, was surrounded in the city of Naha by a demonstration appealing for the "return of Okinawa to Japan." According to the *Okinawa Times*, "Organizations, university students, and high school students—in all more than 10,000 people [...] each held in their hands a Japanese flag [...] and placards in English and Japanese which read 'Return Okinawa.'"[18] The demonstrators faced off with the police and five hundred armed American soldiers who, for a moment, pointed their bayonets at the demonstrators. Eisenhower changed from his planned route to avoid the demonstrators, and from behind the Ryūkyū government building headed toward the airfield. The president's stay lasted only two hours and nine minutes.

The Security Treaty revision consultations had begun in 1958 and America had advocated for Okinawa to be included in the area that Japan and the US jointly defended. Prime Minister Kishi Nobusuke approved. In response, the *Asahi Newspaper* objected, saying, "Okinawa should not be included." "Piling the three layers of Sino-American, Korean-American and Japanese-American defense zones together [...] would cause great distress that Japan might be drawn into international military disputes."[19] In the end, Kishi gave up on the argument for the inclusion of Okinawa. The people of Okinawa recoiled and an editorial in the *Ryūkyū Shimpō* raised the criticism that, "In the event of war, mainland Japan would not want to suffer any injuries for Okinawa, which would most certainly be at the center of the conflict."[20] In June 1959, a US fighter jet crashed into Miyamori elementary school in Ishikawa City (now Uruma City) killing seventeen people, including children.

When Eisenhower arrived for his visit on June 19, 1960, Yui Akiko, Tokyo bureau reporter for the *Okinawa Times*, attended the Tokyo Okinawan Association general meeting at the Kudan Kaikan Hall. When a telegram was read out saying, "The president escaped through the back door," the hall erupted. In an interview, Yui describes: "There was both a feeling of anger in Okinawa of having been abandoned by Japan and a desire to be included in 'peaceful Japan.' The people of Okinawa had these divided emotions but they were not understood by those on the mainland." *Asahi*'s editorial of June 19 took up the issue of the "default approval of the new Security Treaty." While stating that, "there are more than a few improvements (in the new treaty) [...] there is no reason to oppose revision itself." In addition, the paper demanded the government renegotiate to shorten the planned ten-year term of the treaty. On the 21st, the top of the evening edition of the *Asahi* front page read, "Prime Minister Kishi Intends to Resign."

Ryū Shintarō's reflections

In the morning of June 23, 1960, at the official residence of the foreign minister in Tokyo, Japan and America exchanged the ratification papers for the new Security Treaty. The treaty, which had been the focus of widespread opposition, came into effect that day. On the same day, Prime Minister Kishi Nobusuke announced his resignation. There was an unusually long submission in the following day's evening edition of the *Asahi*, in the family-oriented column *Moments* (*Hitotoki*). The piece was written by a 35-year-old housewife from Nakano, Tokyo who had participated in the demonstration at the Diet with her 3-year-old child strapped to her back. She had seen with her own eyes right-wing thugs attacking the demonstrators on the day Kanba Michiko died. The housewife recounted how her child screamed, "I'm scared! I'm scared! I want to go home. [...] And I realized my left sock and sandal were gone but I ran away barefoot anyway." She continued, "I saw the tragedy on television and learned that a female student had died, so I could not sleep the whole night. The following day the newspaper barely mentioned the right-wing attack on the ordinary people and demonstrators."

The July 3 edition of the magazine *Asahi Journal* (*Asahi Jānaru*) contained an eighteen-page special report entitled, "A record of the bloody events of June 15th." The report offered a blow-by-blow description of the event by interviewing about eighty students and reporters who were at the Diet on that day. The opinions and views of police and right-wingers were published as a counter opinion in the next month's issue. However, with Kishi's resignation the wave of demonstrations that had enveloped the Diet immediately evaporated.

In October 1960, a national meeting of *Asahi* bureau chiefs was held in Nagoya. There the *Asahi* director of the editorial board, Ryū Shintarō, reflected on the security treaty, saying that the Japanese people "have a tendency to align themselves with their neighbors when one starts to take action." This "facileness toward action" was not only "in evidence within the students who joined the demonstrations, but also in ordinary people." This is "our responsibility" and we must "reflect on how the media's ability to 'enlighten' is not sufficient to the task." During the Second World War, newspapers were a "guiding engine" of public opinion. Ryū, who joined *Asahi* in 1936, likely carried forward this awareness in his leading role from that time into the postwar. He was looking down on people protesting in the demonstrations from his office on the fourth floor of the *Asahi* offices. In 1962, Ryū retired from his office, a position he had held for fourteen years since 1948 during the American occupation. Five years later, at the age of 66, he passed away.

The Security Treaty of 1960, which split public opinion in two, forced the paper to confront the question: what is "media impartiality?" That question confronts us even now.

High-speed Growth and the Tokyo Olympics

No longer the postwar

The phrase, "the postwar is over," extolled in Japan's 1956 economic white paper, is also used frequently in newspapers. Somehow it was a phrase to be proud of, even though that year's white paper did not exclaim that the grueling lifestyle of the postwar had finished. The banner of the paper read, "Economic Planning Agency White Paper Announces Special Circumstances of Postwar Over."[1] According to the white paper's analysis, 1955 was "the best economic year of the postwar" because exports were favorable without a cost of living increase. The real national per-capita income was rising, along with the mining and manufacturing industrial production. The white paper explained, "The valley into which we descended with the defeat was deep," so climbing back out was quite quick and because there was a chance that growth would slacken off after this, it was necessary to modernize. The report concluded: "we are no longer in the era of the 'postwar.' Presently, we are trying to deal with these new circumstances and face the fact that the growth of recovery after the war is over." The white paper reproved a clinging to the "postwar." An *Asahi* editorial also weighed in: "Furthermore, many problems still exist. However, it is obvious that we should rid ourselves of this persistent attitude of blaming the war and encourage a way to create anew forces for economic development."[2]

The infamous line "the postwar is over" had its roots in an article written by pundit Nakano Yoshio in the February 1956 edition of *Literary Annals* (*Bungei Shunjū*). The title was brazenly "the 'postwar' is over" and it asked, "Isn't it time in this era of searching for new ideals, which has thrown away the dreams of an empire and instead seeks human happiness as a small country, to relinquish this convenient term 'postwar' which has been used to tidy up everything, even the criminal?" At the time, writer Handō Kazutoshi, working at the editorial desk of the same journal, said: "Nakano's piece spoke with awareness. If you took the phrase out of context, separately as used in the economic white paper, it took on a different meaning." The white paper brought on a backlash. The editor-in-chief of *Notebook on Living* (*Kurashi no techō*), Hanamori Yasuji, wrote to the *Asahi* saying, "Don't be ridiculous!!" "You use the phrase 'the postwar is over,' which sounds like something more hedonistic youths would utter, but housing is still insufficient. [...] I don't understand how, thanks to the war, we unwillingly have to live as renters but yet somehow only the 'economy' is no longer in the postwar."

The author of the white paper from the Economic Planning Agency, Gotō Yonosuke, defended himself in the *Asahi* but in October the white paper on public welfare pointed out the disparity for nearly ten million people on low income. Two years later, Nakano wrote in the *Literary Annals* that he had only been explaining that the scars of war still remained everywhere. "Of late, there has been no phrase that has raised such an unfortunate misunderstanding," he lamented.

The three sacred treasures

Prosperity continued into 1956, and the phrase "the best times since Emperor Jimmu" became popular. The "three sacred treasures" began selling well: the black and white TV, the electric washing machine, and the electric refrigerator.[3] Singer Frank Nagai sang of the "13,800 yen" monthly salary for white-collar workers. The price of a washing machine fell between 20,000 and 30,000 yen and that of a black and white television was about 80,000 yen. The first to gain massive popularity was the washing machine and the boom began when Sanyo Electronics started selling the "Jet Style" in 1953. It was half the cost of previous machines with a shorter wash time but washing machines did not sell easily. Makers pushed the idea that washing by hand was hard work and that "the 'labor' of washing weighed one down like an elephant." The *Asahi* household column introduced the Japanese Electrical Manufacturers' Association calculation that a year's worth of laundry for a family of five weighed about 675 kilograms, or "the weight of Hanako, the elephant at Ueno Zoo."[4] Sanyo Electric president Iue Toshio explained:

> It is quite difficult to introduce such appliances into households with elderly people. For the older generation it seems unconscionable to buy such luxuries. [...] They think that it is outrageous how recently young brides only think about how to do things with ease. [...] So, although many wives may want them, and even if their husbands consent, there are many who won't buy them if their elders do not agree.[5]

Asahi also published a cynical article with the headline "The Loud Calls to 'Liberate Women' Without Running Water from 'Tokyo Village.'" The article told of households without running water who still used pumps and who wasted their meager earnings on a washing machine.[6] A submission to the *Moments* (*Hitotoki*) column exclaimed, "I think laundry is a fun and special privilege given only to healthy women."[7] Even with these tongue-in-cheek articles, the 1956 New Year's card lottery prize changed from a sewing machine to an electric washing machine. A full-page ad on New Year's Day from Matsushita Electric Industrial Company (now Panasonic) featured author Tsuboi Sakae saying that doing laundry, which had become more difficult with advancing age, was now something to look forward to. At the end of the year, the household column recapped that "the biggest product to take over housewives' hearts is none other than the washing machine." During the 1950s, while the washing machine was mainly a topic in newspaper household columns, accidents and price wars were news. But a

Figure 30   Flourishing "cultural laundries" similar to today's coin laundry shop. Ten minutes' use of an electric washing machine cost 15 yen in 1955 Kobe, Japan.

column in the financial section introduced the explosive sales: in 1957, 20 percent of households owned electric washing machines, climbing rapidly to 50 percent in 1961 and by 1970 exceeded 90 percent. It was not until 1994 in a special editorial on the fifty years following the war that the revolution in living standards was broached: "For Japanese women who grew up with the reality that 'grandma went to the river to do laundry' was not a line from a fairy tale, the washing machine was a revolution."

The dream of a Tokyo Olympics

The first Olympics in Asia opened in Tokyo in 1964. The selection of Tokyo was made at the May 1959 general meeting of the International Olympic Committee (IOC). The *Vox Populi, Vox Dei* column in *Asahi* revealed: "We were struck by both happiness and unease. [...] It was overwhelming thinking about how bad the roads were, the poor sewers, and worrying about thieves. And what should we do about money?"[8]

The dream of a Tokyo Olympics took hold first in 1936. For Japan this was a major event to celebrate "2600 years of Imperial Rule" and was to be held in 1940. However, in 1937, Japan crossed the Rubicon into a war with China. The Army withdrew the participation of commissioned officers in equestrian events and support dwindled as politicians also expressed that they were opposed. In December, the Japanese Army occupied Nanjing, China. At the beginning of 1938, Britain and several northern European nations began to voice their opposition to the Tokyo Olympics. *Asahi* wrote that such recalcitrance was because the war was dragging on between China and Japan at the time. *Asahi* often quoted Avery Brundage, head of the American Olympic committee who had supported the Tokyo Olympics, writing of the necessity to keep "sports and politics separate." *Asahi* ran copy such as "Don't get sidelined, America supports the Tokyo Games."[9] The March 18, 1938 edition noted that while the boycott of the British equestrians was "incomprehensible" and the opposition from China was "whiney," "justice had prevailed over all manner of obstacles" when the schedule for the Tokyo competition was finalized at the general meeting of the IOC earlier that month. When a *New York Times* editorial voiced antagonism toward the Tokyo Olympics, it was disregarded as "befuddled" in *Asahi*'s June 22 edition. Ironically, counter to the vigor expressed in the papers, in July 1938 the Japanese government decided to relinquish the Olympics as it was "not appropriate for both moral and material reasons." The *Asahi* editorial on July 15 recounted, "in light of the current circumstances in which we are trying to concentrate everything on the objectives of the war, such a decision is sincerely unavoidable."

But there was news behind the news and readers were kept in the dark. *The Washington Post* had reported,

> A contributing factor in the decision may have been the rising tide of sentiment in democratic lands against participation in the 1940 games because of the way in which Japan has acted toward China. The bombardment of unfortified Chinese cities, the barbarous conduct of Japanese troops at Nanking and elsewhere—such and similar actions contravened every canon of sportsmanship exemplified by the Olympic ideal.[10]

Actually, the IOC president Henri de Baillet-Latour met with the Japanese ambassador in April and informed the diplomat that he had received 150 telegrams opposing the Japanese Olympics and recommended that Japan withdraw to save face. Recently, while Musashino Art University professor Aonuma Hiroyuki was conducting research for his book *A History of British Sports*, he came across a document from the British Foreign Office seeking cooperation in the Far East. The document stated that a boycott of the Tokyo Olympics would be unpleasant but that "it was necessary for the Tokyo Olympics to die off naturally." Many people did not understand the reasons behind other countries' opposition to the 1940 Olympics, even as the 1964 Olympics approached.

The peace ceremony

On Saturday, October 10, 1964, the Tokyo Olympics opened. Iwai Hiroyasu from the local news desk at *Asahi* took his position in the press seats and "couldn't keep still." The reporters scattered around the stands came running up to where Iwai was sitting with changes to their draft copies. The opening ceremony, scheduled to begin at 2.00 p.m., would not make the first evening edition of the paper. At such times, previously a pre-prepared "scheduled copy" would be published. According to *Asahi* internal documents, in 1952 the president of the Bank of Japan was scheduled to give a speech "against lowering interest rates," but in his actual delivery he said "lowering interest rates is advisable." Every paper that had printed a pre-scheduled copy published something different from what had actually happened. After that, *Asahi* added "from the draft of the talk" to its stories. At the 1956 Melbourne Olympics, *Asahi* forbade the use of pre-scheduled copy without first confirming and so in 1964 *Asahi* was the only paper with no early evening edition covering the opening ceremony.

For the Tokyo Olympic opening ceremony, the first evening edition began with, "since the morning people have flowed in and [...] we are waiting for two o'clock." A later evening edition finally reported that "everyone was waiting, faces full of anticipation" for the Japanese Olympic athletes marching in the parade. But how do you report what everyone has seen on television? It was the following day's morning edition that printed the real experience:

> The atmosphere unconsciously made you feel as if you wanted to take a deep breath. [...] The only way to describe the opening ceremonies was as a heart-warming spectacle. Processions of young people holding the flags of various countries marched in unison to the music. [...] It is hard to believe that wars have started and people have killed each other under these same flags. Peace really is a wondrous thing.[11]

The author of this *Vox Populi, Vox Dei* column was Irie Tokurō. Before the war he served as a war reporter during the 1939 Nomonhan Incident and he remembers, "If I had made a single mistake I would be dead." If we look back at it now, the most common word *Asahi* used to describe the opening ceremony was "peace," followed probably in close second by the term "war." According to Iwai, who spoke with other reporters about how the Olympics should be treated, someone said "the peace Olympics." Iwai recalled, "That was the atmosphere at the time." The stadium where the opening ceremony was held stood in the same spot where a sendoff party had been held in the rain at the end of the war for students departing for the front. A poem, selected by three judges from *Asahi*'s poetry circle, captured this incongruity.

> *As the ground on which the Olympic torch burns, so does the field. It was raining that day, twenty years ago, when you left for the front.* (Iida Hisao)

Sports reporter Chūjō Kazuo often heard Tabata Masaji—the original chief executive of the organizing committee, which put the Tokyo Olympics on the right track—say: "Japan made war but I want to inform the people of the world that really we are a peace loving people." Chūjō also recalls Tabata saying, "It is because we are at peace that we can have the Olympics. However, having the Olympics does not make us peaceful."

Super-fast dreams

The Tokyo Olympics were called "the one trillion yen Olympic Games." According to official reports, total expenses were about 987.4 billion yen. However, around 97 percent was for "related expenses" and not used directly for the Olympics. Heading the list of expenses was the Tōkaidō Shinkansen (bullet train) project at 380 billion yen. On October 1, 1964, days before the Tokyo Olympics opened, the bullet train began operation. The *Asahi* evening edition made the announcement on the front page, calling it "The Birth of the World's Fastest Train that Travels at 'the Speed of Dreams.'" It was an event for the whole country and even Emperor Hirohito offered remarks at the opening ceremony. A news reporter for the Osaka regional office was on the train from Osaka and wrote, "It reaches top speeds of 200 km/hour. [. . .] Before we knew it the Meishin Expressway was on our left and the cars we passed looked like snails." Until just before the line opened, construction on the rails was still underway and there were some attempts to sabotage the system by placing rocks on the rails. If something went wrong on the first real run, it would have been a terrible disaster. Itō Kunio, in charge of covering the national railways, made a list of the hospitals along the railway line. Itō recalls, "Far from all our poor expectations, it was a huge success. Until then Japan had been all disasters and accidents and we hadn't had many such brilliant achievements. I think everyone was thrilled with the bullet train and the Olympics, deepening our self-confidence."

The city of Tokyo changed before everyone's eyes. Articles from this time convey a leap in emotional pride. With Ginza subway station at its center, "the East's best promenade" was completed. "From close to East Ginza Station, Expressway #1 stretched to Haneda airport. [. . .] The appearance of this wonderful highway seemed to make one think 'so *this* is what you call a road.'"[12] When the Tokyo Metropolitan Expressway opened, it was filled with a continuous parade of people going by car in their pajamas to see Haneda Airport and enjoy the cool evening air. Prime Minister Ikeda Hayato was critical of these revelers and a column in the evening edition of *Asahi* introduced the explanations of some who championed the parade mentality. "At the bottom of feeling ashamed about the pajama revelers is a desire to look good to foreigners. This is a kind of pre-Olympic pathological xenophilia! We do not live for the sake of other people, we live for ourselves," the paper exclaimed.[13]

Figure 31   Bright decorations and a brass band concert send off the "Hikari #1" bullet train departing from Tokyo Station at 6 a.m. on October 1, 1964.

From 1959, when Tokyo won the Olympic bid, the Ministry of Education took public opinion surveys: "Do you think we can put on a fantastic Olympics in which we do not embarrass ourselves in front of foreigners?" In 1964, NHK took a similar survey. At the beginning, 60 percent answered they thought that the Tokyo Olympics could be "outstanding" but after that the numbers fell. Then in June, four months before the opening of the games, the number shot up to 90 percent and after the games 100 percent felt the games had "been outstandingly" managed. In 1964, Japan renovated its image in the world. When Kawabata Yasunari won the 1968 Nobel Prize for Literature, *Asahi* wrote in its editorial, "You could even say instead that the award is already late in coming" and warned against "this self-deprecating tendency" toward the West.

The Polluted Archipelago

Encounter with the unknown

The Sea of Shiranui in Kumamoto Prefecture was known as "a sea overflowing with fish" but the unusual phenomenon that caught media attention had to do instead with cats. The August 1, 1954 *Kumamoto Daily Newspaper* (*Kumamoto Nichinichi Shimbun*) published a short report in the local news section: "Cats completely eradicated by epilepsy in the hamlet of Modō in Minamata City; complaints about the sudden increase in rats." In this fishing village of about 120 households, virtually all one hundred cats had, one after the other, "danced around in circles like they had gone mad" and died. At a loss over what to do because of the sudden increase in the rat population, the residents went to city hall to request better extermination. A *Kumamoto Nichinichi* reporter who happened to be at city hall that day turned the news into an article. This was the first report of Minamata disease.

Shortly before, a reporter from *Asahi* had also noticed something strange. In late July 1954, Minamata correspondent Uemura Makoto had taken a picture of a cat that moved as if it was dancing. Uemura sent the picture and an article to the Kumamoto bureau head but the story never developed. On July 31, Saho Hajime, who had been a reporter at the Kumamoto bureau for three years, also found an account of "insane cats" in Minamata in the records of accidents and events collected by the prefectural police. These stories caught his eye but he said, "I let it go thinking someone had probably spread around rat poison and the cats ate it and got sick." Never in his wildest dreams did Saho think he was letting the first report of a historical event escape his notice.

Other people, too, in particular fishermen and their families, had been falling ill with a strange disease since the end of the previous year. Sufferers complained of numbness in their hands and feet. Before long they were screaming violently, entire bodies cramped, and ultimately they died. Varied diagnoses such as alcohol poisoning, stroke, and beriberi were offered. On May 1, 1956, two sisters were admitted with paralysis to the New Japan Nitrogenous Fertilizer Company factory affiliated hospital.[1] The health department was notified of an outbreak of an "unknown disease of the central nervous system" and it was then recognized as an official disease. The reporting was shoddy and much information was not followed up on or lost. At first, the symptoms were reported as an infectious disease. The *Western Japan Newspaper* (*Nishi Nippon Newspaper*) reported on May 8, "killing or causing madness, a strange

Figure 32   Third outbreak of Minamata disease. Fishermen throw contaminated fish onto the grounds of the chemical factory deemed a source of the mercury waste water. Uto City, Kumamoto Prefecture, June 18, 1973.

contagious disease in Minamata." On May 16, the *Kumamoto Nichinichi* reported: "Origin of a strange disease afflicting children in Minamata, is it the same origin as outbreak among cats?" Three months later on August 25, *Asahi* finally reported: "Kumamoto University and others are investigating in earnest the unknown origins of a mysterious disease with a high fatality rate in the Minamata area of Kumamoto." The article was only published in several western regions of Japan.

Environment-related diseases continued to spread in all areas. Under the heading "The First Recovery from Itai-itai Disease, Cause Noted as 'the Feudalistic Farming Village,'" the May 3 *Asahi* told how a female patient at a hospital in Tokyo was treated with nutritious food and rest and made a complete recovery. Kobayashi Naoki, Professor of Sociology at Hōsei University, continued to investigate reports on the Minamata disease. He said that, "when the scope of an unprecedented situation gradually becomes apparent, there is a strong tendency for the larger media outlets to try to ignore or to force the news into frameworks familiar to them."

The reflex to argue about causes

Even after official confirmation of the mysterious disease that broke out in Minamata City in 1956, there was much debate over causes and reporting wandered directionless.

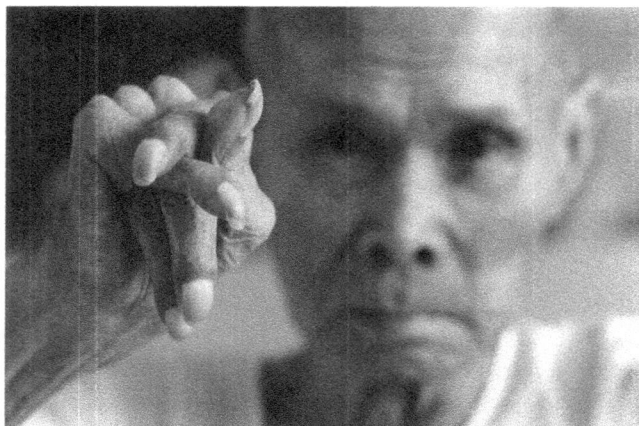

Figure 33 Suffering from Minamata disease symptoms, this fisherman's fingers have become deformed and twisted, Minamata, Kumamoto Prefecture, 1970.

Early on, effluent from the Chisso Minamata factory came under suspicion as the source of the disease because the chemical manufacturing process released various toxic substances into the environment. The March 7, 1957 Kumamoto edition of *Asahi* reported that a medical research unit at Kumamoto University suspected the cause was highly linked to manganese. At first, selenium and thallium were also suspected. It took three years before it was officially announced that the cause of Minamata disease had finally been confirmed. For western Japan, which included the island of Kyūshū and Yamagata Prefecture, this was major news: "Kumamoto Research Unit Confirms on Three Levels—Analysis, Clinical, Pathology—Cause of Minamata Disease is Organic Mercury."[2] This important news did not make it into the Tokyo paper because each region published independently and followed a long-standing trend to prioritize news from its own offices, making it difficult to run stories originating from other offices.

The first mention of mercury as the cause of Minamata disease in the Tokyo edition of *Asahi* was not until four months after it made news in Kyūshū. Even then the news was mentioned as part of a movement to deny the theory of organic mercury. A November 12 article reported the outcome of Tokyo Institute of Technology Professor Kiyoura Raisaku's investigation submitted to the Ministry of International Trade and Industry, which declared "it is not possible that the cause is the factory wastewater." However, on the same day the Ministry of Health, Labor and Welfare's Food Sanitation Investigation Committee backed the Kumamoto University finding that the cause "was some kind of organic mercury compound." Even after this, articles such as "Cause is Poison in Seafood, Mercury Origins of Minamata Disease Invalidated," which repeated Kiyoura's "not mercury theory," continued to appear in Tokyo newspapers.[3] Such articles asserted: "damaged fish were consumed."

Shibata Tetsuji, who served as the head of *Asahi*'s Tokyo science section, recalled: "newspapers carry a considerable responsibility in going along with the machinations to drag out the confirmation of the cause." In Shibata's analysis, the Chisso Company created this state of affairs by repeatedly sending reports to ministries and hosting press conferences in Tokyo, suggesting that "there is conflict in the scientific world about the cause and it has not been confirmed." Shibata points out that Chisso took advantage of the media's tendency to put two arguments side by side as a means to report the news and noted urban newspaper preference to use only stories that emanated from Tokyo. In the shadow of this drawn out controversy over the causes, patients exhausted by their painful lives agreed to receive consolation money from Chisso on December 30, 1959. The allowance to patients, which was backdated to the time they became sick, was 100,000 yen per year (30,000 yen for minors), and upon death condolence money of 300,000 yen. The details of this solatium contract stipulated that even if the cause was later proven to be wastewater from the factory, victims could not seek further compensation. This clause left sufferers dissatisfied. Nonetheless, the following day the Kumamoto edition of *Asahi* wrote that it was an "amicable settlement." Thirteen years later, this compensation contract was invalidated by a court ruling at the first Minamata Disease lawsuit, noting that such a deal was "offensive to the public order and morals."

The accusation brought on by "Cat #400"

Although the Chisso Company completed a compensation agreement in December 1959, management did not admit that the cause of the disease was wastewater from its own Minamata factory and continued to conceal the grave reality. That same year, the chief of the Minamata factory affiliated hospital, Hosokawa Hajime, performed an experiment in which he mixed factory waste liquid into cat food. "Cat #400" subsequently developed Minamata disease on October 7, meaning that Chisso knew the cause of the disease prior to the agreement with patients in December. Tokyo University graduate student Ui Jun and photographer Kuwabara Shisei learned about these experiments on animals such as Cat #400 in the summer of 1962. Ui alluded to the truth in a labor organization bulletin but it garnered little reaction. After the December 1959 settlement there was almost a complete cessation of reports on Minamata disease until the summer of 1968. Patients and their families remained silent while facing discrimination and the media pushed the idea that "the Minamata disease problem is finished." Later, this period was labeled "the eight years of silence."

  Meanwhile, environmental pollution had spread across much of Japan. Leading the charge against this flood were four large environmental pollution trials, including the first Niigata Minamata suit, which opened on June 12, 1967. Galvanized by this proceeding, thirty-six people launched the People's Association Against Minamata Disease (later called the People's Minamata Disease Association) on January 12, 1968. The only person in the press to join was *Asahi*'s Minamata correspondent Nakahara Takanori. He recalls: "I understood the principle of 'journalistic neutrality' but I saw the suffering and destitution of the patients myself and ventured to join." Hiyoshi Fumiko, the president of the People's Association, tells how "Nakahara was able to judge the situation from a distance and offer us advice." Ui, the Tokyo University graduate student, entrusted Nakahara with his privately printed series that totaled five hundred pages. In June, Health and Welfare Minister Sonoda Sunao, who was from Amakusa City in Kumamoto Prefecture, ordered the pollution section of his ministry to acknowledge that Minamata disease stemmed from pollution. The origin of this directive is attributed to a suggestion from Miyazawa Kiichi, director of the Economic Planning Agency.[4] Around this time, plans to shift manufacturing methods that produced organic mercury emissions to those that did not were implemented at various domestic company locations.

In August, to prepare for the anticipated government stand on this problem, Magami Yasunari, a local news reporter for the western region who had experience collecting news about Minamata disease, arrived in Minamata. Magami, who had read Ui's books, took the concealment of Cat #400 as proof of a corporate conspiracy that would deal a decisive blow to the Chisso Corporation. Magami visited Hosokawa Hajime, the now retired hospital chief, in his hometown in Ehime Prefecture. After listening to old stories for the first two hours, Magami put aside his pen and notebook and turned the conversation to the cat experiment. Hosokawa pulled out his notes from that time and then for almost three hours explained the situation in detail. Following this revelation a series of articles on "Minamata Disease," pursuing Chisso's corporate responsibility, continued for almost a year in *Asahi*.

Mercury panic

Around four in the morning Harada Masazumi, an assistant professor at Kumamoto University Medical School, was woken up by phone calls from each of the media companies. On May 22, 1973, *Asahi* printed on its front page, "In the Ariake Sea 'Third Minamata Disease' in Amakusa, Ariake Town with 8 Patients." The Kumamoto University research unit investigating the mercury contamination around Minamata traveled away from the Chisso contaminated area to the Ariake Sea coast. There the team performed medical exams on 904 fishermen. The doctors observed eight people with diminished vision and poor motor coordination, ailments that were indistinguishable from Minamata disease. The chemical plant on the shores of the Midori River, which flows into the Ariake Sea, had been using mercury until 1965. However, the concentration of mercury in the eight patients' hair was low. Based on his experience with Minamata disease, Harada concluded that the contamination was from the past but he also believed that more evidence was needed. The day the *Asahi* article on this story came out, the research unit had submitted its yearly report to Kumamoto Prefecture. At the end of the report, the leader of the research unit, Kumamoto University professor Takeuchi Tadao, wrote: "even if the Ariake area outbreak stems from the past, if the patients can be considered to have organic mercury poisoning, then that would constitute a third outbreak, following the second outbreak of Minamata disease in Niigata. The implications are serious and it is a problem that we must resolve." Sasaki Yoshitaka from *Asahi*'s Kumamoto bureau knew the contents of the report ahead of time and published the news. A further series of articles titled, "The Endless Horror of Mercury," provided a chart of the twenty-two factories around Japan that had a history of using mercury and pointed to the probability that Minamata disease would spread to each of these areas. While the big four pollution lawsuits continued to be won by the plaintiffs, reports of "a new Minamata disease" unleashed a "mercury panic." There were reports of a similar illness in Ōmuta City in Fukuoka Prefecture and along the coastal bay in Yamaguchi Prefecture. The public started buying less fish as a consequence. In July 1973, 12,000 fishmongers held a rally in Tokyo calling for "the return of clean fish." In Minamata, fishermen threw five tons of fish onto the Chisso corporate premises.

The Environment Agency Investigation Committee released its findings in July 1974. Apart from one person in Minamata Bay, the committee "did not find anyone who was judged to be poisoned by organic mercury." The investigation found that diminished movement was due to "spondylosis" and diminished vision to "cataracts." Even now Harada says, "the cases I diagnosed on the Ariake coast were clearly organic mercury poisoning" but "an ill-planned article was not able to topple various [Japanese] social structures in which 'authority' buries the injuries of the weak." Was the report of "Third Minamata Disease" a case of jumping the gun? Half a year before the author Sasaki Yoshitaka died in 2004, he had this to say about the *Kumamoto Nichinichi* coverage: "We couldn't have predicted the panic." He added, "[Japan's manufacturing industry] was changing to methods that did not use mercury. In that sense we accomplished our part. [...] But I do have doubts whether the news was a bit sensationalized."

The narrow acknowledgment of Minamata disease sufferers

On May 30, 1969, the *Asahi* western edition printed at the top of its front page, "Previously Unknown Minamata Disease Patients." In Tsunagi town, Minamata City's neighbor to the north, an 86-year-old town physician died from a stomach hemorrhage. According to the instructions in his will, an autopsy was performed in a Kumamoto University pathology class, which revealed brain shrinkage particular to Minamata disease. In his later life, the doctor had experienced hand tremors but had not connected the symptoms to Minamata disease. Up until this point, 116 people had been certified as suffering from Minamata disease but it became apparent that there were probably many hidden victims of the disease who, like the town doctor, did not show obvious symptoms. Professor of Pathology, Takeuchi Tadao, said at that time: "If we use the metaphor of a mountain the known cases of Minamata disease are only the summit. The fields at the foot of the mountain spread much wider." In this manner, five years later, applications to Kumamoto Prefecture to be recognized as a victim of Minamata disease totaled more than three thousand.

In July 1971, when the Environment Agency was established, a movement began to widen the basis for Minamata disease applications for assistance. On August 7, agency director Ōishi Buichi decided to repeal Kumamoto Prefecture's rejection of Kawamoto Teruo and eight others' application to be recognized as Minamata disease sufferers. Ōishi pushed the idea that in cases where organic mercury poisoning could not be denied, sufferers should still be eligible and it was even made officially public. *Asahi* published this story on the front page with the headline, "Suspicion Alone Will Get You Aid." Actual patients were not pleased with this news. While raising his severely disabled daughter and continuing to support Minamata disease patients, sociologist Saishu Satoru points out that, "Even if *Asahi* had no ill will, it can't be denied that this report marked the time from which there was room to call some sufferers 'fakes.'" "The discrimination and defamation that patients faced is likely well known. They needed to imagine that terms like 'suspicion exists' in huge print on the front page might enflame further discrimination and defamation." In fact, Kawamoto Teruo, while in charge of compensation negotiations with Chisso, continued to be slandered and labeled a "fake victim." Harada Masazumi, who works as the head of the Kumamoto Gakuen University's Open Research Center for Minamata Studies, points out that "*Asahi*'s 1973 article 'Third Minamata Disease,' was later disproven and became the turning point at which certification of patients became more strict."

On July 1, 1977, Ishihara Shintarō, head of the Environmental Agency, established new guidelines for "Acquired Minamata Disease Evaluation Criteria" and made them public. His guidelines added new elements to the certification process. Centering on sensory impairment, the report stipulated that only those with multiple symptoms would be certified as victims of Minamata disease. An editorial in the July 3 *Asahi* evaluated that these new criteria would "have little influence but will make the evaluation wording clearer and serve as a step forward." This forecast was completely wrong. Following this development, more than 10,000 applications were rejected, directly connected to the more restrictive certification process. Despite a 1986 decision that such a policy made the selection "excessively narrow," no revisions have been implemented.

Unforgettable

Nishimura Mikio retired from the *Asahi* but each year he leaves his home in Chiba Prefecture for several months and rents a house in Minamata. He drinks with the aging fishermen and listens to their old stories. What happened here at this place where Minamata disease began? In order to leave a record for later generations, Nishimura has been compiling a detailed account, already reaching close to five hundred pages but still far from complete. When he was just a fledgling reporter, Nishimura was part of the team that covered Minamata disease and even after that he continued to be involved with reporting on the disease alongside his work as a science reporter. "If the newspaper had reported the problem sooner [...] I look back and am full of regrets. Even though I have left this line of work, it is a problem I would like to deal with," he says. Ritsumeikan University professor Kino Shigeru points out, "Minamata disease is a microcosm of Japan's environmental problems." With Toyama Prefecture's Itai-itai disease, the orthopedic surgery association "authority" heaped scorn on the domestic doctor who announced the cause as cadmium. With the asthma problem in Yokkaichi, Mie Prefecture and the second outbreak of Minamata disease in Niigata Prefecture, the regulation of businesses that emitted pollutants was lax, inviting the further spread of damage.

Figure 34   Protests at the Chisso general stockholders meeting, where a protester who lost both parents to the disease confronts company president Egashira Yutaka, November 28, 1970, Osaka.

Reporting on Minamata disease repeatedly "hushed" the actual situation. The author Ishimure Michiko wrote in her book, *Paradise in the Sea of Sorrow* (*Kugai Jōdo*), which describes the misery of Minamata disease, "terrifyingly, the mass media seems to have been busy and forgotten" all about the issue.[5] A current typical example of the same problem would be asbestos. The *Asahi* evening edition on November 17, 1986 reported on its front page: "Asbestos Dust Pollution, Outbreak of Lung Cancer Among Former American Military Base Workers." But over the next twenty years newspapers, including the regional papers, largely remained silent on the health damage. It was only in June 2005 that the *Mainichi Newspaper* reported that there were many deaths around the asbestos factory.

On one hand, the media certainly conveyed the actual harm of environmental pollution. In November 1970, at the Chisso general stockholders meeting, the victims pressed the shareholders to take corporate responsibility in the "one share movement." In June 1972, at the United Nations conference on the human environment in Stockholm, congenital victims of Minamata disease appealed to the public concerning their tragic plight. The more widely the media reported, the more people's interest grew. In his book *Minamata*, a detailed account of the disease, Professor Timothy George at the University of Rhode Island, points out that the source of the great strength of the Minamata disease movement was the strong support it received from ordinary citizens and not connections to any political parties.[6] According to Takamine Takeshi, head of the *Kumamoto Nichinichi* newspaper editorial committee who has followed the Minamata disease problem for more than thirty years, in the end "regardless of whether the coverage is by local or national newspapers, it comes down to a matter of whether there is a journalist who maintains his/her interest. It doesn't really make a difference if it's a national or local paper."

Gazing at the Two Koreas

The younger brother who crossed to the north

"The first mass migration from the free world to the Communist bloc."

The picture at the top of the front page of the *Asahi* evening edition on December 14, 1959 was the image of the first boat leaving Niigata harbor to return Koreans in Japan to the Democratic People's Republic of Korea (North Korea). Because Japan and North Korea did not have diplomatic relations, the Red Cross of the two countries concluded a special agreement and 93,000 Koreans and related Japanese spouses and relatives crossed to North Korea between 1959 and 1984. The January 26, 1960 issue of the *Asahi* introduced a couple heading to North Korea: "I will voyage together with my Korean wife." The Korean wife, Sin Sŏngsuk, waves happily in the picture while her Japanese husband, Shibata Kōzō, says, "I am ready to do manual labor to support my family." Four years later, a letter arrived from Kōzō at the Tokyo house of Shibata Hiroyuki (Shibata Kōzō's elder brother) written in small characters packed onto a scrap of dirty paper: "I'm sorry for always asking so brazenly but could you please send vitamin pills, knitting wool, and two men's wrist watches. Our three-year-old daughter suffers from tuberculosis."

After graduating from Tohoku University, Kōzō had joined the Ministry of Labor and was posted to Takamatsu, Kagawa Prefecture. There he met Sŏngsuk in a small eatery she had opened while looking after the two children she had with her late husband. At New Year's in 1960, Kōzō returned to his family home and informed them, "I want to go to North Korea to help with the reconstruction." His family were strongly opposed and asked "Why?" but he was resolute. He set off only telling his mother that he had gotten married a month earlier. Hiroyuki recalls, "the prejudice against North Koreans in Japan was severe so my brother was probably thinking about the children's education and their future." Letters often arrived from Kōzō in Pyongyang, asking for money to be sent. But he seemed to be doing well sending messages such as, "I am working at a publishing company and teaching Japanese" or "we've had a baby girl." However, in January 1965 sad news arrived from Sŏngsuk: "Kōzō has gone for medical treatment. I also have heart trouble." That was the final letter the elder Shibata received in Japan and then all contact ceased. Hiroyuki asked the Japan Red Cross and the General Association of Korean Residents in Japan (*Chōsen Sōren*) to look into Kōzō's whereabouts but nothing came of it. In 1972, while visiting North Korea on an

Figure 35   Shimane Prefecture staff land on Takeshima and erect signposts marking it as "Takeshima," June 1953, the year before South Korean armed personnel were stationed there.

assignment, a relative who was an *Asahi* reporter asked the authorities to investigate. "He was sick but he recovered and went back to work" was the response the reporter received on the morning he was scheduled to leave Pyongyang. On December 10, 1992, the *Literary Weekly* (*Shūkan Bunshun*) printed an article entitled, "I was imprisoned in a camp with Kōzō." The report revealed the testimony of a man who had escaped North Korea. The international human rights group Amnesty International investigated and received a response from the North Korean authorities. Kōzō had been imprisoned for twenty-six years on charges of espionage but the entire family died in a train accident in March 1990 shortly after he was released. Hiroyuki lamented, "If he had been in Japan he could have lived a happy life."

Heaven on earth

Satō Kunio, an *Asahi* Niigata bureau reporter, went to the lodgings where resident Koreans in Japan stayed before boarding the boat to journey to North Korea. Before their return home, all were giddy with hope. An article that introduced newlywed resident Koreans from Tokyo sat at the top of the front page of the local news section on December 14, 1959. The wife said, "I am happy to be going to a socialist country. My husband designs bridges so [...] maybe he can build a fantastic bridge to connect Japan and North Korea." Not everyone was pleased. Members of the Korean Residents Union in Japan (representing South Korea) tried to stop the train carrying North Koreans to Niigata by sitting on the tracks. Satō thought: "socialism is an ideal society without any difference between rich and poor. These are people who don't understand the changing times." Reporters from the *Asahi, Yomiuri, Mainichi,* and *Sankei* newspapers, as well as *Kyōdō News,* journeyed to North Korea from December 1959 to January 1960 to report on the returnees' welcome. *Asahi* subsequently sent Irie Tokurō, who wrote the *Vox Populi, Vox Dei* column: "I was awoken to the socialist establishment. [...] The roads are lined on both sides with modern style buildings, they are all homes for laborers." He wrote that North Korean Prime Minister Kim Il-Sung "was a kind of smiling amiable sort of elderly uncle." North Korea "completely accepted their poor and ashamed brethren from Japan [...] and guaranteed their livelihood."[1]

It was not only *Asahi* that painted such a rosy impression. *Yomiuri* introduced Japanese wives of returnees who had "bid farewell to their lives of poverty and sometimes disgrace in Japan."[2] They were welcomed into a country of "new dreams" in which they were given their ideal jobs and invited to a new year's party by Kim Il-Sung. On December 25, 1959, *Sankei* reported that "housing has been built in every area and schools have also been readied." According to the *Sankei,* preparations for receiving the returnees were so thorough that "once on board the boat in Niigata the rest was as smooth as being carried along on a conveyor belt." The following day the *Mainichi* evening edition published an article entitled, "Young and Vibrant North Koreans." The paper reported that finding jobs was done through "'state planned deployment' so that even if one remains completely silent he or she will receive a work assignment." The General Association of Korean Residents in Japan called the North Korean motherland "Heaven on Earth."

It did not take long, however, for returnees to awaken from this dream. A man who had returned with his family in 1961 remembers that the shoes of the children who came to meet him at the harbor in North Korea were falling to pieces and their toes were sticking out. There were also people who came to hug him and he remembers they smelled strangely. His father continually apologized until his death that he had been hoodwinked. The man made a daring escape and returned to Japan in 2006. The *Asahi* reporter who went to North Korea, Shimamoto Kenrō, tells how "there was always a guard with us." As soon as he returned to Japan, resident Koreans told him "your story is wrong." Shimamoto regrets having made the mistake.

In the shadow of "humanity"

Why did resident Koreans in Japan return to North Korea in such numbers? A February 5, 1959 *Asahi Newspaper* commentary article provided one answer: after the outbreak of the Pacific War, the number of resident Koreans in Japan increased by a million as a result of those forced into labor or searching for work. When the war ended, there were about 2 million in Japan and in half a year about 1.4 million returned to Korea. At the end of the 1950s, including illegal immigrants, 800,000 resided in Japan. After the war, Japan turned toward reconstruction but life for resident Koreans worsened: one in four was receiving social assistance payments and 80 percent were unemployed. "Life in Japan with such a completely dark future gave birth to crime," and the rates of criminal offences were five times those of the Japanese. The February 5 article also reported the comments of resident Koreans about the difficulty of surviving under such conditions:

"this is death by the roadside [...] if only I had a job, even as a warehouse guard." Another resident claimed, "I was bullied all the way through elementary and junior high school."

While South Korea endured the closing years of Syngman Rhee's administration, the dictatorship and corruption was undeniable. Many repatriating resident Koreans believed: "North Korea developing under socialism is our true motherland. At some point the two Koreas will probably reunite." The parents and four siblings of Sin Ch'ang sŏk, a second-generation resident Korean who lives in Tokyo's Nerima ward, returned to North Korea. He recalled: "We made a living on illegal moonshine [sake] and pachinko. Even if you graduated from university Japanese companies would not hire resident Koreans. We believed without any doubt the advertisements that 'North Korea is heaven on Earth.'" On February 13, the Japanese government acceded in a Cabinet meeting to North Korean repatriation. The editorial in the *Asahi* the following morning stated that "for resident Koreans in Japan to be able to return to where they wish is [...] a basic human right to choose the place in which one lives and everyone has now been given this right." The South Korean government opposed the conditions of return, criticizing it "as a wide humanitarian problem, we cannot but lament this situation." There were also other conditions about which the editorial kept silent.

Three years earlier, *Asahi* had published an article about "Korean people's welfare benefits."[3] About 139,000 resident Koreans were receiving social assistance payments, at a yearly cost of 2.6 billion yen. The article revealed that the Ministry of Health and Welfare was investigating that some families were receiving benefits unlawfully and they forecasted that more than 20 percent of households receiving payments would face a reduction or end of support. When news articles around this time concerned

Figure 36   Resident Koreans in Japan applaud those applying to return to North Korea, June 1959, Edakawa, Tokyo.

Koreans, they noticeably focused on investigations into disturbances at Korean villages or focused on the movements of Korean people's associations that the authorities concerned with public order kept a watch on. To the Japanese government, Korean repatriation meant less responsibility for welfare payments and fewer radical communists. On the other hand, it was said that North Korea, engaged in reconstruction following the Korean War, anticipated the labor force and technical skills of resident Koreans from Japan. The enterprise of large-scale repatriation came to fruition as a result of these entangled forces. News articles told of the poverty and discrimination that enveloped the resident Korean community. However, why were hundreds of thousands of Koreans living in Japan in the first place? Any questioning of Japan's imperial responsibility as a former colonial ruler was relatively muted.

Political gaffes

The treaty normalizing diplomatic relations between Japan and South Korea was signed in Tokyo on June 22, 1965. From the preliminary conference, the process had taken fifteen years of negotiations to reach that moment. That year, on January 7, Takasugi Shin'ichi, who had recently taken up the post as head of the delegation for negotiations with South Korea, told journalists: "Japan ruled Korea but [...] we were trying to help them. I hear that there is not a single tree left on the mountains. [...] If Korea had stayed with Japan for another twenty years then it probably would not have come to this." Takasugi was justifying colonial rule. The Japanese Communist newspaper *Red Flag* (*Akahata*) printed his remarks on the 10th but *Asahi* and the other papers remained silent because Takasugi had made his comments "off the record" and were not meant for attribution. On the 19th, the Korean newspaper, *East Asia Daily* (*Dong-a Ilbo*), reported the incident at the top of its front page: "Delegation Representative Takasugi Makes Enormous Gaffe," and criticism of Japan grew in South Korea. When the socialist party hounded the government in the Japanese Diet over the issue, *Asahi* attempted to explain the incident to its readers. The paper quoted the *Red Flag* and the *Dong-a Ilbo* in a footnote to introduce what Takasugi had said, and added his refutation.[4] *Mainichi* and *Yomiuri* both published a similar footnote in their explanations in evening editions that same day.

   Asahi's Imazu Hiroshi, who shortly after the remark became responsible for foreign affairs coverage at the paper, recounts that, "The media had no idea at the time how outrageous a remark Takasugi had made." In February, Imazu had accompanied Foreign Minister Shiina Etsusaburō on a visit to Korea and covered the initialing of the treaty. Upon their arrival at Gimpo Airport, the planned playing of Japan's national anthem had been cancelled. In the city they were surrounded by student demonstrators who yelled, "We oppose disgraceful diplomacy." When Imazu returned to Japan he wrote, "I pause and cannot help but reflect on the wounds that, even now, Japan has left in the hearts of the Korean people." The *Asahi* editorial about the treaty did not broach the issue of Japan's responsibility for colonial rule but pointed to the fishing industry's dissatisfaction concerning concessions and the shelving of territorial rights over Takeshima (known in Korea as Dokdo Island).[5] On the same page, Imazu's serialized column, "A New Era for Japan and Korea, Volume One," raised the question: "is there a way to somehow wipe away the Korean distrust of Japan and Japanese attitudes of looking down at Koreans?" Imazu pointed out that, "the main cause preventing friendship between the people of Japan and Korea was Japan's thirty-six-year rule over Korea." An article about a symposium of *Asahi* journalists, including Imazu and special correspondents from Korea filled another page. Kwŏn Ogi from the *Dong-a Ilbo*, which had printed Takasugi's remark, said that the Japanese "should understand how the past came to be" to realize that Japan-Korea negotiations were "less about negotiations with neighbors than of negotiation with history." When reading the article on the symposium, Imazu underlined Kwŏn's remarks in red. Even now these words remain clearly in his mind.

Shelving Takeshima

In an expensive residential district in Seoul, at the home of the owner of a big company, South Korean Prime Minister Chung Il-kwon and Japan's Lower House member Uno Sōsuke faced each other. It was January 1965, five months before the signing of the Treaty on Basic Relations between Japan and the Republic of Korea. The subject was the problem of territorial rights over Takeshima Island (Dokdo). Uno read a prepared statement that outlined the contents of a secret agreement. Also present was *Yomiuri* special correspondent in Seoul, Shimamoto Kenrō, who was eagerly taking notes. "The problem of Takeshima/Dokdo was resolved by not being resolved," he said.

Uno was sent as a secret envoy by Kōno Ichirō, head of the LDP's Kōno faction and Japan's Minister of State at the time. Shimamoto, while supporting Uno's work in South Korea, was expected by the Koreans to serve as a conduit to the Japanese political world and thus had access to the Korean Presidential Office. According to Shimamoto, Kōno and a secret Korean envoy had met in Tokyo and agreed to a "secret agreement" concerning shelving a discussion on the territorial rights to Takeshima. The secret meeting in Seoul was held to explain the agreement to the Korean side. However, during formal negotiations a conflict continued until the day of signing concerning whether this issue ought to be brought up as an agenda item or to touch on it in the treaty itself. In the end, the two countries agreed upon a general principle of dispute resolution by not naming Takeshima and therefore the specific problem of the island was postponed. The day after signing, June 23, the *Vox Populi, Vox Dei* column criticized the agreement saying, "it would be logical if the problem of Takeshima was resolved and then holding a formal signing between Japan and South Korea. Signing first and then postponing the resolution of Takeshima until later is backwards." The column continued, "This shuffling creates an Achilles heel in Japan-Korean relations." Conflicts over Takeshima continued to flare between Japan and Korea about every ten years since: in 1977, 1986, 1996, and 2005.

In 2005, Shimane Prefecture enacted an ordinance establishing "Takeshima Day" and in response over several days South Korean newspapers made a show of opposition. The March 17 *Chosun Ilbo* stated: the "Whole country is seething with indignation at Japan's aggressive behavior." However, such a harsh reaction was not always the norm.

In 1977 and 1986, remarks by key members of the Japanese government received a lot of coverage in Korea but were quickly put to rest. Kim Ch'unsik, the Tokyo office chief of *Dong-a Ilbo* from 2002 to 2005, explained "in 1977 and 1986 Korea was under military rule. The newspapers were controlled so the Dokdo Island problem would not interfere with Japan's economic cooperation. The collusion of both countries restrained the press from overheating." In South Korea, with the change to democratic rule, censorship regulations eased and pride rose as the Korean economy grew. With the collapse of the Cold War there was less of a need for cooperation between Japan and Korea as a unified symbol of anti-communism. When friction between Japan and Korea heated up over the regulation for "Takeshima Day," an editorial in *Asahi* touched on the 1965 pact: "Even during negotiations at that time [. . .] it was a realistic and savvy move to shelve the issue but shake hands to restore relations."[6] According to Shimamoto, "the spirit of the secret pact was that there was no resolution plan other than to conduct ourselves as adults and shelve the problem."

Showpiece nation

To report from North Korea it was first necessary to receive an invitation from the authorities. Since the 1959 coverage of the first boat returning Koreans to North Korea, reporters had not visited until 1965 when *Asahi* reporters and NHK television staff traveled there. Then in 1968, twenty years after the establishment of the North Korean state, reporters from the Japan Communist Party Journalists Club were invited. Among them was *Asahi* reporter Iwadare Hiroshi, who was also in charge of covering the General Association of Korean Residents in Japan (*Chōsen Sōren*). Iwadare wrote a report, "As I Saw North Korea" for the October 5 local news section. Other than commenting on the appearance of homes and farms, he quoted the translator on the North Korean side: "A revolution is achieved when a great enlightened person mobilizes and educates the people. Therefore, the history of the Korean revolution is the history of the great leader Kim Il-Sung." Iwadare referenced the impression of Kim Il-Sung in an internal editorial office report: "One comes to feel he is a superior human being. For that reason alone there was widespread doubt that the leader was embarking on taking on anything and everything, so what were the managers of the administration doing?"

Miyata Hiroto, who reported on North Koreans and resident Koreans in Japan from early on, went to North Korea in the autumn of 1971. His articles came out in a twelve-episode series on the front of the *Asahi* evening edition called, "North Korea, Nation of *Juche* Ideology." *Juche* was an ideology of self-reliance created by Kim Il-Sung. The series introduced the young hero who saved his fellow workers by holding up a concrete pillar in a factory with his bare hands when the pillar's supporting cable gave way. The hero did not let go even when he began to bleed profusely. The final installment wrapped up with "teachings" from Kim Il-Sung.

Nowadays, when compared to South Korea, contemporary North Korea has a strong image of being an "impoverished dictatorship" but at that time things were different. Around 1970, North Korea's GNP per capita appeared to exceed that of South Korea and there were many reports that South Korea with a military government was even more of a dictatorship. However, did these reports reflect the real truth? Mark Gayn, a journalist with Canadian citizenship, visited Korea in 1972. In the November 17 issue of *Asahi Weekly* (*Shūkan Asahi*), he called the farmers and children at the kindergarten he saw while reporting on the North Korean side "actors." In the shadow of the show of dressed up dancing kindergartners were children wearing torn clothing. According to Gayn, farmers waited in the paddy fields and only began moving the machines on cue when he was told he could take photographs. Financial journalist Okada Motoharu, after visiting North Korea in 1985, in a column in the financial pages wrote, "I just can't accept the structure that all achievements were 'the results of the leadership and concern of Chairman Kim Il-Sung and Secretary Kim Jong-Il.'" The serialized column pointed out that trade payments were overdue and statistics calculations opaque. According to Okada, "it was obvious we had not covered the most glaring issues." Iwadare believes, "It is the duty of the journalist to enter a country isolated from the news" and he visited North Korea five times. "Readers have their own views about how to think about North Korea but it wasn't fair to criticize without considering the background of the time. They were isolated and unsupported against the severe antagonism between North and South, the relations between Korea and the United States, and the rift between China and the Soviet Union, etc."

An audience with Kim Il-Sung

In the 1970s, Kim Il-Sung's North Korea and Park Chung-Hee's South Korea continued to build their economies under despotic leadership. The Japanese media, without the benefit of diplomatic relations, competed for an audience with the largely unknown Kim Il-Sung. For North Korea, a meeting was also a great opportunity for external publicity and to solidify domestic support for the leadership. In September 1971, Gotō Moto'o, managing editor of *Asahi*'s Tokyo office, concluded an exclusive interview with Prime Minister Kim Il-Sung. According to the *Asahi Newspaper Company History*, the request for the interview was made from the North Korean leader to an *Asahi* executive through the General Association of Korean Residents in Japan. The interview ran in the *Asahi* on September 27. Kim Il-Sung said "this is the first time I've had an interview like this with a gentleman Japanese reporter" and emphasized that he was speaking with the reporter as a friend. The meeting went through lunch and took five and a half hours. The headline at the top of the front page was "Prime Minister Kim Il-Sung Talks about 'Friendship.'" At that time, the meeting with Kim Il-Sung itself was big news. Gotō felt that his role was to raise public opinion about the restoration of diplomatic relations between Japan and its neighboring countries of North Korea and China. One month later, Gotō also had an exclusive interview with Chinese premier Zhou Enlai.

The following year, in 1972, Kim Il-Sung aggressively pursued interviews with other Japanese media outlets. He began with an interview with the *Yomiuri* in January. In April, Kim met with three groups at once—*Asahi*, the Japan Broadcasting Corporation (NHK) and *Kyōdō News*. In September, he spoke with the *Mainichi* and in October the Iwanami publishing company's magazine *World* (*Sekai*). In September 1980, Gotō, now managing director of *Asahi*, gained another exclusive interview with Kim Il-Sung. Kim

Il-Sung told Gotō that as leader, he would not recognize Chun Doo-hwan's South Korean regime and suggested that he would put bilateral discussions between the two countries on hold. North Korea's *Workers' Newspaper* (*Rodong Shinmun*) printed a large commemorative photograph with the *Asahi* media delegation on its front page. In March 1992, managing editor of the Tokyo office, Matsushita Muneyuki, visited North Korea, gaining the final exclusive interview between *Asahi* and Kim Il-Sung. At that time, North Korea's nuclear development was under suspicion. According to reporter Tanaka Yoshikazu, during the interview Matsushita sat up in his chair and asked: "It is probably not a question you want to hear but I would like to ask you about the subject of nuclear inspections." Kim Il-Sung declared he would accept the International Atomic Energy Agency (IAEA) nuclear inspection and this became the front-page news of the April 2 edition. This time the interview, including translation and lunch, lasted two hours. The questions were submitted beforehand and also covered the normalization of North Korea-Japan relations and the relationship between North and South Korea. Tanaka explained, "In a meeting with the highest leader of a country questions with the highest news value are prioritized."

Kim Hyon Hui, perpetrator of the 1987 Korean Air Flight 858 bombing, had testified that a Japanese woman in North Korea had taught her Japanese but the *Asahi* did not touch on this in the interview with Kim Il-Sung. During the Japan-North Korea negotiations in 1991, Japan asked for information about the woman but North Korea denied her very existence and the discussion fell into a deadlock. In the later half of the 1990s the abduction of Japanese became a much debated problem and there were even calls in *Asahi* for Kim Il-Sung to be asked about state terrorism and abduction.

The missing

In September 1977, *Asahi*'s Matsumura Takao was visiting a section of the Metropolitan Police Department to collect information for a story. The section was responsible for looking into incidents involving the Korean peninsula and China. Matsumura was taken aback by what his acquaintance, a veteran detective, told him. A few days later, the detective left a copy of a newspaper article on Matsumura's desk. It was a small article from the *Hokkoku Shimbun*, a regional paper in Ishikawa Prefecture titled, "Man Re-arrested Abetting Those Secretly Departing for the Korean Peninsula." The article told of a resident Korean in Japan who had been arrested on suspicion of secretly smuggling Japanese out of the country through Ishikawa Prefecture's Ushitsu Bay in violation of immigration control laws. While there had been previous incidents of foreign spies sneaking into the country, this was the first time Matsumura had heard of a Japanese citizen being smuggled out of Japan.

Matsumura began researching the story, particularly about the man who had been spirited away. The local news section on November 10 led with the headline, "Mitaka City Office Security Guard to North Korea on a Spy Ship—Is this the First Japanese Defector?" It would later be discovered that the security guard, 52-year-old Kume Yutaka, was a victim of abduction by the North Korean government but at first no one even considered that it had been a kidnapping. "Maybe he was persuaded or he was tricked," people thought. The following year, in the summer of 1978, incidents of couples disappearing in Fukui, Niigata, and Kagoshima Prefectures were reported. All possibilities were considered when the investigations began: crime, accident, and suicide. The former director of the Kagoshima Prefectural police recalls, "usually one then closes in on a criminal profile but this was the first time after several decades of experience that we couldn't form a hypothesis." Three days after the disappearance from Kagoshima Prefecture, a couple returning from swimming in the sea in Toyama Prefecture were attacked by a group of four men. During the abduction, the perpetrators dropped items that could not be obtained in Japan. This clue led the director of the Kagoshima Police department to the belief that "this event has foreign ties." He also heard that very close to the site of the crime suspicious radio signals had been intercepted. At the end of the year the regional paper in Kagoshima, the *South Japan Newspaper* (*Minami Nihon Shimbun*), in a series recalling the events of the year, took up the incidents as "mysterious disappearances." The paper reported, "It seems public security officers are also working under the theory that people were abducted and taken to another country" and mirror "a similar incident in Fukui Prefecture."

At the *Asahi* regional office in Kagoshima, Kitaoki Hirokazu, who was responsible for covering the police, recalled that "detailed information on the incidents in Fukui and Toyama was not forthcoming. We never considered that the Kagoshima incident fitted in as one part of the jigsaw puzzle of the serial disappearance incidents." He added, "It is the role of a national newspaper to use the reporting net of all the regions to put the pieces together, while looking at the whole puzzle. But even so, we could only see the incident that was right in front of our eyes." It was not until February 1997, more than eighteen years later, that the series of disappearances came to be widely recognized after the abduction of Yokota Megumi received news coverage and raised questions in the Diet. Yokota had gone missing in 1977 at the age of thirteen.[7]

21

Youth Revolts

Why the students of developed nations?

In March 2009, an international symposium was held in Berlin to address the topic of Japan, Germany and the United States during 1968. That was the year that young people in developed nations, particularly students, rose up simultaneously in protest in many places around the world. Why would the young people of nations that had for the most part overcome starvation and poverty generate such a radical movement? Today, more than forty years have elapsed and we have the opportunity to look back on 1968 from a global vantage point. Even within Japan, historical sociologist Oguma Eiji's 2009 masterpiece, *1968*, caused a stir. Taking part in the Berlin symposium was Izeki Tadahisa, Associate Professor of Contemporary German History at Chūō University. He explains that unlike the tendency of those in Japan who were involved in the revolts to keep silent, "in Germany the former activists continue to talk about their experiences. It is also characteristic that the young generation is extremely interested."

In 1968, the world was in upheaval. January saw the Viet Cong's Tet Offensive. April witnessed an assassination attempt against the leader of the West Berlin student movement in Germany, the assassination of Martin Luther King, Jr., and the occupation of the university by students at Columbia University in the US. In May, students and police clashed at university campuses in Paris, which led to workers becoming involved in a general strike known as the May Revolution. In August, the Soviet Army invaded Czechoslovakia and in October Liu Shaoqi lost his place as Chinese head of state in the midst of the Cultural Revolution.

Demonstrations in West Germany had been growing following the death of a student at the hands of police a year earlier. At the onset, *Asahi* only described what was happening to the extent that "compared to Japan, the student movements in Europe seem to have less of a political flavor to them."[1] However, the papers closely covered and analyzed the student uprisings in Paris from the initial moments. The students had multiple grievances: dissatisfaction with the universities' move toward popularized and mass-produced education, the gap between generations, the feeling of being constrained by the bounds of society, and anti-Vietnam War sentiment. Seeing that the students were not only resisting the organization of authority in their own countries but were also leading the criticism of Soviet-style socialism, a May 1968 article predicted "it is likely that for several years to come, students will increasingly be driven to behave radically due to these weighty issues."[2] One year after the May Revolution, foreign correspondent Nemoto Chōbē visited the extension campus of Paris' Nanterre University where the riot had begun; but Nanterre now was silent. It had taken General Charles de Gaulle a month to control the situation. Students ranging from conservatives to those on the extreme left co-existed in the same building. "I hitched a ride back to Paris in a car with four or five students from the left and the right, and even though they were traditional rivals there was no trouble." Nemoto still remembers how he was surprised at the difference with Japan's student movements, which were prone to internal strife. Even in Japan, 1968 saw a maelstrom of uprisings.

"Conflict" or "struggle"?

"Commercial Media, you need to be more self critical!"

Shimada Takao was an *Asahi* journalist covering the student disputes at the University of Tokyo. At a meeting in a lecture hall of over one hundred members from the All Student Joint Struggle Committee (*Zengaku kyōtō kaigi*), he was denounced

Figure 37   Students from the Nihon University All Student Joint Struggle Committee demonstrating to democratize the academy, June 11, 1968.

because he reported on moves to control the struggle between students from the university and the Democratic Youth League. On stage the university staff slipped Shimada a memo asking "are you trapped?" but he shook his head. The students, too, as one of the key players in the dispute, had their reasons for acting in this way. The debate carried on for about two hours.

From 1968, campus unrest spread and journalists wrestled over how to report objectively on a situation in which the government, the universities, and various student groups were in opposition to one another. The students called it the "Tokyo University Struggle" but *Asahi* reported it as the "Tokyo University Conflict." Top reporter Kuwashima Hisao felt trapped by *Asahi*'s choice of terms. "The students were against authoritarianism and presented it as a massive problem. It wasn't simply an issue of 'conflict.'" Even now he feels that it may have been better to write, "Tokyo University Struggle." There were various opinions even within *Asahi*. The *Vox Populi, Vox Dei* column was hard on the students and wrote: "intoxicated by big words which you do not properly understand as the basis to unleash ambiguous criticism of the university is utter nonsense."[3] An editorial on September 17, however, explained that it was "incorrect to view the student movement as something induced by radical students, as its roots have deep social origins." The paper pressed students to resolve their problems through discussion. Meanwhile, the magazine *Asahi Journal* was sympathetic to the students, doing such things as introducing the views of the All Student Joint Struggle Committee's polemicists.

At Nihon University, the student protest was sparked by huge unexplained expenditures by the administration. The number of universities involved in uprisings during 1968 reached 115.[4] But how did the students view the media? Former member of the Nihon University All Student Joint Struggle Committee, Matake Yoshiyuki, says: "the struggle at Nihon University, in addition to calling for accounting practices to be made public, was a struggle over democratization and demanded freedom of assembly and the abolition of censorship. Media coverage which conveyed this to the world was a positive step." The former president of the Committee, Akita Akehiro, also explains: "we were in an isolating 'reign of terror' at the mercy of the sports students. When a magazine first wrote about that one part it felt like a small window had opened to the dark cell in which we were trapped."

Former member of the Tokyo University All Student Joint Struggle Committee, Shima Taizō, was more critical: "The mass media only took up phenomena like students fighting among themselves. They neglected their journalistic duty and should have delved into the real problems students were raising such as challenging the university disciplinary system and the content of university education." The way in which people reacted to news depends on their own perspective. "Objective reporting" is a challenge even now.

A reporter's misstep

What exactly is objective coverage? What is neutrality? When one side is so overwhelmingly powerful, should print media not make gestures toward promoting the views of the minority? These were the sorts of questions debated among the younger staff members of *Asahi* publications in 1968, when the student movements were at their peak. Many identified with the activists. These young staff members wrote the *Asahi* labor union's workplace bulletin and named it *5th Arrondissement* (*Dai go gaiku*), in homage to the May 1968 protests in Paris' Latin Quarter.

The *Asahi Journal* was a magazine known for its liberal attitudes in presenting news, commentary, and criticism. During this period, the magazine printed essays like "Bringing Back the Aggressive Intellect" by Tokyo University All Student Joint Struggle Committee representative Yamamoto Yoshitaka, which presented readers with a look inside the minds of "youth in revolt." The *Journal* reached a peak of 263,000 copies in the first half of 1968 but by the time the student movements were drawing to a close, *Asahi* publications had entered a rocky period. First, there was the recall of the March 19, 1971 issue of *Asahi Journal*, which had been the subject of heated discussion at a board of directors meeting. The cover displayed a nude photo and inside was a self-parodying cartoon with the caption, "RED RED ASAHI ASAHI." At a company meeting soon after, executive Watanabe Seiki criticized the *Journal*'s editorial staff saying, "While they claim [...] to promote the views of the minority, they are clearly just writing for themselves." Then in April the *Asahi Weekly* published inaccurate information about a meeting of the Supreme Court justices. These episodes made sufficient waves that on May 24 the Asahi company initiated a major reshuffling of staff between its various publication bureaus. At the *Asahi Journal*, more than half of the editorial staff was changed, including the editor-in-chief and the deputy editor-in-chief.

Kawamoto Saburō was transferred from the *Asahi Weekly* to the *Asahi Journal*'s editorial section, which was going through chaotic reorganization. In January 1972, he was arrested. A man that Kawamoto had met several times in the course of his reporting stabbed to death a Japanese Self-Defense Force official at a defense facility in Asaka, Saitama Prefecture, declaring that he did so in the name of the Red Bolshevik Army. The culprit immediately contacted Kawamoto and the two met secretly to conduct an interview. During this meeting, the man offered Kawamoto the armband and some other items taken off the victim's body as proof of the murder. Kawamoto later had a friend burn these items and was brought up on charges of destroying evidence. It was only his third year since joining *Asahi* but having faced the difficulties and dangers associated with covering anti-establishment movements, Kawamoto came to disregard the protocols for fact checking and protection of sources. After being dismissed from *Asahi*, Kawamoto made a name for himself writing as a critic. Looking back at his disgrace, he states: "Up until the point that the activists launched the All Student Joint Struggle Committee, I don't feel that it was wrong for the *Asahi Journal* to have supported them. But once activist groups started favoring violence we should have spent more time discussing how best to distance ourselves from them."

Jeans and Beheiren

When the writer Yoshioka Shinobu entered Waseda University in April 1967, he was the only one around wearing blue jeans. He started growing out his hair that autumn and recalls, "Most of the students in activist groups or in the Democratic Youth League wore cotton trousers—it was the radicals not affiliated with any group who started wearing jeans." Jeans first appeared in the latter half of the nineteenth century in the western part of the US as work trousers. According to historian Yui Daizaburō, American teens in the 1950s took note of these origins: "The kids in the city were dressing like laborers, challenging the existing norms of society." In the latter half of the 1960s, as the situation in Vietnam grew more intense, jeans became the daily wear of young people who were calling for peace and freedom. Yoshioka joined the anti-war activities of Beheiren (the name is an acronym for *Betonamu ni heiwa o! shimin rengō*; literally, "Citizens League for Peace in Vietnam"). Beheiren harbored US soldiers who had fled the battlefields in Vietnam. The group also started staging "folk guerilla" events—war protest sing-ins at the underground square by the western exit of Shinjuku station in Tokyo. It was a new sort of non-violent citizens' movement.

When American soldiers spoke out after deserting aircraft carriers docked in Japan, *Asahi*'s *Vox Populi, Vox Dei* column on November 15, 1967 sympathized with their comments that "in the middle of the northern bombing campaign this is the desperate human voice that could not be suppressed." The local news page from November 19 reported a flood of donations and letters of support sent to Beheiren for having helped the American soldiers—the jeans-wearing activists received more than one thousand letters in less than a week. After a few months, the police broke up the folk guerilla sing-ins. On May 15, 1969, *Asahi* lamented this absence under the headline: "Shinjuku Local

Figure 38   In January 1971, the popularity of wearing jeans quickly caught on among young people.

Flavor on the Verge of Disappearing," quoting a writer who insisted that "people living in the city needed a space where they could meet for casual but earnest conversation." The author Konaka Yōtarō, who was a leading Beheiren member, remembers this general moment as "a rare case of media and activists being on the same page."

In August 1969, a folk guerilla event on a much larger scale took place in America, when 400,000 young people gathered in the upstate New York countryside over three days for the Woodstock Festival. The event would later be mythologized in terms of long hair, jeans, drugs, and free love. The *Asahi* New York correspondent took a derisive tone in his first article about Woodstock on August 17, reporting on the "Hippie Ruckus" attended only by people with "long and crazy hair." But a few weeks later, on August 30, he changed his position, introducing the view expressed in American newspapers and magazines that "young people hungry for meaning amidst the ruptures of American society" had "come together to soothe their spiritual wounds" and were "crafting a new form of American culture." The counterculture was also alive in Japan and it was not long before that country's young people were also all wearing jeans, the sturdy garment that expressed the spirit of the age. As early as December 1970, the *Asahi* "Home and Family" page declared, "It is rare for an article of clothing to become so firmly a part of everyday wear as jeans have." But as jeans gradually became standard attire so too did their iconic status as a challenge to social norms fade away.

The path to self-destruction

On January 18, 1969, operations began to break the barricade around Yasuda Hall, the Tokyo University building occupied by All Student Joint Struggle Committee activists. Muramatsu Takehiko was with the fifth division of metropolitan riot police at the time, assigned to bring down the section of the barricade in front of the university hall. He recalls that stones, chunks of concrete, and Molotov cocktails rained down on the police from above. They had to protect themselves by holding riot shields overhead, as a direct hit would have been fatal. Muramatsu owns up to being frightened but asserts that the whole troop felt that "if we hadn't done it, who would have?" For the next two days *Asahi* gave broad coverage to the operations, with headlines such as "Police Force Used in Lifting the Tokyo University Occupation," "Battle Lasts More than Ten Hours," and "Yasuda Hall Back Under Control." Muramatsu recounts his impression of the coverage at the time: "It basically reported things as they were actually happening but I remember being furious when I read lines like 'Riot Police Clash with Students'—both parties were being given equal treatment, even though we were the ones upholding the law and regulating the illegal activities of the students."

With the reclamation of Yasuda Hall from the activists, the battle for Tokyo University moved toward its conclusion. The barricade at Nihon University had been removed as well. The All Student Joint Struggle Committee style of activism organized itself around "autonomous individuals"—that is, participants working together without having to formally join anything—but this lost momentum and the various political activist groups of the new left wing came to the fore. Ōba Hisaaki, who had been an All Student Joint Struggle Committee member at Nihon University, shares his experience: "Some of

Figure 39 Yasuda Hall on the Tokyo University Campus enveloped in smoke. Riot police eventually broke up the student occupation, January 19, 1969.

my friends joined the activist groups but I personally witnessed an abhorrent incidence of violence and started to move away from activism." The September 29 evening edition of *Asahi* reported that "Another Student Dies from Intra-Group Violence," the sort of headline that had by that point become a commonplace news item.

In February 1972, five members of the extremist group the United Red Army holed up with firearms in the Asama Mountain Lodge in Nagano Prefecture. It later came to light in the testimony of those who were arrested that the ringleaders had initiated a "reassessment" of the group, after which they executed fourteen members. This macabre episode of killing internal group members was a shock to the wider population of activists. Takahashi Jun'ichi, a former All Student Joint Struggle Committee member at Aoyama Gakuin University, recalls: "It felt like our foundation had suddenly crumbled and collapsed." The United Red Army incident clearly signaled the waning of student activism and new left movements.

Tominaga Hisao was the *Asahi* local news reporter who spent ten snowy days covering the Asama Mountain Lodge affair. He vividly recalls that the five activists who were arrested had the fierce bearing of warriors who had been captured in defeat. Tominaga's co-worker Kimura Takuji was able to enter the mountain lodge immediately after the arrests were made. He remembers: "It was like the place had been both flooded and scorched. I felt like this was the inevitable end result of escalating violence and internal strife." An editorial in the March 11 *Asahi* entitled "What Gave Rise to Lunatic Groups" gave the following assessment: "Extremist groups [. . .] started from a position of skepticism with regards to established values. That much is reasonable. But [...] what awaited them was the trapdoor of dogma."

What was left?

People who had any sort of connection to the global youth unrest around 1968 have been called "The 68 generation"—such as former German chancellor Fritz Schröder, Green Party leader and former German Foreign Minister Joseph Fischer, and current European Parliament member Daniel Cohn-Bendit (known as "Danny the Red" when he was a leader of the Paris May Revolution). In Japan, the 68-er Sengoku Yoshito was appointed Minister of State for Government Revitalization after the 2009 political turnover when the Democratic Party of Japan ousted the Liberal Democratic Party from nearly fifty years of majority rule. Back when he was a Tokyo University student studying for his civil service examinations, Sengoku had helped the All Student Joint Struggle Committee by providing support for arrested activists. He says, "Japan in those days still ran on the democratic ideals of a developing country—we felt that the only way to affect political change was through force. People were saying that trying to change the power structure through elections was nothing but weak social democracy that amounted to sitting around and waiting."

The leaders of European student movements entered politics and learned their statecraft in regional assemblies, in France heading up one faction of François Mitterand's government, and in Germany remaining involved throughout Schröder's administration in 1998. In contrast, Sengoku remarked that Japanese activists were ten years behind. But not all of the 1968 activists in Japan withdrew from the movements. Daidōji Masashi regards himself as a "stubborn survivor from those days." After his experiences with the All Student Joint Struggle Committee, he set off explosives at Mitsubishi Heavy Industries headquarters and was sentenced to death. He is currently in a Tokyo detention center. Although he regrets his role in the explosions, he has not renounced his anti-government position. He had the following to say in an interview through his family:

> After leaving the All Student Joint Struggle Committee, a lot of people got involved with movements against social discrimination or nuclear energy. But there was very little general awareness of how Japan was exploiting the rest of Asia and of its position as aggressor both before and after the war. People were unable to formulate ideas or a movement that had any staying power.

Takagi Masayuki was an *Asahi* senior staff writer who had long covered left-wing movements in Japan. In a 1995 lecture he gave three years before he passed away, he observed: "The waning of the All Student Joint Struggle Committee movement stemmed from an increase in internal violence and the introduction of police force, but also from the movement itself, made up as it was of so many individualized approaches. Activists overestimated its ability to function as 'an organization without organization.'" He was pointing out a paradox: the more importance a movement places on individual subjectivity, the harder it becomes to sustain the movement.

22

Military Bases—Okinawa

Fighting coercion

There was a major reaction to *Asahi* running an article on January 13, 1955 entitled, "Piercing the Veil of the American Military's Civil Administration of Okinawa." Local news writer Iwashita Tadao penned the article and, in a memoir left to his family, records his experience reporting on Okinawa. For several days after writing the article, he received countless letters of support and praise from Okinawans living on the Japanese mainland. But the most forceful response came from the US military's East Asian operations office. Three days after the article's publication, the US released a lengthy statement attacking it. *Asahi* ran the statement in its entirety: "It is quite clear that there are communist elements in Okinawa exploiting the destitute situation of those who have lost their land as a result of the military's building operations. . . ." Terms such as "communist elements" and "exploiting" oozed hostility. Iwashita paid a visit to the military base a few days later. Donald Nugent, a civil administration official in the US military, pointed out that Iwashita's article was not written based on firsthand information gathered in Okinawa. This was not an incorrect observation in and of itself, as the article had been in fact based on material supplied by jurists and scholars from the Japan Civil Liberties Union (JCLU).

In 1954, Iwashita had visited the office of Unno Shinkichi, a lawyer who was serving as executive director of the JCLU. Unno showed Iwashita a letter from Roger Baldwin, chair of the United Nations Human Rights Council. Having heard about the unjust seizure of land in Okinawa, Baldwin was requesting more information for the purpose of negotiating with the American government. His letter said that he assumed "Japanese newspapers were probably reporting on this issue," but in fact mainland Japanese papers tended not to delve too deeply into the hardships ailing Okinawa. Iwashita took on the challenge but he had none of the necessary prerequisite knowledge to cover the story. He called on the prime minister's Southern Areas Liaison Bureau to get permission for travel to Okinawa but was told that the only authorizations granted had been for either entertainers or for those involved in construction on the military bases. When he asked about a reporter's permit for a fact-finding trip, the staff member in charge only repeated that it would be impossible.

Yoshida Shien, a native of Okinawa, was working at the Southern Areas Liaison Bureau and was involved in the movement on the mainland to return Okinawa to

Japanese control. Yoshida asserted that the allegations about the situation on the ground with seizure of land for military bases were all true, and he gave Iwashita reference materials to prove it. Iwashita then applied for a permit to visit Okinawa on the basis of "investigating human rights violations." He was denied, a rejection that ended up helping his case against Nugent. Iwashita wrote in his memoir, "It is the US military that refused to let me go to Okinawa in the first place. [. . .] Is that how it works in America?" Nugent gradually shifted his position, proposing to arrange a discussion between Iwashita and the authorities on bases in Okinawa. Iwashita gladly agreed but that was the last he heard from Nugent. Iwashita was eventually able to go to Okinawa without Nugent's facilitation.

Reporters on the scene

In April 1955, the US military invited reporters from Japan and other countries to Okinawa. This was three months after Iwashita's article had appeared in *Asahi* and it was easy to see that the military was handling this "media tour" as a staged performance. On April 12, *Asahi* reported: "The reporters seemed puzzled at the extravagant welcome they received from Army Commander James Moore and the bouquets of flowers from girls in long-sleeved kimonos." But the gravity of the situation soon became apparent in the contrasting addresses from the American Civil Administration senior official and Okinawan government official, as noted in the April 14 *Asahi*. The US civil administrator said, "As long as the military is here it will need land and as long as there is a need for land someone will have to give ground." But Okinawan government chief executive Higa Shūhei made it clear that "only a very small number of those whose land has been appropriated are satisfied with the arrangement."

Asahi's Iwashita Tadao finally made it to Okinawa in October 1955, to report on the survey being conducted by the US House of Representatives Special Subcommittee of the Armed Services Committee (headed by Charles Melvin Price). Iwashita received permission to go but the military authorities would not yield on the point that he had to travel on a US armed services craft. At first he refused, but then agreed on the condition that he would have full freedom to gather information. Iwashita was given brigadier general level treatment and taken by troop transport from the base in Tachikawa, Tokyo to the one in Kadena, Okinawa where Commander Moore welcomed him. From the *Asahi* on October 28: "The farmers were forced from Isahama and relocated to Misato Village, where they lived in dug-out huts that could barely be called homes." One of the farmers told the surveying group about "a household of eight people who scraped by crammed into a makeshift hut of six *tsubo* [about 215 square feet]." Isahama was a hamlet close to Futenma Air Base and the village land had just been forcibly seized in a large-scale operation called "Bayonets and Bulldozers." The only place Iwashita did not receive permission to cover was Iejima. Like Isahama, the island of Iejima faced hardline measures during the seizures of its land. But Iwashita was otherwise able to move around the Okinawan islands freely and the next month he began a serial feature in the local news pages, "The Face of Okinawa."

The survey team from the US House of Representatives subcommittee publicly released its report the following year. The report touched on the importance of military bases in Okinawa, new land appropriation operations, and even the possibility of stockpiling nuclear weapons there. Within the report, Subcommittee Chairman Price recommended making a lump-sum payment on land to guarantee permanent leasing rights. This recommendation was the trigger that set off the anti-base movement across Okinawa, known as the Island-wide Protest. This movement aimed to bring about a change in occupation policies and it established Okinawa's situation as an issue that the Japanese government could not easily ignore. Nine years later, on August 19, 1965, Prime Minister Satō Eisaku would address a large crowd at Naha Airport: "I know full well that the postwar period will not end until Okinawa is returned."

A case for partial restoration

Prime Minister Satō apparently felt strongly about calling for Okinawa's return to Japan even before he took office. Satō's agenda for his coming term, prepared in May 1964, had originally contained the following passage: "Not only does the Okinawa issue weigh on the American conscience, but holding Okinawa is also no longer of critical importance to American global military strategy." Though this sentence was removed from the final version of his agenda, at a press conference held in July of the same year Satō demanded that America return Okinawa to Japan. But in February 1965, before Satō had given his speech at Naha Airport, the American Army began its bombing campaign in North Vietnam and Okinawa became the main base of US military operations. If it became necessary for the US to consult with Japan beforehand for these attacks, as was the case with bases on the mainland, the Americans thought this would restrict military operations. Further concern surrounded nuclear weapons. The US was stockpiling Mace-B missiles and other nuclear armaments in Okinawa in the face of staunch opposition from the Japanese.

There was talk of a partial restoration plan, which would return various elements of administrative control back to Japan, including education oversight. Some in Okinawa had been calling for this as early as the 1950s. *Asahi* political writer Horikoshi Sakuji asked about this proposal when he paid a visit on the evening of August 22, 1966 to the Setagaya, Tokyo home of Mori Kiyoshi, chief of general affairs in the prime minister's office. At the time, the prime minister's Special Areas Liaison Bureau had jurisdiction over concerns relating to Okinawa and Horikoshi was assigned to cover the story. Three days earlier, Mori had met with Albert Watson, the High Commissioner of Civil Administration in Okinawa. During that meeting Mori sounded out the possibility of restoring authority over education in Okinawa to Japan as part of a restoration plan that allowed for specific administrative functions to be individually restored to Japanese management. Mori told Horikoshi, "I'll bring it up in tomorrow's Cabinet meeting. I've already checked with the Cabinet Legislation Bureau so it should work out."

Horikoshi sped off in his car, back to the newspaper offices in Yūrakuchō, Tokyo. He wrote an article that appeared on the front page of the next morning's paper, under the headline: "Mori to Call for Return of Authority over Education in Okinawa at Today's Cabinet Meeting." The article reported, "Acknowledging the US position of continuing to maintain military bases, [. . .] negotiations are in hand with the Americans for the return of at least education administration to Japan. . . ." This was dubbed the Mori Plan but as *Asahi* noted on the 24th, it was not exactly clear what would be achieved by "returning" education administration to Japan: "Okinawan schools were already using Japanese textbooks and just as on the mainland the Japanese treasury bore the cost of supplying textbooks and subsidizing half of teachers' salaries." In January of the following year, Prime Minister Satō held a press conference in Ōtsu City in Shiga Prefecture, where he called for a "comprehensive return of administrative authority to Japan." With that the Mori Plan vanished. Meanwhile, Horikoshi traveled to Okinawa on assignment for the first time, where he was shocked by how big the bases actually were.

It was around this time that the US government began to seriously consider the question of Okinawa, in terms of both foreign relations and national defense.

America's true intentions

"I don't believe there is a need to stockpile nuclear weapons in Okinawa and I'm sure that at some point in 1969 an agreement will be reached on the reversion of Okinawa to Japan," Edwin Reischauer stated. The former US ambassador to Japan was on the record in a July 23, 1968 interview with *Asahi*'s American correspondent Tominomori Eiji. The interview had not originally been about Okinawa but Reischauer brought the subject up himself and his comment informed the top story on the front page of the next evening's *Asahi*: "Okinawa to Return to Japan with No Nukes—Agreement Likely Next Year." Reischauer's statement covered a few points: first, that it was unrealistic to keep nuclear arms in Okinawa after returning to Japan, given the strong opposition among Japanese citizens; second, there was no particular need to store nuclear weapons there; and finally, the concern that maintaining nuclear-equipped bases in Okinawa after its reversion could open the door for Japan to acquire its own nuclear weapons, which would run counter to US interests.

In November of the previous year, when Prime Minister Satō met with President Lyndon Johnson, there was mutual agreement that the reversion of Okinawa should take place "within two or three years." This position was incorporated into a joint communiqué but there were still formidable obstacles. Tominomori recalls, "There were those at *Asahi* who had their doubts about the truth of a 'no nukes' reversion and it seemed that the lead editors only half believed Reischauer's statement." Reischauer had asserted that reversion would not involve leaving nuclear weapons but he also made other points that were highly suggestive—for example, "Without Japanese cooperation, stationing the Seventh Fleet in the western Pacific would become extremely problematic and costly," and "Japan should do its part to ensure security in Asia, bearing more of the burden."

In March 1967, Satō's older brother and former prime minister Kishi Nobusuke had met with US Defense Secretary Robert McNamara. A summary of their meeting accessed through public records reveals:

McNamara said: "Particularly given its relations with America, Japan should be playing a larger role in Asia."

Kishi responded: "The Japanese people need to know that America is not occupying Okinawa for its own benefit but rather to guarantee stability in Asia."

In 1966, spurred by opinions from Reischauer and others, a joint committee involving members of the State Department, the Defense Department, and the CIA had convened to work on the Okinawa issue. Taking into account the increasing calls for reversion, the group concluded that the best way forward was to explore how reversion could take place without compromising the functioning of the military bases. Kōno Yasuko, a professor at Hōsei University who has researched the US-Japan negotiations surrounding the reversion of Okinawa, states, "The Americans had already begun formulating the conditions under which reversion could accord with their national agenda but the Japanese still did not grasp the implications of these conditions." In March 1969, Prime Minister Satō spoke before the Diet, demanding full reversion with no nuclear weapons, just like on the mainland. Just twenty days later, Kishi told reporters at a press conference during his visit to America that "regarding prior consultation for launching operations from US military bases in Japan, we will not always say 'no' and sometimes might say 'yes.'" Beneath the surface, the issue of bringing nuclear weapons into Japan during emergencies was becoming an issue.

Exploring the idea of bringing in nuclear arms

The reversion of Okinawa to Japan was settled on November 19, 1969 with a top-secret document signed at the White House by Prime Minister Satō and President Richard Nixon. At the end of 2009, Satō's copy of that document was discovered in his personal papers. The agreement which had been announced, in accordance with firm Japanese demands, was that Okinawa would be free of nuclear arms according to the same terms that applied to mainland Japan: all nuclear weapons would be removed from Okinawa and could only be brought back in after prior consultation with the Japanese government. But the secret agreement carried the clear expectation that, in the event of such prior consultation, the answer would always be "yes." The secret agreement is two pages of thick paper folded into thirds, labeled "Record of Agreement Concerning the Joint Declaration." It specifies that, regarding America's "authority to transport nuclear armaments into and through Okinawa" in the event of a "critical situation," the Japanese government "understands all conditions and when consulted in advance will consent to these conditions without delay." Former professor at Kyoto Sangyō University, Wakaizumi Kei, revealed in a 1994 publication his involvement as Satō's secret messenger in the negotiations. It seems that none of the *Asahi* reporters knew the particulars at the time but they nonetheless sensed there was some sort of understanding reached about nuclear weapons.

The top headline on the front page of the November 8, 1969 *Asahi* read: "Bringing in Nukes During Emergency a Focal Point in US-Japan Executive Negotiations on

Okinawa." The article reported that America was sensitive to the request that there be no nuclear weapons but that there were those, particularly in the military, calling forcefully for the right to bring in nuclear arms during times of emergency. Kitani Tadashi, the *Asahi* American bureau chief who had been following the behind-the-scenes negotiations, wrote the article. Tominomori Eiji, on dispatch from *Asahi*'s politics section to cover the deliberations, tells that Kitani "had sources from both governments, particularly from senior officials in the Japanese Foreign Ministry." Reporting from those days on the nuclear arms issue went through two phases: at the time of reversion the concern was whether or not there would be any nuclear weapons, while later coverage focused on the reintroduction of such weaponry during critical situations. The question of reintroduction was the unresolved question.

Directly after the secret accord was reached, the *Mainichi Newspaper* took a further step, reporting on the evening of November 21 that "there is growing agreement among well-informed sources that a top-secret arrangement has been made between officials of both countries with regards to bringing nuclear arms into Japan during emergencies." The 21st also saw the public declaration of the US-Japan joint resolution that Okinawa would revert to Japan in 1972. Tominomori was writing a draft of an article at the *Asahi* American bureau when Kitani returned from reporting on the resolution saying, "I have a gut feeling. Let's go with it this way." The front-page article on the 22nd, under the headline "Reversion of Okinawa Set for 1972," took issue with a particular item in clause number eight, the "no nuclear weapons" section of the joint resolution. This proviso stated: "the system of prior consultation will not compromise the position of the United States," which the *Asahi* article reported as "the American side interpreting the resolution as leaving an open path for the reintroduction of nuclear arms during emergencies." The Japanese government expressed its strong displeasure at this article.

The hidden elements

Foreign Minister Aichi Kiichi in particular was incensed by *Asahi*'s reporting. On November 21, 1969, the day that the joint resolution declaring the reversion of Okinawa to Japan was promulgated, Prime Minister Satō and his retinue moved on from Washington DC to New York, Foreign Minister Aichi included. In New York, *Asahi* American bureau chief Kitani and politics reporter Tominomori met with Aichi to clarify the meaning behind the line in clause eight of the joint resolution, where it stated that there would be no compromise to the US position. The next day's *Asahi* morning edition ran an article interpreting the line as leaving an open path for the reintroduction of nuclear weapons into Okinawa in the event of an emergency.

Aichi refuted this at a press conference on the resolution, citing Japan's Three Non-nuclear Principles. Again expressing anger at recent *Asahi* coverage, the foreign minister assured the audience that "It goes without saying that there will be no nuclear weapons after the reversion and in fact there is no cause for concern about bringing nuclear arms back in the future."[1] But at a meeting between leaders Nixon made reference to nuclear weapons in "the utilization of Okinawa during critical situations." Apparently, Nixon expressed reluctance at the first draft of the joint resolution but agreed to the second draft, which included the item about not compromising the position of the United States. Speaking to the National Press Club after his meeting with Nixon, Satō touched on the issue of prior consultation. He stated his intention "to provide a quick and constructive response" in the event that America approached Japan "to launch military operations against Korea." He said the same would be true for Taiwan. It is clear from US public records that, as of May 1969, America was going to accede to the doctrine of "no nuclear weapons" with the assumption that in times of emergency they could be brought in. At the same time, it had been decided that America would push forward its negotiations with Japan for the "unrestricted use" of bases in the event of a critical situation with Taiwan or Korea. Satō addressed this in his comments before the National Press Club, causing Japanese newspapers much anxiety over the issue of nuclear armaments.

Two and a half years later, another secret agreement involving the reversion of Okinawa came to light. This was revealed at a Lower House budget committee meeting on March 27, 1972. Yokomichi Takahiro, a representative of the Socialist Party, put forth a statement that caused an uproar: "I would like to go through Foreign Ministry documents to bring the facts to light and root out who is responsible for these lies." When the Foreign Ministry documents from June of the previous year were made public, relating to the joint agreement on the reversion of Okinawa, it raised suspicions about the expenditures involved in returning US military property to its original state; the four million dollars of reparations that America was supposed to voluntarily pay were secretly taken on by Japan and folded into the 32 million dollars Japan would pay toward administering reversion. The Foreign Ministry documents found their way to Yokomichi through *Mainichi* reporter Nishiyama Takichi, who had obtained them from a woman working at the ministry. The following month Nishiyama and the female employee were both arrested on charges of national civil employee conduct violations. But this was not the first time that the accusations of Japan taking on US payments had arisen.

Reversion, and then . . .

The details of the reversion of Okinawa were settled in an accord, which was signed on June 17, 1971. The next day Nishiyama Takichi, the *Mainichi Newspaper* writer who covered the Foreign Ministry, wrote an article in his paper's morning edition, voicing suspicions that the Japanese government had secretly taken on the payments that America was supposed to have made toward restoration of the land that the military had been using. The story was titled, "Doubts About Settling Claims—The Underside of the Negotiations." The article suggested that, "an unshakable sense of foul-play lurks behind the reparations. [. . .] There is the nagging question of whether, in the end, it will really be America that will bear these costs. [. . .] Isn't it true that the discussion ended in Congress with the statement that Japan would pay the four million dollars?"[2] *Asahi* had tracked down some information of its own. An article on April 2, 1971 summed up the problematic areas of the negotiations, pointing out that the "slippage in reparation payments" in the return of military land to its original state "had become a focal point of the bilateral deliberations." Then, on April 27 *Asahi* published an article charging that Japan was hoping to solve the "problem of reparations" by "assuming responsibility for a portion of the money owed by America." It was a front-page story, though this analysis was not mentioned in the headline. Nishiyama frequently pressed senior officials at the Foreign Ministry regarding the problem of reparation payments. He recalls, "I thought that if it meant getting Okinawa back, for Japan to pay four million dollars was not a big deal. But the text of the agreement containing falsehoods for the sake of appearances really made the government appear underhanded."

It was raining in Okinawa on May 15, 1972, the day of reversion. The day before, a ceremony was held in Naha at the Shikina Cemetery, honoring the graves of those who had fallen in the war and comforting their spirits with news of the reversion. Reformist political parties opposed the ceremony, questioning whether those who had lost their lives in the war would approve of reversion while US military bases remained. The newspapers reported on a range of problems leading up to the reversion, including the question of nuclear weapons in Okinawa and financial arrangements. Facing an America that was pursuing an agreement assiduously crafted to further its own national interests, Japan was hard pressed and those secret agreements allowed them to reach a resolution. But the bigger issue was that even after this accord, the sprawling US military bases remained. On page four of *Asahi* from the day of reversion, there was a story titled "87 Bases Remain in Okinawa as Before—Japan's Weighty Responsibility as a 'Host' Country." The article did not touch on the distress of the people.

After reversion, the topic of Okinawa, which had been a major theme of *Asahi* reporting since 1955, essentially disappeared from the newspaper's pages. It was not until the rape of a young girl by American soldiers in September 1995 that reporting on the complexities surrounding military bases once again heated up—twenty-three years after reversion.

23

The Cultural Revolution and the Re-opening of Sino-Japanese Relations

Street posters as news sources

On the evening of August 20, 1966, *Asahi* correspondent in Beijing, Nogami Tadashi, was in the busy Wangfujing area when he encountered a group of youngsters shouting slogans like "Rebellion is Justified!" and "Destroy the Four Olds!" That day the Red Guards, vanguard of the revolution, took to the streets and caught the attention of the whole world. Demonstrating their rejection of old modes of thought and culture, they targeted venerated old shops, tearing down signs and wrecking the interiors. Nogami's first article on the subject appeared in the *Asahi* morning edition on August 22, detailing what he saw: "Storm of Cultural Revolution in the streets," "In one night even the names of the neighborhoods were erased," and "Young Red Guards flex their muscle." It was one of the opening episodes of an unprecedented political movement, action that flared up and pulled the masses into what became the Cultural Revolution.

The Cultural Revolution lasted for ten years, and did not end until its instigator Mao Zedong had died and his wife Jiang Qing was arrested together with the other members of the Gang of Four. Today the movement is remembered by the people as having been a disaster and is summed up by a Chinese Communist Party history declaration written in 1981 as "an internal disturbance that brought calamity to the Party, the nation, and the citizenry." For foreign correspondents, official Chinese news sources like the *People's Daily* (*Renmin Ribao*) and *Xinhua* were of very little use; instead, critical information was better obtained from the large print posters plastered up on buildings and walls in public places. The Japanese foreign correspondents in particular were able to use their reading knowledge of Chinese characters to more quickly grasp the inner-workings of the veiled political struggles and regional trends. For a time, the news on China coming out of Tokyo informed the whole world. The *Asahi* company history details: "correspondents and aides from other countries would crowd around the *Asahi* foreign reporting desk from morning to night, clamoring to be shown the newsfeeds coming in from Nogami." The Beijing correspondents of the various Japanese news agencies, nine people in all, won the 1966 Vaughn International Journalism Prize.

After the initial rampage of the Red Guards through the city streets, accusations of capitalist leanings were leveled against the dominant government cliques and this escalated into bloody factional struggles. Concerned that news of the chaos would leak out of the country, Chinese authorities began to regulate the large-print posters. Warnings issued to Japanese correspondents began the following spring in 1967. In July, Red Guards attacked several trading company employees who specialized in Chinese trade at the hotel where *Asahi* and other companies had set up headquarters. These employees were placed under house arrest on suspicion of being spies, accused of having taken unauthorized photos of the large-print posters, and of having Red Guard newspapers in their possession. Nogami had collected a good amount of these sorts of materials and after lengthy consideration decided to dispose of them, shredding them and flushing them down the toilet. Suddenly, on the morning of September 10, all of the Japanese correspondents were called to the Chinese Foreign Ministry. First, the press bureau harshly criticized Prime Minister Satō Eisaku's recent visit to Taiwan as "a grievous political provocation against the Chinese people." Then, the representatives of the *Mainichi*, *Sankei*, and *Nishi Nippon* (representative news agencies that encompassed Hokkaido, Tokyo, and the Nagoya regions) were forced to leave China on the grounds of "anti-Chinese reporting" and replacement reporters were not permitted entry.

Figure 40   When the Cultural Revolution started, Red Guards and others began pasting up large wall newspapers all over China.

Journalist exchanges and the three political principles

In September 1964, nine Japanese news agencies, including *Asahi, Kyōdō News*, and NHK, started dispatching correspondents to Communist China, a country with which Japan had no diplomatic relations. The most effective pipeline between the two countries was the Liao-Takasaki Trade Agreement, which established a framework for an exchange of journalists through which Japanese news agencies realized their goal to report on China. The accord, signed by Liberal Democratic Party (LDP) member Matsumura Kenzō and Premier Zhou Enlai, was intended to steadily expand trade toward the normalization of diplomatic relations. From the outset, Zhou Enlai set forth his "Three Political Principles" as the basis of policy toward Japan. The three points were that Japan not regard China with any hostility; that Japan offer no support toward conspiracies that would create two Chinas (i.e., that the Republic of China in Taiwan not be recognized as a "real" China); and that nothing be done to hamper the movement toward normalizing relations between China and Japan.

On the occasion of the March 1968 shift from the Liao-Takasaki Agreement to the Memorandum Trade Agreement, the parties involved stipulated that Japanese news agencies should also "uphold these three political principles." The journalist exchange arrangement was revised and the number of journalists permitted decreased to five. *Asahi* Beijing correspondent Akioka Ieshige was frequently summoned to the Chinese Foreign Ministry Press Bureau, charged with violating the second principle by writing stories that recognized the Republic of China in Taiwan as a country. According to a memo left by the manager of the foreign news desk at the time, *Asahi* "had to offer a formal apology on each occasion for technical mistakes in articles, such as using the term 'Republic of China' or for recognizing Taiwan as a country." The Chinese Communists even demanded an explanation about an advertisement in the paper for condominiums in Japan, which had a map on it showing the location of the condo in Tokyo and identifying the Republic of China Embassy (Taiwan) as a nearby landmark. The foreign news desk manager was reluctant to apologize for this, claiming that it was only natural for a map of Tokyo to indicate an embassy for a country with which Japan had diplomatic relations. However, his supervisor told him, "just act contrite and it will blow over." The foreign news manager's memo stated: "challenging the complaints of the Chinese government came with a high risk of having correspondents sent back to Japan." In a sense, Japan's news correspondents were held hostage by the three political principles that the Chinese government had forced the media to adopt.

When the journalist exchange agreement was revised in 1968, the conclusion reached between LDP representative Tagawa Seiichi's team and their Chinese counterparts was "to not publicly announce the content" and it was therefore not reported.[1] According to *Asahi*'s company history, one of the reasons why the unclear measures later became a problem was that "they invited criticism from some critics and others that the journalist exchange agreement was incorporated into the three main political principles as a means to restrain journalists from reporting antagonistically about China and this led to a loss of the freedom of the press." With the normalization of diplomatic relations between China and Japan in 1972, journalist exchanges came under the auspices of an administrative governmental accord and were further revised in 2006 when the limit on the number of reporters involved was removed.

Historical witnesses

How should we look at the Cultural Revolution? At the outset of the summer of 1966, *Asahi* observed the events unfolding in China in a calm but critical tone. Beijing correspondent Nogami Tadashi's article from August 29, 1966 asserted that at the heart of the Cultural Revolution was a power struggle: "It was clear that political mainstreamers such as Chairman Mao and National Defense Minister Marshall Lin Biao were planning the total elimination of both the factions that opposed them and national support bases for these factions—one might call it a Mao Zedong coup-d'état, writ large and in bold relief."

Lead editorial articles were critical as well, referencing on August 25 the "abnormal development" of the Red Guard's violent actions and suggesting on August 31 that, "the intentions of the highest echelons of the Chinese Communist Party are becoming more and more dubious." But the next year, amidst the deportation of the *Mainichi* correspondents and other news agents, and the successive cancellation of resident status for employees of the *Yomiuri* and of commercial broadcast companies, there was a subtle change in the tone of *Asahi* reporting. *Asahi* now actively attempted to find some larger significance in what was happening, as can be seen from the editorial lead on August 11, 1967: "It is difficult for us to say that the Cultural Revolution is simply a factionalized power struggle," and that "one might see it as a particular way of spurring on the process of modernization."

Another shocking event took place the following year in June 1968. Veteran *Nikkei* correspondent Samejima Keiji, one of the members of the first journalist exchange groups, was arrested at his home office where he lived and worked. He was held for a year-and-a-half on suspicion of being a spy. In the wake of this incident foreign news chiefs from the various news agencies in Tokyo held an emergency meeting. They agreed that because they did not know all the details of the case, it would be best to proceed cautiously and to avoid writing any speculative articles until the Chinese made a formal statement. In Beijing, the correspondents who still remained from *Asahi*, *Kyōdō News*, and NHK met with representatives at the Memorandum Trade Agreement's Beijing offices. All together there were twenty-some Japanese in Beijing at the time, including correspondents' families. Some pushed for "them all to go back to Japan as a show of protest," but Akioka Ieshige from *Asahi* and others urged that "they stay and provide what support they could to the imprisoned Samejima and seek to resolve the issue in high-level negotiations." In the end, this more circumspect approach won out. Even after returning to Japan, Samejima has never spoken about the incident publicly. When the Cultural Revolution ended in 1977, the Chinese government made an official apology to Samejima and restored his name.

In November 1967, Akioka took over from Nogami as correspondent in Beijing, with instructions from *Asahi* CEO Hirooka Tomoo. Hirooka later related having told Akioka, "There are certain things that will get you deported if you write about them. In

Figure 41 From every region in China and carrying their own sleeping gear, Red Guards gather in Beijing in autumn 1966.

these cases stop just short of writing anything that will get you in trouble. However, if I may say so, it doesn't matter if you don't write anything at all—better that you just see what you can see and not write it. But under no circumstances should you write anything that bends the truth in any way or lie." This attitude would come to be known in *Asahi* as the "Historical Witness Theory."

Asahi CEO Hirooka's visit to China

The ten-year period of the Cultural Revolution, from the summer of 1967 to the end of 1977, almost completely overlaps with Hirooka Tomoo's stint as CEO of *Asahi*. Hirooka was a supporter of normalizing diplomatic relations between China and Japan sooner than later and was always looking for a chance to visit China. In the spring of 1970, when LDP representative Matsumura Kenzō made a trip for the negotiations of the Memorandum Trade Agreement, Hirooka was able to join the trip as a "friend."

The negotiations did not proceed smoothly. In November of the previous year, Prime Minister Satō had made statements during the reversion of Okinawa negotiations that the "security of South Korea and Taiwan was important to the security of Japan." China responded harshly to this and took a tough stance, calling the return of Okinawa "fraudulent" and charging that "Japan was resuming its militaristic ways." The Memorandum Trade negotiations dragged on for nearly a month. Meanwhile, Hirooka nursed a secret hope to interview Zhou Enlai, waiting patiently for his chance. Hirooka later reflected that his long stay in China was unusual and noted that he was "criticized by both *Asahi* employees and outside observers" for spending so much time away from headquarters while serving as CEO, even missing a shareholders meeting. In the end, he never managed to get a one-on-one interview but he did sit in on the meeting between Matsumura's delegation and Zhou Enlai after the conclusion of the negotiations. Hirooka penned an essay entitled "Ending My Visit to China," which appeared on page one of the April 22, 1970 morning edition. In the article Hirooka said:

> I believe that there is a need for more Japanese people to summon up the courage to take a serious look at the realities of the current relationship between China and Japan. If the Japanese firmly believe in peace and disarmament, if they strive to never be pulled into war again, it is essential that they dispel as soon as possible the wariness of the Chinese people. For this to happen there must be an extensive national discussion about how precisely to do this.

Asahi urged the Japanese government, in the January 1, 1971 morning edition and across a three-page special spread, to move forward to restore Japan-China diplomatic relations. The government now needs to change its politics, the special article pointed out. At the company-wide meeting the next day, Hirooka declared before the assembled staff that *Asahi* would devote itself to the normalization of diplomatic relations with China, thus setting the "editorial agenda" for the whole newspaper. As Hirooka expected, 1971 was a year that saw significant shifts in the foreign policy landscape, in particular with regards to China. In July, US National Security Advisor Henry Kissinger made a secret visit to China as a special envoy for the Oval Office, setting the stage for President Nixon's visit to China the following year. At the general assembly of the UN in October, mainland China replaced Taiwan as the "Chinese" representative. Shortly thereafter *Asahi* managing editor Gotō Moto'o succeeded in beating the other news agencies to securing a "one-on-one interview with Zhou Enlai."

But amidst China's return to the international community, the nation was still undergoing profound political shifts and *Asahi*'s coverage of that missed the mark.

The Lin Biao Incident

A political upheaval took place in the innermost circles of the Chinese Communist Party in the autumn of 1971—the Lin Biao Incident. This dramatic episode is still wrapped in mystery but it supposedly involved Lin Biao's failed attempt to assassinate Mao Zedong. Lin was the vice-chairman of the party and national defense minister, who had been officially named in the proceedings of the party as "Mao's closest comrade and successor." It is said that after his failed assassination bid, on September 13 Lin boarded a military plane, intending to flee to the Soviet Union, but he crashed over Mongolia and perished. The Chinese authorities tried desperately to cover up the entire story but little by little news of the disturbance leaked out of Beijing and other regions. The effects were widely felt: annual parades in commemoration of the founding of the People's Republic were cancelled; soldiers had their vacations revoked; a three-day ban on flying over China was instituted from September 13; a Chinese military plane crash was confirmed; Mao's book of quotations and photographs that depicted Mao and Lin together were rounded up; and Lin Biao's name was removed from the speeches of China's allies.

The Beijing correspondent for Agence France-Presse got the scoop about the cancellation of the parades in a story on September 21. France had diplomatic relations with China and even maintained an embassy through the Cultural Revolution, so it can be said that their coverage was more active than that of other countries. In contrast, the *Asahi* correspondent Akioka Ieshige proceeded with caution. He finally submitted an article on the 26th but it emphasized stability, with lines like "Beijing is completely calm," and "It would be a mistake to interpret the current situation as being anything out of the ordinary." Akioka continued to write articles that denied the outbreak of any sort of disturbance. The point at which it become possible to weigh in on the situation was the publication of a number of essays in the December 1971 issue of the journal of Communist thought, *Red Flag* (*Hongqi*). These essays criticized internal sectarianism within the party, making vivid statements such as "Party members at the highest levels are plotting criminal conspiracies," and "The conspirators [...] are orchestrating factional struggles against Chairman Mao." No names were mentioned but many specialists interpreted the essays as referencing the downfall of Lin Biao. *Asahi* noted the shift as well but this did not lead to a change in reporting.

Other news agencies were quick to use foreign news reporting and wasted no time covering the political disturbance around Lin Biao's fall from grace and untimely death. *Asahi* used such reports sparingly, and the Tokyo office wrote political analysis articles that hinted at the upheaval. But the coverage was inconsistent and lagged behind, including a confused story from foreign reports on the February 10, 1972 *Asahi* front page, which outlined an unsubstantiated theory on Lin Biao being alive and well. The wire from *Asahi* correspondents in Beijing that finally confirmed the downfall and death of Lin Biao came on July 28, 1972, the same day that Chinese embassies around the world publicly announced the affair to representatives of local media. Of course, Akioka got his information from various channels "but none of it was certain," he recalls. "It's not that I knew but didn't write anything; rather, I didn't know enough for certain and so I couldn't write anything." It seems that behind this position lay *Asahi* CEO Hirooka Tomoo's doctrine "to not write" any articles that might result in reporters being chased out of China. But Akioka denies that this was the case.

Putting "company policy" first

On November 6, 1971, when information on the Lin Biao affair was still uncertain, *Asahi* ran Tokyo office managing editor Gotō Moto'o's interview with Chinese Prime Minister Zhou Enlai. It spared no detail and took up most of the first three pages. It was Zhou Enlai's first one-on-one interview with any representative of the Japanese media and took place late at night on October 28, just after the UN confirmed mainland China's status as a member nation. How was China's debut on the international stage? There had been no contact from the Chinese side as to the date and time for the interview until immediately before. Prior to his visit to China, Gotō had been in North Korea interviewing Prime Minister Kim Il-Sung. He arrived in Beijing on September 30 and waited for the interview but time passed with no notification. Back in Tokyo, the editorial staff was growing anxious. One executive from the *Asahi* foreign news desk left a memorandum on the matter: "Both before and during Gotō's visit, the offices of the bureau chief were particularly on edge. People were starting to think we should give up [our sensitive reporting surrounding the Lin Biao Incident and related affairs] in order to realize an interview with Zhou."

Interviewing national leaders was one aspect of *Asahi*'s campaign since the beginning of 1971 to stimulate the renewal of diplomatic relations with China. The precedence given to securing these interviews was, however, getting in the way of the daily reporting that is essential to any functioning newspaper, as was clear in the internal memo. An article in the *Asahi Weekly* from December 10, 1971 serves as an example of this sort of "self-regulation" in reporting. Entitled "Following the Mystery of Lin Biao: Survey of Movements During the Past Three Months of 25 Chinese Leaders," the piece was written by *Asahi* foreign affairs journalist Tomono Rō. Tomono suggested that something was amiss surrounding Lin Biao, based on the fact that Lin's name, as well as that of his wife and Politburo member Ye Qun, and those of other high-level military personnel, had disappeared from Chinese media. The *Asahi Newspaper* rejected the report, so Tomono rewrote portions of it and brought it to the *Asahi Weekly* magazine instead. His article sparked fierce protests from the *Asahi Newspaper* staff who were responsible for news on China and who were angry that the *Asahi Weekly* editorial staff machinated to publish an article originally slated for the newspaper but which the "newspaper editorial bureau had refused on the grounds of being biased and subjective." The editorial chief at *Asahi Weekly* who had received the complaint would later say, "I don't recall having thought too hard about whether using a rejected article would offend the editorial bureau. Rather, I felt that the company's position on reporting about China was so gratingly passive that it would have been wrong not to publish the piece." At that point in time, there was a tendency within the company for any critical reporting on China to meet forceful opposition in the name of "company policy" and to be stuck with labels such as "Sinophile" or "Amerophile." Dissatisfaction with the policy of being "historical witnesses" smoldered and some staff members from the foreign news desk invited editorial executives to meetings where they vented their discontent.

The tardy public explanation

From the autumn of 1970, for about three months until the start of 1971, the only full-time Japanese news correspondents in Beijing were those from *Asahi*. *Kyōdō News* had withdrawn its staff and NHK had not received authorization to replace the staff it had sent home. There was a growing backlash against *Asahi*, critics charging that "the paper was toadying up to China" and that "it avoided writing the truth just so that it could keep its correspondents in Beijing." In the autumn of 1970, the Japan Newspaper Association sponsored a roundtable discussion at a newspaper convention on the topic of "Tomorrow's Newspaper." Debate ensued after Kitagawa Chōjirō, CEO of *North Japan Newspaper* (*Kita Nihon Shimbun*), raised a question from the floor: "In the environment where it is not possible to freely cover stories in China, is it necessary to have journalists gathering information there? What exactly is the purpose of sending correspondents to a place where they have no freedom of speech?" *Asahi* CEO Hirooka Tomoo, who was also in the audience, opposed this view. Hirooka countered, "When a country has no freedom of information, or places limits on it, all the more reason that Japan should be sending journalists there." Once again Hirooka was casting the paper as a "historical witness," however his view was not acceptable to the whole company. There was, in fact, simmering dissatisfaction. But protests or formal complaints did not emerge from within the company in any significant way and criticism had no concrete bearing on the way people were carrying out their work. Why was this?

Matsuyama Yukio, a former director of the editorial bureau who had worked at the foreign news desk during part of the Cultural Revolution, says: "There were no specific directives [on this company policy] or instructions but there was a sort of atmosphere enveloping the editorial bureau which suggested we had to write in a certain way if we wanted to avoid having the Beijing branch closed or have our correspondents deported." The submerged voices would not surface until the beginning of the 1980s. In the 1983 summer edition of the editorial bureau circular, Nogami Tadashi, who had been the Beijing correspondent at the outset of the Cultural Revolution, wrote about the "Bias in China Reporting." He said, "China coverage was stilted not only because of the staff stationed in China but also because the home office was growing more anxious not to affront Chinese authorities and disturb the relationship." In the same vein, Hata Shōryū, who had also worked as an editorial supervisor, made the following point in the editorial circular:

> The company at that time was espousing a policy of "pushing toward the renewal of diplomatic relations between China and Japan." It was also espousing the position of "one whole China" and the need for "breaking off relations with Taiwan." [...] But there should have been a rigorous distinction made between that policy and the fair and objective coverage of events. It is unforgiveable that the latter would be subverted for the sake of the former, but at the time there was confusion about this point.

Unfortunately, this sort of critical summation of the coverage of the Cultural Revolution remained within the company. An explanation directed to readers was held off until the 1990s, with publications like the April 1995 special edition entitled, "50 Years of Postwar: A Look at the Media."

The ripple effect of "inconvenience"

The longstanding issue of normalizing relations between China and Japan was finally resolved on September 29, 1972, with a joint proclamation by the two countries immediately following Japanese Prime Minister Tanaka Kakuei's visit to China and negotiations with Zhou Enlai. The joint proclamation set forth that Japan would reflect on its wartime responsibility, as well as recognize the People's Republic of China as the only legal Chinese government. For its part, China would abandon its demands for war reparations. Japanese Foreign Minister Ōhira Masayoshi explained at a press conference, "With today's joint proclamation Japan has closed the books on its dark deeds of the past."

In a front-page article from *Asahi* the day after the proclamation, CEO Hirooka Tomoo, engineer of the company policy of encouraging normalized relations between China and Japan, wrote hopefully about the future now that diplomatic ties had been established. He urged that Japan's course was "to work with China toward peace and progress in Asia." At the same time, the evening edition of *Asahi* on the 29th ran a piece offering observations and opinions from a range of people, including Kyoto University professor Aida Yūji. Aida commented that we "should not forget the lasting psychological wounds the Chinese suffered at the hands of the Japanese." This sort of prudent attitude was already necessary since the events of the welcome reception for Tanaka when he arrived in Beijing on September 25. Zhou Enlai made the initial greetings touching on the issue of wartime aggression during the war, saying "The invasion by Japanese militarists brought great disaster to the suffering Chinese people." Tanaka expressed his contrition by responding, "We caused great 'inconvenience' to the people of China."

The word "inconvenience," *meiwaku* in Japanese, was translated into Chinese in the statement prepared by the Japanese Foreign Ministry as *má fán*, a simple apology that one might use, perhaps, after having spilled water on a lady's dress. The *Asahi* reporter covering the meeting, Nishimura Hidetoshi, noticed that at the moment the interpreters said *má fán*, the applause died and the smiles vanished from the faces of the Chinese attendees. "Tanaka has been riding a wave of popularity," wrote Nishimura in his article, "and expectations are high among Japanese who are looking forward to resuming diplomatic relations, so reporters believed they should not write anything that would dampen the celebratory mood. But it was clear that the Chinese were none too satisfied at the handling of the issue in such flippant terms as 'inconvenience.'" However, Nishimura did write in his article, "the Chinese demonstrated their displeasure over the light use of the word '*meiwaku*.'"

That was the extent of newspaper coverage about the "inconvenience" gaffe, but when Tanaka returned to Japan on September 30 for a general meeting of LDP representatives and reported on the as-yet-unpublicized details of the negotiations, it became clear that his statement had made considerable waves. During the meeting, the day after the welcome reception the situation was strained and Zhou roundly criticized Tanaka, saying that he was inviting the hostility of the Chinese. Chairman Mao also brought up the remark in his meeting with Tanaka.

Why did the Chinese side react so strongly? One clue was unearthed in a special issue of the *Asahi* for the 25th anniversary of the resumption of diplomatic ties entitled "Testimony: The China-Japan Joint Proclamation" (August 27–28, 1997). Leading up to Tanaka's visit, the Chinese government had established a special domestic team designed to smooth over public opinion about Japan. The team worked diligently to win over Chinese people who were saying "they could never welcome the Japanese Prime Minister because members of their families had been killed by the Japanese military." Tanaka's single utterance of the word "inconvenience" could have destroyed the efforts of the Chinese campaign.

Figure 42   Japanese Prime Minister Tanaka Kakuei on the left greets Chinese Premier Zhou Enlai with a historic handshake at Beijing Airport, September 25, 1972.

Breaking off relations with Taiwan

On September 17, eight days before Prime Minister Tanaka arrived in Beijing for the negotiations, LDP Vice-President Shiina Etsusaburō was in the Republic of China (Taiwan). As special envoy from the prime minister, Shiina was there to explain that formal diplomatic ties would have to be severed no matter what. He did not find a warm welcome. Only five media agencies sent reporters along with him, including the *Mainichi Shimbun*, *Kyōdō News*, and Fuji Television. In Taipei, Shiina explained that even with Japan-PRC diplomatic restorations, "the LDP wanted foreign relations, including with Taiwan, to continue just as before." *Asahi* printed a brief mention of Shīna's statement on September 19. Late that night, Zhou Enlai read it as a news feed from *Kyōdō News* and summoned the LDP group led by Kosaka Zentarō and others. Zhou forcefully questioned Kosaka about Japan's intentions. The following evening *Asahi* prominently reported that "Shīna's Statement Received Strong Criticism."

  Asahi had long provided cordial and substantial coverage of Taiwan and from 1952 had intermittently kept a total of six correspondents in Taipei. When the correspondents for Beijing were approved in 1966, the paper kept reporters in both capitals—Beijing and Taipei. According to a memo written at the time by the foreign reporting desk, China persistently protested that *Asahi* was acting as if there were "two Chinas." "*Asahi* ignored these complaints for a time" but eventually in July 1970 the sixth Taipei correspondent, Itō Hitoshi, was called back. At that point, the only remaining Japanese news agency in Taiwan was the *Jiji Press* (*Jiji Tsūshin*). The proposal for the potential for resuming diplomatic relations with China was put forth in the January 1, 1971 *Asahi* laying out the company policy, which ran in line with the claims of the Chinese government: "The People's Republic of China is the only legitimate government representing China. Taiwan is a part of Chinese territory and the handling of the

Taiwan question is an internal issue for the Chinese government." On September 29, 1972, the Japanese government recognized these claims, culminating in the resumption of diplomatic relations. In the pages of *Asahi* the following day—the first day of the new era of Sino-Japanese relations—the *Vox Populi, Vox Dei* column was the only place that gave more than a passing thought to the potential feelings of fourteen million Taiwanese toward Japan in the wake of the severing of relations. "One worry in all this is what happens to the Taiwanese people after relations have been severed?" "We cannot lose sight of the fact that Japan ruled Taiwan for fifty years;" "Taiwan is now China's responsibility but saying that we are no longer concerned does not go down so well. Our hearts go out to the Taiwanese." After cutting off relations, it was not until August 1, 1980 that *Asahi* again covered Taiwan when Beijing correspondent Kondō Tatsuo visited Taipei and wrote a five-installment series, "Looking at the Current Situation in Taiwan."

24

The Lockheed Incident

Naming "Tanaka"

In the autumn of 1975, a US Senate Foreign Relations subcommittee on multinational corporations held a closed hearing investigating the Lockheed Corporation on suspicion of making overseas bribes. Jerome Levinson, the subcommittee's chief legal adviser, directed a question to John Clutter, the Tokyo representative of the major American aircraft manufacturer Lockheed. Clutter murmured his reply: "I was hoping you wouldn't ask that." The subcommittee chairman, Frank Church, broke in and responded: "But he did ask it." The hearing fell under congressional authority and participants testifying were not permitted to decline to answer any question. "All right then," answered Clutter, "The payment was made to Prime Minister Tanaka."

It was in July 1976 that former Prime Minister Tanaka Kakuei was arrested on suspicion of having accepted 500 million yen from Lockheed. Roughly nine months earlier, his name had come up in testimony as the recipient of funds from Lockheed executives. The revelation during the Watergate investigations that President Nixon had taken illegal contributions from American aircraft manufacturer Northrop gave rise to the charge that Lockheed had made payments to foreign political parties and functionaries. Lockheed proactively released a summary of its payouts on August 1, 1975 and the next day *Asahi* reported this in its evening edition. Acting director of the local news section at the time, Saeki Susumu, remembers having a gut feeling that the investigation would come to involve Japan. He assigned the story to Taoka Shunji, who had just returned to Japan after university study in the US. In Saeki's view, the developing story could be a "goldmine" of coverage but there was also information to suggest "Japan was not among the countries that had received payments." When it was clear there was no coherent angle on the story, *Asahi* abandoned it.

At that point, the investigation being carried out by the US Senate subcommittee on multinational corporations cleared several hurdles. Since Lockheed was balking at releasing its records, Levinson changed tack and ordered the company's auditors to submit their files. The auditors' lawyers quickly assented. On February 4, 1976, Levinson and his team held a public hearing where they revealed the results of their investigation. Page two of the next morning's *Asahi* covered the investigation in a brief article under the headline, "Lockheed Made Payments to Marubeni Co. and Kodama Yoshio." It was the first Japanese report on what would become the biggest postwar bribery scandal.

The name "Tanaka" did not appear in that article, as Levinson's team had omitted personal names in consideration of the individual rights of those involved, instead making oblique references to "high-ranking government officials." From the start, Tanaka's name was whispered behind the scenes as being at the heart of the whole affair but it was not until he was arrested on July 27, 1976 that *Asahi* identified him as the recipient of tainted money.

The birth of investigative journalism

Because the Lockheed Incident originated in the United States, Japanese police and prosecutors had virtually no access to information. For reporters in Japan, the main leads on the story were links to names that came up in the congressional hearings and information that came in from the US, and it was a process of trial and error. *Asahi* local news writer Takagi Hattarō focused on other sources such as expenditure receipts from Lockheed in English and receipts that bore the personal seal of major right-wing fixer Kodama Yoshio. With the help of accountants at banks and trading companies, Takagi traced the flow of funds from Lockheed to Kodama, presenting his detailed findings in a graph in *Asahi* on March 10, 1976. Taoka Shunji took Kodama's receipts and went around to shops that made personal seals in Tokyo, following the trail. He uncovered that a Japanese individual living in America, Shigeru "Shig" Katayama, had played a role in Lockheed's money-generating schemes. Taoka brought Katayama to Tokyo on the *Asahi* company jet, conducting several exclusive interviews. His bold reporting methods were later dramatized in a comic strip as part of *Asahi*'s hundredth anniversary celebrations.

Up until that point, it had been standard practice for the authorities to submit their findings from criminal investigation hearings and searches of the premises to the press all at once and only after the matter had come into public view. Then the fruits of the investigation were published in the paper. But in the case of the Lockheed Incident, details started coming to light in America before the Japanese authorities had begun their internal investigation, breaking the standard mold of how reporting was handled. Investigative journalists' focus onto the centers of national authority in both Japan and the United States during the first half of the 1970s changed what it meant to be a reporter. In America, two young reporters for *The Washington Post* pursued the Watergate story, leading to President Nixon's eventual resignation. In Japan, Tachibana Takashi and his team had a role in making the prime minister step down when they published "Investigating Tanaka Kakuei: Channels and Connections" in the November 1974 issue of the *Literary Annals* (*Bungei Shunjū*) magazine. In both cases, the journalists took it upon themselves to target political corruption and reported it.

Nishimura Hidetoshi, who as a roving reporter had the special assignment of bringing together coverage on the Lockheed Incident, recalls: "We were fired up for the fight and thought we should also do it." "The reporters covering the incident had a feeling they were beating criminal investigators to the punch." On October 11, 1983, *Asahi* claimed that the reporting from the Lockheed days was generally considered an unprecedented form of investigative journalism in Japanese history, one that opened a

Figure 43   Front cover of a pamphlet that dramatically depicts the *Asahi Newspaper*'s investigative efforts into the Lockheed Incident.

whole new field. Many media scholars also assess coverage of the Lockheed scandal as the true beginning of Japanese investigative journalism.

Paying a visit to the attorney general

On February 16, 1976, *Asahi* local news chief Saeki Susumu, together with another local news journalist, Nakagawa Shōzō, went on a low-profile visit to lead public prosecutor Fuse Takeshi, about two weeks after the Lockheed story first broke. The examination in the Diet of Tanaka Kakuei's close friend and head of the Kokusai Kōgyō Company, Osano Kenji, had just begun. The purpose of the two journalists' visit was to determine the attitude of the public prosecutor toward the Lockheed Incident. In the summer of the previous year Saeki had assigned roving reporter, Taoka Shunji, to investigate the issue of Lockheed distributing funds overseas but he was unable to gather enough concrete information to write an article. Based on that experience, Saeki felt that the story could not be clearly reported on unless the prosecution initiated a criminal investigation, but that office distanced itself so much from political cases, since the time of the Nittsū Incident (Nippon Express) in 1968, eight years earlier, that it was known as "the sleeping prosecution."[1] An editorial in *Asahi* on February 15 asked, "If America grasps the weakness of the Japanese political sphere can Japan remain prosperous as a country?" Saeki was hoping to use this line of thought to persuade Fuse to act and in the end Fuse said, "Yes, I will do it." Kamiya Hisao, the lead prosecutor in the Tokyo Prosecutor's Office, who was also in attendance at the meeting on the 16th, asked the journalists, "We may have to take some drastic legal measures— would you still support us then?" "Of course," replied Saeki.

On February 18, the top members of the public prosecutorial office held their first meeting about the Lockheed Incident. Fuse declared that they were putting the credibility of the office on the line. Kamiya added his appeal, saying: "if the prosecutor's office did not open an investigation the office would lose the faith of Japanese citizens over the next two decades." Kamiya recalls, "We must have met Mr. Saeki from the *Asahi*, but I can't quite remember now. Even if we did, the lead prosecutor had already made up his mind to open an investigation. Still, it would have been a good thing to have the journalists pay us that visit." Saeki revealed the details of his secret meeting with the lead prosecutor in the Japan Press Club bulletin of May 10, 2000. Criticism had been leveled against this meeting in the magazine *SAPIO* on April 22, 2009: "There was a movement within the ruling party and the public prosecutors office to 'get rid of' Tanaka Kakuei and we suspect that there was broad support for this in the media." Saeki responded to this charge by saying, "I felt that if the newspaper did not work together with the office of the prosecutor this scandal would not be brought to light. In no way were we currying favor or doing the politicians' dirty work."

The *Asahi* column "Today's Problems" (*Kyō no mondai*), in the evening edition on February 19, 1976, called for "an insider" in the Lockheed case. The *Mainichi* also ran a series at the beginning of March soliciting information from internal sources called "Structural Corruption: Whistleblowers Wanted." The investigation was getting closer to the truth and public opinion behind the public prosecutor's investment in the case continued to grow.

The day of the arrest

At 7:27 a.m. on July 27, 1976, a car quickly stopped off in front of the public prosecutor's office in Tokyo. The reporters assigned to keep an eye on the office were astonished when Tanaka Kakuei stepped out of the vehicle. By the time Abe Yoshikazu—the *Asahi* journalist covering the prosecution office—arrived, Tanaka had already gone inside. Abe hurtled up the stairs to the fifth floor, just in time to catch a glimpse of Tanaka entering the hearing room but not in time to take a photo. Not a single Japanese news agency guessed that this would be the day of Tanaka's arrest. Many suspected that the case the public prosecutors were putting together had Tanaka at the center of it all but even if the investigation reached him, most news agencies were more focused on former Secretary-General of the Liberal Democratic Party (LDP) Hashimoto Tomisaburō and other politicians.

Asahi decided to release a special extra but there was no ready-to-go article for a story about the "Arrested Former Prime Minister" and there was no time to write the whole thing from scratch. Instead, the prepared article "Hashimoto Arrested," written by local news reporter Tominaga Hisao, was used as a template. Tominaga recalls, "We changed 'Hashimoto' to 'Tanaka' and 'former Secretary-General' to 'former Prime Minister.' But when we went to print there was still one place where it still said 'former Secretary-General.' I guess we must really have been scrambling." Twelve years later, in the December 17, 1988 edition of *Asahi*, senior staff writer Kunimasa Takeshige wrote about some of what went on behind the scenes with Tanaka's arrest. A week before the arrest, Lower House Speaker, Maeo Shigesaburō, had made a phone call to Tanaka at the urging of Chief Public Prosecutor Fuse Takeshi, telling him that if he resigned from the Diet his sentence would be reduced. Tanaka refused. This conversation suggests that if Tanaka had stepped down the prosecutor's office would not have arrested but indicted him without incarceration. Although Maeo was on good terms with Tanaka he had also cultivated extensive contacts with the public prosecutor's office when he served as justice minister. However, Kamiya Hisao, who had served as chief of the Tokyo Public Prosecutor's Office, claims: "If the lead public prosecutor had proposed such a plan, I would have expected to be consulted about it but I wasn't."

Starting the week before Tanaka's arrest, *Asahi* ran a series of 50 articles in its local news section under the header, "The Grey Areas of the Political Realm." The main contributor was Ninagawa Masao, who worked with the *Asahi* branch office in Nagaoka, Niigata Prefecture while reporting on the town where Tanaka grew up. Ninagawa was a Tokyo reporter but had the idea to find out more about the political climate of Tanaka's hometown and he took up residence there in Muikamachi from 1975 to 1977. Ninagawa spent time drinking with members of Tanaka's election committee (*Etsuzankai*) and took part in local snow removal operations, making himself part of the community as a way to grasp the multi-layered relationship between Tanaka and his local constituency.

Exclusive interview

Former Lockheed vice-chairman Carl Kotchian knew all about the company's machinations to secure overseas contracts and so he was in high demand for one-on-one interviews—not just by Japanese journalists, but also by American, Italian, and Dutch reporters. Finally, on August 21, 1976, almost a month after Tanaka Kakuei's arrest, *Asahi* published its exclusive interview with Kotchian. He gave the details of how Marubeni executive Ōkubo Toshiharu requested that Tanaka be paid 500 million yen. Kotchian explained how, when the agreements seemed about to fall through, he watched Lockheed's secret representative Kodama Yoshio place a phone call to then minister of international trade and industry, Nakasone Yasuhiro, salvaging the situation. Kotchian gave a detailed testimonial of Lockheed's maneuverings over three days of interviews, resulting in four pages of news. Murakami Yoshio from the *Asahi* American bureau had been the one to get Kotchian to talk. "When I saw the earnestness with which Kotchian answered questions at press conferences," he relates, "I knew that if I was going to get the truth, it would be from him." Murakami called Kotchian at home nearly every night, building up trust with conversations about politics and sports, saying, "You have responsibility to reveal to the people of Japan the truth behind what had gone on." Tanaka's arrest served as the impetus for Kotchian to agree to an interview and so with little fanfare Murakami and American bureau chief Matsuyama Yukio boarded a plane to Los Angeles.

While Matsuyama handled the arrangements with headquarters as to how the report would be presented, Murakami holed up in a hotel room interviewing Kotchian for more than sixty hours. Murakami listened, recorded everything in English, and then confirmed with Kotchian. Their talks covered information about Lockheed's dealings with officials in other countries, but Murakami opted not to include this in his reporting since "it did not have to do with Japan." The *Mainichi* also reported the contents of the interview, referencing the testimonial as "according to *Asahi*." The *Asahi* reporter covering the public prosecutor's office, Abe Yoshikazu, was exhausted at the end of the affair, saying, "We've said everything that needed to be said on this, and now we can move on." The following year Murakami was awarded the Japan Newspaper Publishers and Editors Association Prize.

In Kotchian's American court hearing, held before he had spoken to *Asahi*, he testified on the particulars of the contracts for Lockheed's commercial airliners. Had this information not been permitted as evidence in the Japanese courts, it would probably have disappeared. Nakasone, whose name came up in the testimony, challenged the charges of his involvement, saying they were not grounded in fact. *Asahi*'s managing editor of the Tokyo office, Hitotsuyanagi Tōichirō, says: "This denial did not concern me at all because I was well aware of how thorough Murakami's reporting had been." Matsuyama wrote the following in the January 1977 *Asahi* editorial circular: "Kotchian was saying that Lockheed was the victim. He hoped to roll the interview into a book as a way of justifying himself to the shareholders but he made some convenient omissions. I can't imagine he didn't know where the money would go after it had been handed over to Kodama."

The fate of the 500 million yen

What happened to all the money that Tanaka Kakuei had supposedly taken from Lockheed and Marubeni? There was broad speculation but the prosecution shed no light on the matter and it remained a mystery. On January 28, 1989, *Sankei Shimbun*'s top headline read "500 Million Yen of Bribe Money Paid to Tanaka Handed Over to 28 LDP Diet Members." This came thirteen years after the Lockheed Incident was first uncovered and in the intervening time Tanaka had been found guilty in two lower courts and had appealed to the Supreme Court. The article reported that Tanaka had instructed his secretary, Enomoto Toshio, to distribute twenty million yen each to twenty-eight candidates running in the 1974 election for the Upper House of the Diet. Tanaka had personally given out other funds and the article proposed that the 500 million yen from Lockheed was part of the massive combined sum of payouts made by Tanaka and Enomoto. All of this was according to Enomoto's testimony during the investigation. It was a major newsbreak and the first concrete clue as to what happened to the 500 million yen.

After this article appeared, *Asahi* got hold of the transcripts from Enomoto's testimony given to the Tokyo public prosecutor on August 12, 1976, when he was under arrest and awaiting trial. The transcripts contained the list of twenty-eight Diet candidates who had supposedly accepted funds, including individuals who had previously served as justice minister, postal minister, and minister of home affairs. The majority were not members of Tanaka's faction but about twenty had won seats in that election. Enomoto's testimony suggested that the 500 million was not simply handed over to those twenty-eight candidates. He asserted that Tanaka and his cohorts had spread around more than ten billion yen during that Upper House election and claimed that, "even if we assume the five hundred million yen in question went to campaign expenses, there is no way of knowing for sure how it was used." When interviewed by *Asahi*, Enomoto responded: "I marked the names of those who received funds on the list of candidates that the public prosecutor showed me—I recall marking thirty-one names." The prosecutors determined that the testimony and list in question were not necessary to prove the case and did not submit them as evidence to the court. In the *Mainichi* coverage of Tanaka's first public court hearing on April 2, 1981, the paper reported that a portion of the transcript from Enomoto's questioning from August 12, 1976 was oddly omitted from evidence and that one of the lead prosecutors stated in the paper, "For certain reasons it is our intention never to release that portion of the transcript." The prosecutor Murata Hitoshi who questioned Enomoto revealed, "I took down the testimony on the transfer of the five hundred million yen as supporting evidence but how that evidence would be used was up to my superiors." Kamiya Hisao, who had been the head of the Tokyo Public Prosecutor's Office at the time, recalls, "I have a vague recollection of Enomoto making that confession but it's not a given that all depositions taken will be submitted to the court as evidence." If Enomoto's testimony had been submitted in full, it would have resulted in a major political scandal and the public prosecutor's office most likely hoped to avoid throwing the political world into complete chaos.

Critical evidence explodes on television

"It was divided up into cardboard boxes and I made two or three trips to Mr. Itō's residence to pick it up." This was the smoking gun statement made by Tanaka's secretary Enomoto Toshio in reference to having collected boxes containing 500 million yen from former Marubeni executive Itō Hiroshi. Enomoto divulged this secret during an interview with TV Asahi at the beginning of January 1983 just before the public prosecution recommended that Tanaka be sentenced to five years in prison and fined 500 million yen. The statement was broadcast on morning shows after February 10.

During the investigation, Enomoto for the most part corroborated the prosecution's findings that he had on four separate occasions picked up funds either at Itō's home or in meetings on the street, but in court he uniformly denied that these funds went to Tanaka. By the time the trial had reached its final stages, although his account still diverged from the picture painted by the prosecution, Enomoto at last admitted that Tanaka had in fact taken the money. It was TV Asahi producer Shirato Masanao who convinced Enomoto to confess. He had built up a relationship with Tanaka's secretary over a year of visiting the Enomoto household. The *Asahi* newspaper learned the contents of Enomoto's television interview before it aired and made it the top story in the February 8 morning edition. The evening edition, however, ran a story in the local news section entitled, "What is the Truth?", which queried if Enomoto underwent a "conversion" or was "conspiratorial" in his testimony just before a verdict was handed down. An editorial on February 16 called for the trial to be reopened, demanding that Enomoto "Tell the truth!" but the case soon closed. When the judgment was handed down in October, the court accepted the allegations made by the public prosecution and sentenced Tanaka to four years in prison with a fine of 500 million yen. From that point on, Enomoto kept his mouth firmly shut about the case.

According to Inami Tomoyuki, administrative head of the lawyer's team that handled Tanaka's defense, some of the legal team were of the opinion that on the basis of Enomoto's testimony, they should deny the story laid out by the prosecution in the appeals court. Tanaka's lawyers were pressing him to decide whether or not to maintain the strategy of an across-the-board denial but he could not make up his mind. At the end of February 1985, Tanaka suffered a stroke and when the case reached the appeals court his team ended up maintaining the strategy of denying the charges. Kusaka Megumu, an *Asahi* reporter covering Tanaka, tells that he heard directly from Tanaka before his collapse that "the five hundred million yen was part of the money distributed across various industries during the 1974 Upper House election." Tanaka claimed that, "the prosecution is shooting wide of the mark." But, according to Kusaka, "Tanaka could not admit in a public forum the fact that he had received the money because it would be problematic for a prime minister to amass such funds during an election." Kusaka learned of this secret in an off-the-record conversation but could find no corroborating evidence, so he could not write an article about it. When *Asahi* questioned Enomoto further, he responded in writing, claiming: "I received political contributions but never received anything in the street," once again denying the scenario suggested by the prosecutors. Munakata Norio, an attorney who had been in charge of Tanaka's appeal as a prosecutor and had made a close study of the investigation and the initial trial record, had this to say: "There is no mistaking the fact that Tanaka received the five hundred million yen. But there is something not quite right about the story constructed by the prosecution—it may just be that things happened the way Enomoto said they did."

Exemption of criminal liability

On February 22, 1995, eighteen years after the beginning of the Lockheed trials, the Supreme Court handed down its decision on former Marubeni chairman Hiyama Hiro and his associates: "Appeal Rejected," meaning that the guilty verdict stood. When the presiding judge, Chief Justice Kusaba Ryōhachi, was reading the reasoning behind the guilty verdict, a commotion broke out among the press in attendance because they realized the transcripts of the American Lockheed deposition had not been used as evidence, as a special request of the prosecution. Because the arm of Japanese law did not reach Kotchian and other Lockheed employees living in America, Japanese prosecutors extended "criminal immunity" to them, something that does not exist in the Japanese legal system, and after granting them this got them to respond to official questioning. However, given that the judges in the first and second trials found the US depositions as strong enough proof of all the Japanese defendants' guilt for three routes of money funneling—through the Marubeni company, All Nippon Airlines, and private individuals Osano and Kodama—reporters were surprised by its omission as evidence at the Japanese Supreme Court.

Tanaka had already passed away and the case against him had therefore been dismissed. The Supreme Court reached a verdict of guilty based only on the testimony offered by Marubeni representatives. Kimura Kisuke, a Tanaka lawyer who had staunchly protested the legality of allowing the American transcripts as evidence, lamented in his book, "If the transcripts of the American depositions had not been allowed as evidence in the lower courts, it is likely that Tanaka would not have been found guilty."[2] An *Asahi* editorial on June 6, 1976 was in full support of the use of the American depositions, writing that they "will serve as a stepping stone for a mandatory investigation moving forward," and "it is expected that this is the best way of achieving an optimal outcome."

In July 1976, the chief Japanese prosecutor promised Kotchian and the other American Lockheed representatives that no case would be brought against them. At the request of the United States, the Japanese Supreme Court released a declaration of "guarantee" for this promise, after which the transcripts were sent to Japan. Kanatani Toshihiro, who handled the logistics of this matter for the Supreme Court criminal investigation bureau, recalls: "Because the declaration of guarantee was just barely permissible on the level of judicial administrative rules for the purpose of obtaining investigation materials, I knew there might still be a question as to whether or not this sort of transcript could be admissible as evidence in court, but I decided to worry about that later." In September 1978, authorities decided to make use of the transcripts for the Tokyo court case concerning the money funneled through Osano and Kodama. The next day's *Asahi* editorial evaluated this move positively, saying: "This opens up new territory for the handling of criminal procedural law" and "The court has made the appropriate decision." Years later, when the Supreme Court excluded the transcripts as evidence, the *Asahi* editorial from February 23, 1995 read: "It is the responsibility of the Supreme Court to strictly uphold procedures of law. In that sense the Supreme Court's decision can be said to move things back to the way they should be." This view diametrically opposed the earlier *Asahi* editorial take on the issue.

During debates in the editorial room Tsuyama Shōei, who oversaw the writing of the 1995 piece, stressed the importance of strictly preserving court procedure. He says he gave no thought to the need for consistency with the earlier editorial. Tsuyama reflects, "The editorials from back then were the products of a time when a fierce demand for the truth reigned supreme. By the time the case reached the Supreme Court, the situation was such that court decisions could be made in a more measured way."

The reporters covering Tanaka

Political reporters were the journalists able to get the closest to former prime minister Tanaka Kakuei. Starting from July 28, 1976, the day after Tanaka's arrest, *Asahi* ran a series with five installments entitled "The Roots of Corruption." The series was written by veteran reporters of the political section, who used it to level charges against the Tanaka faction, including allegations of financial influence, a byzantine selection process for party leadership, and collusion among politicians, bureaucrats, and business leaders running rampant during the long rule of the LDP. But the *Asahi* political section's foremost areas of interest had always been in the trends of who wielded political power, the movements of various cliques and factions, and how elections were used for political maneuvering. Even after the Lockheed Incident broke, this tendency would not be very quick to change. Tanaka began to play favorites with journalists. Hayano Tōru was an *Asahi* political reporter who had a hard time getting Tanaka to speak to him even after being assigned to cover the politician. Every time Tanaka would return to Niigata Prefecture, Hayano would follow him. In the *Asahi* morning edition from April 17, 1978, one of Hayano's pieces, "Back in Charge: Just a Statesman from Niigata Prefecture," told how Tanaka was putting his energy back again into dialogue with the local voters. From that point on Hayano had free access to Tanaka.

After leaving the LDP, Tanaka expanded his clique, earning the nickname "The Shadow Shogun," and calling the shots during three administrations, including that of Prime Minister Ōhira Masayoshi. For political journalists, Tanaka's revelations about the scene were a treasure trove of potential reporting. But once Tanaka's trial was under way, political articles focusing on him dropped from the pages of *Asahi*. Reporters were gathering information on him but nothing was being published. Yoshida Shin'ichi, responsible for coordinating coverage of Tanaka from 1982 onward, says: "the prevailing mood in political reporting at the time was one of avoiding too much detail on the statements and actions of a defendant under criminal investigation." Hayano Tōru arranged for the chief of the political section, Matsushita Muneyuki, to interview Tanaka and he was able to obtain Tanaka's consent right away. However, Matsushita decided that the "time was not yet right." The moment to report on Tanaka came after the Lower House elections at the end of 1983. Although Tanaka's first trial had just resulted in a guilty verdict, he was nonetheless elected to the Diet to represent the third district of his home prefecture, winning with an unprecedented 220,000 votes. Yoshida says, "The longstanding discontent of reporters covering Tanaka, who could only gather information but not publish anything, exploded with the series 'Tanaka in Control.'" From the end of November 1984, this series was a vivid depiction in thirty installments of how Tanaka tried to orchestrate a dramatic political shuffling by making a key member of his faction, Nikaidō Susumu, the successor to the Nakasone administration.

Nagasaki Kazuo, covering Tanaka for the *Mainichi* at the same time that Yoshida was handling it for *Asahi*, says: "There was talk that some reporters were getting kickbacks from the Tanaka financial system so we went out of our way to keep our noses clean—that's how we won Tanaka's trust." Nagasaki and those like him would cover their own portion when attending dinners with Tanaka and associates, paying by postal bank order so that there would be a receipt of their payments. Yoshida picked up these sorts of tactics from Nagasaki and says, "There was a time when you had to get in good with the boss of a clique if you wanted to get any information. It was probably the Lockheed Scandal which changed this political culture that was previously taken as granted."

What was left out?

The Lockheed Incident involved more than just the United States and Japan. Lockheed came under suspicion of behind-the-scenes dealings to secure aircraft sales contracts in more than ten countries during the 1970s. While most of the cases remained vague in their details, the investigation in Japan led to a criminal prosecution of the prime minister. Voices in America positively evaluated Japan's ability to "clean up corruption," while prominent newspapers in France praised Japan's handling of the situation. There is no doubt that the prosecution was spurred on by the independent inquiries of Japanese journalists in pursuit of the truth, as well as by a public that demanded to know what was really going on.

But even today, some of the details of the affair remain shrouded in mystery.

The biggest unknown is what happened to the 2.1 billion yen identified in the US congressional hearing as having been handed over to major right-wing figure Kodama Yoshio. The front page of the evening *Asahi* from February 14, 1976 reported that the congressional hearing brought to light an agreement that Lockheed would pay Kodama if the company succeeded in winning a sales contract for its P3C anti-submarine aircraft. Many suspected that Kodama used a portion of the more than 2 billion yen for expenses during his machinations to gain the contract. Kodama denied "having accepted anything beyond a fifty million yen annual consultant's fee" and criminal

Figure 44   Kodama Yoshio's burnt-out mansion, incinerated after an actor flew a plane into it in 1976.

investigators gave up on trying to connect him to deals in the political world. Instead, investigators indicted him on charges of tax evasion in the amount of 1.9 billion yen. *Asahi*'s investigation at the time found that Kodama's receipts did not match the sums in question, nor were there any signs that Kodama's assets had made any unusual increases. Kodama passed away during the course of his trial in January 1984 when *Asahi* wrote, "The Dark Side of the Political World: One Aspect of the Lockheed Incident Lost in the Shadows."

Tanaka was embroiled in the criminal investigation but he continued to dominate the political world as a kingmaker. The Lockheed trials became a battleground where the government organ of the public prosecutor's office was locked in a struggle for survival with the political power of Tanaka Kakuei. Magazines published article after article criticizing the evidence that the public prosecution was bringing forth. There are also those who remain dubious of the public prosecution's investigations. Kobayashi Yasuhiro, who did a long stint coordinating coverage of the Lockheed Incident at *Asahi*, says: "The way the media and citizenry evaluate the actions of the public prosecutor is nothing less than a 'reflection of their political maturity.'" Political power breeds corruption and demands oversight. Media coverage of the Lockheed Incident demonstrates to both reporters and readers how important and difficult it is to keep watch on those in positions of political power.

25

The Oil Shock

The eleventh hour

"A crisis in oil energy is approaching" was the lead of the series that ran in the *Asahi* financial section from April 29, 1973, entitled "Burning Up the Earth." It was a large-scale series, running over twelve installments through July, each of which filled an entire page. The reporting covered topics including the difficulties America faced in moving from producing its own oil to importing large quantities, the shifts in power relations between oil-producing countries and the major oil corporations making up the Seven Sisters, and the move toward Japanese government and businesses trying to secure national energy resources.

The forecasted crisis became a reality. Within three months of the end of the series, the entire world was reeling from the effects. Mitsuyu Hisao, a financial reporter and key member of the investigative team, recalls: "There was an awareness that changes were taking place in the oil market, that the cheap prices and plentiful availability of the past were no longer possible. But none of the people who could see the oil shock coming happened to be working in oil companies or in MITI [Ministry of International Trade and Industry]." It was during these days of securing energy resources that oil became a topic with global ramifications. In March 1972, the previous year, the prominent Club of Rome think tank released *The Limits to Growth*, a book that sounded a warning. The think tank was made up of leading business figures from various countries. It cautioned that if population expansion and economic growth were not restrained, then the planet would face a catastrophe of environmental pollution and food shortages. In April, President Richard Nixon sent a special message to Congress on energy issues, calling for institution building and international cooperation. The Japanese government also embarked on oil-related diplomacy. Nakasone Yasuhiro, then Minister of International Trade and Industry, visited the Middle East at the end of April. He stated that he would oppose the US plan for an alliance of oil-consuming countries because "it would invite confrontation with oil-producing countries." He was criticized by the United States of cozying up to oil-producing countries and his efforts met with a chilly reception in Japan as well.

On October 6, the 1973 Arab-Israel War broke out and the oil-producing Arab countries in the Middle East declared that they would raise prices and cut production. These moves sparked the Oil Crisis. At that point, 40 percent of Japanese oil imports were from Arab countries and the other 60 percent through the Seven Sisters, the majority of which were based out of America. Japan was caught between the oil-producing countries and the United States, struggling to reconcile the preservation of both oil resources and diplomatic relations with America. The Japanese government turned to favor the Arab countries. The Chief Cabinet Secretary prepared a statement on the matter but Ōhira Masayoshi, then serving as Foreign Minister, would not sign off on it. Nonetheless, the statement was released on November 22, according to the wishes of Prime Minister Tanaka Kakuei. The center of gravity for Japan's foreign relations was shifting to a position that favored Arab countries, even more so than it had with Nakasone's pronouncement. The analysis in an *Asahi* editorial from December 4 about the Chief Cabinet Secretary's statement read, "There are many in America and elsewhere who see Japan as bending to Arab pressure out of a desire for oil." The paper urged Japan to "grasp the true nature of the problems in the Middle East from a standpoint of international justice and to pursue an autonomous foreign policy."

No toilet paper?

During October 1973 there was a two-week cessation of hostilities in the Arab-Israel War but Arab countries maintained their price increase on crude oil and their decrease in oil distribution. And for some reason Japan was seized by a shortage of paper. On October 23, Osaka-based *Asahi* local news reporter Yoshimura Fumishige was assigned to check out the shortage of toilet paper at supermarkets and headed to Senri New Town. "Toilet Paper Shortage! Sold Out by Evening," ran the headline in the next day's Osaka city edition of the *Asahi*. Yoshimura recalls that after his article his colleagues began competing with one another to cover the run on toilet paper. At the Ministry of International Trade and Industry, the section chief responsible for the paper industry, Muraoka Shigeo, had been keeping a close eye on paper reserves. On October 31, his office telephone rang and the Osaka foreign trade and industry bureau chief in a raised voice asked: "Have you seen the evening *Asahi*?" The paper had run a large photo of a housewife in Nara City who had bought up 180 rolls of toilet paper. The report read, "Dear God, Give us Toilet Paper! Shortage Causing Panic in the Streets." There had been other articles, such as the evening edition of *Sankei* on October 18, that featured a photo of a housewife who had taken her baby out of the stroller in order to load it up with toilet paper, but Muraoka was especially concerned with *Asahi*'s reports that "toilet paper has begun to vanish from stores," and use of the word "panic."

The next day Muraoka went to the press room within the ministry where he warned an *Asahi* reporter that the paper was pouring oil on the fire. That same day there were disturbances at a Senri supermarket, where people were struggling with one another to grab what little toilet paper remained. This story featured prominently in newspapers and on TV. Then on November 2, *Asahi* printed an article with the headline, "Is the Toilet Paper Shortage Real? Investigations Show Production is Up, Ample Supplies Remain." Just as Muraoka thought he could breathe a sigh of relief, the same morning in Amagasaki City, Gunma Prefecture, a mob of housewives descended on a store selling toilet paper and an 83-year-old woman was badly injured in the rush. The hysteria sweeping western Japan calmed down by November 6, with large-scale

Figure 45   A housewife stockpiling toilet paper, October 1973, Nara City.

restocking operations overseen by the Ministry of International Trade and Industry, but people across the rest of the country had also begun buying up large quantities of toilet paper. "Toilet Paper Fever has Spread to Kōchi," read the Kōchi, Shikoku edition of *Asahi* on November 12. The paper reported, "a group of Osaka company employees on vacation took home toilet paper as souvenirs from their trip." It is a newspaper's responsibility to report the facts when people start buying up supplies of a particular item but certain news reports only exacerbated the situation.

According to Shimada Takao, an *Asahi* local news reporter covering issues of market pricing in his role as coordinator of news on the Ministry of International Trade and Industry, "There were plenty of articles that analyzed distribution chains and calmly reported that there were stores of toilet paper. But this reporting just led consumers to think, 'Now's my chance,' and rush out to buy up as much as they could." This sort of stockpiling habit soon spread to detergent, sugar, kerosene, and even to monopoly-controlled goods like salt.

The truth behind the shortages

Immediately after the Oil Crisis broke out in October 1973, Yamagata Eiji, chief administrator of the government's Energy Resources Agency, was called to a Cabinet meeting. Prime Minister Tanaka asked him, "How much oil do we have in reserve?" "About forty-nine days' worth," answered Yamagata and continued, "Forty-five days of that is the stock for industrial distribution. We have four days' worth for everything else."[1] At this Tanaka folded his arms and grunted, then stared up at the ceiling. "Oil Shortage Grows More Acute," ran the top headline from the November 3 morning edition of *Asahi* with the sub-header, "Shell Oil Down Another 17 Percent." The news reported on the broad effects of the crisis, including restraints put on major consumers of oil such as energy companies, limitations set on the use of neon signs in urban centers, and speculative buying of daily household goods.

At the beginning of December, Kuwabara Hideo, the supply and demand supervisor for the industrial group known as the Petroleum Association of Japan, paid a visit to the Energy Resources Office of the Ministry of International Trade and Industry. The ministry was trying to move two oil-related bills through the Diet, one that was aimed at dampening oil consumption, and another toward stabilizing the prices of goods on the market. When Kuwabara showed the Energy Resources Office representative data which suggested that Japan's imports of crude oil had not decreased even after the start of the oil shock, he was told that "this information will make passing the oil bills more difficult and to please keep the data out of the public eye." The top story on the *Mainichi* local news page from December 29 was "The Phantom Oil Shortage: Tracking Down the Supposed '25% Decrease in Imports." Based on information gathered from oil companies and the Coast Guard about the import totals for crude oil in the ports across Japan, the article concluded: "There is no sign of any drastic reduction in imports to the degree of the alarming twenty-five percent decrease originally reported." In actuality, the decrease was no more than 7 percent. According to the trade totals compiled in January 1974, imports of crude oil in December 1973 had actually increased 0.9 percent compared to December of the previous year and the annual total for 1973 showed around a 16 percent increase.

Shimura Kaichirō, an energy journalist for *Asahi*, says: "The Ministry of International Trade and Industry said there was no oil while the Finance Ministry claimed there was. You could even say that it was a struggle between the Trade Ministry, which wanted to increase its power in the government, and the Finance Ministry, which was attempting to prevent that." Itō Saburō, who covered the Finance Ministry, says: "My colleague who covers the Trade Ministry and I discussed that we had to be careful not to let ourselves be manipulated by information obtained from bureaucrats." The evening *Asahi* from January 28, 1974 reported that a Diet member from the Socialist Party "pursued the possibility that the Oil Crisis was fabricated, suggesting before the parliament that 'government and industry likely knew that there was no lack of oil.'" Nakasone Yasuhiro, who was serving as Minister of International Trade and Industry, refuted this "fabricated oil crisis" theory in his book. "This idea ignores the strenuous efforts that the involved parties exerted in taking care of securing crude oil. The whole world was desperate to secure oil." Idemitsu Yūji, who was serving as deputy chief of business affairs for the oil company Idemitsu Kōsan, also asserts: "Saying that there was oil all along is criticism based on hindsight. We had to scramble because there was concern we could not secure enough supply." It was certainly an exaggeration to say that there would be no more oil. But if so, then why was there a crisis? At length, a search began to find the culprit.

The shadow cartel

"Don't send it to me because I won't accept it!" a senior official of the Supreme Public Prosecutor's Office bellowed into his telephone. It was the beginning of 1974 and *Asahi* reporter Matsuura Yasuhiko heard the exchange while he was in the public prosecutor's office on assignment. He guessed that on the other end of the line was someone from the Japan Fair Trade Commission (JFTC).

In November 1973, the JFTC had begun an investigation of the Petroleum Association of Japan, a collection of thirteen leading oil companies and industrial organizations that was facing charges of violating anti-monopoly laws by colluding to raise prices and limit distribution as a sort of "shadow cartel." The JFTC reported to the public prosecutors but that office saw that substantiating the charges was proving difficult and it was reluctant to have evidence sent to them. Although import levels of crude oil had not fallen, consumer goods were still in short supply and prices increased every day, fueling the increasing efforts to produce a culprit. This was the climate when Yamashita Eimei, vice-minister of International Trade and Industry, launched an attack on the oil industry in his remarks at a press conference. He pronounced the members "the root of all evil," which gained their wrath. On February 19, a confident JFTC official denounced the oil industry. The oil industry felt betrayed by the Ministry of International Trade and Industry. Idemitsu Yūji, then deputy chief of business affairs at Idemitsu Kōsan, says: "We adjusted production according to the administrative guidance of the Ministry of International Trade and Industry. I even testified as such before the prosecutors."

Just after the denunciations began, the chairman of the Petroleum Association of Japan stated at a press conference, "We were given forceful administrative guidance by the Ministry of International Trade and Industry and intend to continue compliance by maintaining elevated oil prices." The bureaucratic administrative guidance in question involved everything from the import of crude oil to the increase in gas stations. "The Oil Industry Accused," a series that ran in the *Asahi* financial pages from February 20, made several points in this regard: "These denunciations [. . .] have raised the question of the appropriate means of handling administrative guidance." The paper added, "When it comes to the economy as it relates to the citizenry, we need to rethink the merits and demerits of administrative guidance." At a morning press conference held in the middle of April, a senior official from the public prosecutor's office said as if to himself, "I wonder if Yamashita-san has left by now." *Asahi*'s Matsuura rushed back to the Press Club and sent an article draft to headquarters that vice-minister of International Trade and Industry Yamashita had been questioned by the public prosecutor's office. "The game was fixed," says Matsuura. "The public prosecutors were trying to save face for the Trade and Industry Ministry, while at the same time projecting to the JFTC that the preliminary investigations were finished because they wanted to wrap the whole thing up. With more people calling for the culprits behind the oil crisis to be found, prosecutors had no choice but to press charges against the 'shadow cartel.' "

In May, twelve major Japanese oil companies, the Petroleum Association of Japan, and seventeen executives were indicted. *Asahi* ran a series called "The Oil Cartel on

Trial." In contrast to the industrialists' claims of having formed a "cartel according to administrative guidance," their indictment "contained not a single letter concerning instructions from the Ministry of International Trade and Industry." In the end, there was never a thorough interrogation concerning the issue of administrative guidance in this case.

Sparse information

In October 1973, just after the start of the oil crisis, the vice-president of Esso Standard Oil, Yashiro Masamoto, received a phone call from a higher-up at the Ministry of International Trade and Industry, communicating minister Nakasone's request: "Would it be feasible to set up a hotline between the Ministry and Esso's parent company, Exxon?"

Nakasone wanted intelligence on the major international oil companies. Specialized treatment for a particular country would be difficult, Yashiro demurred, but from that point on he began feeding information he received from Exxon to the Ministry. It was unknown how much the major companies would reduce the amount of crude oil earmarked for Japan amidst the cutbacks in output from the oil-producing Arab countries. There were barely any clues available to the Ministry of International Trade and Industry and the Japanese oil industry that could help answer these questions of extreme significance for the Japanese economy. Whenever Japanese oil companies obtained new information from the major companies, the media would pounce. The October 24 morning *Asahi* reported, "Crude Oil Prices to Rise 30%, Two International Capital Firms Tell Japan," and in the morning paper two days later, "A 10% Drop in Crude Oil Designated for Japan, Notifications from Multiple Major International Capital Firms; To Affect 97% of Imports." Both of these headlines were at the top of the front page.

According to Shimura Kaichirō, the *Asahi* reporter covering energy issues, "The requests from the desk kept coming in for articles about oil and if you submitted one it would be prominently printed." The authorities did not have enough information available to assuage public anxiety. Oil strategy official Matsuo Kunihiko recalls, "There was no information pipeline from oil-producing countries and we were being led every which way by all the claims flying around the rest of the world." Then on the morning of November 20 the *Asahi* front page read, "Cutting Off Diplomatic Relations is the Condition for Relaxing Oil Trade Restrictions." The report told how, after a meeting of OPEC leaders, Ahmed Zaki Yamani, the Saudi Arabian Minister of Oil and Mineral Industries, issued a statement and said, if Japan wanted to avoid a reduction in its share of oil "it would have to break off diplomatic relations with Israel." Hayashi Takashi, Japan's managing director for the Arabian Oil Company in Saudi Arabia, was the only person to meet Yamani at the airport upon his late night return to his country. "Iran is adamant. If things continue to go on this way it could lead to a worldwide financial collapse." When Yamani, who was rushing to report to the Saudi king, told Hayashi this, Hayashi could sense that Yamani was doing everything in his power to prevent an embargo. It would only become clear later that Japan's supplies of crude oil would not be affected. Speaking now Hayashi says, "Neither the Japanese government nor the

Figure 46 People buying up large amounts of kerosene in Ōmiya City in Saitama Prefecture, November 1973.

media could fully grasp the political posturing that forced OPEC and Yamani to issue such ultimatums, and it's likely they took it too literally."

Tanahashi Yūji, who was at that time chief of operations in Dusseldorf for the Japan External Trade Organization (JETRO), seconded by the Ministry of International Trade and Industry, had analyzed the situation he was seeing in Europe. "It's true that Germany used a good deal of coal energy and France had nuclear power but gas prices and electricity bills still went up. Yet, there was not the sort of panic that took place in Japan." Between a lack of information and overreaction to what news did come in, Japan was caught in a vicious cycle of deepening confusion.

Bouncing back from adversity

"The Limits of Civilization" ran the title of the *Asahi* editorial on December 31, 1973, closing out the year of the Oil Crisis. The editorial read: "The astounding economic growth of Japan's postwar years was built on a single-minded dedication to technological advancement. After the collapse of prewar social values Japan was dogmatic in its development of a technological civilization, where the computer is god." This rejection of the path of progress that Japan had itself elected to follow makes clear just how profoundly the oil crisis had shaken the nation.

The Ikeda Cabinet had decided on the plan to double people's income in December 1960, pushing high-speed economic growth into motion. According to the *Asahi* special edition from December 1969, entitled "How Things Have Changed These Ten Years," while wages set at a value of 100 in 1960 had reached a value of 205 by 1967, consumer commodity prices had also increased an average of 5.7 percent each year between 1960 and 1968. Thanks to the new phenomenon of disposable funds, consumer prices continued to rise. The construction boom sparked by Tanaka Kakuei's plan that he encapsulated in the book—*Building a New Japan: A Plan for Remodeling the Japanese Archipelago*—as well as commercial speculation on land and goods, aided such developments. "It was oil that supported that sort of rapid economic expansion, oil that could be gotten cheaply and imported without restriction," opines Makino Nobuhiko, a former *Asahi* editorial committee member. On January 10, 1974, amidst the maelstrom provoked by consumer prices that people were calling "insane," something happened that signaled changes to come in the Japanese economy— Matsushita Electric Industrial Company (Panasonic) announced that they would freeze the prices on their refrigerators. Other appliance manufacturers began to get prices under control by instituting cost-cutting measures in their businesses, competing to develop new energy-saving technologies in response to consumer wariness following the Oil Crisis. Within the next ten years refrigerators of the same size only used one-fifth the electricity of prior models. The oil crisis also spurred advancements in alternative energy sources. An *Asahi* editorial from January 9, 1974 argued, "Judging from the current state of energy technology alternatives to oil, for the time being we need to direct our expectations to the further development of nuclear power." In fact, the various electric companies promoted diversification to nuclear and natural gas energy for fuel, while Japan's reliance on oil continued to decrease. Looking back now, the peak of crude oil imports into Japan was 1973, the year of the oil shock, at around 288 million kiloliters.

On November 16, 1973, shortly after the oil crisis broke out, the British newspaper, *The Times*, commented on Japan's frantic state. It archly observed, "But if the oil situation helps to crystallize Japanese thinking about the medium-term structure of the economy, it will not have performed a disservice."[2] Editorial committee member Makino says: "Having kept up with the world standard in advancements for energy saving and environmental technologies, Japan did not suffer rampant inflation in 1979 during the second oil crisis. The lessons of 1973 had been learned." Though the government, the media, and the public had lost their cool during the first oil crisis, overcoming the difficulties and changing the structures of industry showed the latent strength of the Japanese economy.

26

Yasukuni Shrine Visits

"As a private citizen"

At 12:55 p.m. on August 15, 1975, a black car pulled up to the Yasukuni Shrine in Tokyo and a somber-faced Prime Minister Miki Takeo stepped out, wearing a tuxedo and tails, surrounded by bodyguards. There was a smattering of applause from the shrine's other visitors.[1] A group of journalists asked the prime minister, "What do you think about state support of the Shrine," but Miki declined to answer, disappearing into the main shrine building.[2]

It was the first time that a prime minster had paid a visit to Yasukuni Shrine on the historic day of the end of the Second World War. The day before, Miki had declared that he was visiting the shrine "as a private citizen." The night before the visit, Miki apparently revealed his feelings to his close friend and confidante, acting Secretary General of the Liberal Democratic Party (LDP) Ishida Hirohide, saying: "The world is a strange place. No one seems to have any problem with the prime minister going to a shrine for the Shinto Spring and Autumn Annual Festivals, so why shouldn't it be permissible for him to go to a shrine to pay respects to the dead on the anniversary of the war's end, a totally secular day?"[3] As Miki said, most of his predecessors in the prime minister's office— Yoshida Shigeru, Kishi Nobusuke, Ikeda Hayato, Satō Eisaku, and Tanaka Kakuei— visited Yasukuni Shrine on the occasion of these Shinto dates. The Japanese constitution specifies a separation of state and religion but previously no newspaper ever presented the shrine visits from such leaders as a problem. Yokota Takashi, the *Asahi* local news journalist who reported on Miki's visit to Yasukuni, says: "Newspapers were more or less not paying attention to issues concerning the separation of religion and politics. Making a shrine visit on the anniversary of the war's end, however, had a totally different impact than the visits that had been made up to that point."

At the start of 1975, the LDP abandoned its efforts to pass the National Protection of Yasukuni Bill that would put control of the Yasukuni Shrine in the hands of the state. Christian groups had protested and opposition political parties also resisted. Up until 1974 the bill had been defeated five times, so the LDP shifted its agenda toward having the Emperor and prime minister make public shrine visits. In July 1975, two veteran *Asahi* journalists gave their opinions as unsworn witnesses before the Diet: Aragaki Hideo, who had been a writer for the *Vox Populi, Vox Dei* column, and Ōgiya Shōzō, former editor-in-chief for the *Asahi Weekly*. Aragaki suggested that "the spirits of fallen

Figure 47   Prime Minister Miki Takeo visiting the Yasukuni Shrine on August 15, 1975.

heroes will not be able to rest if the constitutional debate drags on." Ōgiya expressed a similar sentiment, saying: "When I hear about the constitutional debate I feel as if it's an insult to the men I served with." Both men asserted that Yasukuni Shrine stood beyond issues of constitutionality, indicating their support for public visits by the Emperor and prime minister.

Urged on by hawkish elements within his party, Miki decided that he would visit the shrine. "For Miki, who was conservative on matters of constitutionality, visiting as a private citizen rather than as a public servant was the only way for him to not contradict his own political convictions," says Miki's former secretary Nakamura Kei'ichirō. An *Asahi* editorial from August 16 criticized Miki's move, saying that even if he claimed he was going as a "private citizen," the actions of a prime minister "carry political meaning." Three months later the Emperor visited Yasukuni Shrine.

The collective enshrinement of class A war criminals

News that Japan's class A war criminals were enshrined at Yasukuni came to light in mid-April 1979, discovered by *Kyōdō News* senior staff writer Mikano Hirosuke. Over the course of ten years, reporting on how the remains of soldiers from the imperial Japanese military were being handled, Mikano had become concerned about the treatment of class A war criminals. On April 17, 1979, Mikano met with Itagaki Tadashi, Director of the Japan Association for War-bereaved Families (*Nihon Izokukai*). Itagaki was a son of Itagaki Seishirō, a former general in the Japanese Imperial Army who had been sentenced to death during the International Military Tribunal for the Far East (Tokyo Trial). Mikano broached the subject: "And what happened in the case of your father's remains?" "Ahh, well, thankfully [. . .] at last [. . .]," Itagaki swallowed the rest of the sentence. According to Mikano, it was then he was sure that Itagaki's father had been enshrined at Yasukuni.

The next afternoon Mikano visited Yasukuni and in response to his questions Chief Shrine Priest Matsudaira Nagayoshi confirmed that fourteen class A war criminals, including former prime minister Tōjō Hideki and Itagaki Seishirō, had been enshrined in October 1978 as "The Martyrs of Showa." The priest said, "We needed to wait for a suitable time but of course we thought that these individuals should be enshrined." That night Mikano's scoop was transmitted across the country to all of the *Kyōdō News* affiliate newspapers and broadcast stations. *Kyōdō* made a mistake, however. According to Hara Toshio, managing editor at the time, it was customary to alert affiliated news agencies when there was a scoop. In the case of the article on war criminal enshrinement, whomever was responsible to take care of that failed to do so. Perhaps the story got lost in the flood of news but that evening Nihon TV was the only broadcast station to report on it. That same night, Tani Hisamitsu was on duty at the local news desk in the third-floor editorial bureau of *Asahi*'s Tokyo headquarters. When it was nearing 9 p.m., one of the overnight staffers absentmindedly pointed out to Tani, "There is a story on TV about the enshrinement of class A war criminals." "What?" Tani said, shocked to think that those who bore responsibility for the war would be honored together with those who were sacrificed. During the war, Tani was one of the so-called "young war generation" who had listened to Tōjō's speeches on the radio, and he survived the air strikes on his hometown of Nishinomiya in Hyogo Prefecture. "Okay," he said, "Let's cover this story."

Staff members rushed about checking facts and gathering opinions from pundits, putting everything together for an article that appeared as the top story in the local news section of the next morning's paper. On April 19, *Nikkei, Sankei,* and *Tokyo Shimbun* all based their reporting on the original *Kyōdō* story. NHK and other news TV networks covered the story in great detail in their morning broadcasts, while the *Mainichi* and *Yomiuri* reported on it in their evening papers. The Grand Chamberlain of the Imperial Household, Irie Sukemasa, wrote in his diary on April 19: "[The morning papers] have revealed the enshrinement and they speak of it on the TV. I am most vexed."

"Those are my true feelings"

The enshrinement of fourteen class A war criminals at Yasukuni Shrine was a denial of the verdicts reached in the Tokyo Trial. Editorials in various newspapers took a critical stance toward the shrine's position. From the *Mainichi* on April 20: "It is unacceptable to let war responsibility fade from memory." From the same day's *Yomiuri*: "This is a most unfortunate affair." And from the *Hokkaido Newspaper*: "Is it really all right to glorify the story with the passage of time?" On April 21, the *Sankei Newspaper* argued,

"[The Tokyo Trial] was the turning point for a defeated Japan, which ended the nightmare of war and saw the country pick itself back up as a nation of peace. [...] The enshrinement of class A war criminals ignores this historical reality." The paper added, "Certainly there is freedom to honor the dead but freedom does not mean that people can do whatever they want, however they want to do it."

On April 27, *Asahi* featured on its pages an editorial that had originally come from the Singaporean paper, *Sin Chew Daily*. The article stated: "If the Tokyo Trial is considered unjust and illogical, why don't the Japanese do as the Germans did and hold their own trials? They should arrest those responsible for waging a war of invasion, bring them to trial, and thereby prove that there is still such a thing as justice." The opinion from the Singapore paper concluded, "Yasukuni Shrine has become a shrine for war criminals." *Asahi* did not clearly state its own position in any editorials.

Emperor Hirohito was among those distressed by the enshrinement of war criminals. Starting from October 1952, the Emperor had made a personal visit to Yasukuni Shrine every few years, under the new constitution. On May 28, 1959, the Emperor received at his palace twenty representatives from the White Chrysanthemum Bereaved Families Association (*Shiragiku Izokukai*), made up of those whose deceased family members were convicted of war crimes. He said to them, "You lost your flesh and blood in the war and you have been through so much. I offer you my most heartfelt sympathies." Among those attending were relatives of Matsui Iwane, the former general of Japan's Imperial Army in China who commanded the sack of Nanjing and was executed as a class A war criminal.[4] Although the Emperor had expressed his sympathy for the families of war criminals, he would later end his visits to Yasukuni Shrine, after learning that the class A war criminals were to be enshrined. His last visit to Yasukuni was on November 21, 1975. His concern about the enshrinement of class A war criminals is clear from testimony provided by former Grand Chamberlain Tokugawa Yoshihiro in the August 19, 1995 *Asahi* and from a memo documenting imperial statements taken down by former Grand Steward of the Imperial Household Agency Tomita Tomohiko.[5] Tomita's memo about what the Emperor felt reads: "I have learned that at some point A class war criminals will be enshrined, even [former Foreign Minister] Matsuoka [Yōsuke] and [former Ambassador to Italy] Shiratori [Toshio]." "Therefore I will no longer visit the shrine—those are my true feelings." The Emperor was concerned with the fact that "[the enshrinement] will lead to serious problems in the future between us and the countries affected by the war."[6]

In November 1982, Nakasone Yasuhiro came to power, once again changing the debate around Yasukuni.

"A final settling of accounts for postwar Japan"

"Every country has one – America has Arlington, [...] a place where citizens can go and pay their respects to those who fell in defense of their country. It should go without saying that nobody would give their life for the nation if there was no such place." Prime Minister Nakasone Yasuhiro was in high spirits when he uttered these words at an LDP meeting on July 27, 1985. He had been calling for "a final settling of accounts for postwar Japan." Regarding a potential visit to Yasukuni Shrine in August he said, "Members of the Cabinet are discussing the matter in colloquium and I will wait to see what they decide." Despite these words, all of those in attendance understood this to mean that Nakasone would be making an official visit to Yasukuni on August 15.

The "colloquium" he mentioned referred to a personal advisory panel to Chief Cabinet Secretary Fujinami Takao, which had been named "The Cabinet Members' Colloquium on the Yasukuni Shrine Visits Issue" (or "Yasukuni Colloquium" for short). Hayano Tōru, who was head of the *Asahi* team covering the prime minister's offices, recalls: "It was part of a very well thought out re-formatting of the national agenda. Yasukuni Shrine represented the spiritual side of it and breaking through the cap on defense spending that had been set at one percent of the GNP accounted for the tangible side." Having glimpsed Nakasone's true colors as a hawk, journalists re-evaluated their approach to covering him.

The government's position on official shrine visits up to that point had taken into account the separation of state and religion as laid out in Article 20 of the Constitution, and said we "cannot deny that such visits could very well be called unconstitutional." The Yasukuni Colloquium intended to shift this position. According to Fujinami's private secretary from the national police agency, Hirasawa Katsuei, "A course of action had already been decided based on the notion that it was possible to make a shrine visit that was not affected by issues of constitutionality." The deliberations from the Yasukuni Colloquium were not made public, so there was furious competition among journalists to get information about what had been discussed and decided. The Colloquium released its findings on August 9: if the religiosity of an official shrine visit were to be toned down, it would not interfere with the principle of separating religion and the state. "The government was very clever in this," says Fuke Yasunobu, a reporter who had been assigned to cover Fujinami. "[The colloquium members] made it clear that they had listened to the opinions of commentators who were cautious and critical about shrine visits. And then they went ahead with what they said they were going to do."

Some participants of the Yasukuni Colloquium were dissatisfied with the way these events unfolded. One even tendered his resignation in light of the conclusions reached in the Colloquium's discussions. *Asahi* political reporter Wakamiya Yoshibumi persuaded Ashibe Nobuyoshi, a constitutionally conservative scholar, to speak with him. Ashibe's opinions appeared in a long article entitled, "Problems with Keeping the Separation of Religion and the State," published on August 15. At that point, the majority of the articles written on Yasukuni Shrine had to do with the separation of religion and politics. Rarely did they touch on the question that would soon become the main focus: that of the enshrined class A war criminals. With journalists eager to pursue the issue of the government moving past Article Twenty of the Constitution, which seemed to be the issue of immediate concern, no one was paying much attention to any points outside of the constitutional debate. However, there was one person who anticipated the negative reaction that was bound to come from other Asian countries—Nakasone himself. He dispatched to China Lower House member Noda Takeshi, experienced in Sino-Japanese parliamentary diplomacy. Nakasone also conferred with his friends in academia and worked with the Ministry of Foreign Affairs, quietly shoring up foundations.

The perspective of Asian countries

On August 15, 1985, forty years since the end of the war, a blazing sun bore down on Yasukuni Shrine where an agitated crowd of families of those who had died in the war and groups of reporters had been gathering since the morning. Prime Minister Nakasone Yasuhiro arrived at 1:40 p.m. At the front of the lines of people leading up to the shrine, an elderly man with tears in his eyes was waving the Japanese flag and calling out, "Thank you, Prime Minister Nakasone!" The journalists directed the same question to Nakasone and each of the Cabinet members that had come to the shrine with him: "Are you here as a private citizen or as a public servant?" The media were mainly concerned with the question of the separation of religion and state and there was barely any consideration given to the point of view of other Asian countries.

To make it clear that he was not going against the principle of separation of religion and politics, Nakasone did not perform the customary Shinto rite of bowing twice, clapping his hands twice, and bowing again. Instead, he only bowed once before the main shrine building before making a 30,000 yen donation taken from public funds. In *Asahi* the next day, his visit was deemed to have been "handled constitutionally." "A shrine visit of reduced religiosity" was the solution to the problem that proponents of shrine visits had developed. Chief Cabinet Secretary Fujinami Takao had been engaged in closed-door negotiations with Yasukuni Shrine and with the Japan Association for War-bereaved Families up until just before the visit. His final meeting to confirm details with the shrine's head priest Matsudaira Nagayoshi came the day before Nakasone's official visit. Okuno Seisuke, then serving as the chair of the LDP's subcommittee on the Yasukuni issue, was among the politicians who had long hoped to see an official visit to the shrine by the prime minister. He relates, "Matsudaira told me himself, 'I don't want to be known as the head priest who allowed some kind of half-baked visit to the shrine. After spending a sleepless night, I finally made up my mind when the morning came.'"

As Nakasone was signing his name at the register inside a tent set up in front of the main shrine building, Matsudaira furtively waved a sprig of sacred *sakaki* tree behind the prime minister's back in a gesture of ritual cleansing. As the tent walls obscured the view, none of the gathered reporters witnessed the priest's actions. Okuno is still upset by the need to have done this, calling it "a deceitful shrine visit." Meanwhile, at the regularly scheduled press conference held by the Chinese Foreign Ministry on August 14, reporters asked about the official shrine visit. Part of the response touched on the enshrinement of class A war criminals: "It brings grief to the people of Asia, including both the Chinese and Japanese citizens who were so deeply affected by Japan's militaristic national policy." After this in the fall there were broader Chinese protests. The front page of *Asahi* from September 19 carried a story titled, "Anti-Nakasone Demonstration in Beijing; Crowds of Students One Thousand Strong Call for His 'Ousting.'" Nakasone cancelled the customary visit to the shrine on the occasion of the Annual Autumn Festival (a Shinto holiday). Hayano Tōru, *Asahi*'s reporter covering the prime minister's office, can still clearly recall going over the proofs for the article on the Beijing demonstrations the night before it was published. "I could clearly see for the first time that while Yasukuni was a constitutional issue, there was also the question of what other Asian countries were thinking." Wakamiya Yoshibumi, another reporter covering the prime minister, recalls: "Looking at this ostentatious official visit to Yasukuni, the symbol of wartime state Shintō, we started bracing ourselves for the possibility that things might be moving back toward the way they were before the war. Then the protests broke out in Beijing and we thought, well there you have it."

The Yasukuni Shrine problem had entered a new phase.

"I won't let him go next year!"

Itagaki Tadashi, who moved from being Director of the Japan Association for War-bereaved Families to occupying a seat in the Upper House of the Diet, was the son of former Imperial Army General Itagaki Seishirō, who had been executed as a class A war criminal. In November 1985, Itagaki Tadashi was invited to a meeting by Sejima Ryūzō, with whom his father had served in the imperial military. Sejima asked, "Don't you think that your father and the others would have chosen to stand down for the sake of the men who served under them?" He was sounding out the possibility of discontinuing the enshrinement of the class A war criminals. This came to an impasse, however, with staunch opposition from Tōjō Hideki's family. Three months after the official visit to Yasukuni Shrine, on November 5, *Asahi* published a serious analysis of the issue of enshrining class A war criminals. Based on a document summarizing the previously unreleased deliberations of the Yasukuni Colloquium's twenty-one meetings, it reported opinions both for and against the enshrinement of war criminals. Mochida Shūzō, the *Asahi* reporter who had gotten hold of the summary, wrote: "In its haste to realize an official shrine visit the government was far too cavalier about this issue." In China, the background to criticism against the Yasukuni visit was entangled within the domestic situation. The Chinese economy was faltering even as Japanese-made goods were flooding the market, and the Chinese government could no longer ignore the rising tide of anti-Japanese sentiment. Katō Chihiro, *Asahi*'s Beijing correspondent at the time, saw that "the anti-Japanese atmosphere may well have been of some use to the Chinese government as a means of dealing with its domestic crisis."

Japan had underestimated China's response. One year after the official shrine visit, a Japanese high official let slip the following to Hoshi Hiroshi, *Asahi*'s reporter covering the Foreign Ministry: "Before the shrine visit I was assigned by the prime minister to analyze what sort of reaction we could anticipate from China but in consideration of how strongly he felt about the visit I gave an overly optimistic answer." Gotōda Masaharu, who became Chief Cabinet Secretary at the end of 1985, reprimanded the Foreign Ministry: "You guys have grossly underestimated the situation." He also told those around him his position on Nakasone making another shrine visit the following August: "I won't let him go next year!" At the start of the summer in 1986 pressure was mounting against an official shrine visit and on August 14, citing the disapproval of Japan's neighboring countries, Gotōda announced that the prime minister would not be visiting the shrine. The day before, Nakasone's aide and Deputy Chief Cabinet Secretary Watanabe Hideo told Fujinami Takao, the previous Chief Cabinet Secretary who had been instrumental in implementing the official visit the year before, that

Nakasone would not be going. Fujinami was perturbed and said, "Last year we made a visit but this year we will not. [. . .] This is difficult to explain."

By way of rationalization Nakasone said, "I felt the need to make an official visit at least once, [. . .] taking the opportunity on the fortieth anniversary of the war's end." At a September 1986 assembly of the Lower House, Nakasone said with regards to not having made another shrine visit: "The strongest element of democracy is its capacity for repentance and restraint." This statement stands in contrast to the actions of Koizumi Junichirō fifteen years later, who knowingly invited a deterioration in Sino-Japanese relations with his visits to Yasukuni Shrine.

The Bubble Economy

The waterfront

The "Personality" profile in the January 7, 1987 *Asahi* introduced Matsui Masami, CEO of the retail design firm Axe, saying: "He's turning the warehouse district in Shibaura, Tokyo into a play zone." In December of the previous year when they opened, on a corner facing the canal along Tokyo Bay, the club Inkstick Shibaura Factory and the restaurant Tango both had become hot spots among trend-conscious pleasure seekers. Matsui had designed both places, styling himself as a "spatial producer." The dark and sparsely trafficked warehouse block had been rebranded with the English word "waterfront" and transformed into a trendy urban area.

In the second half of the 1980s, low interest rates created circumstances in which significant sums of money had nowhere to go but into land and stocks. The financial page from the October 4, 1986 *Asahi* reported, "Renewed development of warehouses and industrial space along Tokyo's 'Waterfront' point to a solution for the acute shortage of building space in the center of the city. Buyers are now scooping up blue chip stocks, such as Tokyo Gas, Ishikawajima-Harima Heavy Industries, and Nippon Kōkan (NKK), leveraged with extensive property holdings in this area." The price of land shot up and as a result stock prices also rose. It was a system where buying led to more buying. In January 1988, the Tokyo *Asahi* series, "Listening to the Beatles: Tokyo Baby Boomers at 40," featured Matsui as "the guy who makes it special—sometimes called a professional property value raiser." Venues that Matsui worked on were guaranteed hits; the crowds would gather while the surrounding land values continued to rise.

The weekend *Asahi* special feature, "Weekend Finance," ran a small column called "New Winds, New Currents," written by hip concept designers like Matsui and Nishikawa Ryūjin, and profiling the clubs and venues in which Matsui had been involved. Inamura Ryūji, the *Asahi* staff member responsible for the column, said: "It was a way to note the latest trends and what was happening in the pages of the paper." University students were joining tennis clubs, organizing dance parties and going on ski trips. At the Maharaja Disco in Tokyo's Azabu Jūban district, partygoers were admitted based on what they were wearing and inside they would dance atop raised platforms. On Christmas morning, long lines of couples in hotel lobbies were waiting to check out after spending the night together. Looking back Matsui says, "In the midst of the bubble we didn't actually know that it was a bubble. No one had ever experienced anything like it before." The two venues that Matsui had designed in Shibaura both closed their doors after three years, which was as he had planned. In May 1991, a new disco opened in Shibaura: Juliana Tokyo, the club said to have symbolized the bubble. By that point, however, the bubble economy had already started to collapse.

Steadily growing stock prices

"First Big Issue of NTT Stock; Mass Buying Fever" ran the headline in the evening *Asahi* on February 9, 1987, which announced the telecommunications company NTT's public tender. Orders came pouring in so quickly that they could not all be filed. The price when the stock went public was about 1.19 million yen; the next day the stock opened at 1.6 million yen, so anyone who sold their newly acquired stock would have already made approximately 400,000 yen (at that time roughly US$2,600). An article reported the phenomenon of "housewives buying and selling stock who were smiling but clearly bewildered." NTT became representative of Japan's steadily rising stock prices, the sort that lured first-time buyers to the stock market. In January 1987, the Nikkei average surpassed 20,000 yen and it broke 30,000 yen by December 1988. On December 29, 1989, the market stood at 38,915, nearly doubling its value in just three years. "Heavy Trading with Influx of Surplus Funds; Ease of Credit Spurring Speculation." On March 28, 1986, *Asahi* assessed the situation surrounding high stock prices. The paper included an opinion from an economic analyst, saying: "If left alone the current situation will lead to even greater purchases of stocks and properties in urban centers. [...] Rising stock prices and real estate values in urban areas should be considered a warning sign." *Asahi* also quoted a trust bank auditor's comment when the Nikkei broke the 20,000 yen mark: "Having so much surplus money in the economy is like overinflating a balloon."

At the same time that alarm bells were ringing there were also articles that reproduced the unfounded bullish forecasts of securities trading companies. A column written by a division chief from a major securities firm appeared in the evening *Asahi* on October 4, 1986, saying: "I want to believe that stocks will remain high through the end of this year and into the beginning of next. This is not based on logic but on the momentum of the market...." Even as the columnist acknowledged that "these days the high stock prices are for the most part not reflective of corporate revenues," he asserted that "the purchase of stocks is an index for our dreams of the distant future." The securities broker recommended buying stocks according to theme. As an example, he offered "waterfront brands," referring to steel and shipbuilding companies whose coastal holdings had skyrocketed in value. On December 30, 1989, *Asahi* produced an article making projections for the next year's market conditions based on the record high reached by stock prices the previous day. The newspaper pointed out that "securities companies are setting the tone with their confident assertions 'that this year's momentum will continue and that at this time next year we can expect to see stock averages as high as forty-five thousand.'"

Kishiro Yasuyuki, *Asahi* writer in charge of covering securities firms, recalls: "Climbing so high and then looking back down for the first time, we were suddenly aware of the yawning gulf below us." As the calendar dawned on 1990, stock prices began to slide. In

Tokyo's Kabutochō ward, there is an eel restaurant that has been in business there for a long time, nestled amidst the blocks of securities firms. In the past, employees from the firms in that city's quarter would take their clients there in celebration of negotiations concluded earlier in the day and things would often get rather lively. Kishiro can still clearly recall when the shop's owner, Emoto Yoshio, muttered, "I wonder how long this can go on." Looking back now Emoto says, "Come to think of it, there was an article on the front page of a trade publication where the president of a mid-level securities firm had made some lavish claim about stocks going up to one hundred thousand."

Neither that securities firm nor the trade publication exists today.

An encouragement of personal finance management

At the beginning of 1986, the major newspapers in Japan began to feature weekly financial management advice pages, jumping on the bandwagon one after the other. *Mainichi* was the first paper to do so with its January 8 debut of a column entitled "Money and Life." The two-page spread appeared in the paper every Wednesday morning and it centered around a "Money Management Game," where contributors competed to see who could best manage a fund of thirty million yen. The next to appear was *Asahi*'s "Weekend Economy," established as a regular feature in the Saturday evening paper on January 25, addressing financial issues including stocks, taxes, and pensions. On February 20, the *Yomiuri* unveiled its new weekly, *Yomiuri Home Finance Newspaper*, issued separately from the regular *Yomiuri Shimbun*. It ran "The Kabutochō Derby," a contest where readers could bet on the climbing values of brands as if they were betting on horse races. In response to these encroachments on its territory, the *Nihon Keizai Shimbun* (*Nikkei*) launched the "Monday Nikkei" in its morning edition on February 24, packed with information on finances, the stock market, and news about high-level personnel decisions.

The financial management boom swept the nation. After the Plaza Accord of September 1985, as the value of the yen rose and interest rates in Japan fell, all sorts of new financial products appeared and significant differences in investment yields grew. Rising numbers of people began adopting financial strategies that involved a risk of losing principal value for stocks, investment trusts, and foreign currency. Newspaper readers were demanding more information on financial matters. "Posturing from the Major Papers—Info War with Special Editions on Finance," wrote the *Literary Weekly* (*Shūkan Bunshun*) on March 13, 1986. The magazine criticized newspapers for tempting amateurs into risky investments, asking "Is it really okay if housewives get burned?"

Who was to blame?

The 1985 Plaza Accord enabled the continued rise of the yen while the government maintained its policy of reducing interest rates as a shield against economic downturn. Stock prices and property values soared thanks to the glut of money. But who was responsible for inflating the bubble in the first place?

There have been strong accusations leveled at the Bank of Japan, charging that the official discount rate was lifted too late and that low interest rates were maintained for too long. In fact, according to Tsukuda Ryōji, one of the bank's board members, directors of the board of the Bank of Japan quietly confirmed at their September 1987 coordination committee meeting that they would soon set out to raise the interest rate. Both Japan's Ministry of Finance and the United States were opposed to raising interest rates. Facing this stubborness, Tsukuda and the other executives took the desperate measure of encouraging higher interest rates on interbank short-term borrowing and lending. But they realized there was a limit to how much interest rates could be adjusted with clever tricks and decided to take a more direct approach. Just as they were about to do this, the US stock market suffered a major crash on October 19, 1987—Black Monday. The Bank of Japan executives held off on raising interest rates.

Asahi also favored maintaining a low interest rate. There were good opportunities to raise it in the summer of 1988, when West Germany and the United States both raised their rates, but a column on the finance page from September 9 boasted, "Japan's financial authorities have won the world's approbation with their decision not to follow Europe and America in raising interest rates." *Asahi* opposed raising rates as late as February 26, 1989, with an editorial that read "Japan, the largest creditor in the world, is working hard to hold on to its low interest rates as long as possible. . . ." The unbridled expansion of public expenditures also stimulated excesses of funds, marking the Ministry of Finance as another culprit. The 1986 Maekawa Report indicated a structural shift toward a focus on domestic demand. In May 1987, due in part to requests from America and a sluggish economy foundering on the high yen, the Japanese government worked out an emergency economic plan to the tune of six trillion yen. According to economic estimates the government issued shortly thereafter, the domestic economy had bottomed out in November 1986 after which it began its expansion.

Asahi editorials actively encouraged the mobilization of public finances. An opinion piece published on February 24, 1987—before the emergency countermeasures had been announced—argued that "the pressing challenge is to study how to correct our austerity orientation." Another piece on May 30 called for financial mobilization. At the same time, *Asahi* editorial committee member Ōtani Ken's June 12 article suggested, "The lion's share of the expansion of domestic demand went to property owners, and that money once more flowed into real estate and securities, [. . .] which ended up supporting high prices on the stock market."

The economic bubble was the consequence of factors emanating from both the US and Japan, resulting from a form of international cooperation: the United States had requested that Japan increase its domestic demand as a means of alleviating the US trade deficit and Japan responded by lowering interest rates and mobilizing public finances. *Asahi* criticized these measures in its pages on February 21, 1987, saying, "The official discount rate has become a tool of foreign economic policy, effectively giving the United States a leadership role," and noting that "The official discount rate has been used to conceal the government's lack of a plan for increasing domestic demand." Thus, there was a gap between the editorial writers who supported the authorities and the reporters on the ground who adopted a more critical stance.

Individuals who triggered colossal investments

During the bubble, many individuals who had close connections to financial institutions and large corporations poured significant funds into real estate and stocks. When the bubble burst, the majority of these investors were unable to recoup their losses or pay their debts and some even faced criminal charges. Despite this involvement, during the bubble newspapers barely delved into the actions of these individual investors.

Takahashi Harunori was one of these individuals. He bought up major hotels, resorts, and office buildings across the world during the 1980s, earning him the nickname "Resort King of the Pacific Rim." He borrowed funds from institutions like the Long-Term Credit Bank of Japan, assuming debt of nearly one trillion yen and he was a close associate of politicians as well. Takahashi had been the chairman of the board of the Tokyo-Kyōwa Credit Association, which went under in December 1994. The following year he was summoned to testify before the Diet after which he was arrested and indicted on charges of criminal breach of trust. Takahashi's name only appeared in the pages of *Asahi* twice during the bubble years, in May 1987 and May 1989. Both were brief articles mentioning his building purchases in Hong Kong. Internal documents from the Long-Term Credit Bank that had loaned Takahashi so much money identified a particular element of his business operations as one of the secrets to rapid growth: "Keeps a low public profile." Although Takahashi was moving around sums in excess of 100 billion yen, news coverage of him was virtually nil and he maintained no public persona to speak of. The Long-Term Credit Bank judged that because he was relatively unknown it was possible for him "to act autonomously when initiating both domestic and foreign ventures or when considering acquisitions," and that this anonymity was one of "the attributes of a new breed of entrepreneurs." Yamada Atsushi, an *Asahi* finance reporter in the economics section, says that he "had heard about Takahashi as an up-and-coming contender." When Yamada was dispatched to London in April 1984 he interviewed Takahashi, who was in Europe investigating a development opportunity, but it never turned into an article. Despite the fact that Takahashi was working with several hundred billions of yen, the greater industrial world viewed him as no more than "an active small to medium sized enterprise." Takahashi was mentioned in *Asahi* a third time on April 26, 1991, this time in an article with the headline, "The Worldwide Real Estate Bubble Has Burst; Creditors' Meeting Requests Tabling Debts."

The Recruit scandal

When Recruit, a human resources company, was certain that prices were going up, it distributed shares of its not-yet-publicly-traded real estate subsidiary company to politicians, bureaucrats, and financiers. This soon erupted into a scandal. The first report came out on June 18, 1988 when *Asahi* ran it as the top story on its local news page: "Recruit Temptation in Kawasaki City, Deputy Mayor Receives Associated Stock; Shares Go Public to Profits of 1 Billion Yen." Junior *Asahi* reporters at the Yokohama and Kawasaki branch offices dug up the story through exclusive interviews, revealing that the

Kanagawa prefectural police had refrained from pursuing a case on the Kawasaki City deputy mayor, suspected of accepting a bribe. Both branch offices worked to shed light on who had been accepting stocks that had not yet gone on the market, turning up one recipient after another. The front-page top story on July 6 reported that there were even some involved who were close to former Prime Minister Nakasone Yasuhiro and Finance Minister Miyazawa Kiichi. "Alchemy for Easy Money" became a buzz term. According to Yamamoto Hiroshi, the Yokohama reporter who headed up the investigation, some at *Asahi* wanted to be cautious and limit the story to the local Kanagawa edition but the local news editors judged that it should be handled as national news.

Recruit had grown rapidly as a company through its job placement magazine. With all the surplus money floating around, the company had received substantial loans from financial institutions and expanded into real estate holdings, nurturing expectations for a high priced stock once its subsidiary companies went public. Recruit's founder, Ezoe Hiromasa, was a graduate of Tokyo University and a venture capitalist who appeared on television and in newspapers, as well as serving on government advisory panels. The Tokyo Prosecutors Office joined the investigation on the heels of the journalists and charges were brought against seventeen individuals, including Ezoe and two politicians, all of whom were found guilty.

Ezoe looked back on the affair in his 2009 book, *The Recruit Scandal: The Truth According to Ezoe Hiromasa*, writing, "I did not think I was doing anything particularly wrong by providing profit from stocks that were rising in value."[1] With regards to distributing funds to politicians he says, "I was hoping that it would go some small way toward improving national politics." He was also candid about what he was feeling back then. "I was motivated by the strong sense that I always had to be learning and growing, and I was always alone and on edge. I tried to balance myself by making significant political contributions whenever asked." Ezoe also had the following to say about Yamamoto, who orchestrated *Asahi*'s investigative journalism: "The list of people who had acquired stock was supposed to be private information but he must have somehow gotten his hands on it. Then he parceled out the names a few at a time, attracting the attention of other newspapers and turning it into a major story that lasted for a long while—a very clever way of doing things." Yamamoto, who has had a long career in investigative journalism, refutes this theory:

> Newspapers have an obligation to the public to clarify suspicions about the government, bureaucracy, and industry. To that end we need inside information. I can't reveal my sources but I gathered all sorts of information. I didn't give out details about private individuals, only those of politicians and public figures for which I found corroborative information, and this I put into news stories.

Learning from history

"Fluctuating asset values that deviate from actual values on account of speculation are the phenomenon known as a 'bubble.'" This is the definition given for "bubble" by Bank of Japan employee Okina Kunio in an essay he wrote for *Financial Research*, a Bank of Japan Financial Research Institute bulletin published in April 1984. Okina had researched the theory and history of economic bubbles at the University of Chicago, earning his PhD in 1983. Yamada Atsushi, who covered finance for *Asahi* starting in 1985, was familiar with the definition as explained by Okina and when property values and stock prices started to climb he said to his co-workers, "What we have here is a bubble."

In the first half of 1986, the finance pages of *Asahi* launched a major weekly series entitled "Filthy Rich Japan," focusing on the new sort of strain the country was feeling as a result of wallowing in money. The first installment featured the story of a retired "salaryman" who had lost six million yen trading bond futures. The column's writer, Inamura Ryūji, recalls: "By that point we could already see the dark side of the bubble, the forewarnings of collapse." On February 20, 1987, the Bank of Japan decided to reduce the official discount rate. Yamada wrote, "[The economy] is extremely swollen. The seeming dynamism of a swift rise built on an easy money market comes with a major backlash. One might say that rushing after the short term profits dangling right in front of our noses propagates the impending crisis." At that time he avoided the term "bubble," unfamiliar as it was to readers, rendering the idea instead as "easy money." In July of the same year, *Asahi* senior staff writer Hayabusa Nagaharu met with renowned Harvard Economics Professor Emeritus John Kenneth Galbraith, who told him the following: "There is no doubt that Japan is already in a bubble. Why aren't Japanese scholars and journalists writing about it?" But Hayabusa did not put this in the paper. He says, "*Asahi*'s corporate atmosphere at the time was not one where we wrote such articles." People only truly understand a bubble once it bursts. While the bubble is still inflating, it is very difficult to identify it and step on the brakes.

"Bubble economy" took second place in the annual Word of the Moment contest at the end of 1990, the year that had opened with a steep drop in stock prices. "Writing the truth is a newspaper's job," says Inamura, but "there were certain difficulties in doing this before the bubble collapsed and now I regret not having sounded the alarm." Okina, who became a professor at Kyoto University, wrote the following on his online profile: "Despite the experience of the panic that followed the collapse of the bubble, people are not sufficiently aware of the magnitude of its effects. Looking at the recent situation in America, I can keenly feel how difficult it is to learn something from historical experience." In order to prevent future mistakes, we must identify the lessons of the past and humbly investigate what history teaches us.

Translator's Conclusion

This investigative book by the *Asahi Newspaper* Company concerns the political and social history of Japanese media and its interaction with the ebb and flow of Japanese and international history. At times the newspaper, and Japanese media in general, seemed to take an active role in shaping the paths Japan journeyed; other times the newspaper and media seemed cowed by the government, authority and military. As readers will have noticed during the course of the book, there was not one avenue but many that Japan followed over this period, which covered its rise in the 1920s, through the Second World War, defeat, and the reconstruction in the postwar. But luckily, the story does not end there. The original Japanese version continues for almost another 100 pages, breaking the longer history of the Showa period (1926–1989) into shorter thematic segments and offering more personal insights and interviews than could be shared with the audience that will enjoy the translation. Unfortunately, this more inclusive version was untenable for an English translation that needed to come in at a shorter length for publishing parameters and readability to a wider international audience. In addition, foreign audiences are not always focused on the same issues that engage Japanese readers. With these factors in mind, I spent time trying to cull what I assessed as examples extraneous for non-Japanese readers but keeping the journalistic flow of the text smooth and informative.

However, these efforts do not mean that the book can end without a conclusion. Over the 63 years of the Showa era, Japan slowly gravitated from being a country on the fringes of the Pacific, to a great imperial power, to a shattered former empire, and finally after rebuilding over decades to an economic powerhouse that worried the rest of the world with its winning success formula. What *Asahi*'s team of investigators uncovered throughout this process is that at no time was war "inevitable" and at no time was conflict pre-ordained as some dark fate that awaited the archipelago, etched into the sands of time for historians to decipher the causes of later. What happened to Japan prewar, during the war and in the postwar was the result of the action, or frequent inaction, of the people in all their shapes and sizes—as leaders, politicians, writers, military officials, and of course journalists. As this research has ably shown, media do not just merely "report" on a given situation. Media shape perceptions, set the agenda, create a lexicon that the population then uses to calibrate or give voice to events as they happen and later as they become fuel for historical memory. As former *Asahi* editor-in-chief Funabashi Yōichi wrote in the foreword to this volume, history probably does not repeat itself, but we certainly need to reflect carefully and diligently on its provenance and our own role in its evolution. This is not only the case with elected officials, who theoretically represent the people's choice for leadership, but with the unofficial representatives of the people—the mass media, whose very presence plays a crucial role in any viable democracy to bring scrutiny to authority and to speak truth to power. In our age especially, given what we know about leaks and government surveillance that seem to be creeping more and more into our quotidian lives, the media with their access and reach still have formidable power to champion truth in the face of adversity and challenge authority even when we cannot as individuals.

Japan's Showa era was unique in modern history. Under the reign of one emperor, the nation began as an upstart, enthralled the West and then terrified it, only to vanish as a sovereign nation after the defeat and during the occupation. It is testament to the Japanese courage and determination to rebuild, as well as the rather forgiving postwar world order, and the tenets of the Cold War that later allowed Japan to grow postwar as a victor rather than villain, which assisted the country to reform and become an economic superpower by the 1980s.

What happened to Japan following the end of the Showa era, after 1989, is a question that belongs to chapters on the postwar and modern Japan, but it is also grist for another volume. Of course, Japan struggled with many of the issues that seeded themselves in earlier decades, such as the economy, foreign policy, and how to envision its own history. One aspect of the post-Showa era, which is only tangentially touched on toward the end of this book, is the roots of what came to be called Japan's "lost decades." Precisely how the decades after Japan's surrender and the years of eminent economic growth during the 1980s were painted by the media, which portrayed Japan as "number one" and the new economic leader of East Asia, are important factors when looking at contemporary Japan and its international role as it confronts many new difficulties in the twenty-first century. We should position ourselves critically to not only observe how media companies perform their roles, and how *Asahi* performed its own, but also keep in mind that we have the duty and ability as citizens to demand change not only politically but also as consumers of this media. If there is one moral lesson to be gained from these pages, it is that a country's own citizens are also never short of blame and need to take responsibility for their own government's action as much as expecting their media to do the same. Media shape social discourse, but they equally respond to political apathy.

The interaction between the various Japanese media companies, which arguably wanted to see themselves as a fourth estate, and history is the long running theme in this book. As such, we should be struck by the remarkable daring demonstrated by many throughout the long years of censorship, conflict, desperation, rebuilding, and success that Japan experienced at various moments during the twentieth century. Even in its darkest moments the country had pockets of men and women talented and able enough to arguably change the course of their own national history and thus the course of Japan's role in the world.

Notes

Chapter 1

1. *The Times*, January 7, 1989.

Chapter 2

1. *The New York Times*, October 25, 1929.
2. *Asahi*, March 15, 1927, morning edition.
3. *Asahi*, March 24, 1927, morning edition.
4. James R. Lothian, "A History of Yen Exchange Rates," in William T. Zemba et al., eds, *Japanese Financial Market Research* (Elsevier, 1991). According to Lothian, the ¥/$ nominal rate between 1922 and 1929 was 0.51.
5. *Asahi*, March 18, 1927.
6. *Asahi*, June 7, 1932, evening edition.
7. Imamura Takeo, *Hyōden: Takashi Korekiyo* (Zaisei keizai kōhōsha, 1950). Unless otherwise noted, all Japanese books are published in Tokyo.
8. *Asahi*, January 22, 1932, evening Tokyo edition.
9. Takahashi Kamekichi, *Bungei shunjū*, December 1929.
10. The Manchurian Incident is also known as the Mukden Incident in English.
11. *Asahi*, March 16, 1936, Tokyo edition.
12. Asahi shimbun hyakunenshi henshū iinkai, ed., *Asahi shimbun shashi* (Asahi shimbunsha, 1990–1995).
13. *Kaizō*, August 1932 (censored "XX" in the original).
14. *Asahi*, June 11, 1933, Tokyo morning edition.
15. *Asahi*, June 28, 1933, evening edition.
16. *Asahi*, June 20, 1930, evening edition.
17. *Asahi*, June 25, 1932.
18. *Asahi*, December 7, 1932.

Chapter 3

1. *Asahi*, December 1, 1929, evening Tokyo edition.
2. Takamiya Tahei, *Ningen Ogata Taketora* (Hara shobō, 1979).
3. Satō Shintarō, *Chichi, Satō Ichirō ga kakinokoshita gunshuku kaigi hiroku* (Bungeisha, 2001).
4. Itō Takashi, ed., *Kaigun: Katō Hiroharu nikki* (Misuzu shobō, 1994), part of the series, *Zoku, Gendaishi shiryō* (vol. 5).
5. Itō Kinjirō, *Ikite iru kaishō Katō Hiroharu* (Showa shobō, 1942).
6. Itō Masanori, *Shimbun seikatsu nijū nen* (Chūō kōronsha, 1933).

7. Harada Kumao, *Saionji Kō to seikyoku* (Iwanami shoten, 1950–1956).
8. Nakashima Yadanji, "Hamaguchi Osachi shushō o omou," *Meisō*, January 1953.
9. Ōita kenritsu sentetsu sōsho, *Hori Teikichi shiryōshū*, vol. 1 (Ōita kyōiku iinkai, 2006).
10. *The Times*, March 19, 1930.
11. Ikei Masaru, ed., *Hamaguchi Osachi nikki, zuikanroku* (Misuzu shobō, 1993).
12. Seki Shizuo, *Rondon kaigun jōyaku seiritsushi* (Minerva shobō, 2007).
13. Yamanashi Katsunoshin, *Rekishi to meishō: senshi ni miru rīdashippu no jōken* (Mainichi shimbunsha, 1981).
14. Yamaura Kan'ichi, ed., *Mori Tsutomu: tōa shintaisei no senku* (Mori Tsutomu denki hensankai, 1940).
15. *Asahi*, April 26, 1930.
16. *Asahi*, April 30, 1930.
17. *Asahi*, May 4, 1930, Osaka edition.
18. Bōeichō bōei kenkyūjo shusenshishitsu, ed., *Daihon'ei kaigunbu: rengō kantai 1* (Asagumo shimbunsha, 1975).
19. Asahi shimbunsha, *Taiheiyō sensō e no michi: shiryōhen* (Asahi shimbunsha, 1963).
20. Kobayashi Tatsuo, "Tōsuiken kanpanron to kaigun gunreibu jōrei no kaisei," *Kokugakuin hōgaku* 2, 1968.
21. *Asahi*, September 2, 1930, Tokyo edition.
22. Imai Seiichi et al., eds, *Gendaishi shiryō 4* (Misuzu shobō, 2004).
23. Ikeda Kiyoshi, *Nihon no kaigun* (Asahi sonorama, 1993).
24. Kōno Tsukasa, ed., *2.26 jiken* (Nihon shūhōsha, 1957).
25. Takahashi Masae, ed., *Gendaishi shiryō 5* (Misuzu shobō, 2004).
26. Hori Makiyo, "Hamaguchi shushō sogeki jiken: Sagoya Tomeo no dōki to haigo seiryoku ni tsuite," *Seinan gakuin daigaku hōgaku ronshū* 11, 1986.
27. *Asahi*, May 5, 1931, Tokyo edition.
28. *Asahi*, August 8, 1931, Osaka edition.
29. *Asahi*, August 27, 1931, Tokyo edition.

Chapter 4

1. Yosano Akiko, *Travels in Manchuria and Mongolia*, translated by Joshua A. Fogel (Columbia University Press, 2001), p. 119.
2. Yosano, *Travels*, p. 119.
3. Yosano, *Travels*, pp. 122–123.
4. *Rōnin* was a word used to describe masterless samurai during the Tokugawa era; in this context, a *Manshū rōnin* was someone who worked in Manchuria but in a rather loose and lawless way.
5. *Asahi*, January 23, 1929, evening edition.
6. The "Manchurian Incident" (*Manshū jihen*) in modern history books has now come to signify the Manchurian (Mukden) Incident that occurred in 1931, but in the wake of the Zhang Zuolin Incident several years earlier a similar term (*Manshū jiken*) was in use to refer to this previous 1928 plot.
7. Terasaki Hidenari and Mariko Terasaki Miller, *Shōwa tennō dokuhakuroku, Terasaki Hidenari goyōgakari nikki* (Bungei shunjū, 1991), p. 22. Hirohito delivered this memoir after the war to a small circle of advisers, during five secret meetings in March and April 1946.

8. Fang Zheng, *Ichi rōchūgokujin no kaisō: gekidō no jidai o hōkō shita shōgai* (Fang Zheng sensei kaisōki kankōkai, 2008).
9. Gotō Takao, *Shingai kakumei kara manshū jihen e: ōsaka asahi shimbun to kindai chūgoku* (Misuzu shobō, 1987), p. 376.
10. Kiyosawa Kiyoshi, *Hijō nihon e no chokugen* (Chikura shobō, 1933), p. 25.

Chapter 5

1. *Asahi*, April 12, 1928, Tokyo morning edition.
2. Ōyama Ikuo kinen jigyōkai, ed., *Ōyama Ikuo den* (Chūō kōronsha, 1956).
3. *Hōritsu shimbun*, February 25, 1928.
4. *Asahi*, April 30, 1928.
5. *Asahi*, March 6, 1929, Osaka evening edition.
6. *Asahi*, March 8, 1929, Tokyo edition.
7. Extracts and summary of records of the Lower House.
8. *Asahi*, July 26, 1933, Tokyo evening edition.
9. Following the examples respectively: *Asahi*, August 25, 1933, Tokyo evening edition; *Yomiuri*, September 20, 1933, evening edition; and *Asahi*, November 9, 1933, Tokyo morning edition.
10. *Asahi*, August 19, 1933, Tokyo morning edition.
11. *Asahi*, September 16, 1933, Tokyo evening edition.
12. October 1935 issue of the magazine *Hanashi* (*Stories*) by the Bungei shunjū company.
13. *Asahi*, November 23, 1934, Tokyo evening edition.
14. *The Times*, February 27, 1936.
15. Asahi shimbun hyakunenshi henshū iinkai, eds., *Asahi shimbun shashi* (Asahi shimbunsha, 1990–1995), vol. 2, p. 453.
16. Igarashi Chiyū, *Rekishi no shunkan to jānaritsutotachi: asahi shimbun ni miru nijūseiki* (Asahi shimbunsha, 1999).
17. From the records of the Lower House.
18. *Asahi*, July 15, 1936, evening edition.

Chapter 6

1. Minobe had opined that the Emperor consulted his ministers and was thus an element of the state structure, not necessarily completely above it.
2. Okada Sadahiro, ed., *Okada Keisuke kaikoroku* (Chūō kōronsha, 1987).
3. Kobayashi Isamu, *Sekirekisō shujin: hitotsu no Iwanami Shigeo den* (Kōdansha, 1993).
4. Miyazawa Toshiyoshi, *Tennō kikan setsu jiken: shiryō wa kataru* (Yūhikaku, 1970), vol. 1.
5. Mikiso Hane, trans., *Emperor Hirohito and his Chief Aide-de-Camp: the Honjō Diary, 1933–36* (University of Tokyo Press, 1982), p. 133.
6. Japan, however, did not declare it a war and it was described as a "conflict" in domestic media.
7. *Asahi*, July 12, 1937, Tokyo edition.
8. *Asahi*, August 16, 1937.
9. Yanaihara Tadao, *Yanaihara Tadao zenshū* (Iwanami shoten, 1964), vol. 18.
10. *Seikai ōrai*, March 1953.

11. Kurita Naoki, *Ogata Taketora* (Yoshikawa kōbunkan, 2001), pp. 79 and 82.
12. Kaji Ryūichi, *Ogata Taketora* (Jiji tsūshinsha, 1962).
13. Kashihara Shrine is situated on the legendary site of the enthronement of Emperor Jimmu, and is dedicated to him.
14. *Asahi*, July 7, 1938.
15. In Japanese mythology the sacred three-legged crow (*yatagarasu*) was sent by the Sun Goddess Amaterasu to guide Jimmu on his expedition to conquer eastern Japan. In wartime propaganda, the bird acquired symbolic significance as a force to guide the direction of Japan's modern imperium in Asia.
16. *Hakkō ichiu* means "Eight corners of the world under one roof." This phrase was attributed to Emperor Jimmu and appeared in the *Nihonshoki* (also known as the *Chronicles of Japan*). The "eight corners of the world" refers to the eight geographic directions and represents the entire planet. In wartime Japan, this term became a political slogan that embodied Japan's mission to unite "the whole world under one roof."
17. According to Japanese mythology, Mount Takachiho (in Miyazaki Prefecture) was the site where the Sun Goddess Amaterasu's grandson, Ninigi no Mikoto, descended from the heavens as the first divine ruler. It was from here that his descendant, the first Emperor Jimmu, set out east to establish his governance over all of Japan.

Chapter 7

1. Hamada Tsunejirō, *Taisen zen'ya no gaikō hiwa: tokuhain no shuki* (Chiyoda shoin, 1953).
2. Hara Yoshihisa, *Yoshida Shigeru: sonnō no seijika* (Iwanami shoten, 2005).
3. Miwa Kimitada, *Matsuoka Yōsuke: sono ningen to gaikō* (Chūō kōronsha, 1971).
4. Sugimoto Ken, *Kaigun no shōwashi: teitoku to shimbun kisha* (Bungei shunjū, 1982).
5. *Asahi*, August 23, 1939.
6. Ogata Taketora, *Ichi gunjin no shōgai: teitoku Yonai Mitsumasa* (Bungei shunjū, 1955), p. 3.
7. May 16, 1940 in *Danchō-tei nichijō*, in *Kafū zenshū* (Iwanami shoten, 1962–1965), vol. 23, pp. 34–35.
8. Matsumoto Shigeharu, *Konoe jidai: jānarisuto no kaisō* (Chūō kōronsha, 1986–1987).
9. Ogata Taketora, *Meiji makki kara taiheiyō sensō made* (Asahi shimbunsha, 1951).
10. Ogata Taketora denki kankōkai, ed., *Ogata Taketora* (Asahi shimbunsha, 1963).
11. Miyamoto Tarō et al., *Kasumigaseki no seisho: sūjiku gaikō o meguru* (Ikuseisha, 1941).
12. *Asahi*, September 28, 1940.
13. Uchikawa Yoshimi, ed., *Masu media tōsei, gendaishi shiryō 41* (Misuzu shobō, 1973–1975), pp. 274–276.
14. *Asahi*, September 28, 1940.
15. Suzuki Bunshirō, *Beiō hentenki* (Zenkoku shobō, 1943), p. 333.
16. Nogami Yaeko, *Nogami Yaeko zenshū* (Iwanami shoten, 1985), vol. 7.
17. Ejiri Susumu, *Berurin tokuden* (Kyōdō tsūshinsha, 1995).
18. Sugimoto Ken, *Kaigun no shōwashi: teitoku to shimbunkisha* (Bungei shunjū, 1982).
19. Muno Takeji, *Taimatsu jūrokunen* (Iwanami shoten, 2010).
20. *Asahi*, June 24, 1941, evening edition.
21. *Asahi*, February 16, 1940.
22. Awaya Kentarō and Nakazono Hiroshi, eds, *Senji shimbun ken'etsu shiryō* (Gendai shiryō shuppan, 1997).

23. Asahi shimbun hyakunenshi henshū iinkai, ed., *Asahi shimbun shashi* (Asahi shimbunsha, 1990–1995), vol. 2, pp. 564–565. The internal review section was the newspaper's own office that assisted with internal censorship before being submitted to the government authorities.
24. Asahi shimbun hyakunenshi henshū iinkai, ed., *Asahi shimbun shashi* (Asahi shimbunsha, 1990–1995), vol. 2, pp. 555–556.
25. Satō Kenryō, *Daitōa sensō kaikoroku* (Tokuma shoten, 1966).
26. *Asahi*, August 16, 1941, evening edition.
27. Tōgō Shigenori, *Tōgō Shigenori gaikō shuki: jidai no ichimen* (Hara shobō, 1967), p. 251.
28. *Asahi*, December 5, 1941, evening edition.
29. Asahi shimbun hyakunenshi henshū iinkai, ed., *Asahi shimbun shashi* (Asahi shimbunsha, 1990–1995), vol. 2, p. 577.

Chapter 8

1. *Asahi*, November 7, 1943.
2. Shigemitsu Mamoru, *Gaikō ikenshoshū 2* (Gendaishiryō shuppan, 2007), p. 284.
3. Hatano Sumio, *Taiheiyō sensō to ajia gaikō* (University of Tokyo Press, 1996), pp. 161–168.
4. http://www.nato.int/cps/en/natolive/official_texts_16912.htm.
5. *Asahi*, November 11, 1943.
6. Ishii Itarō, *Gaikōkan no isshō* (Yomiuri shimbunsha, 1950).
7. *Asahi*, November 17, 1943, Tokyo morning edition.
8. Kaji Ryūichi, *Hito to kokoro to tabi* (Asahi shimbunsha, 1973).

Chapter 9

1. *Mokusatsu* literally means "to kill with silence," but it is often translated as "to ignore" and may also have been intended to indicate "no comment." See John Toland, *The Rising Sun: The Decline and Fall of the Japanese Empire, 1936–1945* (Random House, 2003), p. 774.
2. Tokyo terebi, ed., *Shōgen: watakushi no shōwashi 5* (Ōbunsha, 1985), p. 243.
3. Suzuki Kantarō, *Suzuki Kantarō jiden* (Heibonsha, 1981), pp. 258–259.
4. *The New York Times*, July 30, 1945.
5. Shimomura Kainan, *Shūsenki* (Kamakura bunko, 1949), p. 98.
6. *The New York Times*, August 7, 1945.
7. *The New York* Times, August 7, 1945.
8. Barack Obama, "Remarks by President Barack Obama in Prague" (April 5, 2009), http://www.whitehouse.gov/the_press_office/Remarks-By-President-Barack-Obama-In-Prague-As-Delivered/.
9. Soviet Declaration of War, Avalon Project at Yale: http://avalon.law.yale.edu/wwii/s4.asp.
10. Satō Naotake, *Kaiko hachijūnen* (Yumani shobō, 2002), p. 499.
11. Suzuki Kantarō, *Suzuki Kantarō jiden* (Heibonsha, 1981), pp. 260–261.
12. Toyoda Soemu, *Saigo no teikoku kaigun* (Sekai no nihonsha, 1950).

13. Takami Jun, *Haisen nikki* (Chūō kōron shinsha, 2005), pp. 294–295.
14. Shimomura Kainan, *Shūsenki* (Kamakura bunko, 1949), p. 98.
15. *Mainichi shimbun hyakunenshi* (Mainichi shimbunsha, 1972), p. 209.

Chapter 10

1. Ōgiya Shōzō, *Nihon no ichiban atsui hi: shōwa 20-nen 8-gatsu 15-nichi* (PHP kenkyūjo, 1982).
2. Taken from the original translation made by Tadaichi Hirakawa, which he read aloud on an international broadcast at the same time. William Theodore De Bary and Richard Lufrano, eds, *Sources of Japanese Tradition: From Earliest Times to 1600*, vol. 1 (Columbia University Press, 2000), p. 1016.
3. The serialized articles were later compiled as a full-length book: Kase Hideaki, *Tennōke no tatakai* (Shinchōsha, 1983), p. 221.
4. *Bungei shunjū*, February 2005.
5. Kageyama Kōyō, "Namida no kōkyo mae hiroba," in *Kageyama Kōyō shashinten* (Ritsumeikan daigaku kokusai heiwa myūjiamu, 2003), p. 42.
6. Katō Shūichi, *A Sheep's Song: A Writer's Reminiscences of Japan and the World*, translated by Chia-ning Chang (University of California Press, 1999), p. 204.

Chapter 11

1. Takeyama Akiko, *Gyokuon hōsō* (Banseisha, 1989), p. 31.
2. Kōseishō, ed., *Hikiage to engo sanjūnen no ayumi* (Kyōsei, 1978), p. 25.
3. Katō Kiyofumi, *Dainippon teikoku hōkai* (Chūō kōron shinsha, 2009), p. 57.
4. Wakatsuki Yasuo, *Sengo hikiage no kiroku* (Jiji tsūshinsha, 1995), p. 50.
5. Morita Yoshio, *Chōsen shūsen no kiroku* (Gannandō shoten, 1950), pp. 10 and 39.
6. http://www.presidency.ucsb.edu/ws/index.php?pid=12261.
7. Kōseishō, ed., *Hikiage to engo sanjūnen no ayumi*, p. 55.
8. *Asahi*, December 22, 1949.
9. *Asahi*, July 30, 1949.
10. *Asahi*, December 5, 1949.
11. *Asahi*, September 8, 1947.
12. *Manshū kaitakushi* (Zenkokutakuyū kyōgikai, 1966).
13. *Asahi*, October 30, 1947.
14. *Asahi*, September 17, 1949.
15. *Manshū kaitakushi*.

Chapter 12

1. Takami Jun, *Haisen nikki* (Chūō kōron shinsha, 2005), p. 363.
2. *The New York Times*, September 25, 1945.
3. *The New York Times*, September 29, 1945.
4. *The New York Times*, September 29, 1945.
5. Toyoshita Narahiko, *Shōwa tennō: Makkāsā kaiken* (Iwanami shoten, 2008).

6. *Asahi*, October 26, 1945.
7. The Yokohama Incident signifies six cases where charges were brought against writers and intellectuals for violating the Peace Preservation Law toward the end of the Second World War in Japan. See Nishimura Hideki, "The Retrial of the 'Yokohama Incident': a six-decade battle for human dignity," *Japan Focus* (http://www.japanfocus.org/-Nishimura-Hideki/2025).
8. October 1954, special edition of *Bungei shunjū*.
9. *Shūkan shinchō* editorial department edition, "MacArthur's Japan" (*Makkāsā no nihon*).
10. Takemae Eiji, *Inside GHQ: the Allied occupation of Japan and its legacy*, translated by Robert Ricketts and Sebastian Swann (Continuum, 2002), p. 181.
11. Arai Naoyuki, *Shimbun sengoshi* (Kurita shuppankai, 1972).
12. Mark Gayn, *Japan Diary* (W. Sloane Associates, 1948), p. 331.
13. Ariyama Teruo, *Sengoshi no naka no kenpō to jānarizumu* (Kashiwa shobō, 1998).

Chapter 13

1. *Asahi*, September 12, 1945.
2. Awaya Kentarō, *Shiryō nihon gendaishi* 2 (Ōtsuki Shoten, 1980), p. 344.
3. Kido Kōichi, *Kido Kōichi nikki* (Tokyo daigaku shuppankai, 1966).
4. Higashino Makoto et al., eds., *Shōwa tennō futatsu no dokuhakuroku* (Nihon hōsō shuppan kyōkai, 1998), p. 22.
5. *Asahi*, September 16, 1945.
6. Awaya Kentarō, *Shiryō nihon gendaishi* 2, p. 335.
7. Awaya Kentarō, *Shiryō nihon gendaishi* 2, p. 339.
8. Fujita Hisanori, *Jijūchō no kaisō* (Kōdansha, 1961), p. 187.
9. Fujita Hisanori, *Jijūchō no kaisō* (Kōdansha, 1961), pp. 187–190, 202–204.
10. *Asahi*, May 4, 1946.
11. *Shūkan asahi*, October 10, 1948.
12. Ōgane Masujirō, *Junkō yohō* (Shinshōsetsusha, 1955).
13. *Asahi* internal records.
14. John Dower, *Embracing Defeat: Japan in the Wake of World War II* (W.W. Norton, 1999), p. 508. Originally quoted from the Japanese magazine *Van*.
15. William J. Sebald, *With MacArthur in Japan; A Personal History of the Occupation* (The Cressef Press, 1965), pp. 162–165.
16. Okudaira Yasuhiro, *Bansei ikkei no kenkyū* (Iwanami shoten, 2005), p. 193.
17. Togashi Junji, *Tennō to tomoni gojūnen* (Mainichi shimbunsha, 1977), p. 112.
18. "Tōkyō saiban no hanketsu," *Asahi hyōron*, December 1948.
19. Watanabe Kazuo, "Nisenikki shōji II," in *Watanabe Kazuo chosakushū* 11 (Chikumashobō, 1976).
20. Hagi Shūgetsu, *Tennō heika o kataru* (Aika shoin, 1953).
21. *Diamondo*, March 1952.

Chapter 14

1. Ebata Kiyoshi, ed., *Kaisō Ryū Shintarō* (Asahi shimbunsha, 1969).
2. *Shūkan asahi*, May 14, 1958.

3. Ryū Shintarō, *Nihon no shisei, sengo 20nen* (Nansōsha, 1965).
4. Kusunoki Ayako, *Yoshida Shigeru to anzen hoshō seisaku no keisei* (Mineruva shobō, 2009).
5. *Asahi*, April 28, 1952, evening edition.

Chapter 15

1. Okada Akira, *Mizutori gaikō hiwa: aru gaikōkan no shōgen* (Chūō kōronsha, 1983).
2. Miyagi Taizō, *Bandon kaigi to nihon no ajia fukki* (Sōshisha, 2001), p. 124.
3. *Shūkan asahi*, June 12, 1955.
4. *Asahi*, April 22, 1955.

Chapter 16

1. *Asahi*, September 11, 1952, evening edition.
2. Hatoyama Ichirō, *Hatoyama Ichirō kaikoroku* (Bungei shunjū, 1957), p. 178.
3. *Asahi*, June 6, 1956.
4. Hatoyama Ichirō, *Hatoyama ichirō kaikoroku*, p. 196.
5. The Kuril Islands are a long archipelago chain off the coast of Hokkaido but known in Japan as *Chishima rettō* (literally the "thousand island archipelago"). Prewar Japan had mainly controlled four: Habomai, Shikotan, Etorofu, and Kunashiri. Sakhalin Island is a separate island, just off the northeast coast of Russia, but was known to prewar Japanese as Karafuto and the southern half of that island came under Japanese control until the end of the Second World War.
6. Kokuren kōhō sentā, *Kaisō nihon to kokuren no sanjūnen* (Kōdansha, 1986), p. 30.
7. *Asahi*, December 15, 1957.
8. *Asahi*, December 15, 1957.

Chapter 17

1. *Asahi*, September 24, 1959.
2. *Asahi*, May 10, 1960. English quoted from *The New York Times*, May 10, 1960.
3. *Asahi*, May 20, 1960.
4. *Aera*, May 24, 1988, p. 78.
5. Kobayashi Tomi, *"Koe naki koe" o kike: hansen shimin undō no genten* (Dōjidaisha, 2003), pp. 11–13.
6. *Asahi jānaru*, June 19, 1960.
7. This is a demonstration that zigzags to occupy the entire street. *Mademoiselle*, August 8, 1960.
8. Kantō Radio is now known as Radio Nippon.
9. Itō Takashi et al., eds, *Watanabe Tsuneo kaikoroku* (Chūō kōron shinsha, 2000), p. 175.
10. Aoki Akira, *Shimbun to no yakusoku* (NHK shuppan, 2000), p. 128.
11. Ikematsu Fumio, "Shichisha seimei no ondo o toru," in Ebata Kiyoshi, ed., *Kaisō Ryū Shintarō* (Asahi shimbunsha, 1969), p. 46.
12. Hanzawa Sakuichirō, *Kyoboku kayasan: ishoku no tōdai moto gakuchō* (Chūō kōron jigyō shuppan, 1985).
13. Mori Kyōzō, *Kisha henro* (Asahi, 1974).

14. Danno Nobuo, "Anpo nokoro," in Ebata Kiyoshi, ed., *Kaisō Ryū Shintarō*, p. 225.
15. *Aera*, May 24, 1988.
16. *Asahi*, June 19, 1960, morning edition.
17. *Asahi*, June 19, 1960.
18. *Okinawa taimusu*, June 19, 1960, evening edition.
19. *Asahi*, November 2, 1958.
20. *Ryūkyū shimpō*, January 16, 1959.

Chapter 18

1. *Asahi*, July 17, 1956, morning edition.
2. *Asahi*, July 17, 1956, morning edition.
3. The original "sacred treasures" of the modern era were the vacuum cleaner, the washing machine and the refrigerator.
4. *Asahi*, June 15, 1953, evening edition.
5. *Bungei shunjū*, June 1955.
6. *Asahi*, May 1, 1954, evening edition.
7. *Asahi*, July 28, 1955, evening edition.
8. *Asahi*, May 27, 1964.
9. *Asahi*, January 20, 1938.
10. *The Washington Post*, July 16, 1938.
11. *Asahi*, October 11, 1964.
12. *Asahi*, August 31, 1964.
13. *Asahi*, September 3, 1964.

Chapter 19

1. *Shinnihon Chisso Hiryō*, later the company name was changed to Chisso in 1965.
2. *Asahi*, July 14, 1959.
3. *Asahi*, April 12, 1960, evening addition.
4. Hashimoto Michio, *Shishi kankyō gyōsei* (Asahi shimbunsha, 1988).
5. Ishimure Michiko, *Kugai jōdo: waga minamatabyō* (Kōdansha, 1969).
6. Timothy George, *Minamata: Pollution and the Struggle for Democracy in Postwar Japan* (Harvard University Asia Center, 2001), p. 281.

Chapter 20

1. *Asahi*, December 26, 1959, evening edition.
2. *Yomiuri*, January 9, 1960.
3. *Asahi*, April 26, 1956.
4. *Asahi*, February 15, 1965, evening edition.
5. *Asahi*, June 23, 1965.
6. *Asahi*, April 9, 2002.
7. Yokota's case became news after her family received a telephone call with information about her abduction. Yokota is still missing, and while North Korean officials have admitted to her abduction they make conflicting claims about her death.

Chapter 21

1. *Asahi*, February 17, 1968, evening edition.
2. *Asahi*, May 20, 1968, evening edition.
3. *Asahi*, September 7, 1968.
4. *Asahi*, December 27, 1968.

Chapter 22

1. *Asahi*, November 23, 1969.
2. *Mainichi*, June 18, 1971.

Chapter 23

1. Tagawa Seiichi, *Nicchū kōshō hiroku* (Mainichi shimbunsha, 1973).

Chapter 24

1. The Nittsū Incident was a corruption scandal involving the Nittsū Company and its monopoly over the transport of grains.
2. Kimura Kisuke, *Tanaka Kakuei kesareta shinjutsu* (Kōbundō, 2002).

Chapter 25

1. Denki kyōkai shimbun, ed., *Shōgen daiichiji sekiyu kiki: kiki wa sairaisuru ka* (Nihon denki kyōkai shimbunbu, 1991).
2. *The Times*, November 16, 1973.

Chapter 26

1. *Asahi*, August 16, 1975.
2. *Mainichi*, August 15, 1975, evening edition.
3. *Ekonomisuto*, September 16, 1975.
4. *Kaikō*, July 1959.
5. *Nihon keizai shimbun*, July 20, 2006.
6. Okano Hirohiko, *Shōwa tennō gyosei: shiki no uta* (Dōhōsha media puran, 2006).

Chapter 27

1. Ezoe Hiromasa, *Rikurūto jiken: Ezoe Hiromasa no shinjitsu* (Chūō kōron shinsha, 2009).

Index